A SHORT TREATISE

ON

Canadian Constitutional Law

BY

A. H. F. LEFROY

AUTHOR OF 'CANADA'S FEDERAL SYSTEM' AND 'LEGISLATIVE POWER
IN CANADA'

With an Historical Introduction

BY

W. P. M. KENNEDY

DEPARTMENT OF MODERN HISTORY, UNIVERSITY OF TORONTO

THE LAWBOOK EXCHANGE, LTD.
Clark, New Jersey

ISBN 978-1-58477-777-9

Lawbook Exchange edition 2008, 2019

The quality of this reprint is equivalent to the quality of the original work.

THE LAWBOOK EXCHANGE, LTD.
33 Terminal Avenue
Clark, New Jersey 07066-1321

*Please see our website for a selection of our other publications
and fine facsimile reprints of classic works of legal history:*
www.lawbookexchange.com

Library of Congress Cataloging-in-Publication Data

Lefroy, A. H. F. (Augustus Henry Frazer), 1852-1919.
   A short treatise on Canadian constitutional law / by A.H. F. Lefroy,
with an historical introduction by W. P. M. Kennedy.
      p. cm.
   Originally published: Toronto : Carswell. 1918.
   Includes index.
      ISBN-13: 978-1-58477-777-9 (cloth : alk. paper)
      ISBN-10: 1-58477-777-X (cloth : alk. paper)
   1. Constitutional law--Canada. 2. Canada--Politics and government.
   I. Kennedy, W. P. M. (William Paul McClure), 1879-1963. II. Title.

   KE4219.L44   2007
   342.71--dc22   2006036095

Printed in the United States of America on acid-free paper

A SHORT TREATISE

ON

Canadian Constitutional Law

BY

A. H. F. LEFROY

AUTHOR OF 'CANADA'S FEDERAL SYSTEM' AND 'LEGISLATIVE POWER
IN CANADA'

With an Historical Introduction

BY

W. P. M. KENNEDY

DEPARTMENT OF MODERN HISTORY, UNIVERSITY OF TORONTO

TORONTO:
THE CARSWELL COMPANY, LIMITED

LONDON:
SWEET & MAXWELL, LIMITED
1918

TO THE MEMORY OF MY SON

FRAZER KEITH LEFROY

SECOND-LIEUTENANT, ROYAL FIELD ARTILLERY,

WHO WILLINGLY GAVE HIS LIFE

FOR CANADA AND THE EMPIRE,

AND FOR THE PRINCIPLES OF A CHRISTIAN CIVILIZATION,

ON THE WESTERN FRONT IN FRANCE,

ON APRIL 7th, 1917,

IN HIS 23rd YEAR,

I DEDICATE THIS BOOK.

PREFACE

This Short Treatise upon Canadian Constitutional Law, which I now offer to the profession and the public, embodies the two-fold scheme, of providing a text concise and simple enough for the purposes of University students and law students, and, at the same time, supplying in the Notes all the requirements of the practical lawyer called upon to advise upon some question arising under the British North America Act, or otherwise in relation to the Federal Constitution of the Dominion of Canada. In the Notes my aim has been to cite practically every scrap of authority, direct or indirect, which exists upon these matters. I have had the ideal throughout of completing my task absolutely regardless of the trouble involved. I do not think that anyone who turns over the pages of the Notes, or looks at the Table of Cases, every one of which has been carefully studied, will harbour any doubt as to the labour which I have put into this volume.

Will anyone ask whether my subject is worth such an expenditure of time and trouble? From a commercial point of view it may not be: but a man must take very short views, and be possessed of little imagination, who does not see the interest and importance of those constitutional rules and arrangements which lie at the basis of the national life of this Dominion. The greatest pessimist, if he possesses normal intelligence, cannot any longer doubt the glorious future which lies before the British Empire when, with the favour of Heaven, the allied nations have victoriously completed the present titanic struggle against the diabolism and grasping ambition of modern Germany, nor the place which this Dominion is destined to hold within it.   But however glorious the future of Canada may be it may well be worked out, so far as concerns her internal affairs, upon the basis which the Fathers of Confederation laid in the British North America Act, 1867.

That Act, it may surely be said, is the most successful piece of constitutional legislation which has ever emanated from the Parliament at Westminster. Much of the credit of that success must no doubt be accorded to the men who have lived and worked under the system created by it,—that sturdy blend of English, Irish, and Scotch, which forms the predominating element in the British Canadian provinces, whose staunchness and constancy is now winning recognition on the battle fields of Europe.   But while making every allowance for this aspect of the matter, the fact remains that the more thought and labour one expends on the Constitution of Canada under our Federation Act, the greater grows one's admiration for the wisdom and prescience of those to whose constructive genius it is due.   I have said something on that subject in the concluding portion of this Treatise, and there is no need to repeat it here.

I have had the good fortune to enlist the services of Professor W. P. M. Kennedy, of the University of Toronto, in contributing an Historical Introduction which I feel sure will be found to add very materially to the interest and value of the book.

A. H. F. LEFROY.

JULY 1ST, 1918.

TABLE OF CONTENTS

TABLE OF CASES[1]

A.

[1] A,-G.=Attorney-General; n.=note; nn.=notes; p.=page.
When the reference is to a note, the relevant text should be
referred to.

B.

G.

H.

I.

J.

K.

M.

T.

TABLE OF STATUTES REFERRED TO[1]

[1] n.=note; nn.=notes; p.=page.

TABLE OF ABBREVIATIONS[1]

A. L. R. ....Alberta Law Reports: Toronto.
Alta. .... Alberta Law Reports.
B. C. .... British Columbia Law Reports: Victoria,
      B.C.
C. A. .... New Zealand Court of Appeal Reports.
Cass. Dig. S. C........ A digest of cases decided by the Supreme
      Court of Canada, by Robert Cassels,
      Q.C.: Carswell & Co., Toronto, 1893.
Clement's L. of L. C... Clement's Law of Canadian Constitution:
      Toronto, 1916.
C. L. J. .... The Canada Law Journal: Toronto.
C. L. R. .... Commonwealth (Australia) Law Re-
      ports: Melbourne.
C. L. T. .... Canadian Law Times: Toronto.
Con. Stat. N. B. ...... Consolidated Statutes of New Brunswick.
D. L. R. .... Dominion Law Reports: Toronto.
Dor. Q. A. or Q. B..... Decisions of the Court of Appeal
      (Queen's Bench) Reports: Quebec, by
      L. C. W. Dorion, Montreal.
Ex. C. R. .... Reports of the Exchequer Court of Can-
      ada: Ottawa.
Gr. .... Reports of cases in the Court of Chan-
      'cery of Upper Canada, and afterwards
      of Ontario, by Alexander Grant: To-
      ronto.
Hannay .... Reports of cases in the Supreme Court of
      New Brunswick, by James Hannay,
      1870-5: Fredericton and St. John, N.B.
Haw. Rep. .... Hawaian Reports: Honolulu.
Hodg. Prov. Legisl. ... Correspondence, reports of the Ministers
      of Justice, and Orders in Council, upon
      the subject of Dominion and Provin-
      cial Legislation, 1867-1895, by W. E.
      Hodgins, M.A., Ottawa, 1896.
Imp. Un. and Brit. Dom.Imperial Unity and The Dominions, by
      A. Berriedale Keith: Oxford: Claren-
      don Press: 1916.
Jl. Comp. Leg. .... Journal of Comparative Legislation, New
      Series: London.
J. R. N. S. S. C. ...... New Zealand Jurist Reports, New Series,
      Supreme Court.
Knox (N. S. W.)...... Cases in the Supreme Court of New
      South Wales, by George Knox, Sydney.

[1] The abbreviated methods of citing the *English Law Reports*, and some few other abbreviations, are omitted from this table as being too well known to need explanation.

L. C. J. .... The Lower Canada Jurist, being a collection of decisions of Lower Canada:
Montreal.

L. C. R. .... Lower Canada Reports

L. N. .... Legal News: Montreal.

L. T. .... Law Times Reports: London.

Man. .... Manitoba Law Reports.

M. L. R. (S. C.) ...... Montreal Law Reports, Superior Court:
Montreal.

M. L. R. (Q. B.) .... Montreal Law Reports, Queen's Bench:
Montreal.

M R. .... Manitoba Law Reports.

N. B. .... New Brunswick Law Reports.

Nfd. Dec. .... Newfoundland Decisions: St. John's, Nfd.

N. S. .... Nova Scotia Law Reports.

N. S. W. .... New South Wales Reports.

N. W. T. .... Reports of the Supreme Court of the
North-West Territories.

O. A. R. .... Ontario Appeal Reports: Toronto.

O. L. R. .... Ontario Law Reports (Superior Courts,
and Ontario Court of Appeal): Toronto

O. P. R. .... Ontario Practice Reports: Toronto.

O. R. .... Reports of decisions in the High Court of
Justice for Ontario: Toronto.

O. W. N. .... Ontario Weekly Notes: Toronto.

O. W. R. .... Ontario Weekly Reporter: Toronto.

P. & B. .... Reports of cases in the Supreme Court of
New Brunswick, by Wm. Pugsley and
G. W. Burbidge: Saint John, N.B.

P. E. I. .... Prince Edward Island Reports; Charlottetown, P.E.I.

Pugs. .... New Brunswick Reports, by Wm. Pugsley.

Q. L. R. .... Quebec Law Reports.

Q. P. R. .... Quebec Practice Reports.

R. & C. .... Russell and Chesley's Nova Scotia Reports: Halifax, N.S.

R. & G. .... Russell and Geldert's Nova Scotia Reports: Halifax, N.S.

R. G. in D. .... A. Berriedale Keith's *Responsible Government in the Dominions* (3 vols), by
A Berriedale Keith: Clarendon Press,
1912.

R. J. Q. (S. C.) .... Les Rapports Judiciaires de Quebec:
Cour Superieur: Montreal.

R. J. Q., Q. B. or K. B.. Reports in the Quebec Court of Queen's
Bench, or King's Bench, in same series
as last.

R. L. .... La Revue Legale: Montreal.

Russ. Eq. .... Russell's Nova Scotia Equity Decisions:
Halifax, N.S.

S. A. L. R. .... South African Law Reports.

ADDENDA

P. 56. The letter H. should precede the word *Quebec* in the 24th line. .

Pp. 63-64. As to the recent Federal disallowance of a British Columbia Act on the report of Mr. Doherty, Minister of Justice, of May 21st, 1918, on the ground of interference with proprietary rights, see *Canadian Law Times,* Vol. 38, pp. 445-9, 584.

P. 69. As to law Courts not being concerned with the motives of the legislature in legislating, see now *per* Meredith, C.J.O., in *Currie* v. *Harris Lithographing Co., Ltd.* (1917), 41 O. L. R. 475, 490-1.

P. 143. Note *Re An Application by the Hudson Bay Co. and Heffernan* (1917), 3 W. W. R. 167, where the Saskatchewan Full Court held that a provincial legislature has not the power to prohibit the keeping of liquor within the province for export to other provinces or foreign countries.
Also *Rex* v. *Shaw* (1917), 28 Man. 325, where the Manitoba Court of Appeal (Haggart, J.A., dissenting), held *intra vires,* as a matter of a merely local or private nature in the province, an enactment of the provincial legislature prohibiting residents of the province from taking orders from any person within the province for 'purchasing or supplying of liquor for beverage purposes within the province. . .' Fullerton, J.A., inclined to think it justifiable also as an Act relating to civil rights within the province.

P. 152. As to *bona vacantia* in Quebec, see *The King* v. *Rithet,* 40 D. L. R. 670.

P. 158. Among the works dealing with the Constitution of Canada should undoubtedly have been mentioned A. Berriedale Keith's *Responsible Government in the Dominions* (3 Vols.), often referred to in the 'Notes; and also his *Imperial Unity and the Dominions:* 1916: Clarendon Press.

P. 232, n. 244. *Currie* v. *Harris Lithographing Co.* in appeal is now reported 41 O. L. R. 475.

P. 260-1, nn. 360, 367. See, also, *Ottawa Separate School Trustees* v. *Quebec Bank* (1918), 41 O. L. R. 594.

LEADING GENERAL PROPOSITIONS[1]

1. Although the British North America Act, 1867, or as it may be called for shortness sake, the Federation Act, is the sole charter by which the rights claimed by the Dominion and the provinces respectively can be determined, those legal decisions which embody the common law Constitution of Great Britain are equally authoritative in Canada; and we may say of both the Dominion and provincial governments that that great body of unwritten conventions, usages, and understandings which have in the course of time grown up in the practical working of the British Constitution form as important a part of the political system of Canada as the fundamental law itself which governs the federation . . . . .p. 40

2. The powers of legislation conferred upon the Dominion parliament and the provincial legislatures respectively by the Federation Act are conferred subject to the sovereign authority of the Imperial parliament . . . . .p. 47

3. The Crown is to be considered as one and indivisible throughout the Empire, and cannot be severed into as many distinct kingships as there are Dominions and self-governing colonies; and the prerogative of the Crown runs in Canada to the same extent as in England, where not expressly limited by statute . . . . .pp. 59-60

[1] Although almost the whole of the text of this Treatise may be said to consist of general propositions, which are illustrated and amplified in the notes, it is hoped and believed that the student will be assisted by the selection here made.

4. The Crown is a party to, and may be bound, by express mention or necessary intendment, by Dominion and provincial statutes so far as such statutes are *intra vires* ....pp. 60-61

5. The Crown is represented in Dominion affairs by the Governor-General, and in provincial affairs by the Lieutenant-Governors of the provinces; and the latter are as much the representatives of His Majesty for all purposes of provincial government as the former is for all purposes of Dominion government ....p. 61

6. The Governor-General in Council has power to disallow any provincial Act within one year after the receipt thereof by him ....pp. 62-66

7. Neither the Dominion parliament nor the provincial legislatures are to be considered as in any sense delegates of or acting under any mandate from the Imperial parliament, and they have the same powers as the Imperial parliament would have, under the like circumstances, to delegate to a municipal institution or body of their own creation authority to make by-laws or regulations as to subjects specified in their enactments, with the object of carrying such enactments into operation and effect; or to legislate conditionally, as, for example, subject to local option ....pp. 66-69

8. If it be once determined by competent judicial authority that the Dominion parliament or a provincial legislature has passed an Act upon any subject within its area of power, its jurisdiction as to the terms of such legislation is as absolute as that of the Imperial parliament would be if legislating over a like subject; and Courts of law have

no right whatever to enquire whether such jurisdiction has been exercised wisely or not; or to pronounce the Act invalid because it may affect injuriously private rights, or destroy vested rights, or
be otherwise unjust, or contrary to sound princi-

9. The object and design of an Act may be one
of the things to be determined in order to ascertain
the class of subject to which it really belongs, but
assuming such Act falls within the powers conferred
by the Federation Act upon the legislature passing
it, the motive which induced such legislature to ex-

10. The Dominion parliament cannot under colour of general legislation deal with what are provincial matters only; and, conversely, provincial legislatures cannot, under the mere pretence of legislating upon one of the enumerated matters confided to them by the Federation Act, really legislate
upon a matter assigned, to the jurisdiction of the

11. The language of the sections of the Federation Act conferring legislative powers upon the Dominion parliament and provincial legislatures respectively, and of the various heads which they contain, obviously cannot be construed as having been
intended to embody the exact disjunctions of a perfectly logical scheme. The way in which provisions
in terms overlapping each other have been placed
side by side in these sections shows that those who
passed the Act intended to leave the working out
and interpretation of these provisions to practice

12. The scheme of the Federation Act comprises a fourfold classification of legislative powers: firstly, over those subjects which are assigned to the exclusive power of the Dominion parliament; secondly, over those assigned to the exclusive power of the provincial legislatures; thirdly, over two subjects, and two subjects only, agriculture and immigration, which are assigned concurrently to the Dominion parliament and the provincial legislatures, Dominion legislation, however, having the predominance; and, fourthly, over a particular subject, namely, education, which, for special reasons, is dealt with exceptionally, and made the subject of special provisions ....pp. 72-74

13. With the exception of agriculture and immigration, which are dealt with specially, there is no subject-matter over which there can (strictly speaking) be said to exist concurrent powers of legislation in the Dominion parliament and the provincial legislatures. The powers of the Dominion parliament and of the provincial legislatures to deal directly and in their entirety, and as matters of separate and detached legislation (as distinguished from subjects merely ancillary to the main subject of legislation, as to which see Proposition 19) with the various classes of subjects enumerated in sections 91 and 92 of the Federation Act are in each case special and exclusive ....pp. 80-82

14. A general undefined and unrestricted residuary power is given to the Dominion parliament by the Federation Act to make laws for the peace, order and good government of Canada in relation to all matters not coming within the subjects assigned to the provincial legislatures; but such Dominion legislation should be strictly confined to such

matters as are unquestionably of Canadian interest and importance. The Dominion parliament cannot legislate under this residuary power in relation to matters which in each province are substantially of local or private interest upon the assumption that these matters also concern the peace, order, and good government of the Dominion. But some matters in their origin local or provincial (not being subjects specifically mentioned in the Federation Act as provincial subjects), may attain such dimensions as to affect the body politic of the Dominion, and justify the Dominion parliament in passing laws for their regulation or abolition in the interests of the Dominion. This, however, will not prevent provincial legislatures still dealing with such matters in their local or provincial aspect, but, in case of conflict, Dominion legislation will prevail ....pp. 74-77

15. The sections of the Federation Act relating to the distribution of legislative power exhaust the whole range of such power so far as the internal affairs of Canada are concerned, and whatever is not thereby given to the provincial legislatures in relation to such internal affairs, rests with the Dominion parliament. ....pp. 77-79

16. The Federation Act has to be construed as a whole, and when some specific matter is mentioned as within the exclusive power of the Dominion parliament or provincial legislature, as the case may be, which, but for that reference, would fall within the more general description of a subject-matter expressed to be confided to the other, the statute must be read as excepting it from that general description .... pp. 82-3

17. Where in respect to matters with which provincial legislatures have power to deal, provincial legislation directly conflicts with the enactments of the Dominion parliament, whether the latter immediately relate to the enumerated classes of Dominion subjects, or are only ancillary to legislation upon such subjects, or are enactments for the peace, order, and good government of Canada in relation to matters not coming within the classes of subjects assigned exclusively to the provincial legislatures, nor within the enumerated Dominion subjects, the provincial legislation must yield to that of the Dominion parliament. For as to Dominion laws we have a quasi-legislative union. They are the local laws of the whole Dominion, and of each and every province thereof. ....pp. 84-85

18. The legislative authority of the Dominion parliament over the enumerated Dominion subjects is exclusive. Whenever, therefore, a matter is within one of these specified classes of subjects, legislation in relation to it by a provincial legislature is incompetent. Thus a provincial legislature cannot enact a bankruptcy law or a copyright law for the province, even though the Dominion parliament may not have itself legislated upon those subjects.
pp. 85-86

19. The due exercise of the enumerated power conferred upon the Dominion parliament by the Federation Act may occasionally and incidentally involve legislation upon matters which are *prima facie* committed exclusively to the provincial legislatures. The Dominion parliament may deal with such local or private provincial matters where such legislation is necessarily incidental to the exercise

of its own enumerated powers; or to the extent of
such ancillary provisions as may be required to prevent the scheme of one of its own laws from being
defeated... ....pp. 87-88, 93-94

20. There is no restriction upon the Dominion
parliament when legislating upon one of its enumerated classes of subjects, to prevent it passing a
law affecting one part of the Dominion and not
another, if in its wisdom it thinks the legislation
desirable in one and not in the other.....pp. 88-90

21. The Dominion parliament can, in matters
within its sphere, impose duties upon any subjects
of the Dominion, whether they be officials of provincial Courts, other officials, or private citizens.....
pp. 90-91

22. The provincial legislatures have no powers
to make laws save upon the sixteen enumerated
subject-matters confided to them, except the powers
given to them to make laws in relation to education, and in relation to agriculture in the province,
and immigration into the province. They cannot
legislate beyond the areas of the prescribed subject-
matters ....p. 91

23. Co-equal and co-ordinate legislative powers
in every particular were conferred by the Federation Act on the provinces. The Constitutions of all
provinces within the Dominion are on the same level.
p. 93

24. Whatever powers provincial legislatures
have as included within the enumerated subject-
matters committed to them, when properly understood, those powers they may exercise, although in

so doing they may incidentally touch or affect something which might otherwise be held to come within the exclusive jurisdiction of the Dominion parliament under some of the enumerated Dominion subject-matters . . . `. . . . . .pp. 95-97

25. A provincial legislature is not incapacitated from enacting a law otherwise within its proper competency merely because the Dominion parliament might, under its own powers, if it saw fit so to do, pass a general law which would embrace within its scope the subject-matter of the provincial Act.
pp. 97-98

26. Subjects which in one aspect and for one purpose fall within the enumerated provincial legislative powers, may, in another aspect and for another purpose, fall within the Dominion legislative powers, and so be proper for Dominion legislation, by "aspect" being meant the aspect or point of view of the legislator in legislating, the object, purpose, and scope of the legislation. Any merely incidental effect a law may have over other matters does not alter its own character. . . . . .p. 98

27. Although part of an Act, either of the Dominion parliament or of a provincial legislature, may be *ultra vires,* and, therefore, invalid, this will not invalidate the rest of the Act if it appears that the one part is separate in its operation from the other part, so that each is a separate declaration of the legislative will, and unless the object of the Act is such that it cannot be attained by a partial execution . . . . .p. 100

Historical Introduction.

The British North America Act, 1867, which con-
federated the British colonies of Canada, Nova
Scotia, New Brunswick and potentially the rest of
British North America, stands at the close of a·cen-
tury of constitutional experiment. Goldwin Smith's
aphorism that '' deadlock was the father of Canadian Confederation '' is only a half-truth, for Canadian Confederation is, from many points of view, the
logical outcome of antecedent attempts at govern-
.ment, none of which in reality failed and each of
which brought with it its own quota of development.
Responsible federal government in Canada is an
evolution through a hundred years of anxious questionings, of difficult and complicated situations, of
wisdom and folly, of insight and blindness, of de-
spair and faith. It is true, as will appear in the
course of this Introduction, that deadlock accele-
rated the development, and it is well to realize
clearly in connexion with the British North America
Act that there is very little of the dramatic and
brilliant faith which launched the Union of South
Africa. Almost every step towards Canadian Confederation was taken in the light of past experience in constitution making in Canada. On every
side along the difficult and treacherous road there
were finger-posts marked "danger." The Fathers of Canadian Confederation had behind them
a history which not only pointed out the solution to
Canadian difficulties, but also emphasized the pit-
falls which it was necessary to avoid. There hung

round the Quebec Conference an historical atmosphere of hope and fear, and in such an atmosphere Canadian Confederation was born—the child of experience, remote and immediate.

An historical background is, as a consequence, emphatically necessary for a Treatise on Canadian Constitutional law. This Treatise traces in detail the interpretation of the Constitution during the last fifty years. We shall see that the British North America Act was almost necessarily an outline, in which, however, as Edward Blake said in *The Ontario Lands' Case,* "a single line imported into the system that mighty and complex and somewhat indefinite aggregate called the British Constitution." Thus, there was wide scope for amplification, for discussion, for differences of opinion, for legal decisions, which, indeed, have occupied no inconsiderable place in legal and historical circles. With this aspect of the Canadian Constitution I have, in this Introduction, no concern. My object is to trace the historical evolution to which reference has already been made. There are, of course, obvious limitations. It would be impossible to elaborate the history, to enter fully into the *pros* and *cons* of constitutional problems, complicated as they are with political and social considerations, to examine judicially many theories which lend colour to present day controversies. My work is in some respects more difficult. It is not a mere retelling of a story. It is an attempt to interpret a development. It is not a mere summary of facts. It is an attempt to find in facts the complex characters and diverse conditions out of which they grew. It is an attempt to animate documents and manuscripts—petitions, letters, ordinances, despatches, Acts of Parliament —with something of the vital energy which once

called them into being; to see the history with contemporary eyes; to reconstruct contemporary standards and ideals; to judge objectively the storm and
stress of the human will, and in all the difficult process to give a true and adequate, but above all a
living setting to Canadian Confederation.

The Peace of Paris in 1763 left England with
practically a free hand to do with a conquered
people almost as she wished. We are not here concerned with the various pictures of Canadians and
Canadian life which General Murray vividly drew in
his earliest reports to the British government: the
"litigious disposition" of the whole community;
the vanity, the contempt for trade, the petty tyranny
of the seigniors; the French dignitaries of the
Church; the rank and file of Canadian clergy;
shrewd and hardy traders and hunters; "strong,
healthy, virtuous and temperate" peasants; a residuum "allured and debauched" by the Indian
trade. It is a strange and suggestive picture standing as it does in violent social contrast with the
southern Colonies. The contrast, however, goes further and affords for our immediate purpose an interesting and important point of view. The government—where it extended at least—was fixed and
rigid in State and Church, being only rescued from
monotony through the doubtful varieties provided
by the unreliability of despotism and corruption.
If the letter was paternalism, the spirit was auto-
cratic conservatism. England took over a people, from prelate and seignior down to habitant
and hunter, who had not only no training in political
thought, but were as far removed as it is possible to
conceive from contemporary British and colonial
conceptions of free citizenship. On the surface the
situation did not seem very complicated. It looked

a simple enough thing to become rulers over a people
so undeveloped and inexperienced in government.
More careful examination shows that the problem
was pregnant with difficulties.

In the first place, Britain never before had ac-
quired half a continent, so to speak, in which another
white race had made colonizing experiments. The
problem was then a problem of inexperience—how
to govern a conquered white race? The problem
was rendered all the more difficult, when it was
mixed up with the question of ruling them in
relation to adjoining British colonies, alien in race
and religion, and highly advanced for the age in
political thought. Would the southern Colonies wel-
come their conquered neighbours as fellow citizens?
Would the southern Colonies prove aggressive,
either socially or economically? Many questions
pressed forward for an answer. Were this survey of
the situation complete, it would have presented an
ambiguous enough outlook. There was, however, the
Indian question, and more difficult still there was
the presence of British settlers already in Canada—
a complication to which we shall return.

British statesmen approached their task by
selecting General Murray as first " Captain-General
and Governor-in-chief." When he began his new
work in August, 1764, he had two documents on
which he could fall back for guidance—his own Commission of the previous November and the Royal
Proclamation of the previous October. The latter
outlined possibilities in a broad spirit of wisdom,
but throughout there was a tactful ambiguity. Canada was to be given, as far as possible and expedient,
those customs and institutions which the British
valued. It would appear that the intention was an
immediate introduction of English law, and the

establishment of courts of justice in which civil and criminal cases should be tried " as near as may be agreeable to the laws of England "—an important clause. In addition, representative institutions were promised, but only as soon as circumstances would permit: a proviso reinforced, and its importance emphasized in Murray's Commission as Governor. This Commission set up a form of government something akin to what we know to-day as that of a " Crown Colony." Until the opportune moment came for calling a popular "General Assembly of the freeholders," the Governor was empowered to make Ordinances on the advice of a nominated Council. In other words, executive and legislative government were exercised by the Governor on the advice of the Council—the creation of the Crown. In due course, a system of Courts was established, in which English law, broadly speaking, was to be administered, and trial-by-jury introduced without any religious tests.

Such was the scheme under which some 70,000 French-Canadians began their new life. To them it must have appeared by no means hard and tyrannical when they remembered that as a conquered people they had every reason to expect the application of contemporary standards. To the British Government it must have appeared generous and equitable. What more could " the new subjects " want than the hopes of colonial self-government, English law, English law-courts and English justice? The citizen of the twentieth century may see the humour of the question; but to the eighteenth century Englishman there was a pleasing condescension in promising to the Canadians all that he most valued, and round which the sacrosanct atmosphere of unreasoned awe and reverence had gradually gathered. If in the issue he did not find pronounced graltitude for his gift, it was because of difficulties which Murray and his successor, Sir Guy Carleton, understood.

Reference has already been made to the fact that there were British settlers in Canada. The earliest difficulties in the Canadian situation were largely caused by the extreme claims which were put forward by these few hundred settlers alien to the Canadians in race, speech, and religion. We must allow for the irritation which their assumed superiority caused Murray; for his description of some of them as "the most immoral collection of men I ever knew"; for his extreme condemnation of their arrogance, which sought to place the entire government of the country in their own hands. On the other hand, Murray was a high-minded man of upright principles, who could not fail to see that the spirit displayed by this small section of the community was highly detrimental. His opinion cannot be idly overlooked. It is confirmed many times over by his successor, a man of equally high principles and character. Nor was the situation rendered any more easy by the type of official sent out from England — men who called forth the almost impassioned condemnation of both these Governors. Indeed, the evident good-will of England to give to the Canadians in the future institutions which she thought must be instinctively valued by everyone was in itself a source of weakness. As we have seen, the Canadians could not in the least understand the type of government with its many unedifying disputes, under which the English colonists to their south lived. With their roots in the immemorial past of paternalism, they were immeasurably removed from the appreciation of any form of self-government, and they were certainly not likely to be enamoured of it, when their fellow citizens of alien speech, race and religion loudly demanded it for Canada. So, too, English systems of law and justice were inexplicable. Before long, chaos reigned.

It will be well, however, to point out that an historical judgment on the state of affairs is not forced to rest on the reports of Governors alone, self-evident though their honesty may be. Many documents from the minority itself help us. For example, the Grand Jury at Quebec claimed that they were "the only body that represented the colony, . . . that they, as British subjects, have a right to be consulted, before any Ordinance, that may affect the body that they represent, be passed into law." The document might be left to the judgment of history, were it not necessary to point out that the six French Canadians who signed it along with fourteen British, could not understand it. Murray described the authors as "licentious fanatics" who wished to expel the Canadians. Nor does the Grand Jury's presentment stand alone. Some of the minority almost immediately petitioned for Murray's recall on the grounds of anti-Protestant and anti-British rule, and incidentally because he did not go to church on Sunday. They asked for a House of Assembly composed exclusively of Protestants, for whom, however, the Canadians might be permitted to vote! These documents taken with Murray's reports, show how far a sense of superiority curtails a sense of humour.

Murray's successor, Carleton, went through a somewhat similar experience. Things reached an absurd position when he was somewhat officiously called to task by the minority for his method in

asking advice. His reply was stinging in its high
sense of dignity and in its well merited snub. But
nothing could disturb the smug self-satisfaction of
the minority, who, had they had their way with a
popular Assembly, would have made it almost certain that Canada would have become a fourteenth
State of the Union.

While the body politic was thus disturbed, in the
legal world all was confusion. The Proclamation
of 1763 was never fully enforced, and it would have
been an utter impossibility at any given moment to
have stated in anything like clear terms what the
law of Canada really was. The State-papers of the
period abound in reports on the Canadian judicial
and legal system, and in suggestions drawn up on
the advice of the home government for the better-
ment and simplification of the confusion. It is true
that Carleton managed to make some necessary
improvements in the law and procedure relating to
the recovery of debt, that he pruned the wings of
the inefficient justices of the peace. This necessary
Ordinance was a mere detail however in the chaotic
state of affairs. Of course, English criminal law
largely prevailed from the beginning of Murray's
administration, but in civil law anarchy was supreme. Canadian lawyers, utterly ignorant of English law, pleaded in French before English-speaking judges who knew nothing of French law. In
fact, nobody really knew what civil law was in force,
and as a result all the evils of corruption, exces-
sive fees, and worst of all of real injustice, prevailed—while high above the whirl of confusion
rose the voice of the minority demanding the immediate and complete introduction of English civil
law and procedure.

It at last became evident that the new colony could no longer be carried on on a system, which, if at times highly humourous, tended to reduce respect for law. Carleton, the most enlightened man in Canadian affairs, saw that the situation was little likely to enhance British rule in the eyes of the new subjects, and certainly was most detrimental to their political development. Amid the mass of suggested changes, his stands out in interest. He wished the retention of the entire French civil code, subject to a few sensible and necessary amendments, with the English code, as before, for criminal proceedings. There was no small amount of intelligent and fair-minded inquiry, and when Carleton went to England in 1770, it was an open secret that an Act of Parliament would be brought forward to deal with the Canadian situation. Carleton remained in England four years, and to England we must now turn to follow the course of Canada's fortunes—or misfortunes as the point of view may be, for Carleton did not return until the Quebec Act of 1774 had, for good or ill, become law.

From the constitutional point of view, two influences seem to have been at work which gave the Quebec Act its final form. One was the unmistakable attitude taken up by Carleton; the other was the growing breach between England and the American Colonies. Carleton was convinced that an injustice would be done were the government of the Canadians handed over to a small British minority by providing a House of Assembly to which the latter alone should send representatives. This equitable opinion was emphasized doubtless by the fact that, if Canada was not to go the way which the Thirteen Colonies were evidently going, it would be necessary to save the Canadians from a Govern-

ment which would have been more or less inclined
to accept for them the proferred hand of southern
friendship. With what greater insinuation would
that offer have been made had there been no Quebec Act, when the Act itself was made the occasion
for asking the Canadians to desert Britain? As a
consequence, the Quebec Act did not contain any
provision for the immediate summoning of an Assembly—the time was considered "inexpedient"—
and the government remained much the same as
before—that of a " Crown Colony." English criminal law was continued in the Province, while the
civil law of France was to govern "all matters of
controversy relative to property and civil rights."
The religious question was dealt with along lines
laid down by previous experience. Freedom was
granted to the Roman Catholic Church, a simplified
oath of allegiance was provided, and the clergy were
confirmed in their rights to their "accustomed
dues" from their parishioners.

The Bill may be summed up as a confession of
failure and a confession of strength. Canadian
civil law was restored, and the proposal for a popular Assembly postponed *sine die*. Thus any severe
construction of the Proclamation of 1763 was ruled
out of Court—indeed the Proclamation was by name
repealed by the fourth section. On the other hand,
trial by jury in criminal suits, toleration in religion,
and a Council to which men of any creed might be
called were guaranteed. There can be seen in every
section the guiding hand of Carleton, who kept his
balance at a moment when chaotic failure, bitter
recrimination and inability to understand the Canadian situation were only too widespread. Perhaps, too, we may see in it the tracings of the finger
already writing "Mene" on the wall of British
colonial experiment.

We are not concerned here with the wisdom or unwisdom of the Act, but no student of Canadian Constitutional history ought to overlook the debates[1] on the measure as it passed through the British parliament. These debates must be read as a whole, and extracts from them would only discount their illustrative value. They not only throw light on the failings of great men—North, Burke, Fox, Chatham—who had passed through years of embittered parliamentary struggle, but they provide the best contemporary comment on Canadian affairs of which I know, as they contain the evidence of Governor Carleton, the judicial fair-minded gentleman; of Chief Justice Hey, no less honourable and sincere; and of Masères, whose honesty shines out all the more clearly on account of the limitations which his Huguenot ancestry imposed on him of approaching the Canadian situation in a spirit entirely unprejudiced. The interested reader will find enough in the course of his study to convince him that the Quebec Act was no sudden, subtle, and well arranged attack on their freedom, as the citizens of the Thirteen Colonies claimed. He will see how it comes logically out of the difficulties inherent in Canadian government, and, while the ''colonial troubles'' doubtless coloured the Act, they had little or nothing to do with the broad framework.

. These ''colonial troubles,'' however, affected the Quebec Act in another way, which the student of constitutional history, anxious to study experiments in their workings, 'may be inclined to deplore. The breaking out of hostilities between Britain and her

[1] See Cavendish, *Debates on the Canada Bill in 1774* (London, 1839).

Colonies almost rendered the Act still-born. In the general lining up of all the forces which she could command in the greatest struggle in her history, there was little time or opportunity for seeing in full how the experiment of giving parliamentary recognition to a French colony within the Empire would work. The isolated demands for a new Constitution were drowned in the noise of battle. If they require an answer from the constitutional historian, it can best be found in Haldimand's despatch of October 25th, 1780, to Lord George Germain: "It requires but little penetration to discover that, had the system of government solicited by the old subjects been adopted in Canada, this colony would in 1775 have become one of the United States of America." But these isolated demands soon became reinforced by those of the colonial citizens known to history as the United Empire Loyalists, many of whom took up new homes in Canada — mostly in those districts which compose the modern province of Ontario—during and after the Revolutionary War. When a petition for "a free constitution," signed by the British of Quebec, Montreal and Three Rivers, was presented to the King almost immediately after the conclusion of peace, it was no longer a mere repetition of the twenty-year old demand, but a finger-post pointing to a new experiment. The arrival of the ex-soldiers and the new citizens practically made a change necessary, and we must now turn to consider the events which led up to another mile-stone on the road of Canadian constitutional development.

The problem at once caused anxious questionings and poignant debates both in England and in Canada. When Carleton, now Lord Dorchester, returned for the second time as Governor in October, 1786, it was clear that there lay before him a more difficult task than that which confronted him previous to the passing of the Quebec Act. The "ancient subjects" were as persistent as ever, their demands now including not merely a House of Assembly, but the right of taxation and some control over the executive. The last point is worthy of more than passing notice. It is a long time until we again hear of it in either express or implied terms in Canadian history; but doubtless the emphasis on it during the American Revolution and the too flagrant abuses connected with British official appointments in Canada might have lent it such weight at this time as to have hastened the solution of Canadian problems, had not the "ancient subjects" been forced, as we shall see, to defend another position. The United Empire Loyalists, while they had stood out solidly for the monarchical position, yielded nothing to the Fathers of American Confederation in their claims to representative institutions. They were, indeed, more developed in political thought than contemporary Englishmen, and it soon became apparent, as Dorchester informed the home Government, that those who had sacrificed their homes and fortunes and political rights to begin life again in the wilds of Canada would not sit down calmly under the constitutional system erected by the Quebec Act. Then there were the French-Canadians, still children in political experience, to whom representative institutions and all their appendages were meaningless and undesirable. Heirs to the apathy born of absolutism, they knew nothing of and cared less for all the constitutional safeguards which the United Empire Loyalists and "ancient subjects" claimed as their most valued political possessions. To them a House of Assembly was but "une machine anglaise pour nous taxer." Out of such opposed forces would it be possible to present any adequate and just solution to a problem which was pressing itself forward with insistent demand?

The first on the scene were the "ancient subjects" fortified by petitions from their supporters in England, who claimed for them "the blessings of British law and British government." For some months petitions, counter-petitions, and a voluminous correspondence occupied the attention of the Government, but it was only on the motion of a private member that Canadian affairs came before the House of Commons in April, 1786, when a bill was introduced to amend the Quebec Act in such a way as to meet the new situation, and to overturn "the complete despotism and slavery" of the existing system. Once again, Fox stands forth with all the phrases of the new political philosophy on his lips. Pitt, however, took matters in hand. His practical mind realized that doctrinaire theories must be tested by a careful analysis of Canadian affairs, and by a close scrutiny of them on the part of those most competent for the work. On his advice the debate was postponed until Dorchester had once again applied himself to the complicated subject and sent in further reports.

For some months Dorchester was at work on the Canadian problem with a judicial minded energy to which many despatches bear witness. A new impetus was given in 1788 by the arrival of Adam Lymburner in London as the representative of the British minority in French Canada. His arrival forced the hands of the Government, who had already decided, with Dorchester in agreement, that there was no plan easily available, which could be justly offered to take the place of the existing Constitution. Lymburner at the bar of the House dwelt largely on the legal intricacies and the inadequate constitutional condition of Canadian government. In the ensuing debate, in which great names once more figure, the point of view is rather one of melancholy insularity. Fox reached the old heights of academic eloquence. Burke piled sentence on sentence with the command of words which had now become fatal. Pitt's good sense rescued the scene from hollowness and unreality, and he promised a full dress debate next session.

As a consequence of this promise the Government in the autumn of the same year seems to have decided on the presentation of a bill for the division of the province—at any rate this project was referred to Dorchester in September, and did not receive his full approval. He was prepared, however, to help if the home Government insisted. Delays caused by discussions over land-tenure occupied a year. In October, 1789, the draft of the new Constitution was sent to Dorchester containing provisions for popular institutions in each new province. Grenville's covering despatch is interesting, containing as it does the now famous description of the Act, which in a short time was to appear in General Simcoe's speech in closing the first Parliament of Upper Canada—"an image and transcript of the British Constitution." In addition we find in the same despatch an elaborate explanation of the proposal to found a kind of Canadian House of Lords as a bulwark against the dreaded democracy of the new Republic. The proposal was quashed by Dorchester, although it was inserted as a permissive clause in the bill, and later on General Simcoe played with it in a highly characteristic and amusing manner.

Of more interest, perhaps, to the student is the opinion obtained about this time by Dorchester from William Smith, Chief Justice of Canada—an opinion to which Dorchester himself lent support. The proposal was in reality one for a federation of British North America. It is true that neither Smith nor Dorchester foreshadowed Canadian self-government as we know it to-day, but both of them displayed remarkable insight in seeing how some kind of federation would tend to eliminate the meticulous pettiness of small and jealous provinces. If Franklin's proposal of 1754 aimed at the federation of the Thirteen Colonies against an external foe, the proposal made by Dorchester and Smith aimed at saving provinces from foes of their own household. However, the times were not ripe for such a scheme, and in March 1791, Pitt introduced the Constitutional Act.

The passage of the Act through the British Parliament cannot be dealt with at length, but certain points deserve at least a passing notice. Lymburner once more appeared on behalf of his friends, who were now to be hoist on their own petard—an Assembly—but on terms of equality with their old neighbours, the French-Canadians. He opposed the division of the Province, as he and his did not relish in such company an isolation from the United Empire Loyalists of the western districts. It never seems to have occurred to the section of the Canadian public which he represented that there was any possibility of the French-Canadians being anything more than passive citizens, to be ruled and used by the superior British. Lymburner's evidence well repays reading, were it only to provide a lesson on the fatuous folly of "the liberty of prophesying." The debate itself is, alas, too often only

recalled from the fact that the breach of friendship
between Burke and Fox occurred during it; but,
however pregnant with heart-searching the future
proved to be, the debate will convince the student
that the Government of the day did not lightly dole
out of its treasures a new Constitution for Canada.
Doubtless, it did not satisfy the abstract theorists,
but it was based on facts studied and grasped as
far as possible, and the honesty of the Government
cannot be questioned because they happened to lack
political omniscience and the wisdom which we possess! I think we shall see that the weakness of the
Act lay in what it did not give, more than in what
it gave. Grenville's letters, too, at this time mark
the beginnings of England's new colonial policy.
He wrote of the graciousness of immediate conces-
sions, which, if delayed, might be extorted without
discretion. Pitt also turned his back on the past
when in introducing the bill he repudiated England's right to impose taxes except for the regulation of trade and commerce, and, "in order to
guard against the abuse of these powers, such taxes
were to be levied and disposed by the Legislature
of each division."

It is necessary to note somewhat carefully the
provisions made for Canadian government by the
Constitutional Act of 1791. In each province was
set up a Legislative Council appointed by the King
for life, which with the House of Assembly in each
province, had power to make laws. Permissive
power was given to the King to annex to hereditary
titles the right of being summoned to the Legislative Council. The appointment of the Speaker of
the Council lay in the hands of the Governor. The
right to vote for members of the House was vested,

in the counties and towns, in those who had a small property qualification. Legislative Councillors and clergymen could not hold seats in the Assembly. The Governor and all public officials were to be appointed by the Crown. Freedom for the Roman Catholic religion was granted, and a proportion of uncleared Crown lands was set aside for the support of the Protestant clergy. The entire executive authority was left in the hands of the Crown, and the possession of vast lands made it possible for the Government to be independent of parliamentary taxation. The administration of justice was practically passed over, the Governor or Lieutenant-Governor and the Executive Council in either province being constituted a Court of appeal in civil cases. There was no definition of the relationship of the Legislative Councils to the Houses of Assembly, but Grenville informed Dorchester in a covering despatch that, as far as the latter made claims for granting money, the claims were " so consistent with the spirit of our Constitution that they ought not to be resisted." Nor was any attempt made to define the legislative relationship of the provincial parliaments to the British parliament.

With such a system, which lasted almost half a century, Canada started her new constitutional life. These years are perhaps the most complicated in Canadian history and any detailed survey of them must naturally lie outside the scope of my work here. However, it is well to point out a danger into which the student of Canadian history is liable to fall. Overwhelmed in documents, dumbfounded by the *minutiæ* of endless quarrels, wearied by petition and counter-petition, he may turn aside from the task of careful study of these years, convinced that they are too largely filled with valueless detail. The years are, however, the most vital in Canadian history if a proper historical perspective is to be obtained and the present judicially estimated. It is true that the mass of historical material is almost colossal, but it will repay all the work spent on it, for out of it will, I think, emerge valuable considerations in constitutional experiment and illustrations of constitutional growth, without a knowledge of which the present cannot be properly and fairly understood. On the surface the life of the period is petty, dull, and common-place, but beneath can be traced streams of development which later came to light and met in the full river of responsible government. Difficult then though the history may be, it is possible to consider it under several generalizations and to sum up the half century's contribution to the growth of the Canadian Constitution.

The first problem to which I would draw attention is connected with supply. The Governor had at his disposal crown-revenues, and he could always draw on the military chest which was replenished by the home Government, while the Assembly had control only over monies raised by provincial legislation. Thus the Governor—that is the Crown in Canada—could at any time work the machinery of government as he wished. The history of the period is full of painful illustrations of the Crown's independence of grants and of its carrying out the administration of the country without monies voted by the legislature. As long as the Crown was able to control effectively the government, there was a certain farcical element in representative institutions. This was one of the broad issues. It is true that the protagonists of the Assembly in this connexion were too frequently factious and recalcitrant demagogues, but behind the wearisome reiteration of their claims there lies the great constitutional truth that there can be no safe element in self-government unless the elected Assembly has control over appropriation.

Secondly, since there was in the Act no definition of the legislative sphere peculiar to the British and provincial Parliaments, issues in themselves strictly affecting the provinces and yet of vital importance to the entire scheme, were reserved for consideration to the British Parliament. Among these was the power to amend the provincial Constitutions. To any one only superficially acquainted with the new system it must be clear that there were bound to be clashes between the various constituent parts of the Government which only constitutional amendments could remove. At first the Assembly of Lower Canada tried petitions, but when England failed to provide the remedy which apparently was within her sphere to provide, the Assembly passed from point to point until it claimed the power itself of changing the Constitution, a position which erected another barrier between the Crown and the popular house.

Thirdly, there was the fact that the Crown had no constitutional responsibility to the House of Assembly, and yet there could be no legislation without the House of Assembly. The question was how to link up the chief Executive authority with the elected Chamber. As a matter of fact no answer to that question was found within these years. The executive was financially and, worse still, constitutionally independent, and the House of Assembly, in seeking vaguely to cure a disease which it had not in reality diagnosed, frequently overstepped its sphere, with the result that it was dissolved time after time. Constitutionally the Governor had as much right to dissolve it as the King had to dissolve Parliament, but in the latter case the King would act on the advice of responsible ministers in a spirit of nebulous, if royal, neutrality, whereas the Governor in Canada was driven to act in the capacity of a political party leader. As a consequence, respect for the Executive Government diminished, while the House of Assembly became more and more aggressive in asserting its rights. Nor did the fact that in Lower Canada a considerable proportion of the Executive Council were members of the hated unelected Legislative Council help the situation—in Upper Canada the entire Executive Council belonged to the Legislative Council. The Executive and Legislative Councils were used by the Crown as bulwarks against the popular Assemblies, and appointments to them were as a rule confined to those who supported the administration. The whole system was vitiated by an irresponsible Executive.

Two consequences of a serious nature followed. In Upper Canada control passed into the hands of a clique, known to history as "the family compact," but there was little popular fury, as the rebellion in that province was but the shadow cast by its flamboyant leader. In Lower Canada the situation passed from point to point of pathetic folly, for which both the Crown and the Assembly were responsible. It was a fatal move to suggest the union of the provinces in 1822, and I believe that that suggestion and the bill which embodied it gave the French-Canadians a national cause. It was fatal, too, for French Canada to pass through the storm and stress of struggle under leadership too often undisciplined. On the other hand, there was in reality no remedy at hand, and if foolhardy rebellions in both provinces closed the constitutional experiment under the Constitutional Act, the Crown had nothing to replace it, just as Oliver Cromwell had no workable system ready at the close of the Civil War. As we read the history to-day in the light of fifty years and more of full Canadian responsible government, it is of course quite easy to see the exact points in which the whole scheme was weak, but no one at that moment in history had worked out the problem. The sovereignty of the Crown seemed an insurmountable barrier to anything like responsible colonial government. Thus, for example, in Lower Canada where the situation was always graver, and the necessity always greater, the House of Assembly continued to believe that the introduction of the elective system into the Legislative Council would solve all difficulties.[1] For our purpose, then, Lord Durham's words perhaps best sum up the entire situation: "representative government coupled with an irresponsible Executive... constant collision between the branches of the Government; the same abuse of the powers of the representative bodies, owing to the anomaly of their position, aided by the want of good municipal institutions, and the same constant interference of the Imperial administration in matters which should be left wholly to the provincial Governments."[2] The period closed in darkness with the suspension of the Constitution and the provision for the temporary government of Lower Canada early in 1838. In darkness but not in failure, for with the arrival of Lord Durham in Canada in May, 1838, there began

---

[1] Of course, on the eve of the Rebellion, there were demands for "responsible government" and for "a responsible Executive"; but no one in either Province knew clearly the meaning of these demands.

[2] Lucas, *Lord Durham's Report*, Vol. II. p. 194 (Oxford, 1912).

another and better era, to which these years, tragic though they were in religious and racial hatred and bloodshed and thick with constitutional errors, brought an invaluable quota of experience. Indeed Canada had from one point of view and in a lesser degree re-enacted a phase of the constitutional history of England.

Lord Durham's *Report on the Affairs of British North America* is, with all its limitations and especially those in connexion with Upper Canada, the worthy outcome of the noble purpose which he outlined for himself in the House of Lords on the eve of his departure from England. Standing as it does among the greatest State-papers in British history, it must be read as a whole, if any adequate estimate is to be formed of its insight, its grasp of Canadian affairs, and its modest if in places dogmatic assurance. It is not too much to say that it laid the foundation not only for the future government of Canada but for every future self-governing Dominion. Durham, like Lord Dorchester and Chief Justice Smith, looked forward to a federation of British North America. If the time was not at hand he hastened it by the proposal of restoring the Union of the Canadas under one legislature. He diagnosed the constitutional disease of Canada: " I know not how it is possible to secure harmony in any other way than by administering the government on those principles which have been found perfectly efficacious in Great Britain. I would not impair a single prerogative of the Crown; on the contrary, I believe that the interests of the people of these Colonies require the protection of prerogatives which have not hitherto been exercised. But the Crown must, on the other hand, submit to the necessary consequences of representative institutions; and if it has to carry on the government in

unison with a representative body it must carry it
on by means of those in whom that representative
body has confidence.[1] He saw, too, the necessity—
belated though it was in England's own constitutional struggle—of placing the judges on the same
footing in Canada as they had been placed in England by the Act of Settlement: '' the independence
of the judges should be secured, by giving them the
same tenure of office and security of income as exist
in England.''[2] It remained for Lord Durham and
his assistants to gather up the broken and half-
uttered suggestions of previous workers in the same
difficult field and to give them the solidarity and
vitality of a constitutional creed. Responsible government alone can galvanize into life representative
institutions. The *Report* instinctively sums up the
situation, and in the main and along broad generous
lines of statesmanship, pointed the only safe road
for Britain to follow. Mistaken though it may have
been in proposing a fusion of races, yet the scheme
for immediate union under responsible government
brought together the British and French as never
before. Turbulent though the experience itself was,
it pointed the way to and made all the more rosy-
red the dawn of Canadian Confederation.

It was a fortunate coincidence that to such
a man as Lord John Russell should have fallen
the lot of being the official recipient of Lord Durham's *Report,* and that under his guidance the
Act of Union was passed, embodying as far as possible, as he informed Lord Durham, the general
principles of his survey. It was still more fortunate that the government chose Poulett Thomson,
afterwards Lord Sydenham, to carry out the actual

1 Lucas, *op. cit.,* p. 278.
2 *Ibid.,* p. 327.

reconstruction. '' It is rare,'' said Joseph Howe of
him, '' that a statesman so firm, so sagacious, and
indefatigable follows in the wake of a projector so
bold.'' It is true that at the passing of the Act,
Lord John Russell was not prepared to accept *in
toto* Lord Durham's theory of responsible government, but he at least set up a jumping-off place, if I
may be allowed the expression, in his advice to
Thomson, who explained in answer to an address
from the Upper Canadian House of Assembly, that
he had '' received her Majesty's commands to administer the government of these provinces in accordance with the well understood wishes and
interests of the people, and to pay to their feelings,
as expressed through their representatives, the
deference that is justly due to them.''[1] The despatches authorizing this statement were, in 1841,
submitted to the legislature of the united province.
In them Lord John Russell instructed the Governor-
General '' to call to his councils and to employ in
the public service those persons, who, by their position and character, have obtained the general confidence and esteem of the inhabitants of the province.''[2] This was at least the recognition of a new
principle. If Thomson preferred to be his own
first minister, to choose the best men independent
of numerical support in the Assembly, and did not
feel anxious to drive responsible government to its
logical conclusion—cabinet government, yet his
method tided Canada over a trying period in her
history, with the rebellions in the near past, with
the French-Canadians full of suspicion and ominous
apprehension lest Lord Durham's suggestions for
their absorption might be present in some subtle

[1] *Journals of the House of Commons of Canada, 1841.* Appendix, BB.
[2] *Ibid.*

way in the mind of the new Governor. Indeed, with
no provision in the Act itself for responsible government, Thomson worked wonders.

It is hardly necessary to analyse the Act in detail. The general scheme of government was little
changed. There was erected one Legislative Council, members of which held office for life on good
behaviour, and one House of Assembly, the members
of which were to consist of an equal number from
each old province, and must possess property worth
at least £500. The Speaker of the Council was to
be nominated by the Governor, and of the Assembly
to be elected by its members. The status of the
Roman Catholic Church, of the Church of England,
of waste lands and of religious toleration was
clearly defined and protected. Arrangements were
made for a consolidated fund out of which the expenses of the judiciary, Government, and pensions
might be paid. The rest of the revenue was at the
disposal of the United Legislature which assumed
the debts of the two provinces. Appropriation and
taxation originated with the Governor-General and
were then open to discussion in the House of Assembly.

Sydenham's success was a personal one, and
even he could not bring together the best men of
the opposing races, nor even of the British race.
He succeeded in stamping on the Government, into
which he called no extremists, his own strong per-
sonality. I always think of him as a man whose
great and constructive energy was relieved by an
inner spirit of subtle humour, for I can never
imagine him responsible to any one but to himself
and Lord John Russell, however much he may have
hinted at responsible government. His death anticipated his resignation which he had already sent in,

but it may not be a reflexion on his fine and courage-
ous character to say that it was perhaps fortunate,
as, had he remained to govern Canada, his very
success might have proved his undoing. His successor, Sir Charles Bagot, determined to continue his
policy. Bagot, however, had not Sydenham's
strength and his very impartiality led him to accept
a reform ministry—the reforming parties in both
sections of the province having joined hands—under
Baldwin and Lafontaine—a thing, I imagine, Sydenham would not have done. Bagot's successor, Sir
Charles Metcalfe, had little belief in responsible
government, and under him the thorny question
arose of the relation of the Governor to the Executive Council. Was it that of the Sovereign to his
responsible and constitutional ministers? The
question widened out. Was the Governor in the
final analysis the servant of the Colonial office with
his Council in Canada merely advisory? On both
questions Metcalfe had clear-cut and definite opinions: "With reference to your views of responsible
government," he said, " I cannot tell you how far I
concur in them without knowing your meaning,
which is not distinctly stated. If you mean that
the Governor is to have no exercise of his own judgment in the administration of the government and
is to be a mere tool in the hands of his Council, then
I totally disagree with you. That is a condition to
which I never can submit, and which her Majesty's
Government, in my opinion, can never sanction. . .
If you mean that the Governor is an irresponsible
officer, who can, without responsibility, adopt the
advice of his Council, then you are, I conceive, entirely in error."
It was fortunate for Canada that Lord John
Russell came into power on the fall of Sir Robert

Peel's ministry, with Earl Grey as Secretary of
State for the Colonial Department. Almost immediately it was decided to give the colonies full
responsible government and the principle was laid
down by Earl Grey himself: "This country has no
interest whatever in exercising any greater influence
in the internal affairs of the colonies, than is indis-
pensable either for the purpose of preventing any
one colony from adopting measures injurious to
another, or to the Empire at large."[1] The principle of course meant party government.

Space has prevented me from tracing the growth
of representative institutions in the Maritime Provinces, where Joseph Howe, in four magnificent
letters[2] to Lord John Russell, outlined the necessity
and justice of responsible government. They hold
a place in the literature of British constitutional
development, perhaps unrivalled for insight, logical
power, and skilled discussion. Nova Scotia and New
Brunswick passed into their promised land somewhat more easily and more quickly than Canada.
The transition was never at any time as complicated
and the passage was practically uneventful. In
Canada, however, for eight years all the difficulties
of establishing Cabinet Government, which England
had gone through in the eighteenth century, were
re-enacted. It remained for Lord Elgin to get the
system into full working order. Elgin did not allow
himself to be affected much by theories of government. He faced immediate issues and left any
possible difficulties about the status of the Governor
to take care of themselves as they arose. With him
responsible government triumphed. His rule is

[1] Earl Grey, *The Colonial Policy of Lord John Russell's
Administration*, Vol. I. p. 17. (London, second edition, 1853).
[2] J. H. Chisholm, *The Speeches and Public Letters of Joseph
Howe*, Vol. I. pp. 221 ff. (Halifax, 1909).

summed up by Earl Grey: "In conformity with the
principle laid down, it was his object in assuming
the government of the province to withdraw from
the position of depending for support on one party
into which Lord Metcalfe had, by unfortunate circumstances, been brought. He was to act generally
on the advice of his Executive Council, and to receive as members of that body those persons who
might be pointed out to him as entitled to be so by
their possessing the confidence of the Assembly.
But he was careful to avoid identifying himself with
the party from the ranks of which the actual Council
was drawn, and to make it generally understood that
if public opinion required it, he was equally ready
to accept their opponents as his advisers uninflu-
enced by any personal preferences or objections."[1]
Once more, however, another advance in Canadian
constitutional development was handicapped by a
set of new difficulties, a consideration of which will
lead up to Confederation.

Cabinet government, if it is to be successful,
postulates strong party government. As a rule two
strong parties make it most effective. The difficulty
in Canada arose from the fact that there were many
parties—Upper Canadian Reformers, Upper Canadian Conservatives; later on French-Canadian Conservatives and French-Canadian Radicals, with a
small group that carried on the traditions of "the
family compact." Even supposing it had been
possible to combine the Conservatives or Radicals
from each section, there was no clearly defined foundation of a common Conservatism or a common
Radicalism between them. Similarity of party names
did not in the least mean similarity of party plat-
forms. As a consequence of the many parties the
Government was always a coalition. As a consequence

[1] Earl Grey, *op. cit.* p. 213.

of no common political principles among parties of the same name, there was added to the limitations inherent in coalition government a further serious limitation — the Government in power was never secure in its measures. In addition, there was the religious difficulty which was emphasized under the stress of parliamentary and political oratory. It was a human impossibility for Upper Canadian and Lower Canadian to act together on questions which crossed the thin line of theological controversy. Nor were the issues at stake frequently of more than a local nature in which French-Canadian and Upper Canadian had no common interest.

During this period the consequences of these difficulties complicated the government of the United Province. Thus we find two premiers, one French, one British. Before long we find a kind of unwritten constitutional convention at work, which demanded that a Ministry must have a distinct majority from French-speaking Canada and from English-speaking Canada. The actual workings out of government further illustrated the anomalous position. Each division, for example, demanded an equal expenditure of public funds. A Ministry risked its existence if this demand were unsatisfied. Thus the whole system degenerated into a life-in-death condition, and for years there dragged on government as unreal as government well could be. Ministries quickly followed one another to defeat.

Other difficulties soon appeared. As Upper Canada developed and exceeded Lower Canada in population there arose a party which, gathering strength with the years and drawing into its ranks both Conservatives and Radicals, demanded representation by population. Such a programme could not command adherence in Lower Canada, strong in its legal guarantees for an equal number of seats. Once again it became clearer and clearer that new developments were at hand. In 1858 the Canadian Government fell back on the untried suggestion of Lord Durham and advocated a federation of British North America—Alexander Galt, who lived to benefit the final scheme by his financial abilities, coming into the Ministry on that understanding. For the moment Britain was not prepared to re-open the Canadian question, but the fact that in the following year an attempt was made to unify the opposition in the Canadian parliament by a proposal to govern the two sections of the Province on a kind of federal basis proves that the federal idea was gaining ground in Canada. It is here that we touch hands with Goldwin Smith's saying. Party deadlock was the immediate cause of Confederation.

In addition, the American Civil War and the "Trent affair" of 1861 emphasized in Canada the consciousness of constitutional weakness; while the anticipated revocation by the United States of the Reciprocity Treaty, which had been arranged by Lord Elgin, turned the eyes of Canadian statesmen to economic problems with which a Canadian federation could best deal. Indeed John A. Macdonald laid weight on these considerations in words of measured firmness during the Confederation debates in the Canadian parliament: "If we are not blind to our present position, we must see the hazardous situation in which all the great interests of Canada stand in respect to the United States. I am no alarmist. I do not believe in the prospect of immediate war. I believe that the common sense of the two nations will prevent a war; still we cannot trust to probabilities. The Government and Legislature would be wanting in their duty to the people if they ran any risk. We know that the United States at this moment are engaged in a war of enormous dimensions—that the occasion of a war with Great Britain has again and again arisen, and may at any time in the future again arise. We cannot foresee what may be the result; we cannot say but that the two nations may drift into a war as other nations have done before. It would then be too late when war had commenced to think of measures for strengthening ourselves, or to begin negotiations for a union with the sister provinces. At this moment, in consequence of the ill-feeling which has arisen between England and the United States—a feeling of which Canada was not the cause—in consequence of the irritation which now exists, owing to the unhappy state of affairs on this continent, the Reciprocity Treaty, it seems probable, is about to be brought to an end—our trade is hampered by the passport system, and at any moment we may be deprived of permission to carry our goods through United States channels—the bonded goods system may be done away with, and the winter trade through the United States put an end to. Our merchants may be obliged to return to the old system of bringing in during the summer months the supplies for the whole year. Ourselves already threatened, our trade interrupted, our intercourse, political and commercial, destroyed, if we do not take warning now when we have the opportunity, and, while one avenue is threatened to be closed, open another by taking advantage of the present arrangement and the desire of the Lower Provinces to draw closer the alliance between us, we may suffer commercial and political disadvantages it may take long for us to overcome.''[1]

[1] *Parliamentary Debates on the subject of the Confederation of the British North American provinces,* p. 32: (Quebec, 1865).

Other forces, more subtle, were at work. The forces of history which had brought responsible government drove men to larger visions. There began to dawn before some of the greatest Canadians of the day outlines of a larger Canada from Atlantic to Pacific linked up by bonds of steel. Joseph Howe and George Brown saw the vision, and even the stalwart Conservative champion had his Pisgah moment when he realized that the United States might claim lands as yet constitutionally unlinked to either Canada or the United States. As the vision broadened out it lent weight to the situation created by party deadlock, and it seemed no impossible thing to extend to British North America a federal system based on the constitutional experience of the previous century. The issue was almost rendered secure by the singular coincidence that delegates from the Maritime Provinces assembled at Charlottetown in 1864 to discuss a federation of those Provinces. To this Convention delegates from Canada were permitted to go, and in due course the Conference adjourned to Quebec to consider the wider union. In eighteen days, October 10th to 29th, 1864, seventy-two resolutions were passed which became substantially the British North America Act. This was the assembly of the greatest Canadians in public life—Taché, the aged French-Canadian premier; Cartier, who bore the olive branch of union to his countrymen; Macdonald and Brown, the Upper Canadian foemen, who shed party for the higher vision; Galt, whose genius saved the proposal from wreck on the dangerous shoals of financial difficulties; Tupper and Tilley and others of less note, but of no less necessity at the moment. It may be fanciful, but I cannot look at the picture of the Fathers of Canadian Confederation without something akin to emotion. I always connect it with the great ventures of faith in history—and it is faith which raises politics into the realms of constructive statesmanship. A federal scheme was outlined in which a general government should be given control over the wider interests, while local governments for each of the Canadas and for the Maritime Provinces should control local affairs. At the same time, provision was made for admitting British Columbia, Vancouver, and the North-West Territory.

George Brown left for England, where he laid the scheme before the British Government, who received it with "prodigious satisfaction." In February, 1865, the Quebec Resolutions were debated by the Canadian Parliament, being presented for acceptance or rejection as a whole, and as solemn agreements between equal contracting parties. In spite of able opposition, they passed by substantial majorities in the House of Assembly and the Legislative Council. Their progress led to speeches which are vital to a clear understanding of the actual state of affairs. With the debates on the Quebec Act, Lord Durham's *Report,* John Howe's letters, and Lord Elgin's despatches, they are among the most valuable commentaries that we possess on Canadian constitutional development.

The later history is too well known to detain us. In due course the British North America Act became law, and out of the gropings of the years emerged a new Canada to develop side by side with the first great experiment in federal government. Few of those alive in England or in federated Canada realized the richness of the future, and perhaps not a few anticipated that there was near enough at hand an independent Canada as the next step in her constitutional history. The student, at any rate, can hardly find a century richer in constitutional experiment. The British North America Act was almost necessarily a skeleton, and there has gathered round it in the course of its workings many legal decisions which are dealt with in the following Treatise. Round it, too, has grown up a sentiment which has made it Canadian in the widest sense of the word, and has carried the principles for which free institutions and responsible government stand from the local life of every province of the Canadian Confederation into the world Federation struggling in a death grapple with ancient autocracy and arbitrary government.

[NOTE. — I have used the documents published by the Canadian Archivists, by Professors Egerton and Grant, by Mr. W. Houston; The British Parliamentary Papers relating to Canada; The Parliamentary Journals of the various Canadian Provinces.]

A SHORT TREATISE

ON

Canadian Constitutional Law

Sec. I. Formation of the Dominion of Canada —Its Component Parts—Canadian Constitutional Acts. The Dominion of Canada was first established by the union or confederation[1] in 1867 by the Imperial British North America Act (sometimes referred to in these pages, for shortness sake, as "the Federation Act"), which was passed on March 29th, 1867, and came into force on July 1st of the same year, of the British North American provinces of Nova Scotia, New Brunswick, and Canada, the last of which had been formed in 1840 by a union of the provinces of Upper Canada and Lower Canada, and was now in 1867 re-divided under the names of Ontario and Quebec, as two separate provinces of the new Dominion. British Columbia was admitted as a province of the Dominion by Order-in-Council of May 16th, 1871, and Prince Edward Island by Order-in-Council of June 26th, 1873.[2]

The North-West Territories, which comprise all the area of the Dominion not included from time to time within the limits of any province, and now consist only of the territory north of the 60th parallel of latitude and east of the Yukon, were ceded to the Dominion by Imperial Order-in-Council of June 24th, 1870, pursuant to power conferred by section 146 of the British North America Act, 1867, and full authority was conferred upon the Parliament of

Canada to legislate for the future welfare and good
government of the said territories. In 1870 the
province of Manitoba was carved out of these North-
West Territories by Dominion Act, 33 Vict. c. 3,
confirmed by Imperial Act, 34 Vict. c. 28, and
made one of the provinces of the Dominion. The
province of Alberta was constituted out of these
territories in 1905 by Dominion Act, 4-5 Edw. VII.,
c. 30, and the province of Saskatchewan, also in 1905,
by Dominion Act, 4-5 Edw. VII., c. 42, both under
the authority of Imp. 34 Vict. c. 27, known as the
British North America Act, 1871. The above
Orders-in-Council admitting new provinces, as also
the Dominion Acts establishing the provinces of
Manitoba, Alberta, and Saskatchewan,[3] all provide
that the provisions of the British North America
Act, 1867, shall, with some minor variations in each
case not affecting the main features of the Constitution, be applicable to each of the said provinces
' in the same manner and to the like extent as they
apply to the several provinces of Canada, and as if
(each of the said provinces) had been one of the
provinces originally united by the said Act.' The
Imperial Act, 49-50 Vict. c. 35, passed in 1886,
known as the British North America Act, 1886, gave
the Parliament of Canada power to provide representation in the Senate and House of Commons for
any territories which for the time being form part
of the Dominion of Canada, but are not included in
any province thereof.[4]

This treatise, then, will be mainly concerned with
the provisions and interpretation of the British
North America Act, 1867, especially with those portions of it which distribute legislative power over
the internal affairs of the Dominion between the
Federal or Dominion Parliament, on the one hand,

and the various provincial legislatures on the other.
The written portion of the Constitution of the Dominion, in the sense in which that phrase is generally used, is to be found in it, supplemented or
amended by the British North America Act, 1871,
Imp. 34 Vict. c. 28, as to the power of the Dominion
Parliament to establish new provinces in any territories of the Dominion and provide for their constitution and administration, and also to alter the
limits of existing provinces and to legislate for territories not included in any province—the Parliament of Canada Act, 1875, Imp. 38-39 Vict. c. 38,
substituting a new section for section 18 of the
British North America Act, 1867, as to the privileges, immunities, and powers of the Dominion Senate and House of Commons and of the members
thereof respectively — the British North America
Act, 1886, Imp. 49-50 Vict. c. 35, as to the representation in the Parliament of Canada of territories which
for the time being form part of the Dominion, but
are not included in any province — the British
North America Act, 1907, making further provision
with respect to the sums to be paid by Canada to the
several provinces of the Dominion;[5] the British
North America Act, 1915, Imp. 5-6 Geo. V., c. 45,
making certain changes in the composition of the
Dominion Senate while preserving its quasi-federal
character. To these may be added the Canada
(Ontario Boundary) Act, 1887, Imp. 52-53 Vict.
c. 28; the Statute Law Revision Act, 1893, Imp. 56
Vict. c. 14, repealing certain sections of the British
North America Act, 1867, which had by lapse of time
become unnecessary, and the Canadian Speaker
(Appointment of Deputy) Act, 1895, Imp. 59 Vict. c.
3. In these statutes is to be found the written
portion of the federal Constitution of Canada.

But it must always be remembered that those great constitutional documents which comprise almost the whole of the written portion of the Constitution of Great Britain—Magna Charta, the Petition of Right, the Bill of Rights, and the Act of Settlement—are equally included in Canada's constitution, while as to the unwritten part of the Constitution, those legal decisions which embody the common law Constitution of Great Britain are equally authoritative in Canada, and we may say of both the Dominion and provincial governments that ' that great body of unwritten conventions, usages, and understandings which have in the course of time grown up in the practical working of the English Constitution, and which are so admirably dealt with in Dicey's "Law of the Constitution," form as important a part of the political system of Canada as the fundamental law itself which governs the federation.' ⁶

SEC. II. SYNOPSIS OF THE SCHEME OF THE CANADIAN CONSTITUTION AS CONTAINED IN THE BRITISH NORTH AMERICA ACT, 1867—ITS GENERAL ANALOGY TO THE CONSTITUTION OF THE UNITED KINGDOM. A royal proclamation, issued on May 22nd, 1867, to take effect on July 1st, 1867, established the Dominion of Canada under the provisions of the British North America Act, 1867, which recites that the provinces of Canada, Nova Scotia and New Brunswick had expressed their desire to be federally united into one Dominion under the Crown of the United Kingdom of Great Britain and Ireland with a Constitution similar in principle to that of the United Kingdom. It seems proper to first give a short account of the general features of the scheme thus provided, for the better understanding of what is to follow. Under the provisions of this fundamental Act the executive government and authority of and over Canada continue and are vested in "the Queen," a term which is expressed (section 2) to ' extend also to the heirs and successors of Her Majesty, Kings and Queens of the United Kingdom of Great Britain and Ireland.' The Sovereign, acting, of course, by and with the advice of responsible Ministers, appoints a Governor-General as chief executive officer to carry on the government of Canada on his behalf and in his name. This he has to do by and with the advice of "the Queen's Privy Council for Canada," whose members are nominally chosen and removed by himself, and who in accordance with the system of responsible cabinet government existing in Canada comprise the Ministry of the day so far as active functions are concerned, though ex-Ministers retain after retirement the titular rank of Privy Councillors. There is one Parliament for Canada, consisting of the Sovereign, an Upper House styled the Senate, and the House of Commons, which is required to hold a session once at least in every year. The Senate, under the (Imp.) British North America Act, 1915, is to consist of ninety-six members, appointed by the Governor-General, from time to time, in the name of the Sovereign, twenty-four from the province of Ontario, twenty-four from the province of Quebec, twenty-four from the Maritime provinces and Prince Edward Island (being ten from New Brunswick, ten from Nova Scotia, and four from Prince Edward Island), and twenty-four from the western provinces (being six from Manitoba, six from British Columbia, six from Saskatchewan and six from Alberta). Thus this Act preserves, or rather restores, the Senate's original quasi-federal aspect which had become impaired, the original idea of the composition of the Senate having been that of affording protection to the smaller provinces which they might not always enjoy in a House when the representation was based on numbers only. Senators hold their office for life; and to be a senator a man must be thirty years of age, a natural born or naturalized subject of the King, a resident of the province for which he is appointed, and possessed of a property qualification of $4,000 over all liabilities. It cannot be said that the Senate holds either a strong, or a popular, position in Canada, although it may be said to have been in its favour that the one departure was made from the principle of following, wherever possible, the analogy of the British Constitution. For it is expressly provided in the Federation Act that at no time shall more than six additional senators be appointed over and above the number prescribed in that Act; or, we must now add, in the subsequent Acts or Orders-in-Council adding other provinces to the Union. The British unlimited prerogative power to add new members to the Upper House does not, therefore, exist in Canada. The Governor-General appoints from among the senators a Speaker of the Senate, and may remove him and appoint another. As to the Dominion House of Commons, it is summoned to meet from time to time by the Governor-General, who may also dissolve it. Unless sooner dissolved it continues for five years. Its numbers may be from time to time increased by the Dominion Parliament, but Quebec is always to have a fixed number of sixty-five members, and each of the other provinces a corresponding number of members in proportion to population, as ascertained at each decennial census. At present it consists of 221 members.[6a] Except in the case of Saskatchewan, Alberta, and the Yukon

Territory, the provincial voters lists determine the federal electorate, as well as the provincial, by virtue of express Dominion enactment. In all the provinces the franchise is a very low one. In nearly all an adult male British subject, not being an Indian, has a vote if he has resided in the province for one year, and in the electoral district for three months. Manitoba, Alberta, and Saskatchewan have, within the last year or two, given women the vote for their provincial elections, which will in the case of Manitoba, apparently, though not in the case of Saskatchewan and Alberta (see Dominion *Elections Act,* R. S. C. 1906, c. 6, ss. 10, 32), secure them also the federal vote. The Dominion Parliament has power over the qualification of members of the House of Commons, over the right to vote for such members, the proceedings at elections, the trial of controverted elections, etc., which last is, as in England, delegated to the Courts. The House of Commons elects its own Speaker. The relations between the House of Commons and the Senate in respect to money bills, and otherwise, are analogous to those which existed between the House of Lords and the House of Commons in England prior to the English Parliament Act, 1911.

When a bill has passed both Houses it is presented to the Governor-General for the King's assent, who then declares either that he assents thereto in the King's name, or that he withholds the King's assent, or that he reserves the bill for the signification of the King's pleasure. When he assents to a bill in the King's name, a copy of it is sent to the Imperial Government in England, and may be disallowed within two years after receipt thereof. As a matter of fact since Confederation only one Act of the Dominion Parliament appears to

have suffered this fate, viz., 33 Vict. c. 14, commonly
known as the Oaths Bill, which was disallowed in
1873 as being *ultra vires* of the Parliament of Canada.[7] Of course this power of disallowance, as also the
like power possessed by the Governor-General over
provincial Acts, is exercised subject to usage and
convention with which we are not at the present
moment concerned, but which is briefly dealt with
infra pp. 60-66.

For each province of the Confederation the
Constitution provides a Lieutenant-Governor, appointed by the Governor-General in Council,
who holds office during the pleasure of the latter,
but may not be removed within five years except
for cause assigned. When appointed, however,
he represents the King, not the Governor-General,
as we shall presently see. He is, in each case,
assisted in the discharge of his duties by an
Executive Council, appointed by himself, comprising
the provincial Ministry, and discharging in regard
to the province functions similar to those discharged
by the Dominion Privy Council in regard to the Dominion. Each province has also a legislature of its
own, consisting, in the case of Ontario, New Brunswick, Manitoba, British Columbia and Prince Edward Island, of a single house styled the Legislative
Assembly, but in the case of Quebec and Nova
Scotia, of a Legislative Council and a Legislative
Assembly, the members of the former being appointed by the Lieutenant-Governors, and holding
office for life. The Prince Edward Island legislature is, however, an amalgamation of the old Legislative Council (the members of which were, and
their present representatives still are, elected by
voters possessed of a small property qualification),
and the House of Assembly. The Lieutenant-Gov-

ernors are a part of their respective provincial legislatures, as the Governor-General is of the Dominion Parliament, and have analogous functions in regard to bills which have passed the House or Houses, either assenting to them, or withholding assent, or reserving them for the consideration of the Governor-General; and any provincial Act may be disallowed by the Governor-General within one year after he has received a copy of it. It must of course be remembered that in all such cases Governor-Generals and Lieutenant-Governors alike act under the advice of their respective Ministers. To the Dominion Parliament on the one hand, and the provincial legislatures on the other, the British North America Act, 1867, assigns certain legislative powers, for the most part exclusive, over specific subject-matters, and in addition confers upon the Dominion Parliament power to make laws for the peace, order, and good government of Canada in relation to all matters not coming within the classes of subjects assigned exclusively to the legislatures of the provinces. These legislative powers will be referred to hereafter in detail. The Governor-General appoints the judges of the Superior, District and County Courts in each province, and the provincial Courts have cognizance of all matters of litigation, whether relating to the federal Constitution, or arising under Dominion statutes or not, except proceedings against the Crown (Dominion)[8] and petition of right in Dominion cases, which are within the exclusive jurisdiction of the Exchequer Court of Canada. There is no such system of federal Courts in Canada as exists in the United States. The only federal Courts are the Supreme Court of Canada, and the Exchequer Court of Canada. The latter deals with the matters just mentioned, and has also concurrent original jurisdiction with the ordinary provincial Courts in revenue cases, and in all cases of conflicting applications for any patent of invention, or for the registration of any copyright, trade mark, or industrial design, or in which it is sought to impeach or annul the same, or in which a remedy is sought respecting the infringement of any patent of invention, trade mark, or industrial design, and in certain other matters. See Audette's ''Practice of the Exchequer Court of Canada'' (Ottawa, 1909). The Supreme Court of Canada deals with appeals from the Exchequer Court and from the various provincial Courts, generally of last resort, as provided in the Supreme Court Act, R. S. C. 1906, c. 139, and the amendments thereto.[8a]

Reverting again to the recital in the British North America Act, 1867, already referred to, the analogy of the above to the Constitution of the United Kingdom is very apparent. The Sovereign of Great Britain occupies the same relation to the Canadian legislatures as to the Parliament of Great Britain, acting, however, through his appointed representatives, and on the advice of different sets of ministers. The relation between the House of Lords and the popular House in Great Britain, as it was before *The Parliament Act,* 1911, is reproduced, as far as may be, in those between the Dominion Senate and provincial Legislative Councils, where such exist, on the one hand, and the Dominion and provincial popular Houses on the other. The absence of any provision prohibiting members of the Dominion Cabinet or the provincial Executive Councils from being members of the legislature during their continuance in office, together with the power of dissolution of the popular Houses possessed by the Governor-General and the provincial Lieutenant-Governors, preserves in Canada the British system of parliamentary cabinet government. And other and less obvious features might also be cited, such as the plenary character of legislative power in Canada, which illustrate the way in which the framers of the scheme of Canadian confederation sought to follow, so far as was possible under federal conditions, the British model.[9]

SEC. III. THE IMPERIAL PARLIAMENT—ITS PARAMOUNT AUTHORITY. The powers of legislation conferred upon the Dominion Parliament and the provincial legislatures respectively by the British North America Act, 1867, are conferred subject to the sovereign authority of the Imperial Parliament.[10]

SEC. IV. THE GENESIS OF CONFEDERATION—THE PRE-CONFEDERATION CONSTITUTIONS. These are subjects upon which it seems right to say a few further words before passing to a detailed consideration of the present Constitution of Canada.

The Constitutions of Nova Scotia, New Brunswick, and Prince Edward Island, as they existed at the time these provinces respectively became included in the Canadian Confederation, did not rest upon any formal charter, but were derived from the terms of the royal commissions to the Governors and Lieutenant-Governors, and from the instructions which accompanied the same, moulded from time to time by despatches from Secretaries of State conveying the will of the Sovereign, and by Acts of the local legislature assented to by the Crown; and the whole to some extent interpreted by uniform usage and custom in the colony. In each there was an Executive Council to advise and assist the Governor, a Legislative Council and a general elective Assembly. In the Governor, Legislative Council and Assembly was vested the local law-making power. In all these colonies the system of responsible parliamentary government was in operation. In British Columbia, by virtue of the Imperial Act to provide for its government, 21-22 Vict. c. 99, the Queen appointed a Governor who, by his commission, was authorized to make laws, institutions, and ordinances for the peace, order, and good government of the colony, by proclamation under the public seal. A Legislative Council was afterwards introduced, which was, however, by local ordinance No. 147 of 34 Vict., abolished immediately prior to the entrance of this province into the Union, and a Legislative Assembly of wholly elective members was established in its stead. New Brunswick has also abolished its Legislative Council, so that in Quebec and Nova Scotia alone of all the provinces of Canada, is a Legislative Council now to be found.

The present provinces of Ontario and Quebec represent respectively the provinces of Upper and Lower Canada, into which the province of Quebec, as created and established by royal proclamation of 1763 and the Quebec Act, Imp. 14 Geo. III., c. 83 (1774), had been divided by the Constitutional Act of 1791, 31 Geo. III., c. 31, as explained in the Historical Introduction to this Treatise. In 1840 the Union Act, Imp. 3-4 Vict. c. 35, again united these two provinces into the province of Canada and provided for the united province a Legislative Council appointed for life by the Governor, and an elective Legislative Assembly. The system of responsible government was shortly afterwards introduced. In

1856, by local Act, 19-20 Vict. c. 140, the legislative council was made elective.

In 1864 a conference of delegates from the different provinces met at Quebec and drew up a number of resolutions upon which, as revised by the delegates from the different provinces in London, the British North America Act, 1867, was based, receiving the royal assent on March 29th, 1867, and called into operation by proclamation on July 1st, 1867. This Act specially provides (ss. 64, 88), that the constitution of the executive authority and of the legislature of Nova Scotia and New Brunswick respectively, shall, subject to the provisions of the Act, continue as they existed at the union, until altered under the authority of the Act; and a similar provision was contained in the Imperial Orders-in-Council under which Prince Edward Island and British Columbia entered Confederation. See, also, B. N. A. Act, 1867, s. 129. But by reason of the division of the existing province of Canada into the provinces of Ontario and Quebec, the Federation Act contains special provisions as to the Constitution of the executives and legislatures therein respectively. As to Manitoba, Alberta, and Saskatchewan, these possess legislatures consisting of the Lieutenant-Governor, and one House, styled the Legislative Assembly of the province, Manitoba having abolished the legislative council, which it originally had, in 1876; and, as already stated, the Dominion Acts constituting these provinces provide that the provisions of the British North America Act, 1867, shall, with some minor exceptions not necessary to refer to here, be applicable to them in the same way and to the like extent as they apply to the original provinces, and as if they had been among the provinces originally united by the said Act.[11]

Sec. V. English Law in Canada—Systems of
Law in the Different Provinces. We may also,
by way of preliminary, say something on these subjects before proceeding further.

A. *Imperial statutes in force in Canada proprio
vigore.* It must of course be remembered that
any Imperial statute which, by express reference
or necessary intendment, applies to the overseas
Dominions of the British Crown creates law binding upon them.[12] The parliament at Westminster is
an Imperial parliament still, and the number of Imperial statutes even to-day which, or some parts of
which, are operative in the colonies, is considerable.[13]

B. *English case-law.* It is also necessary, in
dealing with the subject of English law in Canada,
to distinguish from the rest of English law that
part of English case-law which deals with common
law or equitable principles apart from statutes, or
the interpretation or application of statutes. The
part of English case-law thus referred to is now,
and has always been, binding in Canada upon Courts
of equal or inferior jurisdiction to the English
Court so declaring the law, in the absence, in the
case of Courts of equal jurisdiction, of prior decisions here directly the other way. The hierarchy
of Courts in the case of Canada extends across the
Atlantic. The Privy Council have also expressly
laid it down[14] that when a colonial legislature has
passed an Act in the same terms as an Imperial
statute, and the latter has been authoritatively construed by a Court of Appeal in England, such construction should be adopted by the Courts of the
colony. The Ontario Courts have, however, affirmed this modification,—and so have those of British Columbia, and probably the Courts of the other

provinces would follow them in this respect,—that when a decision of the Court of Appeal in England is at variance with one of the Court of Appeal in their province, the latter should be followed in their province, for, as the Ontario Courts put it, the Court of Appeal in England is not a Court of Appeal from it.[15] Quebec we deal with separately *infra* pp. 57-8.

The only Appellate Court outside the Dominion from the decisions of Canadian Courts is the Judicial Committee of the Privy Council. The judgments of this tribunal, although not binding upon other Courts in Great Britain or Ireland, are binding upon all Colonial Courts, even as against any possible conflicting judgments of the House of Lords itself.[16]

C. *General principles with regard to the recognition of English statutes as in force in Canadian provinces.* And now as to statute law, we shall see that the question of the applicability of English statute law generally in the Canadian provinces only arises as to such English statute law as it existed at such and such a date, the date differing in different provinces. But there are certain principles in regard to the matter which may be first noted. The fundamental principle is, of course, the applicability of the statute in question to the circumstances of the provinces.[17]

But these further points may also be noticed. Part of such English Acts may be held in force, and part not.[18] Again a British statute may be held to be in force, and yet not to apply to certain subject matters in the province.[19] And the fact that a clause here and there in an English statute might be carried into effect in the province, will not make it part of the provincial law when its main object and tenour is foreign to the nature of the provincial institutions.[20] But English statutes otherwise applicable may be worked out by the existing machinery of the local Courts in a Canadian province, notwithstanding that special tribunals are created by those statutes to work them out in England.[21] Where an English statute is local in its character it will not be held in force.[22]

D. *The Maritime Provinces.* With these preliminary remarks we can now proceed to consider first, the maritime provinces of the Dominion, to wit, Nova Scotia, New Brunswick, and Prince Edward Island, for we shall find that the application of English statutes, and of English law generally, stands on different footings in the different provinces.[23] Now the Canadian provinces, other than Quebec, being colonies by settlement, or so regarded (see the recital in the Nova Scotia Act, 33 Geo. II., c. 3), the ordinary rule applies that the settlers took with them, at the time of settlement, all the common and statute law of England, applicable to their situation, subject of course to be afterwards amended or repealed in respect to their local application by the local legislatures, and the maritime provinces have, upon this principle, always assumed English law to be so in force in them as from the time of settlement without any special enactments of their own in that regard; but 1784, when New Brunswick was separated from Nova Scotia and made into a separate province, is the date taken in those two provinces, while Prince Edward Island takes 1773, the year when the first statute (13 Geo. III., c. 1) of that province was passed. The other provinces, on the other hand, have by local legislation adopted English law, as existing at certain specified dates, expressly stating in all cases, except Ontario, that they do so only so far as such English law be applicable to them. But in Nova Scotia the principle was laid down from an early date, that whereas the English common law will be recognized as in force there excepting such parts as are obviously inconsistent with the circumstances of the country, none of the statute law will be received except such parts as are obviously applicable and necessary.[24] It cannot be said that the Courts of New Brunswick have taken quite the same view. Thus the Courts there have adopted the principle expressed by Sir William Grant in *Attorney-General* v. *Stewart*,[25] that the question depends upon whether the English Act in question is a law of local policy adapted solely to the country in which it was made, or a general regulation of property equally applicable to every country in which property is governed by the rules of English law.[26]

E. *Ontario.* The first statute of the legislature of Upper Canada, 32 Geo. III., c. 1, passed on October 15th, 1792, enacted (sec. 3) that 'from and after the passing of this Act, in all matters of controversy relative to property and civil rights, resort shall be had to the laws of England, as the rule for the decision of the same;' also (sec. 5), that ' all matters relative to testimony and legal proof in the investigation of fact, and the forms thereof, in the several Courts of law and equity within this province, shall be regulated by the rules of evidence established in England.' These two provisions still hold their place in the statute books of the province, known since the British North America Act, 1867, as Ontario, and are to be found in R. S. O. 1914, c. 101, s. 2, the words being added, which of course were implied in the Act of George III.: ' except so far as such laws and rules have been since repealed, altered, varied, modified or affected by any Act of the Imperial Parliament still having the force of law in Ontario, or by any Act of the late province of Upper Canada, or of the province of Canada, or of the province of Ontario, still having the force of law in Ontario.' It is also provided in a sub-section that ' nothing in this section shall extend to any of the laws of England respecting the maintenance of the poor.'[27]

As to criminal law it was enacted by Upper Canada statute, 40 Geo. III., c. 1, that 'the criminal law of England, as it stood on September 17th, 1792, shall be and the same is hereby declared to be the law of this province,' saving (sec. 2) any ordinance of the province of Quebec made since (Imp.) 14 Geo. III., c. 83. This has, however, lost its importance since in 1892 the Dominion Parliament, having exclusive jurisdiction over criminal law (*infra,* pp. 116-9), enacted a Criminal Code. This Code is in the main a reproduction of that drafted by Sir Fitzjames Stephen for the English Royal Commissioners in 1898, but never enacted. But unlike this English draft Code, it does not contain any clause abrogating the common law of crime. Consequently the common law as to crime is still operative in Canada, notwithstanding the Code, unless there be some repugnance in its express provisions. Moreover, it expressly provides that, subject to any enactments having local application repealing, amending, or affecting it, the criminal law of England as it existed on September 17th, 1792, shall be the criminal law of Ontario (s. 10); as it existed on November 19th, 1858, the criminal law of British Columbia (s. 11); and as it existed on July 15th,

1870, the criminal law of Manitoba (s. 12). And the Criminal Code being a federal law, its provisions extend to all the provinces including Quebec, where English criminal law has been in force since 1763, subject to local modification. See, also, sec. 9 as to its application in Saskatchewan, Alberta, and the Northwest Territories.[28]

F.—*British Columbia.* This province takes the civil and criminal laws of England as the same existed on November 19th, 1858, so far as the same are not from local circumstances inapplicable, and, of course, so far as the same have not been abrogated or amended by legislation operative in British Columbia, which was taken into the Union by Imperial Order in Council of May 16, 1871.[29]

G.—*Manitoba, Alberta, Saskatchewan, Yukon Territory, North-west Territories.* All these were included in what was formerly known as Rupert's Land and the North-Western Territory, which were admitted into and became part of the Dominion of Canada by Imperial Order in Council of June 23rd, 1870.[30] By Dominion Act, 49 Vict. c. 25, originally, and now by R. S. C. 1906, c. 62, s. 12 ("The Northwest Territories Act"), it is enacted:—'Subject to the provisions of this Act, the laws of England relating to civil and criminal matters, as the same existed on July 15th, 1870, shall be in force in the Territories, in so far as the same are applicable in the Territories, and in so far as the same have not been, or are not hereafter, as regards the Territories, repealed, altered, varied, modified, or affected by any Act of the Parliament of the United Kingdom or of the Parliament of Canada, applicable to the Territories, or by any ordinance of the Territories.' This still governs the reception of English law in the above provinces and the

Yukon Territory, the Alberta Act (4-5 Edw. VII., D. c. 3, s. 16) and the Saskatchewan Act (4-5 Edw. VII, c. 42, s. 16) and the above Yukon Territory Act, now R. S. C. 1906, c. 63, s. 19, containing express provisions continuing existing laws, while R. S. M. 1913, c. 46, s. 11, enacts, in accordance with the Manitoba Act of 1874, that ' the Court of Queen's Bench shall decide and determine all matters of controversy relative to property and civil rights, both legal and equitable, according to the laws existing, or established and being in England, as such were, existed, and stood on July 15th, 1870, so far as the same can be made applicable to matters relating to property and civil rights in the province.' [31]   Moreover, R. S. C. 1906, c. 99, s. 6 (an enactment first passed in 1888, 51 Vict., c. 33, s. 1, D.), provides that the laws of England relating to matters within the jurisdiction of the Dominion parliament as the same existed on July 15th, 1870, were from the said day and are in force in Manitoba, in so far as applicable to the province and not repealed or altered by any competent legislature.[32]

Quebec. It remains to speak of this province which presents a very complicated legal situation. Although the Quebec Act (14 Geo. III., c. 83, s. 8), provided that in the province of Quebec—' in all matters of controversy relative to property and civil rights, resort shall be had to the laws of Canada as the rule for the decision of the same,' —*i.e.,* that the law existing in the province at the time of the Conquest relative to property and civil rights should continue to govern, subject of course to variation or alteration by provincial legislation, and although this provision has never been abrogated, there is a great deal of English law in the province of Quebec. To begin with, Quebec is an integral part of the Empire, and as such, her constitutional and administrative law ' so far as it depends upon custom is governed upon the rules of law applied in like matters in England, and so far as it has been reduced to statute, has been so reduced in statutes framed on English models. Neither in national nor in local affairs have French governmental institutions been copied, and, in cases in which public law has to be applied, it is not usual to refer to French authorities.'[33] Then Quebec is one province only of the Dominion, and statutes of the Dominion parliament—very many of which are based upon Imperial legislation—are as applicable to her as to any other province, where she is not expressly excepted. In the third place the Quebec Act, 1774, by sec. 11, enacted that the criminal law of England should 'be observed as law in the Province of Quebec' and that provision stood until the Dominion Criminal Code was enacted in 1892 (see *supra,* p. 54) and became operative as well in Quebec as elsewhere through Canada. It is only when all these are eliminated that we come down to the provincial law of Quebec properly so called. Of this the primary source in Quebec is the *Civil Code* which came into force on August 1st, 1866. Speaking concisely it covers the law of persons and the law of property, and includes succession, gifts, obligations in general, special contracts, registration, prescription, and to some extent the law of merchant shipping (see *supra* p. 47, n. 10), and insurance. This Civil Code was prepared by a commission under instructions from the legislature directing them to follow as far as possible the French codes; and, accordingly, they largely followed the Code Napoléon, utilizing, however, the commen-

taries of French jurists upon it, which have great
weight before the Quebec Courts where the texts
are identical. So, too, the decisions of the French
Courts, especially of the *Cour de Cassation,* are
very frequently quoted as authority and gain great
consideration. The position, however, is complicated by the fact that the commissioners who prepared the Quebec Code drew many provisions from
the English law, and the rule is that when a provision is derived from the French law it is to be
interpreted by reference to French authority, and
when it is derived from English law, by reference
to English authority. Again in the matter of commercial law, which includes the law of corporations
and the mercantile law, the codifiers availed themselves freely of English and Scottish as well as of
French authorities. The practice in this branch of
the law is to refer both to French and English
authorities.[34] As to the authority of decided cases
the position in Quebec may be described as a sort
of middle term between the French system on the
one hand, and the English on the other. Mr. Walton
says as to this: 'Under our system as matter of
theory previous decisions are not absolutely binding. But in practice they enjoy greater authority
than they do in France, though less than they do
in England, and the tendency is toward giving them
greater weight than was formerly the case. This
is inevitable seeing that the Privy Council and the
Supreme Court of Canada, the two highest courts
of appeal, act upon the principle that previous decisions are binding.'[35]

I. *Canadian adoption of English statutes.* Before leaving the subject of English law in the
Canadian provinces we must not omit all reference
to the fact that in the region of what is sometimes

called "lawyers' law," to say nothing of statutes dealing with governmental and administrative matters, and quite apart from the general receptions of English law of which we have spoken (*supra,* pp. 52-6), the more important English statutes have, at all times, been largely borrowed from, adopted and re-enacted, in Canada. No one who has not actually practised law in Canada is likely to appreciate the extent to which the "Mother of Parliaments" has always, and still does, in this sense, legislate for the Dominion. By "lawyers' law" is meant the law governing the private relations and transactions of men, such as the law of real and personal property, the law of contracts, and the law of domestic relations, to which may be added the law of evidence in civil actions. Thus the provisions of the leading English statutes relating to the law and transfer of property such as what lawyers know as "Lord Cranworth's Act," or the Fines and Recoveries Act, 1833, and the Prescription Act, and those regarding the law of landlord and tenant, and the Married Women's Property Acts, and the Settled Estates Acts, and Lord Brougham's Act and Lord Denman's Act as to the admissibility of evidence of parties to actions, and of interested persons, have been generally adopted by re-enactment in the Canadian provinces; while the Dominion Bills of Exchange Act is a re-enactment of the English Bills of Exchange Act, 1882.

SEC. VI. THE CROWN IN CANADA. Proceeding now to grapple more closely with the principal subject of this article, we first deal with the Crown in its relation to Canada.

A. *The Crown one and indivisible.* The Crown is to be considered as one and indivisible throughout the Empire; and cannot be severed into as many distinct kingships as there are Dominions, and self-governing colonies.[36]

B. *The prerogative of the Crown in Canada.* As a corollary of the unity and indivisibility of the Crown through the Empire, the prerogative of the Crown runs in Canada to the same extent as in England. The prerogative of the King, when it has not been expressly limited by Imperial statute, or by valid local law or statute, is as extensive in His Majesty's colonial possessions as in Great Britain itself.[37] Thus His Majesty's prerogative rights over the Dominion of Canada as the fountain of honour, or of mercy, have not been in the least degree impaired or lessened by the British North America Act, though, of course, in Canada, as everywhere where parliamentary responsible government exists, the royal prerogative can be constitutionally exercised, only on the advice of responsible ministers.[38] So again, whatever rights, prerogatives, and priorities, the Crown has when suing in respect of Imperial rights, it has the same when suing in the Colonies. Thus the Crown (Dominion), when claiming in New Brunswick as creditor of a bank, was held entitled to priority over other creditors of equal degree according to the general rule of English law.[39]

Imperial veto power. The veto power of the Crown (Imperial) is specially preserved as to Dominion statutes by the British North America Act, 1867, but its exercise is limited to a period of two years after receipt by a Secretary of State of an authentic copy from the Governor-General.[40]

C. *Prerogative may be bound by Dominion or provincial statute.* This has already been intimated. The Crown is a party to and bound by both Dominion and provincial statutes, so far as such statutes are *intra vires*, i.e., relate to matters placed within the Dominion and provincial control respectively by the British North America Act. A gift of legislative power carries with it a corresponding executive power, even where such executive power is of a prerogative character, unless there be some restraining enactment, and this notwithstanding that sec. 9 of the British North America Act, 1867, declares that ' the executive government and authority of and over Canada continues and is vested in the King.' [41]

D. *The representatives of the Crown in Canada.* The Crown, however, is represented in Dominion affairs by the Governor-General, and in provincial affairs by the Lieutenant-Governors of the provinces, which latter are as much the representatives of His Majesty for all purposes of provincial government as the Governor-General himself is for all purposes of Dominion Government.[42] It is expressly provided in the British North America Act, 1867, that though provincial legislatures have an exclusive power to amend the provincial Constitution, this does not extend to the office of Lieutenant-Governor because he represents the Crown: sec. 92, No. 1.[43] A colonial Governor, however, under the British system is not a viceroy, but is vested with an authority limited by the terms of his commission and instructions, and, of course, by any valid statute conferring authority upon him, or regulating his powers. Such powers of the Crown as are not expressly or impliedly conferred by the British North America Act, or dealt with by statute, local or imperial, exist, whether in the Governor-General or in the provincial Lieutenant-Governors, only by delegation from the Sovereign, and until so controlled by statute law, can be withdrawn or modified and regulated, by the Sovereign, acting under the advice of his Imperial Ministers, as to the Governor-General, directly, and as to Lieutenant-Governors mediately through the Governor-General.[44]

E. *The Federal disallowance power.* By virtue of secs. 56 and 90 of the Federation Act, an authentic copy of every provincial Act has to be sent to the Governor-General, and if the Governor-General in Council, within one year after the receipt thereof, thinks fit to disallow the Act, such disallowance, being signified by the Governor-General in the manner prescribed, annuls the Act from and after the day of such signification. Thus one year only is allowed for such disallowance, and however detrimental, from the point of view of the federal Government, experience of its working may have shewn a provincial Act to be, it cannot afterwards be vetoed. This federal power of disallowance is one of the features of the Constitution of Canada which specially distinguishes it from that of the United States.[45] No direct power of confirmation or disallowance of Acts of the provincial legislatures rests with the Imperial authorities, owing to which fact, *inter alia,* as Mr. Keith observes (R. G. in D. Vol. II, pp. 1052-3) it has never been found possible to admit the securities of the Canadian provinces to the benefits of the Imperial Act of 1900 respecting colonial stocks and investments of trust funds. The Imperial Government, however, not infrequently intervenes, through the Secretary of State for the Colonies, by despatch to the Governor-General, with proposed or actual provincial legislation, by way of objection thereto when occasion arises.[46]

F. *Principles on which Federal disallowance is exercised.* It may, perhaps, be said that there are four main grounds upon which the Federal veto of provincial Acts may conceivably be exercised or advocated:— (1) because the provincial Act in question is an abuse of power and contrary to sound principles of legislation, as *e.g.,* amounting to spoliation, or a violation of property and vested rights, under contracts or otherwise: (2) because it is *ultra vires,* and therefore invalid; (3) because it conflicts with Imperial treaties or Imperial policy; (4) because it conflicts with Dominion policy or interests.

Disallowance of provincial Acts as violating vested rights or otherwise unjust. As to (1) in the early days of confederation and even as late as 1893, the authoritative view was that if provincial legislation interfered with rights of property, or contracts, without providing compensation, that circumstance afforded sufficient reason for the exercise of the power of disallowance; but, at any rate since 1901, Ministers of Justice, upon whose reports the power of disallowance is exercised or abstained from, have, until the accession to office of the present Minister of Justice, Mr. Doherty, consistently expressed a different view, viz.: that each provincial legislature, within the sphere of its authority and jurisdiction, should be supreme and amenable only to the electors of its own province, and have refused to disallow provincial Acts upon such grounds. In 1912, however, Mr. Doherty, in a report of January 20th, 1912, though refusing to recommend the exercise of the power in the case with which he was dealing, nevertheless states that ' he entertains no doubt that the power is constitutionally capable of exercise, and may on occasion be properly invoked for the purpose of preventing, not inconsistently with the public interest, irreparable injustice or undue interference with private rights or property through the operation of local statutes *intra vires* of the legislatures.' And Mr. Doherty reiterated similar views in another report of March 23rd, 1912, though, again, for reasons stated, abstaining from disallowance. It is possible, therefore, that we may yet see a revival of the exercise of the federal veto power in such cases, especially as such legislation may be deemed no merely local provincial matter, but injurious to the credit, and therefore injurious to the interests of the Dominion as a whole.[47]

Disallowance of provincial Acts as ultra vires. As to (2), the exercise of federal disallowance upon provincial Acts upon the ground that they are *ultra vires,* although as late as 1909, a Saskatchewan statute incorporating certain loan and investment and trust companies with power to do business beyond the limits of the province (since held to be permissible by the Privy Council in the *Bonanza Creek Gold Mining Co.* v. *The King* [1916] A. C. 566), and as late as 1910 a Quebec Act, amending the charter of a Trust Company which conferred powers of a banking character, were vetoed on such ground, it seems unlikely that many such cases of disallowance will occur in the future, unless the provincial Acts in question are seriously injurious to Imperial or Dominion policies or interests. As objected by the Government of British Columbia in 1905, to adopt such a course of action is to make the Minister of Justice the highest judicial dignitary in the land for the determination of constitutional questions, rather than the Supreme Court of Canada, or the Imperial Privy Council.[48]

(3) *Disallowance of Provincial Acts as contrary to Imperial treaty, policy, or interests.* As to the exercise of federal disallowance on the ground that the provincial Act in question conflicts with the Imperial treaties or Imperial policy, or on other grounds of Imperial intervention, there is little difference in substance between an Imperial veto where that can be exercised directly, and the intervention of the Imperial Government, through the Governor-General, against a proposed Act of a Canadian provincial legislature: and that the Imperial Government might veto a colonial Act where Imperial interests of great importance are imperilled is explicitly recognized by Mr. Joseph Chamberlain, as Secretary of State for the Colonies, in a despatch to the Governor of Newfoundland in 1898-9.[49] Again, although the Imperial Government may sometimes intervene in cases affecting the rights of persons not resident in the Dominion, and press for fair treatment of such persons, yet it does not seem to have ever gone further than to make such representations on the subject as could be used to a friendly foreign power. There certainly does not appear to be any case in which the Dominion Government has disallowed a provincial Act because of Imperial intervention on such grounds.[50] On the other hand, the Governor-General in Council may always be relied upon to veto provincial Acts contrary to Imperial treaties, which are placed under the special care of the Dominion Parliament by sec. 132 of the British North America Act, 1867.

Disallowance of Provincial Acts as contrary to Dominion policy and interests. (4) As to the disallowance of provincial Acts on such a ground as this, for many years the railway policy of the Dominion was carried out by disallowance of provincial legislation which conflicted with it. Between 1882-7 provincial Acts incorporating provincial railways were disallowed in accordance with a guarantee ratified by the Dominion Parliament in the session of 1880-1, that the Dominion Government would not permit for twenty years the construction of any line of railway south of the Canadian Pacific Railway from any point at or near the latter, except such as should run south-west.[51] So provincial Acts which discriminate against foreign immigrants and resident aliens have, quite apart from any question of Imperial treaty, been frequently disallowed, and in recent years, as *e.g.,* British Columbia Acts in 1899 and 1901. For it is the policy of the Dominion Government to promote immigration, and large sums of money are annually expended from the Dominion Treasury to that end. Moreover, of course, such legislation affects directly the relations of the Empire with foreign States.[52]

SEC. VII. CERTAIN INTRODUCTORY MATTERS AND GENERAL PRINCIPLES OF INTERPRETATION OF THE BRITISH NORTH AMERICA ACT, 1867.

A. *Plenary powers of Canadian legislatures.* Before dealing with the respective powers of the Dominion parliament on the one hand, and of the provincial legislatures on the other, there are still certain introductory remarks to be made, and certain general principles of interpretation established by the authorities to be pointed out. Thus it is important to notice that neither the Dominion parliament nor the provincial legislatures are to be considered as in any sense delegates of or acting under any mandate from the Imperial parliament, whereas in the United States the State legislatures are held to possess only a delegated power themselves, and, therefore, to be unable to delegate their powers to any other person or body. There is no such restriction upon Canadian legislatures. If it be once determined that the Dominion parliament or a provincial legislature has passed an Act upon any subject which is within its jurisdiction to legislate upon, its jurisdiction as to the terms of such legislation is as absolute as that of the Imperial parliament in the United Kingdom over a like subject. Thus it is the proper function of a Court of law to determine what are the limits of the jurisdiction committed to them; but when that point has been settled, Courts of law have no right whatever to enquire whether their jurisdiction has been exercised wisely or not.[53] This supremacy of legislatures under the Constitution of Canada may be deemed to be one of the points in which, in the words of the preamble of the Federation Act, it is a ' Constitution similar in principle to that of the United Kingdom.' For as Professor Dicey says in his Law of the Constitution (3rd edition, p. 37), ' the sovereignty of Parliament is (from a legal point of view) the dominant characteristic of English political institutions.'

B. *Imperial Treaties.* In view of the plenary powers of Canadian legislatures the question suggests itself whether a Dominion or provincial Act could be held void and unconstitutional merely because in conflict with an Imperial treaty, unless, of course, such treaty has been confirmed by Imperial statute, for there is no provision in the Canadian Constitution similar to that of Article VI of the Constitution of the United States, which provides that—' All treaties made, or which shall be made

under the authority of the United States, shall be
the supreme law of the land.' It is little likely,
however, that the Dominion parliament would, at
any time, persist in passing a Bill at variance with
an Imperial treaty, and if it did, the Governor-
General would, doubtless, reserve it to await His
Majesty's pleasure, or if he failed to do so, the
Imperial veto power would be available to save the
situation. Provincial Acts might, however, conflict
with Imperial treaties, and have, perhaps, done so
in such matters as immigration. But as to these
there is not only the Dominion veto power available,
but the Federation Act, by sec. 132, especially provides:—

' 132. The Parliament and Government of
Canada shall have all powers necessary or proper
for performing the obligations of Canada or of any
province thereof, as part of the British Empire towards foreign countries, arising under treaties
between the Empire and such foreign countries.'[54]

C. *Power of Canadian legislatures to delegate
their functions.* Accordingly Canadian legislatures have the same power which the Imperial parliament would have, under the like circumstances,
to confide to a municipal institution or body of their
own creation authority to make by-laws or regulations as to subjects specified in the enactment, and
with the object of carrying the enactment into
operation and effect; and, also, power to legislate
conditionally, as, for instance, by enacting that an
Act shall come into operation only on the petition
of a majority of electors.[55] So, of course, a provincial legislature can delegate to the Lieutenant-
Governor in Council the power to make rules, regulations, and by-laws auxiliary to carrying into
operation the provisions of an Act; and legislation

by one legislative body by reference to the enactments of another legislative body is defensible on
the same principle.[56] It is scarcely necessary to discuss the question, which has not yet actually arisen,
whether the Dominion parliament or a provincial
legislature could create in Canada and arm with
general legislative authority within the limits of
their own respective spheres a new legislative body
not created or authorized by the British North
America Act. It would seem, however, that provincial legislatures could, under No. 1 of sec. 92 of
the Federation Act, whereby they may amend the
Constitution of the province, save as to the office
of Lieutenant-Governor; and as to the Dominion
parliament there is the very wide power ' to make
laws for the peace, order, and good government of
Canada ' in relation to all matters not coming
within the classes of subjects assigned exclusively
to the provincial legislatures. See *infra,* pp. 74-7.[57]

D. *Law Courts are not concerned with the
motives of the legislature in legislating.* This is
an obvious corollary to the plenary nature of legislative power in Canada. Of course, the object and
design of an Act may, as we shall presently see
(*infra,* p. 98), be one of the things to be determined
in order to ascertain the class of subject to which
it really belongs—its true aspect—but assuming it
falls within one of the powers conferred by the
Federation Act upon the legislature passing it the
motive which induced the legislature to exercise its
power is no concern of the Courts.[58]

E. *Colourable legislation.* The parliament of
Canada cannot, under colour of general legislation,
deal with what are provincial matters only,[59] and
conversely, provincial legislatures cannot, under

the mere pretence of legislating upon one of the matters enumerated in section 92, really legislate upon a matter assigned to the jurisdiction of the parliament of Canada.[60] And if the Dominion parliament or the provincial legislatures have no power to legislate directly upon a given subject-matter, neither may they do so indirectly.[61]

F. *Law Courts not concerned with justice of legislation.* Again it is not competent for any Court to pronounce either a Dominion or a provincial Act invalid merely because it may affect injuriously private rights, or destroy vested rights, or be otherwise unjust, or contrary to sound principles of legislation, any more than it would be competent for the Courts in England, for the like reason, to refuse to give effect to a like Act of the Parliament of the United Kingdom.[62]

There are no provisions in the Canadian Constitution similar to those in that of the United States, that 'no State shall . . pass any Bill of attainder, *ex post facto* law, or law impairing the obligation of contracts '; and, as to Congress itself, that ' no bill of attainder or *ex post facto* law shall be passed.' All of which forcibly brings out the difference between the sovereign power of Canadian legislatures when legislating on the subjects committed to their jurisdiction, and the limited powers of legislatures in the United States.

G. *Some introductory remarks as to the distribution of legislative power within Canada.*

1. *Generality of language used in the British North America Act, 1867.* The language of sections 91 and 92 of the Act conferring legislative powers upon the Dominion parliament and provincial legislatures respectively, and of the various heads which

they contain, obviously cannot be construed as
having been intended to embody the exact disjunctions of a perfectly.logical scheme. The draughts-
man had to work on the terms of a political agreement, terms which were mainly to be sought for in
the resolutions passed at Quebec in October, 1864.
Of these resolutions, and the sections founded on
them, it may be said that if there is at points obscurity in language, this may be taken to be due,
not to the uncertainty about general principle, but
to that difficulty in obtaining ready agreement about
phrases which attends the drafting of legislative
measures by large assemblages. For these reasons
it is impracticable to attempt with safety definitions
marking out logical disjunctions between the various powers conferred by the 91st and 92nd sections,
and between their various subheads *inter se*. Lines
of demarkation have to be drawn in construing the
sections in their application to actual concrete cases,
as to each of which individually the Courts have
to determine on which side of a particular line
the facts place them.[63] It may be added that
the way in which provisions in terms overlapping each other have been placed side by side
in these sections shows that those who passed the
Federation Act intended to leave the working out
and interpretation of these provisions to practice
and to judicial decision. The framers of that Act,
purposing, as they state in the preamble, to give
to Canada ' a Constitution similar in principle to
that of the United Kingdom,' restrained their
hands, and in the distribution of legislative powers,
as in devising the other features of the Constitution, they used general language, and allowed as
free scope as in the nature of the case was possible,
for that process of organic growth of the Constitution coincidently with the development of the

national life generally which is one great virtue
of the Constitution of Great Britain. The general
terms employed show that the wish was to give a
general elasticity in the Constitution. It would,
indeed, have been impossible to make a complete
enumeration of all the powers to be vested in the
Dominion parliament and the provincial legislatures.[64] With this structure of sections 91 and 92,
and the degree to which the connotations of the
expressions overlap, and the use of general terms,
there comes the risk of some confusion whenever
a case arises in which it can be said that the power
claimed falls within the description of what the
Dominion, on the one hand, or the provinces, on
the other, are to have; while it becomes unwise for
the Courts to attempt exhaustive definitions of the
meaning and scope of the expressions used. Such
definitions must almost certainly miscarry. It is
in many cases only by confining decisions to concrete questions which have actually arisen in circumstances the whole of which are before the tribunal that injustice to future suitors can be
avoided.[65]

H. *The general scheme of the distribution of
legislative power.* The scheme of the Federation
Act comprises a fourfold classification of legislative
powers; firstly, over those subjects which are
assigned to the exclusive power of the Dominion
parliament; secondly, over those assigned to the
exclusive power of the provincial legislatures;
thirdly, over two subjects, and two subjects only,
agriculture and immigration, which are assigned
concurrently to the Dominion parliament and the
provincial legislatures by section 95, but with the
proviso that 'any law of the legislature of a province,
relative to agriculture or to immigration, shall have

effect in and for the province as long and as far only
as it is not repugnant to any Act of the Parliament
of Canada'; and, fourthly, over a particular subject,
namely, education, which, for special reasons, is
dealt with exceptionally, and made the subject of
special legislation: see *infra,* pp. 143-9.[65a]

As to the first class, the subjects assigned to the
exclusive power of the Dominion parliament comprise generally the power ' to make laws for the
peace, order, and good government of Canada in
relation to all matters not coming within the classes
of subjects assigned exclusively to the legislatures
of the provinces.' But inasmuch as the unequivocal
intention was to place within the power of the
Dominion parliament all matters which, although
they might appear to come within the description
of " provincial," or " municipal," or " local or
private," were deemed to possess an interest in
which the inhabitants of the whole Dominion might
be considered to be alike concerned,—therefore
section 91 expressly enacts that—' *notwithstanding
anything in this Act* (this is known as " the *non
obstante* clause ") ' the exclusive legislative authority of the Parliament of Canada extends to all
matters coming within the classes of subjects next
hereinafter enumerated,' being twenty-nine enumerated classes of subjects presently to be considered *seriatim* (see *infra,* pp. 101-124), but that
this enumeration is not to be construed as restricting
the generality of the preceding power to make laws
for the peace, order and good government of
Canada in relation to non-provincial subjects; and,
further, that ' any matter coming within any of the
classes of subjects enumerated shall not be deemed
to come within the class of matters of a local or
private nature comprised in the enumeration of the
classes of subjects assigned exclusively to the

legislatures of the provinces,' which the Privy
Council have interpreted to mean " shall not be
deemed to come within any of the classes of matters
assigned to the provincial legislatures.'' See *infra*
p. 87.

As to the legislative powers assigned to the
provincial legislatures all of these are by section 92
expressed to be assigned to them ' exclusively ': and
the section, instead of indicating them in general
terms as all matters of a purely local or private
nature in the province, enumerates, under items 1
to 15 inclusive, presently to be considered *seriatim*
(see *infra*, pp. 124-143), certain particular subjects of
a purely provincial, local, or private character, and
then winds up with item 16—' generally all matters
of a merely local or private nature in the province '
(see *infra*, p. 143) to prevent the particular enumeration of the local and private matters included in
items 1 to 15, being construed to operate as an exclusion of any other matter, if any there might be,
of a merely local or private nature.[66]

I.   *The Dominion residuary legislative power.*
The great importance of that feature of the Federation Act (sec. 91) whereby a general undefined and
unrestricted power to make laws for the ' peace,
order and good government of Canada ' in relation
to all matters not coming within the classes of subjects assigned exclusively to the legislatures of the
provinces by section 92 is given to the Dominion
parliament, is obvious. Yet it may mislead to
speak, as is often done, of the residue of legislative
power under the Canadian Constitution belonging
to the Dominion parliament, because the provincial
legislatures under section 92 also have a residuary
power to make laws in relation to ' generally all
matters of a merely local or private nature in the

province ' (see *infra* p. 143).[67]   The exercise of legislative power by the Dominion parliament in regard
to all matters not enumerated in section 91 ought,
therefore, to be strictly confined to such matters as
are unquestionably of Canadian interest and importance. It derives no jurisdiction from section 91,
when legislating on any subject not included within
the classes of subjects enumerated in that section,
to deal with any matter which is in substance local
or provincial, and does not truly affect the interest
of the Dominion as a whole. When so legislating
it has no. authority to trench or encroach upon any
class of subjects which is exclusively assigned to
provincial legislatures by section 92.   It cannot
legislate in relation to matters which in each province are substantially of local or private interest
upon the assumption that these matters also concern
the peace, order, and good government of the
Dominion.[68]   There is only one case, outside the
heads enumerated in section 91, in which the
Dominion parliament can legislate effectively as
regards a province, and that is where the subject
matter lies outside all of the subject matters
enumeratively entrusted to the province under section 92.[69]   But it must be remembered that some
matters in their origin local or provincial may
attain such dimensions as to affect the body politic
of the Dominion, and justify the Canadian parliament in passing laws for their regulation or abolition
tion in the interests of the Dominion; though this
will not prevent provincial legislatures still dealing
with the matter in its local or provincial aspect; but
in case of conflict Dominion legislation will prevail
(*infra*, pp. 84-5). Great caution must be observed
in distinguishing between that which is local and
provincial, and, therefore, within the jurisdiction of
the provincial legislatures, and that which has

ceased to be merely local or provincial, and has become a matter of national concern, in such sense as to bring it within the jurisdiction of the parliament of Canada.[70] It must also be borne in mind that to say that the Dominion parliament when legislating under its residuary power may not trench or encroach upon provincial subjects of legislative power, is not to say that when so legislating it may not incidentally affect such subjects. Few, if any, laws could be made by Parliament for the peace, order, and good government of Canada, which did not in some incidental way affect property and civil rights; and it could not have been intended to exclude the Parliament from the exercise of this general power whenever such incidental interference may result from it.[71] Perhaps the matter cannot be illustrated better than it was by Mr Upjohn on the argument before the Privy Council in the *Insurance Companies case*,[72] who gave as an example legislation in the form of a Sanitary Act in the case of an epidemic of disease, and said:—'' Then the fact that a person in a province is affected either in his property, if he is the owner of infected property, or in his person if he himself is infected and subject to the disease, does not show that the Dominion parliament has interfered with the exclusive jurisdiction of the provincial parliament over 'property and civil rights.' ''

Under this residuary power the Dominion Parliament can *primâ facie* pass any kind of laws provided it does not trench or encroach upon the subject-matters placed under the exclusive powers of the provincial legislatures by section 92, which, however, it would do if it legislated upon a matter of a merely local or private nature in the provinces. The legislation, as

we have seen, must be confined to such matters
as are unquestionably of Canadian interest and importance. As Lord Haldane expressed it on the
argument in the *Insurance Companies case*,[73] "it
must be something done for the Dominion in the
interests of the Dominion."

In the *Riel case*,[74] their lordships say that the
words in which this residuary power is given in
section 91, are apt to authorize the utmost discretion of enactment for the attainment of the
objects pointed to quite irrespective of the English
common law or legislation. In *Russell* v. *The Queen*,[74a]
they held that they fully authorised the Canada
Temperance Act, which abolished all retail transactions between traders in liquor and their cus-
tomers within every provincial area in which its
enactments had been adopted by the majority of the
local electors as in the Act provided. Would they
authorise the Dominion parliament even changing
the federal Constitution of Canada, without, of
course, affecting the Constitutions of the provinces?
On one of the arguments before the Judicial Committee Lord Davey suggested that they might even
do that. The balance of opinion seems, at present,
to be against that view.[75] There seems a certain
special significance in the word ' order,' in the
phrase ' peace, order, and good government of
Canada,' in section 91. In the previous Canadian
Constitutional Acts the phrase used in respect of
law-making powers had been ' peace, welfare, and
good government.' The substitution of "order" for
"welfare" appears clearly to place in the hands of
the federal power of the Dominion the right and
responsibility of maintaining public order throughout the whole country.

J. *The distribution of legislative power between the Dominion and the provinces is exhaus-*

tive. ,It is clear from the sections of the Federation
Act relating to the distribution of legislative power
to which we have been referring, that they exhaust
the whole range of legislative power, so far as the
internal affairs of Canada are concerned, and that
whatever is not thereby given to the provincial
legislatures rests with the Dominion parliament.
" The powers distributed between the Dominion on
the one hand, and the provinces on the other hand,
cover the whole area of self-government within the
whole area of Canada." [76] It has been well said by
a British Columbia judge that in these sections of
the Federation Act we have that distribution of
legislative power which " may one day, though in
the perhaps distant future, expand into national
life." [77] We have here two important points of
contrast between the Constitution of Canada and
that of the United States. Under the latter there
is a residuum of powers neither granted to the
Union nor continued to the States, but reserved to
the people, who, however, can put them in force
only by the difficult process of amending the Constitution. The scheme of the Canadian Federation
Act was to have no such reserved powers; but that
there should be in Canada the same kind of supreme
legislative power as there is in the British parliament, so far as consistent with the federation of
the provinces, and the position of Canada as a
Dominion within the Empire, in accordance with the
promise in the preamble of the Act, that the provinces were to be federally united ' with a Constitution similar in principle to that of the United
Kingdom.' Again, under the Canadian Constitution
all powers of legislation not expressly assigned to
the provincial legislatures, are vested in the Dominion parliament (see *supra*, pp. 74-7), whereas in
the United States, as expressed in the 10th amend-

ment: ' The powers not delegated to the United
States by the Constitution, nor prohibited by it to
the States, are reserved to the States respectively,
or to the people.' The intention of the framers
of the Canadian Constitution was that " the general
legislature should be stronger, far stronger than
the federal legislature of the United States in
relation to the States Governments." [78] In Canada,
then, if the subject-matter of an Act is not within
the jurisdiction of the provincial legislatures, acting,
either severally or in concert with each other, it is
within the jurisdiction of the Dominion parliament;
while on the other hand, if the subject matter of an
Act, other than agriculture and immigration (see
sec. 95 of Federation Act, and *infra.* p. 149) is
within the jurisdiction of the Dominion parliament,
it is not (in its entirety) within the jurisdiction of
the provincial legislatures, whether acting severally
or in concert with each other, although some of the
provisions of such Act, ancillary to the main subject
of legislation, may, as we shall see, be within such
provincial jurisdiction,[79]

K. *Extra-territorial legislation is, generally
speaking, invalid.* It is no doubt true, as a general
statement, that the Dominion parliament cannot
legislate except for Dominion territory, nor a provincial legislature except for provincial territory.[80]
But this, of course, does not affect the power of the
Imperial parliament to give the legislatures of self-
governing Dominions within the Empire, the power
to pass statutes, which shall operate outside their
borders, though within the Empire itself.[81] Moreover, bearing in mind the plenary character of the
powers of Canadian legislatures, see *supra,* pp. 66-7,
and the expressed intention to confer upon the
Dominion a Constitution similar in principle to that

of the United Kingdom, it may well be that they
have the same power to bind their own subjects
everywhere as the Imperial parliament has to bind
British subjects everywhere. For the expression
" subject of a colony " has high judicial authority,
and perhaps, may be taken to mean British subjects
domiciled in the colony.[82] It is, furthermore,
still a moot question whether colonial statutes,
purporting to have an extra-territorial operation,
are, nevertheless, not valid and binding within the
territory and upon the Courts of the lawmaker,
unless repugnant to some Act of the Imperial parliament; but it is quite a different question whether
foreign courts will recognise them, and judgments
obtained in legal proceedings initiated under them.[83]

Sec. VIII. Concurrent Legislative Power. We
have seen that to effect some legislative objects, a concurrent exercise of their respective legislative powers by the Dominion parliament and the
provincial legislatures, or by the provincial legislatures *inter se,* may be necessary (*supra,* p. 79), but
this is quite a different thing to concurrent legislative
power existing in both federal and provincial legislatures. With the exception of agriculture and immigration (see sec. 95 of the Federation Act, and *infra*
p. 149), there is no subject-matter over which there
can (speaking strictly) be said to exist such concurrent powers of legislation. But this must not be
understood as meaning that, if a given Act is *intra
vires* of the Dominion Act, a precisely similar Act
could under no circumstances be *intra vires* of a
provincial legislature. For, as we shall see (*infra,*
p. 98) subjects, which in one aspect and for one
purpose fall within the provincial powers of section
92 of the Federation Act, may, in another aspect
and for another purpose, fall within sec. 91; and

when the Federal parliament is legislating upon one of the subjects enumerated in sec. 91, there is no restriction upon its passing an Act which shall affect one part of the Dominion only; consequently it seems quite possible that a particular Act, regarded from one aspect, might be *intra vires* of a provincial legislature, and yet, regarded from another aspect, might be also *intra vires* of the Dominion parliament. In other words what is properly to be called the subject-matter of an Act may depend upon what is the true aspect of the Act.[84] At any rate it certainly must not be supposed that the Federal parliament and the provincial legislatures can, for no purpose whatever, or under no circumstances whatever, legislate in relation to the same matter. Thus the fact that the former can declare a thing a crime, will not, it would seem, exclude the powers of a province to deal with the same thing in its civil aspect, and impose sanctions for the observance of the law, as, *e.g.*, in the matter of providing against frauds in the supplying of milk to cheese factories.[85] And where federal legislation is under the residuary Dominion power, and not under any of the enumerated Dominion powers, it by no means follows that a provincial legislature cannot make a local law of a similar character, as is well illustrated by the various cases upon temperance legislation (see *notes* 127, 356-7). And certainly legislation by the latter is not necessarily *ultra vires* because it may interfere with or even render nugatory perfectly constitutional legislation by the Dominion. As we shall see, in certain cases, provincial legislation may by indirect means render inoperative such federal legislation, and *vice versa* (*infra,* pp. 96-7). And legislation by the Federal parliament on the enumerated Dominion sub-

jects may comprise ancillary provisions touching
and trenching upon provincial law and jurisdiction,
and *pro tanto* placing it in abeyance (*infra*, p. 94).
Moreover, legislative power as to certain broad
general subjects of legislation (*e.g.*, notably pro
perty and civil rights) is rested partly in the
Federal and partly in the provincial legislatures
(*infra*, pp. 134-7). Thus the most that can be said
with accuracy is that the powers of these legislatures respectively to deal directly and in their entirety, and as matter of separate and detached
legislation (as distinguished from legislative provisions merely ancillary to the main subject of
legislation) with the various classes of subjects
expressly enumerated in sections 91 and 92 of the
Federation Act are, in each case, special and exclusive.

Sec. IX. General Principles of Construction
of the Sections of the Federation Act Respecting
the Distribution of Legislative Power.

A. *Federation Act to be construed as a whole.*
It will be found that the subject-matters of legislation enumerated in sections 91 and 92 of the
Federation Act, and confided to the Dominion parliament and provincial legislatures in certain cases
" overlap," or, as it has also been called, " interlace
with " each other. In such cases the principle
applied is that the British North America Act, 1867,
has to be construed as a whole, and when some
specific matter is mentioned as within the exclusive
power of the Dominion parliament or provincial
legislature, as the case may be, which, but for that
reference, would fall within the more general description of a subject-matter expressed to be confided to the other, the statute must be read as excepting it from that general description. Thus it

comes about that legislative power may reside in
the provincial legislatures over certain matters,
notwithstanding that these matters fall within the
general description of some one of the classes of
subjects enumerated in sec. 91, and there confided
to the exclusive jurisdiction of the Federal parliament, and *vice versa.*[86] Moreover, in construing a
particular class of subject enumerated in section 91,
or section 92, it may be necessary to consider the
other subjects enumerated in the same section, although confided to the same legislature. In other
words, if the two sections are taken separately, in
some instances, the subjects enumerated in the same
section overlap each other. Thus the expression
' civil rights in the province ' '' is a very wide one,
extending if interpreted literally, to much of the
field of the other heads of section 92, and also to
much of the field of section 91. But the expression
cannot be so interpreted, and it must be regarded
as excluding cases expressly dealt with elsewhere
in the two sections, notwithstanding the generality
of the words.''[87]

B. *Overlapping legislation.* As, then, the
classes of subjects enumerated in sections 91 and 92
of the Federation Act, in many cases, '' overlap,''
so may Dominion and provincial legislation upon
certain matters included in them. In such case
neither legislation will be *ultra vires* if the field is
clear; but if the field is not clear, and in such domain
the two legislations meet, then, the Dominion legislation must prevail. Thus, for example, in the case
of the law of master and servant, the servants may
be workmen employed on a Dominion railway, and
the Dominion may deal with the subject so far as
they are concerned as ancillary to its railway legislation, in a different way to that in which provincial

legislatures deal with it as concerns workmen generally.[88]

C. *Rules for testing validity of Acts in Canada.* In determining the validity of a Dominion Act, the first question to be determined is whether the Act falls within any of the classes of subjects enumerated in sec. 92, and assigned exclusively to the legislatures of the provinces. If it does, then the further question will arise, whether the subject of the Act does not also fall within one of the enumerated classes of subjects in section 91, and so does not still belong to the Dominion parliament. But if the Act does not fall within any of the classes of subjects in section 92, no further question will remain. In like manner in determining the validity of a provincial Act, the first question to be decided is whether the Act impeached falls within any of the classes of subjects enumerated in section 92 of the British North America Act, and assigned exclusively to the legislatures of the provinces, for, if it does not, it can be of no validity, and no further question would then arise. It is only when an Act of a provincial legislature *primâ facie* falls within one of these classes of subjects that the further question arises, namely, whether, notwithstanding this is so, the subject of the Act does not fall within one of the enumerated classes of subjects in section 91, and whether the power of the provincial legislature is, or is not, thereby overborne. For, *notwithstanding anything in the Federation Act,* the exclusive authority of the parliament of Canada extends to all matters coming within the classes of subjects enumerated in section 91.[89]

SEC. X. PREDOMINANCE OF DOMINION LEGISLATION. Where in respect to matters with which provincial legislatures have power to deal, provincial legislation directly conflicts with the enactments of the Dominion parliament, whether the latter immediately relate to the enumerated classes of subjects in sec. 91 of the British North America Act, or are only ancillary to legislation on such subjects, or are enactments for the peace, order, and good government of Canada in relation to matters not coming within the classes of subjects assigned exclusively to the provincial legislatures, nor within the enumerated classes of section 91, the provincial legislation must yield to that of the Dominion parliament. For before the laws enacted by the federal authority within the scope of its powers, the provincial lines disappear. As to these laws we have a quasi-legislative union. They are the local laws of the whole Dominion, and of each and every province thereof.[90] Nor does it make any difference whether the provincial enactments be prior in date to the conflicting Dominion enactments, or subsequent.[91] But, of course, provincial legislation which is merely supplemental to Dominion legislation may be perfectly good, at any rate when the latter is not within one of the enumerated Dominion subjects.[92] And the Privy Council have certainly not received with favour the contention which has been raised in certain cases, that provincial powers of legislation are restricted or placed in abeyance by the very inaction of the Dominion parliament, or by reason of the fact that the latter has legislated *in pari materia,* though conditionally only upon the exercise of local option, which latter has not been exercised in favour of the operation of the Act.[93]

SEC. XI. EXCLUSIVENESS OF DOMINION ENUMERATED POWERS. As is expressly stated in the Federation Act, notwithstanding anything in that Act, the exclusive legislative authority of the Dominion parliament extends to all matters coming within the classes of subjects enumerated under the various items of section 91. Whenever, therefore, a matter is within one of these specified classes, legislation in relation to it by a provincial legislature is incompetent. Thus a provincial legislature cannot enact a bankruptcy law or a copyright law for the province, even although the Dominion parliament may not have itself legislated upon those subjects. Nor can a provincial legislature enact fishery regulations and restrictions for the province. That is not saying that provincial legislation is necessarily *ultra vires* because it may have some relation to fisheries. It is only that subject-matter which is within the proper meaning and interpretation of one of the enumerated classes of section 91 that is for the exclusive legislative jurisdiction of the Dominion parliament; and we must not take too narrow and literal a view of the words by which these classes are described. The important thing to notice is that under the Federation Act, legislative power is distributed by subjects and not by area, and this will be further illustrated by what we shall have to say as to locally restricted Dominion laws (*infra* pp. 88-90).[94]

SEC. XII. GENERAL CHARACTER OF THE POWERS OF THE DOMINION PARLIAMENT. The principle of the 91st section of the British North America Act is to place within the legislative jurisdiction of the Dominion parliament general subjects which may be dealt with by legislation as distinguished from subjects of a local or private nature in the province.[95] All the great questions which affect the general interests of the Confederacy as a whole, are confided to the Federal parliament, while the local interests and local laws of each section are preserved intact, and entrusted to the care of the provincial legislatures. The Dominion powers relate to matters necessarily and naturally proper for federal administration. For example, the Dominion power to make laws in relation to the regulation of trade and commerce, like that relating to bills of exchange, or interest, or weights and measures, or legal tender, or bankruptcy and insolvency, was a necessary incident to the Union to secure a homogeneous whole.[96]

SEC. XIII. THE RELATION BETWEEN THE DOMINION ENUMERATED POWERS AND THE PROVINCIAL POWERS. It was apparently contemplated by the framers of the Federation Act that the due exercise of the enumerated powers conferred upon the Dominion parliament by section 91 might occasionally and incidentally involve legislation upon matters which are *primâ facie* committed exclusively to the provincial legislatures by section 92. In order to provide against that contingency the concluding part of section 91 enacts that—' Any matter coming within any of the classes of subjects enumerated in section 91 of the British North America Act shall not be deemed to come within the class of matters of a local or private nature comprised in the enumeration of classes of subjects by the Act assigned exclusively to the legislatures of the provinces.' This language was meant to include, and correctly describes, all the matters enumerated in the sixteen heads of section 92 which comprise the provincial legislative power, as being, from a provincial point of view, of a local or private nature. But the exception thus expressed was not meant to derogate from the legislative authority given to provincial legislatures by those sixteen sub-sections

save to the extent of enabling the parliament of
Canada to deal with matters local or private in
those cases where such legislation is necessarily
incidental to the exercise of the powers conferred
upon it by the enumerated heads of section 91. It
has no application to matters which are not specified among the enumerated subjects of legislation,
and in legislating with regard to them, the Dominion
parliament has no authority to encroach upon any
class of subjects which is exclusively assigned to
the provincial legislatures by section 92.[97] It has,
however, the further significance—although perhaps unnecessary in view of the fact that the Dominion enumerated powers had been previously
expressed to be exclusive ' notwithstanding anything in the Act '—that provincial legislatures cannot legislate on any of those enumerated Dominion
subjects, under the pretence or contention that the
legislation is of a provincial or local character, as
for example, incorporate a bank for the province.

SEC. XIV.   LOCALLY RESTRICTED DOMINION LAWS.
Although in the course of the argument before the
Judicial Committee of the Privy Council in
Canadian Pacific R. W. Co. v. *Bonsecours,*[98] Lord
Watson apparently suggested that the Dominion
parliament has under section 91 no power given it to
legislate in relation even to the enumerated classes
of subjects in that section (as to its residuary power
see *supra,* pp. 74-7), unless it can be predicated
of such legislation that it is legislation for the peace,
order, and good government of Canada—it would
seem that, when legislating upon one of these enumerated subjects, there is no restriction upon that
parliament to prevent it passing a law affecting
one part of the Dominion and not another, if in its
wisdom it thinks the legislation desirable in one

and not in the other.[99]   And although in *L'Union St. Jacques de Montreal* v. *Belisle*,[99a] Lord Selborne, delivering the judgment, says: "Their lordships observe that the scheme of enumeration in that section is to mention *various categories of general subjects* which may be dealt with by legislation"; and that "there is no indication in any instance of anything being contemplated except what may be properly described as general legislation"; and although in *Cushing* v. *Dupuy*[100] the Privy Council say that "It is a necessary implication, that the Imperial statute in assigning to the Dominion parliament the subjects of bankruptcy and insolvency intended to confer on it legislative power to interfere with property, civil rights, and procedure within the provinces, *so far as a general law relating to those subjects might affect them*"—special or private bill legislation by the Federal parliament is of yearly occurrence and has never been seriously questioned.[101]   And it is well to point out that section 91 says that the gift of exclusive legislative authority over the enumerated classes of subjects, is to be read ' not so as to *restrict* the generality of the foregoing terms of this section.' It is not said that they are not to be read so as to ' *enlarge* ' the apparent restriction in the foregoing terms of the section of Dominion legislative power to legislation for the peace, order and good government of Canada.

As to whether the Dominion parliament has a like power of enacting statutes to operate in certain provinces, or a certain province only, when legislating under its general residuary power to pass laws for the peace, order and good government of Canada upon non-provincial subjects, it must be admitted that direct authority on the point is not

to be found in the reported decisions. It is submitted, however, that they certainly have the power,
for as we have seen, the distribution of legislative
power under the Act is exhaustive, and such legislation, though confined to two or three provinces
only, might be called for in the general interests of
the Dominion: *supra,* pp. 77-9.[102] It may be, however,
contended that all matters not admitting or calling
for legislation applying to the Dominion as a whole,
and not within the enumerated Dominion subjects,
must be considered matters of ' a merely local and
private nature,' in the provinces concerned, and left
to be dealt with by the legislatures of the provinces
concerned.

Sec. XV. Dominion Power over all Canadian
Subjects. The Dominion parliament can, in matters within its sphere, impose duties upon any
subjects of the Dominion, whether they be officials
of provincial Courts, other officials, or private citizens.[103] But although the Dominion parliament can
impose jurisdiction on provincial Courts in
Dominion matters, it is not so clear that it can
divest the provincial Courts of concurrent jurisdiction, although, of course, it can establish additional
Courts of its own for the better administration of
the laws of Canada, and then, perhaps, it can give
such Dominion Courts sole jurisdiction on Dominion
subjects.[104] It would appear that in matters within
their sphere, provincial legislatures can impose
duties upon Dominion officials in certain cases, for
the Supreme Court of British Columbia has held
that they can under No. 14 of sec. 92 of the Federation Act, which gives them exclusive power to make
laws in relation to ' the administration of justice in
the province, including the constitution, maintenance, and organization of provincial Courts, both of

civil and criminal jurisdiction,' enact that a County Court judge appointed for one district might, under certain circumstances, act as judge of another district, and that, until a County Court judge of Kootenay had been appointed, the judge of the County Court of Yale should act as such.[105]

SEC. XVI. THE GENERAL CHARACTER OF PROVINCIAL LAW-MAKING POWERS.

A. *None except the enumerated ones.* The provincial legislatures have no powers to make laws save upon the subject-matters enumerated in section 92 of the Federation Act, except the power given them to make laws in relation to education by sec. 93 (see *infra,* pp. 143-9), and in relation to agriculture in the province, and immigration into the province, given them by sec. 95 (see *infra,* p. 149). They cannot legislate beyond the areas of the prescribed subject-matters.[106] But, it must, of course, be always remembered that No. 16 of sec. 92 gives them a general residuary power to make laws in relation to 'all matters of a merely local or private nature in the province,' *supra,* p. 143. It is scarcely necessary to add that, although uniformity of legislation on provincial subjects can, of course, be produced in different provinces by their respective legislatures enacting similar laws, the sphere of law-making power of each legislature remains identically the same as before.[107]

B. *Inherent powers of legislatures, apart from law-making.* Apart, however, from law-making, provincial legislatures have by virtue of being legislative bodies at all, such powers and privileges as are necessarily inherent in and incident to such bodies; and, having them, may regulate their exercise by statute or by standing rules,

if they see fit to do so; as, *e.g.*, the power to remove
any obstruction offered to the deliberations or
proper action of the legislative body during its
sittings; some power of suspending members guilty
of obstructing, and disorderly conduct, but not extending to unconditional suspension for an indefinite time, or for a definite time depending only on
the irresponsible discretion of the Assembly itself;
and whatever, in a reasonable sense, is necessary
to the existence of such a body, and the proper
exercise of the functions which it is intended to
execute.[108] Such powers, however, are protective
and self-defensive only, not punitive, and cannot be
measured by powers of the parliament of Great
Britain under the ancient *lex et consuetudo parliamenti,* which is a law peculiar to and inherent in
the two Houses of Parliament of the United Kingdom.[109] However, the practical importance of this
subject does not appear to be very great, seeing
that No. 1 of sec. 92 of the Federation Act whereby
provincial legislatures may amend the Constitution
of the province, except as regards the office of
Lieutenant-Governor, confers the power ' to pass
Acts for defining the powers and privileges of the
provincial legislature.'[110] As to the power of the
Dominion parliament in respect to these matters,
sec. 18 of the Federation Act as amended by Imp. 38-
39 Vict. c. 38, expressly provides that:—' The privileges, immunities, and powers to be held, enjoyed
and exercised by the Senate and by the House of
Commons, and by the members thereof respectively,
shall be such as are, from time to time, defined by
Act of the parliament of Canada, but so that any
Act of the parliament of Canada, defining such
privileges, immunities and powers, shall not confer
any privileges, immunities or powers, exceeding
those at the passing of such Act, held, enjoyed, and

exercised by the Commons House of Parliament
of the United Kingdom of Great Britain and Ireland and by the members thereof.' [111]

C. *Provincial powers co-equal and co-ordinate.*
Co-equal and co-ordinate legislative powers in every
particular were conferred by the Federation Act
on the provinces. The Constitutions of all provinces
within the Dominion are on the same level. [112]

SEC. XVII. POWER TO REPEAL OR ALTER STAT-
UTES OF THE OLD PROVINCE OF CANADA. Powers are
conferred by sec. 129 of the Federation Act upon
the provincial legislatures of Ontario and Quebec,
to repeal and alter the statutes of the old parliament
of the province of Canada, which powers are made
precisely co-extensive with the powers of direct
legislation with which these bodies are invested by
the other clauses of that Act; and the power of the
provincial legislature to destroy a law of the old
province of Canada is measured by its capacity to
reconstruct what it has destroyed. And in no case
can an Act of the old province of Canada applicable to the two provinces of Ontario and Quebec,
be validly repealed by one of them, unless the nature
of the Act is such that it still remains in full vigour
in the other. [113]

SEC. XVIII. DOMINION INTRUSION ON PROVINCIAL
AREA. ANCILLARY LEGISLATION.

A. *Indirect interference.* An Act of the Dominion parliament is not affected in respect to its validity by the fact that it interferes prejudicially with
the object and operation of provincial Acts, provided
that it is not in itself legislation upon or within one
of the subjects assigned to the exclusive jurisdiction
of the provincial legislature. Thus Dominion legis-

lation imposing conditions of a prohibitory character on the liquor traffic throughout the Dominion may be none the less valid because it destroys a profitable source of income to the provinces derived from licenses granted to taverns for the sale of intoxicating liquors.[114]

B. *Direct intrusion.—Powers by implication.* In *Russell* v. *The Queen,*[114] the legislation was under the general residuary power of the Dominion parliament, in which case, although that parliament may indirectly interfere with the operation of provincial Acts, it cannot directly encroach upon the provincial area: see *supra,* pp. 75-7. But when it is legislating upon the enumerated Dominion subject-matters of sec. 91 of the Federation Act, it is held that the Imperial parliament, by necessary implication, intended to confer on it legislative power to interfere with, deal with, and encroach upon, matters otherwise assigned to the provincial legislatures under sec. 92, so far as a general law relating to those subjects may affect them, as it may also do to the extent of such ancillary provisions as may be required to prevent the scheme of such a law from being defeated. The Privy Council has established and illustrated this in many decisions.[115]

C. *Rule of necessity as applied to such Dominion interference.* When it is sought to find some rule regulating the power of the Federal parliament thus incidentally to deal with matters which are under the jurisdiction of the provinces, it does not appear that any has been, or it may be, can be formulated beyond this, that such power does not extend any further than is reasonable to enable it to legislate on the general subjects committed to its jurisdiction by the Federation Act.[116]   It would

appear, in words of Anglin, J., to be sufficient if the
intrusive legislation is "eminently germane, if not
absolutely necessary," to the main legislation.[117]
At the same time in the very case last cited, on appeal to the Privy Council, their lordships say that
"it must be shown that it is necessarily incidental to
the exercise" of the Dominion power, that it should
trespass in the way it has done on the provincial
area; and they use this expression "necessarily incidental" not less than three times.[118]   And they
used the same expression "necessarily incidental,"
in the same connection in their previous judgment
in the *Liquor Prohibition Appeal, 1895.*[119] Still
their judgment in *City of Toronto* v. *Canadian Pacific Railway Co.*,[116] seems to show that
the words "necessarily incidental" must not be
read so strictly as to mean that without the provision which encroaches on the provincial area "it
would be impossible to carry into effect the intention
of the (Dominion) legislature, or that probably no
other provision would be adequate.   On the contrary
it seems that if such provision might, under certain
circumstances, be beneficial, and assist to more fully
enforce such legislation, then it must, at all events,
on an appeal to the Courts, be held to be necessary,
that is, necessary in certain events."[120]

SEC. XIX.   PROVINCIAL INTRUSION ON DOMINION
AREA.   There seems to be no authority to support
the view that provincial legislatures can at all legislate upon any of the Dominion subject-matters
enumerated in sec. 91 of the Federation Act by way
of provisions ancillary to their own Acts.   What
judicial authority there is does not seem to carry
the matter further than this, that whatever powers
the provincial legislatures have as included within
the enumerated subject-matters of sec. 92, when

properly understood, those powers they may exercise, although in so doing they may incidentally touch or affect something which might otherwise be held to come within the exclusive jurisdiction of the Dominion parliament under some subject-matter enumerated in sec. 91.[121] The Dominion residuary area (see *supra,* pp. 74-7) is a different matter. The provincial legislatures may well have power incidentally to invade this area, without having any power to invade the area of the enumerated Dominion subjects.

SEC. XX. PROVINCIAL INDEPENDENCE AND AUTONOMY.[122]

A. *Incidental interference with Dominion legislation does not invalidate provincial Acts.* Although when provincial legislation and Dominion legislation directly conflict with each other, the latter must prevail (*supra,* pp. 84-5), and although the construction of the enumerated powers conferred upon the Dominion parliament may be said to over-ride the construction of sec. 92 of the Federation Act conferring the provincial powers, yet the Canadian provinces have not, as the several States of the Union have, a general power of legislation subject only to certain specified powers conferred by themselves upon the Federal body,—but they as well as the Dominion parliament, have received from one and the same source, namely, the Imperial parliament, certain express powers of legislation upon specified subjects, which are theirs exclusively; and, therefore, their power to legislate upon these subjects cannot be denied, as is the case with the American States, merely because in doing so they may interfere with, or restrict the range of, Federal legislation.[123] But, on the other hand, the Dominion Government possesses what the United States

Government does not possess, namely, a veto power over all provincial legislation (see *supra* pp. 62-6).

B. *Injustice does not invalidate Acts.* In so far as they possess legislative jurisdiction, the discretion committed to the legislatures of the Dominion or of the provinces is unfettered. It is the proper function of a Court of law to determine what are the limits of the jurisdiction committed to them; but when that point has been settled Courts of law have no right whatever to enquire whether their jurisdiction has been exercised wisely or not. The supreme legislative power in relation to any subject-matter is always capable of abuse. If it is abused, the only remedy is an appeal to those by whom the legislature is elected.[124]

C. *Possibility of Dominion legislation superseding them does not invalidate Provincial Acts.* A provincial legislature is not incapacitated from enacting a law otherwise within its proper competency merely because the Dominion parliament might, under sec. 91 of the Federation Act, if it saw fit so to do, pass a general law which would embrace within its scope the subject matter of the provincial Act.   Thus the fact that under No. 7 of section 91, the Dominion parliament legislating in respect to military and naval defence, might take any of the land of a province for the purpose of such defence, but has not actually done so, does not deprive the provincial legislature of legislative jurisdiction over the lands of the province in the meanwhile.[125] On the other hand the abstinence of the Dominion parliament from legislating to the full limit of its powers cannot have the effect of transferring to any provincial legislature any part of the legislative power assigned to the Dominion by sec. 91.[126]

SEC. XXI. ASPECTS OF LEGISLATION. Subjects which in one aspect and for one purpose fall within sec. 92 of the Federation Act and so are proper for provincial legislation may, in another aspect and for another purpose, fall within sec. 91, and so be proper for Dominion legislation. And as the cases which illustrate this principle show, by "aspect" here must be understood the aspect or point of view of the legislator in legislating, the object, purpose, and scope of the legislation. The word is used subjectively of the legislator, rather than objectively of the matter legislated upon.[126a]

SEC. XXII. SOME OTHER CONSIDERATIONS RELEVANT TO THE QUESTION OF THE CONSTITUTIONALITY OF STATUTES.

A. *The object and scope of the legislation.* It follows as a necessary corollary of the principle just discussed regarding different aspects of statutes, that "the true nature and character of the legislation in the particular instance under discussion— its grounds and design, and the primary matter dealt with—its object and scope, must always be determined in order to ascertain the class of subject to which it really belongs, and any merely incidental effect it may have over other matters does not alter the character of the law."[127] But, of course, as has already been stated, *supra,* p. 69, when once it is clear to what class any particular Act belongs, and, therefore, whether it is within the jurisdiction of parliament, or within that of the provincial legislature, the motive which induced Parliament, or a local legislature, to exercise its power in passing it cannot affect its validity.

B. *Presumption in favour of the validity of Acts.* It is not to be presumed that the Dominion parliament has exceeded its powers, unless upon grounds really of a serious character.[128] And as regards provincial Acts, where the validity of such an Act is in question, and it clearly appears to fall within one of the classes of subjects enumerated in sec. 92 of the Federation Act, the onus is on the persons attacking its validity to show that it also comes within one or more of the classes of subjects specially enumerated in sec 91.[129] But it is not so clear, although some Canadian Courts have so laid it down,[130] that there is any general presumption in favour of provincial Acts, inasmuch as the provinces have only specially enumerated powers of legislation, and what is not given to them is given to the Dominion parliament.[131]

C. *Declarations of the Dominion parliament upon the interpretation of the British North America Act* are not, of course, conclusive, but when the proper construction of the language used in that Act to define the distribution of legislative power is doubtful, the interpretation put upon it by the Dominion parliament, in its actual legislation, may properly be considered; and, no doubt, this applies *a fortiori*, when the provincial legislatures have, by their legislation, shown agreement in the views of the Dominion parliament as to their respective powers.[132] So, too, views acted upon by the great public departments, as expressed in Imperial despatches, or otherwise, carry weight in the absence of judicial decision.[133]

D. *Continued exercise of a legislative power does not make it constitutional.* If the Dominion parliament does not possess a legislative power,

neither the exercise, nor the continued exercise,
of a power belonging to it can confer it, or make
its legislation binding. And the same is, of course,
true of legislation by provincial legislatures.[134]

SEC. XXIII. STATUTES UNCONSTITUTIONAL IN
PART ONLY. NULLITY OF UNCONSTITUTIONAL STAT-
UTES. Although part of an Act, either of the
Dominion parliament or of a provincial legislature,
may be *ultra vires,* and therefore invalid, this will
not invalidate the rest of the Act, if it appears that
the one part is separate in its operation from the
other part, so that each is a separate declaration of
the legislative will, and unless the object of the Act
is such that it cannot be attained by a partial execution.[135] And, in the same way, an Act may sometimes be *intra vires* in some of its applications, while
ultra vires in others.[136] Nor must it be supposed
that Acts incorporating companies must necessarily
be invalid altogether because *ultra vires* in respect
to part of the powers conferred upon the company.[137]
It is scarcely necessary to say that a transaction
which is *ultra vires* of the parties to it, can derive
no support from an Act which is itself *ultra vires*
of the legislature passing it; nor will the right of
those affected by it to treat it as of no legal force
or validity, be interfered with by such an Act. So,
likewise, incapacities imposed upon persons guilty
of certain practices by an Act which is *ultra vires*
will not enure to or affect those persons.[138]

SEC. XXIV. LEGISLATIVE POWER AND PROPRIETARY
RIGHTS. The fact that legislative jurisdiction in
respect of a particular subject-matter is conferred
on the Dominion parliament or provincial legislatures affords no evidence or presumption that any
proprietary rights with respect to it were transferred by the Act to the Dominion or provinces

respectively.[139]   Accordingly the Dominion parliament and provincial legislatures have no power by virtue of their legislative jurisdictions under sections 91 and 92 respectively to confer upon others proprietary rights where they possess none themselves, unless under such of the enumerated items in those sections as necessarily imply the power so to deal with property, although not vested in the Crown as represented by the Dominion or provincial Governments.[140]   And although the Dominion parliament and provincial legislatures have unquestionably the right to legislate as to, and to dispose of any property belonging to the Dominion or the provinces, respectively, they have been thought to have only the right to dispose of the interest they have in such property.[141]

SEC. XXV. SPECIFIC LEGISLATIVE POWERS—DOMINION AND PROVINCIAL.   Having now set forth the sections of the British North America Act, 1867, which construct the framework of the Constitution of the Dominion of Cànada, and having discussed the place and functions therein of the Crown, in which is vested the executive power, and having stated and explained such general propositions and principles bearing upon its general scheme and operation as the discussion of it in the Courts and elsewhere, since Confederation, have discovered, we have next to explain the various specific and enumerated legislative powers in sections 91 and 92 so far as the authorities have thrown light upon them, and then to treat of the property provisions of the Act.

A. *Dominion powers.*

1. '*The public debt and property.*'   The subject of Dominion and provincial property under the Federation Act is treated *infra*, pp. 151-3.

2. *'The regulation of Trade and Commerce.'*
It is absolutely necessary that the literal meaning
of these words should be restricted in order to afford
scope for powers which are given exclusively to the
provincial legislatures. They must, like the expression ' property and civil rights in the province,'
in sec. 92 (see *infra,* pp. 134-7) receive a limited interpretation.[142] They "may have been used in some
such sense as the words ' regulations of trade ' in
the Act of Union between England and Scotland
(6 Anne, ch. 11), Article 6 of which enacted that all
parts of the United Kingdom, from and after the
Union, should be under the same ' prohibitions, restrictions, and regulations of trade.' Parliament
has at various times since the Union passed laws
affecting and regulating specific trades in one part
of the United Kingdom only, without its being supposed that it thereby infringed the Articles of
Union."[143] In the same way there have been very
numerous decisions in Canadian Courts holding
provincial legislation of a local, sanitary, or police
character, valid notwithstanding any effect it might
have on particular trades,[144] while, on the other
hand, the Dominion authority to legislate for the
regulation of trade and commerce does not extend
to the regulation by a licensing system of a particular trade in which Canadians would otherwise be
free to engage in the provinces.[145] Nor does the importance of the particular trade or business affect
the matter. Many highly important and extensive
forms of business in Canada are freely transacted
under provincial authority. When the British North
America Act has taken such forms of business out
of provincial jurisdiction, as in the case of banking,
it has done so by express words.[146] It may be well
to note that the words of the Act are ' regulation
of trade and commerce,' not ' regulation of *trades*

and commerce.' It may be that regulation of the customs tariff was principally in the mind of the legislature.[147] Regulation of trade and commerce includes "political arrangements in regard to trade, requiring the sanction of Parliament, regulation of trade in matters of inter-provincial concern, and may, perhaps, include general regulations of trade affecting the whole Dominion, but it does not comprehend the power to regulate by legislation the contracts of a particular business or trade, such as the business of insurance, in a single province."[148] Under this power over 'the regulation of trade and commerce' in combination with that (No. 25) over 'naturalization and aliens,' the Dominion parliament has jurisdiction to require a foreign company to take out a license from the Dominion minister, even in a case where the company desires to carry on its business only within the limits of a single province.[149] So, too, this power "enables the parliament of Canada to prescribe to what extent the powers of companies the objects of which extend to the entire Dominion should be exerciseable, and what limitations should be placed on such powers." But this does not mean in the case of companies incorporated by the Dominion not under one of its enumerated powers (see *infra,* pp. 122-4), but under its residuary power, — that because the status given to it by the Dominion parliament enables it to trade in a province, and thereby confers on it civil rights to some extent, "the power to regulate trade and commerce can be exercised in such a way as to trench in the case of such companies on the exclusive jurisdiction of the provincial legislature over civil rights in general" (see *infra,* pp. 134-7); but, on the other hand, "the province cannot legislate so as to deprive a Dominion company of its status and powers . . . The status and powers of a Dominion company as such cannot be destroyed by provincial legislation,'' as, for example, by compelling the Dominion company to obtain a provincial license or to be registered in the province as a condition of exercising its powers and of suing in the Courts. A province cannot '' interfere with the status and capacity of a Dominion company in so far as that status and capacity carries with it powers conferred by the parliament of Canada to carry on business in every part of the Dominion.'' [150] So much, then, as to what we call the positive aspects of this Dominion power so far as the same have been up to the present time defined by the authorities. We may add, however, that it is no doubt in reliance on this power that the Dominion has passed such legislation as the *Conciliation and Labour Act,* R. S. C. 1906, c. 96.[151] And now as to the negative aspects of this Dominion power, it does not prevent provincial taxation of the persons or companies regulated.[152] Nor does it prevent a provincial legislature requiring every brewer, distiller, or other persons, though duly licensed by the Government of Canada for the manufacture and sale of fermented, spirituous, and other liquors, to take out licenses to sell the liquors manufactured by them, and pay a license fee therefor.[153] Nor does it prevent a provincial liquor Act including divers prohibitions and restrictions affecting the importation, exportation, manufacture, keeping, sale, purchase and use of intoxicating liquors, which may interfere with licensed trades in the province, and indirectly with business operations beyond the limits of the province.[154] Nor does it prevent a provincial Act validating a municipal by-law granting certain persons an exclusive right of establishing a system of electric lighting for a certain term of years in the city, notwithstanding that electric light is a commercial commodity.[155] Nor does it prevent a provincial Act making police or municipal regulations of a merely local character for the good government of taverns licensed for the sale of liquor by retail.[156] And, as we have already stated, there are very numerous decisions in Canadian Courts holding provincial legislation of a local, sanitary or police character valid, notwithstanding any effect it may have on particular trades: *supra,* p. 102.

3. '*The raising of money by any mode or system of taxation.*' This Dominion power is obviously not intended to over-ride the provincial power under No. 2 of sec. 92, in respect to ' direct taxation within the province, in order to the raising of a revenue for provincial purposes.'[157] All other power to impose direct taxation, however, is exclusively in the Dominion under this subsection. On the other hand, notwithstanding the exclusive provincial power under No. 9 of sec. 92 to make laws in relation to ' shop, saloon, tavern, auctioneer, and other licenses in order to the raising of a revenue for provincial, local or municipal purposes,' the Dominion parliament also can tax by means of licenses.[157a] Under this power the Dominion parliament can impose a customs duty upon a foreign-built ship to be paid upon application by her in Canada for registration as a British ship, there being no repugnancy between this and any Imperial enactment extending to Canada.[158] In conclusion we may notice that, in entire accordance with the plenary powers within their sphere of Canadian legislatures (*supra,* pp. 66-7), which is one of the points in which, in the words of the preamble of the Federation Act, the Dominion has ' a Constitution similar in principle to that of the United Kingdom,' there is no such necessity for uniformity and equality of

taxation as exists in the United States (Art. 1, sec. 3; Art. 1, sec. 8).

4. *'The borrowing of money on the public credit.'*

5. *'Postal Service.'*

6. *'The Census and Statistics.'* [159]

7. *'Militia, Military and Naval Service and Defence.'* It has been held that the Dominion parliament has no right under this power to impose in the Militia Act civil obligations upon any provincial municipality for the payment of the troops.[160] It would be absurd to contend that under it, the Dominion parliament has authority to confer the provincial franchise upon the militia.[161]

8. *'The fixing of and providing for the salaries and allowances of Civil and other officers of the Government of Canada.'* [162]

9. *'Beacons, Buoys, Lighthouses, and Sable Island.'*

10. *'Navigation and Shipping.'* This power entitles the Dominion parliament to declare what shall be deemed an interference with navigation.[163] Nevertheless it does not appear to include the right to authorize the erection of booms for securing lumber in the rivers of the province. Rather 'Navigation and Shipping' would seem to mean the right to prescribe rules and regulations for vessels navigating the waters of the Dominion.[164] It would seem to relate to such matters as the law of the road, lights to be carried, how vessels are to be registered, evidence of ownership and title, transmission of interest and such matters.[165] And although exclusive legislative authority is thus given to the

Dominion with regard to shipping, there is, nevertheless, under item 10 of sec. 92 (*infra*, pp. 128-9) a
power relating to shipping of a certain class reserved to the provincial legislatures, viz.: ' Local
works and undertakings other than . . . lines
of steamships between the province and any British
or foreign country.' Thus this Dominion power
does not prevent the valid incorporation of provincial navigation companies, the operations of which
are limited to the province.[166] But such a provincial
corporation may find that, in order to the effectual
execution of its corporate purposes, it may have to
have recourse to the Dominion parliament or authorities, as, *e.g.*, to obtain leave to construct and
maintain a bridge across a harbour, or to construct
works upon a harbour bed, or in or over navigable
waters.[167] Again a provincial legislature may have
power to regulate, with a view of preventing the
spread of infectious diseases, the entry or departure of boats or vessels at the different ports in the
province, in relation to transport from one of such
ports to another, subject, of course, to any regulation on the subject of quarantine by the federal
authority; but it would, probably, not be competent
for it to legislate as to the arrival of vessels, vehicles,
passengers, or cargoes from places outside the province.[168] Lastly, it was under this Dominion power
in conjunction with the power over the ' regulation
of trade and commerce' (*supra*, pp. 102-4) and with
that under sec. 101 to establish additional Courts for
the better administration of the laws of Canada
(*infra*, pp. 149-151), that the Supreme Court affirmed the validity of the Dominion Act constituting
the Maritime Court of Ontario.[169]

11. '*Quarantine and the establishment and
maintenance of Marine Hospitals.*'[170]

12. *'Sea Coast and Inland Fisheries.'*[171] This
Dominion power is confined to the enactment of
fishery regulations and restrictions, and does not
extend to direct interference with proprietary rights
in fisheries, as by authorizing the giving by lease,
license, or otherwise, the right of fishing in navigable
or non-navigable lakes, rivers, streams, and waters,
the beds of which had been granted to private proprietors before Confederation, or not having been
so granted are assigned to the provinces under the
Federation Act. Nevertheless Dominion legislation
under it may affect proprietary rights, as, *e.g.,* by
prescribing the times of the year during which fishing is to be allowed, or the instruments which may
be employed for the purpose. The enactment of
such fishery regulations and restrictions is within
the competence of the Dominion exclusively, nor can
the provincial legislatures deal with the subject even
in the absence of Dominion legislation. Not that
provincial legislation is necessarily incompetent
merely because it may have some relation to
fisheries. For example, prescribing the mode in
which a private fishery is to be conveyed or otherwise disposed of, or the rights of succession in
respect to it, or the terms and conditions upon which
the provincial fisheries may be granted, leased or
otherwise disposed of, would be within provincial
powers over ' property and civil rights in the province,' (*infra,* pp. 134-7), or the management and
sale of public lands belonging to the province (*infra,*
p. 127).[172] And this decision of the Privy Council
must not be interpreted as meaning that the Dominion parliament has not power to absolutely prohibit
foreign nations from fishing within the three-mile
limit of the coast of Canada; or that the federal
Government has no police jurisdiction.[173]

13. '*Ferries between a province and any British or foreign country, or between two provinces.*' Under this power the Dominion parliament has authority to, or to authorize the Governor-General in Council to, establish or create ferries between a province and any British or foreign country, or between two provinces.[174]

14. '*Currency and Coinage.*'[175]

15. '*Banking, incorporation of Banks, and the issue of paper money.*' "The obvious reason why the incorporation of banks was assigned to the Dominion and not left with the provinces was that the whole subject of banking and its adjuncts was being assigned to the Dominion, and if the provinces were allowed to incorporate provincial banks with the rights properly and necessarily belonging to a bank, the whole subject of banking would have been left in inextricable confusion. And so far from having a national banking system to-day of which we are justly proud, we would have a series of systems, some conservative and others more in accordance with what western ideas are popularly supposed to advocate."[176] 'Banking' is an expression wide enough to include everything coming within the legitimate business of a banker, and the Dominion powers of legislation under this, as under the other enumerated items of sec. 91 of the Federation Act, are exclusive, and necessarily imply the right to affect the property and civil rights of individuals in the province so far as is necessary in order to their exercise. Thus the Dominion parliament can legislate in respect to warehouse receipts taken by a bank in the course of its business, though it thereby modifies civil rights in the province, and may conflict with provincial statutes relating to

warehouse receipts and other negotiable documents which pass the property of goods without delivery.[177] Provincial legislatures have no right to license private banks. At any rate the Dominion Government has always objected to their so doing.[178] Neither can the provincial legislatures confer banking powers upon provincial corporations, as, for example, upon trust companies.[179] But provincial legislatures may impose direct taxes on banks doing business in the province,[180] or make laws which will control real estate owned by a bank in the province for the purpose of its business, or establish the procedure under which it may be seized and sold upon an unsatisfied judgment against the bank, or for non-payment of taxes.[181]

16. '*Savings Banks.*'

17. '*Weights and Measures.*' This power appears to relate merely to the fixing of standard weights and measures.[182]

18. '*Bills of Exchange and Promissory Notes.*' The mere fact that provincial legislation may incidentally touch such negotiable instruments does not necessarily make it *ultra vires.* Thus the Dominion power is not incompatible with the right of the provincial legislature to confer authority on a provincial corporation to become a party to instruments of this nature as a matter incidental to such corporation.[183]

19. '*Interest.* We must await a Privy Council decision for a finally authoritative interpretation of this Dominion power.[184] So far as the authorities go at present it would seem to refer to preventing individuals under certain circumstances from contracting for more than a certain rate of interest,

and fixing a certain rate when interest was payable
by law without a rate having been named, and to
regulations as to the rate of interest in mercantile
transactions, and other dealings and contracts between individuals, and not to taxation under municipal institutions and matters incident thereto.[185]
Thus the Dominion Act (R. S. C. 1886, c. 127, s. 7),
regulating interest recoverable under mortgages of
real estate, was held *intra vires* under it.[186]

20. *' Legal Tender.'*

21. *' Bankruptcy and Insolvency.'*[187] It would
seem that the only exclusive power which the
Dominion parliament possesses under this subsection in respect to such legislation as is usually re-
sorted to in order to secure a rateable distribution
of the assets of a person financially insolvent, is the
power of providing for a compulsory process
whereby this end may be attained, authorizing, in
other words, proceedings *in invitum* against the insolvent. But provided they base themselves upon
a voluntary assignment to a trustee for the general
benefit of his creditors previously executed by the
insolvent, provincial legislatures have full power,
under their jurisdiction over property and civil
rights in the province, and procedure in civil
matters in the province, to give to such an assignment, once executed, precedence over judgments and
executions, and over such subsidiary processes as
garnishee orders, attachments, or interpleaders.
While, on the other hand, such latter provisions
being properly ancillary to bankruptcy and insolvency legislation, strictly so called, there is nothing
to prevent the Dominion parliament including them
in a law relating to bankruptcy and insolvency, in

which case, of course, the provisions of the
Dominion Act would place in abeyance those of the
provincial legislation (*supra,* p. 85).[188]   As a fact
there has been no Dominion bankruptcy or insolvency Act since 1880, save as to corporations.[189]
In assigning this power to the Dominion parliament,
the Imperial Act, by necessary implication, intended
to confer on it legislative power to interfere with
property, civil rights, and procedure within the provinces, so far as a general law relating to these subjects might affect them.[190]   And notwithstanding
the provincial power under No. 14 of sec. 92 (see
infra pp. 137-140) over the administration of justice,
including the constitution of Courts in the province,
there can be no doubt of the power of the Dominion
to institute an Insolvency Court, and regulate its
procedure.[191]   Nor is there any doubt that the
Dominion parliament can impose new jurisdiction
in bankruptcy and insolvency upon provincial
Courts.[192] The circumstance that the Dominion parliament may not, in fact, have exercised its power
of legislating in relation to bankruptcy and insolvency, does not give provincial legislatures the right
to legislate thereon.[193]   But this does not prevent
the latter dealing incidentally in their legislation
with assignees in insolvency;[194] or with insolvent
debtors, as, *e.g.,* by defining the conditions under
which a writ of *capias* can be obtained, though, in
some cases, applicable only to insolvent traders;[195]
or, as we have seen (*supra* p. 111) making all such
provisions in the case of voluntary assignments for
the benefit of creditors as are necessary to secure
a rateable distribution of the assets of an insolvent
among his creditors. Finally, as we have also seen
just above, Dominion legislation in relation to
bankruptcy and insolvency may contain, as ancillary
provisions, enactments dealing with such matters,

and then provincial legislatures would be precluded
from interfering, and any existing provincial enactments which did conflict would be superseded by the
Dominion legislation.[196]

22. *'Patents of Invention and Discovery.'*[197]

23. *'Copyrights.'* The intendment of this sub-
section is " to place the right of dealing with colonial
copyright within the Dominion under the exclusive
control of the parliament of Canada, as distinguished from provincial legislatures."[198] But it
in no way interferes with the power of the Imperial
parliament to legislate for the whole Empire in
respect to copyright by statutory provisions made
expressly applicable to every part of the British
Dominions; nor did it exempt Canada from the
binding force of such Imperial legislation un-
repealed at the time of Confederation.[199]

24. *'Indians and Lands Reserved for the
Indians.'*[200] " The fact that the power of legislating for Indians, and for lands which are reserved
to their use, has been entrusted to the parliament of
the Dominions is not in the least degree inconsistent
with the right of the provinces to the beneficial interest in these lands, available to them as a source of
revenue whenever the estate of the Crown is dis-
membered of the Indian title."[201] The general subject of Indian lands will be found discussed *infra*
pp. 152-3, where property under the Federation Act
is dealt with. Lands surrendered by Indians to the
Crown, though for a consideration in the nature of
an annuity by way of interest accruing from the
proceeds of the sale of the lands, do not come within
this subs. 24 of sec. 91 as ' lands reserved for
Indians '; but, on such surrender, become ordinary

unpatented lands, and upon being sold to private
purchasers are liable to assessment under provincial
Acts, even before patent granted.[202]   There is, of
course, nothing in this Dominion power over Indians
to debar provincial legislatures enacting that
Indians shall not exercise the provincial franchise.[203]

25. ' *Naturalization and Aliens.*' This subsection of section 91 of the Federation Act '' does not
purport to deal with the consequences of either
alienage or naturalization. It undoubtedly reserves
these subjects for the exclusive jurisdiction of the
Dominion—that is to say, it is for the Dominion
to determine what shall constitute either the one or
the other; but the question as to what consequences
shall follow from either is not touched. The right
of protection and the obligations of allegiance are
necessarily involved in the nationality conferred by
naturalization; but the privileges attached to it,
where these depend upon residence, are quite independent of nationality.[204]   As to aliens the net
result of the authorities in reference to this
Dominion power seems to be that provincial legislatures cannot legislate against aliens, whether before or after naturalization, merely as such aliens,
so as to deprive them of the ordinary rights of the
inhabitants of the province, although they may so
legislate against them as possessing this or that
personal characteristic or habit, which disqualifies
them from being permitted to engage in certain oc-
cupations, or enjoy certain rights generally enjoyed
by other people in the province. The Dominion
parliament alone can legislate in relation to them
merely as aliens. But it is a different matter when
rights and privileges which have to be specially conferred are in question, such as the right to exercise
the franchise. It is within the power of provincial

legislatures to refuse to confer such rights upon
-aliens or any other class of people in the province;
and especially is this clear in the case of the legislative franchise, for the qualifications for the exercise of that are an integral part of the Constitution
of the province, which by No. 1 of section 92 of the
Federation Act is expressly assigned exclusively to
the provincial legislature.[205] It appears that under
this Dominion power the Federal parliament can, by
properly framed legislation, require a foreign company to take out a Dominion license, even where the
company desires to carry on its business only
within the limits of a single province.[206] It is not,
of course, to be supposed that provincial legislation
may never even incidentally relate to aliens, as *e.g.*,
by providing that aliens may be shareholders in
provincial companies, and entitled to vote on their
shares, and be eligible as directors.[207]

26. '*Marriage and Divorce.*'[208] In a recent
decision the Privy Council have, in defining the scope
of the provincial power over the 'solemnization of
marriage in the province' under No. 12 of sec. 92 of
the Federation Act (*infra* pp. 133-4, where the case
will be further considered), determined that this
Dominion power does not cover the whole field of
validity of marriage, but that provincial legislatures
may enact conditions as to solemnization which may
affect the validity of the contract.[209] Consequently,
and as the effect of this decision, the Dominion parliament could not enact, as was proposed by the so-
called 'Lancaster Bill,' that any marriage performed by any person authorized to perform any
ceremony of marriage by the laws of the place
where it is performed, and duly performed according to such laws, shall everywhere within Canada
be deemed to be a valid marriage, notwithstanding

any difference in the religions of the persons so married, and without regard to the person performing the ceremony; because a province has power to enact that no marriage solemnized within its borders shall be valid where the parties of one of them is of a particular religion, unless solemnized before some special class of persons authorized in that province to solemnize marriages, *e.g.*, a Roman Catholic priest.[210]   As to divorce, in 1907, the Ontario legislature assumed to enact that the High Court of Justice in Ontario should have jurisdiction, subject to certain conditions and qualifications, to declare and adjudge a ceremony of marriage gone through between two persons either of whom is under eighteen years of age, without consent of father, mother, or guardian, not to constitute a valid marriage.   There are conflicting decisions as to the validity of this enactment, which must still be considered undecided.   It is submitted in the light of the Privy Council judgment in *In re Marriage Legislation in Canada* [1912] A. C. 880, that it is valid.[211]

27. '*The Criminal Law, except the Constitution of Courts of Criminal Jurisdiction, but including the Procedure in Criminal Matters.*'   This subsection reserves for the exclusive legislative authority of the parliament of Canada " the criminal law in its widest sense."[212]   This suffices to dispose of the suggestion made in several provincial cases, that to come within the meaning of ' criminal law ' in this subsection 91 of the Federation Act, and so to fall under the exclusive jurisdiction of the Dominion parliament, an offence must be of that kind which is esteemed to be *malum in se*, quite apart from it also being *malum prohibitum*.[213]   The above Privy Council decision in *Attorney-General for*

Ontario v. *Hamilton Street R. W. Co.* also seems to displace the view of Wetmore, J., in *Queen* v. *City of Fredericton, supra,* that "to ascertain the jurisdiction given to parliament in reference to criminal matters, we must look at the law as it stood at the time the British North America Act was passed; although there are cases where, in construing that Act, it is pertinent to consider the condition of things before Confederation (*supra* p. 93). And the question whether before Confederation certain offences have been embraced within the criminal law, may, perhaps, determine the power of provincial legislatures to deal with such offences after Confederation.[214]   Two things, however, create difficulty in the construction of No. 27 of sec. 91 of the Federation Act, namely, that whereas ' criminal law ' is thus assigned to the Dominion parliament, ' the imposition of punishment by fine, penalty, or imprisonment for enforcing any law of the province made in relation to any matter coming within any of the classes of subjects enumerated in this section,' is by No. 15 of sec. 92, assigned to the provincial legislatures; and that whereas 'procedure in criminal matters ' is assigned to the Dominion parliament, ' the constitution, maintenance, and organization of provincial Courts, both of civil and criminal jurisdiction,' is, by No. 14 of sec. 92 assigned to the provincial legislatures.   As to the first of these points we must, in accordance with the principle of construction already noticed, read No. 15 of sec. 92 as excepted out of criminal law assigned to the Dominion by No. 27 of sec. 91.   We shall deal more particularly with it hereafter (*infra* pp. 140-3), but may observe here that—" a provincial legislature has, of course, no power to authorize any Act which has been constituted an offence by parliament." [215] Neither can provincial legislatures alter or amend

the criminal law, using that term in the sense in
which it is used in No. 27 of sec. 91.[216] On the other
hand, although it cannot be denied that parliament
may draw into the domain of criminal law acts
which have hitherto been punishable only under a
provincial statute,[217] it does not follow that provincial legislatures may not still have the right to pass
laws in regard to such acts in another aspect.[218] The
Dominion parliament, moreover, can give jurisdiction to provincial Courts in criminal matters, in
spite of any provincial statutes relating to such
Courts,[219] but, of course, cannot regulate the procedure under a provincial penal statute. Provincial
legislatures alone have power to regulate the procedure under the penal laws which they have authority to enact under No. 15 of sec. 92 of the Federation Act.[220] As to the second point of difficulty
above mentioned, namely, to distinguish ' procedure
in criminal matters ' in No. 27 of sec. 91, from ' the
constitution . . of provincial Courts . . of
criminal jurisdiction' in No. 14 of sec. 92, it was
held by the Ontario Court of Appeal in *King* v.
Walton[221] that a provincial legislature has power to
determine the number of grand jurors to serve at
Courts of oyer and terminer, and general sessions,
this being a matter relating to the constitution of
the Courts; but that the selection and summoning
of jurors, including talesmen, and fixing the number
of grand jurors by whom a bill may be found, relate
to procedure in criminal matters in respect of which
the Dominion parliament alone has power to legislate.[222] In another case it has been held that a
Dominion Act authorizing the Court of General or
Quarter Sessions of the Peace to try an appeal
from a summary conviction without a jury where
no jury is demanded by either party, is *intra vires*

of the Dominion parliament.[223] In another it has been held that it is not within the power of a provincial legislature to regulate or control the inspection of the jurors' book or jury panel so far as it relates to criminal causes or matters.[224] In yet another it has been held that a provincial Act, creating stipendiary and police magistrates a Court with all the powers and jurisdiction which any Act of the parliament of Canada had conferred or might confer, is *intra vires.*[225]

28. '*The establishment, maintenance, and management of penitentiaries.*'[226]

29. '*Such classes of subjects as are expressly excepted in the enumeration of the classes of subjects by the British North America Act assigned exclusively to the legislatures of the provinces.*' The classes of subjects expressly excepted from those assigned exclusively to the legislatures of the provinces are: (1) the office of Lieutenant-Governor, which, by No. 1 of section 92 of the Federation Act is expressly excepted out the provincial power over the ' amendment from time to time, notwithstanding anything in this Act, of the Constitution of the province .   .   .   .,'[227] and the classes of ' local works and undertakings ' expressly excepted in No. 10 of section 92, whereby a general power subject to such express exceptions is given to provincial legislatures to make laws in relation to ' Local Works and Undertakings.' These exceptions are: (a) ' Lines of Steam or other Ships, Railways, Canals, Telegraphs, and other Works and Undertakings connecting the Province with any other or others of the Provinces, or extending beyond the limits of the Province; (b) Lines of Steam Ships between the Province and any British or Foreign Country; (c) Such Works

as, although wholly situate within the Province, are
before or after their execution declared by the Parliament of Canada to be for the general Advantage
of Canada or for the advantage of two or more of
the Provinces.' [228]   The effect of this sub-section 10
of section 92 is to transfer the excepted works mentioned in sub-heads (a), (b) and (c) of it into
section 91, and thus to place them under the exclusive jurisdiction and control of the Dominion parliament.   These two sections must then be read and
construed as if these transferred subjects were
specially enumerated in section 91, and local railways as distinct from federal railways were specifically enumerated in section 92.[229]   And the first
point to notice is that when acting under it the
Dominion parliament can confer upon a corporation
all powers necessary to effectuate its corporate purposes.   Thus parliament may entrust an electric
power company whose work or undertaking extends
beyond the limits of one province, or the works of
which have been expressly declared to be for the
general advantage of Canada, and so brought under
Dominion jurisdiction, with freedom to interfere
with municipal and private rights.[230]   In the same
way a Dominion corporation for carrying on such
an undertaking as comes within the exceptions to
item 10 of section 92 is not subject, in carrying on
its business as authorized by its charter, to the provincial laws of the province where it does so.[231]   It
is otherwise when the Dominion is incorporating
not under one of its exclusive enumerated powers,
but under its general residuary power, as, e.g., incorporating an insurance company, or a building
and investing company.   In such cases it can grant
no more than the power of acting as a corporation
throughout the Dominion, but subject in each pro-

vince, as is any other person, to the laws of that province.[232] The Privy Council have, also, decided that, for the purposes of a Dominion railway company, the Dominion parliament has power to dispose of provincial Crown lands, and therefore, of a provincial foreshore to a harbour.[233] And what we have been stating about Dominion railway companies is only an example of the general principle that the Dominion parliament has all necessary incidental powers when legislating upon the subject-matters comprised in its enumerated powers in section 91 of the Federation Act. But the powers assumed under this principle must in fact be necessarily incidental to the exercise by the Dominion parliament of its exclusive control over such subject-matters.[234] And the fact that legislative control of Dominion railways, *qua* railways, belongs to the Dominion parliament, does not make such railways cease to be part of the provinces in which they are situated, or exempt them in other respects from the jurisdiction of the provincial legislatures. Thus provincial legislatures can impose direct taxation upon such portions of a Dominion railway as are within the province, in order to the raising of a revenue for provincial purposes. So, again, provincial legislation requiring a ditch belonging to a Dominion railway company, and running along the side of the railway track on the lands of the company for the purpose of their railway, to be kept in good order and free from obstruction which would impede the water-flow, but not regulating the structure of the ditch, would not be *ultra vires*.[235] On the other hand provincial legislation would be *ultra vires* which purported to enable a railway company authorized under it to take possession of lands belonging to a Dominion railway company, ' and to use and enjoy any portion of the right of way, tracks, terminals, stations, or station grounds, of such railway company . . in so far as the taking of such lands does not unreasonably interfere with the construction and operation of the railway whose lands were taken,' for this is legislation as to the physical tracks and works of the Dominion railway.[236]

As to declarations by the Dominion parliament, under subs. (c) of section 92, as embraced in No. 29 of section 91 (*supra* pp. 119-120), that works wholly situate in one province, are ' for the general advantage of Canada, or for the advantage of two or more of the provinces.'[237]   When such a declaration is made, the railway to which it refers is withdrawn from the jurisdiction of the provincial legislature and passes under the exclusive jurisdiction and control of the parliament of Canada, however small and provincial it may be.[238]   But the Dominion parliament can revoke any such declaration or repeal the Act containing it, and the railway or railways to which such declaration refers will then cease to be under Dominion jurisdiction, and come again under provincial jurisdiction.[239]   The question still remains whether such declaration by the Dominion parliament must be express or whether it can be implied. On the whole the balance of authority at present seems in favour of the view that it need not be a declaration in express words.[240]

Dominion corporations generally.[241] The power of the Dominion parliament to incorporate companies is not based exclusively on No. 29 of section 91 of the Federation Act or on any other of its enumerated powers. It can incorporate companies by virtue of its general residuary power to make laws for the peace, order, and good government of

Canada; but as this residuary power, by express provision of section 91, can only be exercised in relation to matters not coming within the classes of subjects by that Act assigned exclusively to the provincial legislatures, no Dominion incorporation under it can give the company incorporated exemption or immunity from the general provincial law.[242]

Nevertheless it is within the scope of the Dominion exclusive legislative power in respect to 'the regulation of trade and commerce' to authorize all companies incorporated by it under its residuary powers, and, *a fortiori*, all companies incorporated under its enumerated powers, to carry on their business throughout Canada, and to give such companies power to sue and be sued, and to contract by their corporate name, and to acquire and hold personal property for the purposes for which they were created, and to exempt individual members of the corporation from personal liability for its debts, obligations, or acts, if they do not violate the provisions of the Act incorporating them; and the status and powers of such a Dominion company cannot be destroyed by provincial legislation, although, as already stated, when incorporated, not under any of the enumerated Dominion powers, but solely under the residuary Dominion power, such a company cannot exercise its powers in contravention of the laws of the province restricting the rights of the public in the province generally. But provincial legislation must not strike at capacities which are the natural and logical consequences of the incorporation by the Dominion Government of companies with other than provincial objects.[243] Thus the Privy Council have vindicated the objection which Ministers of Justice at Ottawa have constantly taken to provincial Acts imposing the necessity upon companies incorporated by Dominion charter, even though under the residuary power only, of taking out a provincial license before doing business in the province. Such provincial legislation they hold to be *ultra vires* although they quite admit that provincial taxation may be by way of license.[244] In the same way power conferred by a provincial legislature on an industrial company in its incorporating Act to carry on its corporate enterprise to the exclusion of every other company in a designated territory will be without effect against a company constituted for similar ends by a previous Dominion statute, with power to carry on business throughout Canada.[245] It is scarcely necessary to add that the Dominion parliament can alone incorporate companies with chartered powers to carry on business throughout the Dominion, seeing that provincial powers of incorporation are by No. 11 of section 92 of the Federation Act expressly confined to ' companies with provincial objects,' as to which see *infra* pp. 130-3;[246] but there seems nothing to prevent a Dominion corporation confining its operation to one or more provinces, subject of course to the requirements of its charter.[247]

B. *Provincial powers.*[248]

1. ' *The amendment from time to time, notwithstanding anything in this Act, of the Constitution of the province, except as regards the office of Lieutenant-Governor.*' [249] The *non obstante* clause in this subsection must be read subject to the *non obstante* clause of section 91 (see *supra* pp. 73-4), otherwise, as Ramsay, J., says in *Ex parte Dansereau*,[250] No. 1 of section 92, in its widest sense, would amount to a power to upset the Feder-

ation Act. The saving clause as to the office of
Lieutenant-Governor is manifestly intended to keep
intact the headship of provincial government, forming, as it does, the link of federal power. It does
not, however, apparently inhibit a statutory increase
of duties germane to the office.[251] The Privy Council
have held that under this subsection provincial
legislatures have power to pass Acts for defining
their own powers, immunities, and privileges as regards their independence from outside interference,
their protection, and the protection of their members
from insult while in discharge of their duties.[252]
They can also under this head of power exclude
aliens, whether naturalized or not, from exercising
the provincial franchise, notwithstanding the
Dominion exclusive power to legislate in relation to
' naturalization and aliens ' (*supra* pp. 114-5).[253]

   2. ' *Direct taxation within the Province in
order to the raising of a revenue for provincial
purposes.*' It is obvious that it could not have been
intended that the general Dominion power under
No. 3 of section 91 to make laws in relation to ' the
raising of money by any mode or system of taxation'
(*supra* pp. 105-6) should override this particular
provincial power in respect to taxation.[254] We may
further observe, by way of preliminary, that no
Canadian legislature, Dominion or provincial, is
subject in matters of taxation to that restriction
which exists under the United States Constitution,
and requires ' all public taxation to be fair and equal
in proportion to the value of property, so that no
class of individuals, and no species of property, may
be unequally or unduly assessed.'[255] Proceeding
now to interpret the terms of this provincial power
the question what is to be understood by '' direct
taxation '' has been before the Privy Council in five

cases, with the result of establishing that it is to
be interpreted in accordance with John Stuart
Mills's definition of a direct tax as ' one which is
demanded from the very persons who it is intended
or desired should pay it,' as distinguished from indirect taxes, which are ' those which are demanded
from one person in the expectation and intention
that he shall indemnify himself at the expense of
another.' [256]   And although the power to tax is expressed to be ' in order to the raising of a revenue
for provincial purposes,' this is not to be understood
as meaning that the provincial legislature may not,
whenever it shall see fit, impose direct taxation for
a local purpose upon a particular locality within the
province;[257] but a province can only tax property
within it.[258]   The person to be taxed, however, need
not be domiciled or even resident within it. Any person found within the province may be legally taxed
there if taxed directly.[259]   And a provincial legislature can place a tax upon property locally situate
inside the province to which a person succeeds under
a will or on intestacy, notwithstanding that the deceased owner was domiciled outside the province at
the time of his death, provided it excludes by the
use of apt and clear words the application of the
maxim *mobilia sequuntur personam*.[260] The question
remains : Can a provincial legislature indirectly place
a succession duty tax on property locally situate
outside the province by placing the tax, not directly
on the property, but on the transmission of the property by succession to a person in the province? In
King v. *Cotton*,[261] the majority of the Supreme
Court of Canada held that it can. It must not be supposed, moreover, that provincial legislatures can
tax all property whatever if it be within the province. Section 125 of the Federation Act enacts

that, 'no lands or property belonging to Canada or any province, shall be liable to taxation.'[262] But the provinces can tax Dominion officials notwithstanding that No. 8 of section 91 gives the Dominion parliament exclusive authority over ' the fixing of, and providing for, the salaries and allowances of civil and other offices of the Government of Canada;'[263] and Dominion corporations, as, for example, banks;[264] and Dominion licensees.[265]

3. ' *The borrowing of money on the sole credit of the province.*'

4. ' *Provincial Offices and Officers.*'[266]

5. ' *The management and sale of the public lands belonging to the province, and of the timber and wood thereon.*'[267]

6. ' *The establishment, maintenance, and management of public and reformatory prisons in and for the province.*'

7. ' *The establishment, maintenance, and management of hospitals, asylums, charities and eleemosynary institutions in and for the province, other than marine hospitals.*'

8. ' *Municipal Institutions in the province.*' This '' simply gives provincial legislatures the right to create a legal body for the management of municipal affairs,'' to which they can then give any powers which come within the subject-matters with which they are entitled to deal.''[268] Having created such municipal bodies they can delegate to them any powers they themselves possess;[269] and have all incidental powers necessary to carry on and work such municipal institutions.[270]

9. ' *Shop, saloon, tavern, auctioneer, and other licenses, in order to the raising of a revenue for provincial, local, or municipal purposes.'* Many judges in Canadian Courts, though not all, have felt themselves constrained to interpret "other licenses" by the rule of *ejusdem generis,*[271] but the Privy Council judgments can scarcely be said to encourage any stress being laid upon this.[272] Taxation by license under this subsection is direct taxation.[273] Such licenses, moreover, as it authorizes may be imposed on wholesale just as much as on retail business.[274] The object of all such licenses, however, must be ' in order to the raising of a revenue.'[275] The Dominion parliament, also, can, of course, both tax and regulate in matters within their jurisdiction, by means of licenses.[276]

10. ' *Local works and undertakings other than such as are of the following classes:*

(a) *Lines of steam or other ships, railways, canals, telegraphs and other works and undertakings connecting the province with any other or others of the provinces, or extending beyond the limits of the provinces:*

(b) *Lines of steamships between the province and any British or foreign country:*

(c) *Such works as, although wholly situate within the province, are before or after their execution declared by the Parliament of Canada to be for the general advantage of Canada or for the advantage of two or more of the provinces.'*[277]

It must be pronounced to be still an unsettled point whether under this subsection of section 92 of the Federation Act provincial legislatures can authorize

the construction, or operation of such works and
undertakings ' as railways, or electric light and
power transmission lines or telephone lines, extending to the provincial boundaries, where they may,
and probably will, connect with similar works and
undertakings in other provinces, or in the United
States; and it seems to have become a sort of tra-
dition in the Department of Justice at Ottawa to
object to provincial Acts authorizing the construction of railways to the boundary line of the province.[278] It is submitted, nevertheless, with all
proper deference, that such legislation is *intra vires.*
The plenary powers of provincial legislatures
(*supra,* pp. 66-9), are not to be restricted by construction save so far as is necessary to allow for the
enumerated Dominion powers under section 91, and
what are placed under Dominion jurisdiction by the
subsection we are considering, are such lines of
steam or other ships, railways, canals, telegraphs,
and other works and undertakings as themselves
connect, under their own charter powers, the province with any other or other of the provinces, or
extend beyond the limits of the province.[279]

A provincial legislature may, it would seem, when
incorporating a local undertaking restrict its powers
of operation to six days a week, thereby securing
Sunday observance,[280] although legislation directly
requiring observance of the Lord's Day might be
ultra vires as matter of criminal law.[281] The
Minister of Justice at Ottawa, however, has pronounced *ultra vires* and disallowed British Columbia
legislation incorporating railway companies with a
provision that no Chinese, Japanese, or other alien,
shall be employed thereon.[282] Provincial corporations are, of course, just as subject to Dominion
laws, validly enacted, as individuals are.[283]

11. ' *The incorporation of companies with provincial objects.*' [284]   This subsection of section 92 of the Federation Act is concerned with the incorporation of private companies with objects outside the exclusively Dominion matters.   As to other kinds of corporations, the creation of municipal corporations would fall under No. 8 of section 92; of charitable and other similar corporations under No. 7 (*supra,* p. 127); of what may, perhaps, be called Governmental corporations, such as the Hydro-Electric Power Commission of Ontario, under No. 1, No. 4 or No. 14 (*supra,* pp. 124-7; *infra,* p. 137); and of educational under section 93 (*infra,* pp. 143-9). ''Incorporation'' includes ''the constitution of the company, the designation of its corporate capacities, the relation of the members of the company to the company itself, the powers of the governing body. How much more it would include may be left to be determined in each concrete case in which the point arises ''; but '' you cannot by any permissible process infer from the language of No. 11 any limitation upon the jurisdiction of the provinces in relation to companies not within No. 11 in regard to matters which do not fall within the strictly limited subject of ' incorporation.' '' [285]   The contentions which have arisen over this clause have centred round the words ' with provincial objects,' contentions which appear to have been finally set at rest by the Privy Council in the recent case of *Bonanza Creek Gold Mining Co.* v. *The King.*[286] The majority of the judges of the Supreme Court of Canada had adopted the view that the introduction of the words '' with provincial objects '' imposed '' a territorial limit on legislation conferring the power of incorporation so completely that by or under provincial legislation no company could be

incorporated with an existence in law that extended
beyond the boundaries of the province. Neither
directly by the language of a special Act, nor indirectly by bestowal through executive power, did
they think that capacity could be given to operate
outside the province, or to accept from an outside
authority the power of so operating."[287] The Privy
Council, however, hold that, by virtue of section 65
of the Federation Act, which in conjunction with
section 12 makes a distribution of executive power
between the Dominion and the provinces corresponding to the distribution which it makes of
legislative power,—there was in the Lieutenant-
Governor, that is, in the provincial executive, a
power to incorporate companies with provincial objects, but with an ambit of vitality wider than that
of the geographical limits of the province. The
powers of incorporation which the Governor-
General or Lieutenant-Governor possessed before
the Union must be taken to have passed, by virtue
of section 65, to the Lieutenant-Governors so far as
concerns companies with this class of objects; and
there can be no doubt that prior to 1867 the
Governor-General was for many purposes entrusted
with the exercise of the prerogative power of the
Sovereign to incorporate companies throughout
Canada. Under sections 12 and 65 the continuance
of the powers thus delegated to the Governor is
made by implication to depend on the appropriate
legislature not interfering; and in the case of
Ontario (under whose Companies Act the Bonanza
Creek Mining Company had been incorporated, and
which Act expressly recognizes as supporting the
charters granted under it, any powers with which
the Lieutenant-Governor might be vested in respect
to granting charters of incorporation apart from its

provisions), such powers had not been interfered
with. Section 92 of the Federation Act, and especially the words " with provincial objects," their
lordships held, " confine the character of the actual
powers and rights which the provincial Government
can bestow, either by legislation or through the
Executive, to powers and rights exercisable within
the province. But actual powers and rights are one
thing and capacity to accept extra-provincial powers and rights is quite another. . . The words
' legislation in relation to the incorporation of companies with provincial objects ' do not preclude the
province from keeping alive the power of the
Executive to incorporate by charter in a fashion
which confers a general capacity analogous to that
of a natural person; nor do they appear to preclude the province from legislating so as to create,
by or by virtue of statute, a corporation with this
general capacity. What the words really do is to
preclude the grant to such a corporation, whether
by legislation or by executive act according with the
distribution of legislative authority, of powers and
rights in respect of objects outside the province,
while leaving untouched the ability of the corporation, if otherwise adequately called into existence, to
accept such powers and rights if granted *ab extra*.
It is, in their lordships' opinion, in this narrower
sense alone that the restriction to provincial objects
is to be interpreted. It follows as the Ontario
legislature has not thought fit to restrict the exercise
by the Lieutenant-Governor of the prerogative power
to incorporate by letters patent with the result of
conferring a capacity analogous to that of a natural
person, that the appellant company could accept
powers and rights conferred on it by outside authorities." [288] There can be, it is submitted, no

doubt that a provincial corporation existing in one province may be incorporated with similar rights and powers in another province by the legislature of the latter.[289] It is likewise impossible now to acquiesce in the *dicta* of Davies, J., in *Hewson* v. *Ontario Power Co.*[290] as to a provincial legislature not being able to give an electric light and power company of its creation, the right to connect its wires with those of a local company in another province, or with those of a company in the United States. Provincial companies, as we have seen (*supra,* p. 107), may need Dominion assistance in order to the effectual execution of their corporate purposes; but the Dominion parliament, of course, cannot enlarge the charter powers of a provincial company, although it might incorporate the members of the provincial company as a Dominion company.[291] Nor can the Dominion parliament, under colour of incorporating a Dominion company, infringe the exclusive provincial power under the clause we are considering, to incorporate companies with provincial objects.[292]

12. '*Solemnization of Marriage in the Province.*' This provincial power must be considered as excepted out of the general exclusive jurisdiction in respect to 'Marriage and Divorce' given to the Dominion parliament, by No. 26 of Section 91 of the Federation Act (as to which see *supra,* pp. 115-6).[293] It must not be supposed that the provincial power extends only to the directory regulation of the formalities by which the contract of marriage is to be authenticated, and that it does not extend to any question of validity. Provincial legislatures may enact conditions as to solemnization which may affect the validity of the contract. The whole of what " solemnization "

ordinarily meant in the systems of law of the provinces of Canada at the time of Confederation is
intended to come within the subsection under consideration, including conditions which affect validity.
For it was not the common law of England nor the
law of Quebec that the validity of marriage depended
on the bare contract of the parties without reference
to any solemnity. Thus for example, a provincial
legislature has power, and the exclusive power, to
enact that no marriage solemnized within its borders
shall be valid where the parties or one of them is
of a particular religion, unless solemnized before
some special class of persons authorized in that province to solemnize marriage, e.g., a Roman Catholic
priest.[294] But, of course, this does not mean that a
provincial legislature can validly enact that inhabitants of the province of which it is the legislature,
shall not be validly married if they cross the border
and are married according to the solemnities and
under the conditions prescribed by the legislature
of another province for marriages within the borders of that province.[295]

13. 'Property and civil rights in the Province.'[296] It may, perhaps, be said that there is no
area of legislative power conferred by the Federation Act the delimitation of which occasions more
trouble than that of the provincial power under this
subsection. To begin with it cannot be ascertained
without at the same time ascertaining the power
and rights of the Dominion under sections 91 and
102 of the Federation Act.[297] It is very obvious
that many of the enumerated Dominion powers
involve, in a more or less direct way, the right to
affect property and civil rights in the different
provinces.[298] Moreover the words 'property and
civil rights in the province' must be regarded as

excluding also cases expressly dealt with elsewhere in section 92 itself. In truth " an abstract logical definition of their scope is not only, having regard to the context of the 91st and 92nd sections of the Act, impracticable, but is certain, if attempted, to cause embarrassment and possible injustice in future cases.'' [299] So far as Dominion powers are concerned, the true constitutional rule would seem to be as follows:—The provincial legislatures have general jurisdiction, and they alone have general jurisdiction, over ' property and civil rights in the province '; but this is not to be understood, on the one hand, as meaning that they can legislate upon anyone of the subjects assigned exclusively to the parliament of Canada by section 91; nor is it to be understood, on the other hand, as meaning that the parliament of Canada cannot incidentally affect property and civil rights by its legislation so far as such power is implied in its power to legislate upon the subjects exclusively assigned to it by section 91, or so far as is required as ancillary to the power to legislate effectually and completely, on such subjects (*supra,* pp. 94-5); and as, on the one hand, the operation of Acts of the provincial legislatures respecting property and civil rights in the province, or other provincial subjects, may be interfered with by reason of the operation of Acts of the Dominion parliament, so, also, Dominion Acts may be interfered with by reason of the operation of Acts of the provincial legislature (*supra,* pp. 95-7), although Dominion legislation, whether on one of the enumerated classes in section 91, or by way of provisions properly ancillary to legislation on one of the said enumerated classes, will over-ride and place in abeyance, provincial legislation which directly conflicts with it (*supra,* pp. 93-5). And even when legislating only under its general residuary

power, the Dominion parliament cannot possibly be
restricted from incidentally affecting property and
civil rights in the different provinces, if it is to
legislate at all.[300]   But in no case must Dominion
interference with property and civil rights in the
provinces be more than the effectual exercise of its
own powers requires.[301]   And to determine whether
the Dominion parliament has power, in any given
case, over property or civil rights in a province, it
may be necessary to consider the nature and present
position of the subject-matter in question, as, for
example, property originally belonging to the
Dominion may have been disposed of by it.[302]   The
limitation contained in the words " in the province "
in the clause under consideration occasions considerable difficulty.   It would seem, however, now
established by decisions of the Privy Council that
this provincial power over property and civil rights
extends only to such as have a local position within
the province; and if, in any case, provincial legislatures cannot legislate in relation to such property
or civil rights without at the same time legislating
in relation to property or civil rights in another
province, that is a case beyond their powers of legislation altogether.[303]   It remains to mention section
94 of the Federation Act, which enacts that 'notwithstanding anything in this Act, the parliament of
Canada may make provision for the uniformity of
all or any of the laws relative to property and civil
rights in Ontario, Nova Scotia, and New Brunswick,
and of the procedure of all or any of the Courts in
those three provinces, and from and after the passing of any Act in that behalf, the power of the parliament of Canada to make laws in relation to any
matter comprised in any such Act shall, notwithstanding anything in this Act, be unrestricted; but

any Act of the parliament of Canada making provision for such uniformity shall not have effect in
any province unless and until it is adopted and
enacted as law by the legislature thereof.'[304]

14. ' *The administration of justice in the Province, including the constitution, maintenance, and
organization of provincial Courts, both of civil and
of criminal jurisdiction, and including procedure
in civil matters in those Courts.*'[305] In a notable
report of his as Minister of Justice on a certain
Quebec Act respecting District Magistrates, Sir
John Thompson says that—' the most remarkable
instance in which provincial legislation has over-run
the limits of provincial competence, has been the
legislation in reference to the administration of
justice.' He is referring, especially, to provincial
legislatures interfering with, or trespassing upon,
the power given to the Governor-General in the
matter of the appointment of judges by section 96
of the Federation Act.[306] This section enacts as
follows :—

96. ' The Governor-General shall appoint the
Judges of the Superior District and County Courts
in each province, except those of the Courts of Probate in Nova Scotia and New Brunswick.'

Before, then, considering what the provinces may
do in the matter of the appointment of judicial officers, or otherwise, under No. 14 of section 92, which
we are about to treat of, it may be well to consider
what, under the authorities, they may not do by
reason of this section 96, and its general interpretation.[307] There can be no doubt, as Sir John Thompson
points out in his Report already referred to, that the
words ' Judges of the Superior, District, and County
Courts ' include all classes of judges like those
designated, and not merely the judges of the par-

ticular Courts which at the time of the passage of
the Federation Act happened to bear those names.[308]
And provincial legislatures have no power to settle
the qualifications of judges to be appointed by the
Governor-General under section 96, as they have
sometimes attempted to do, as, *e.g.*, by providing
that they must be barristers of not less than ten
years' standing.[309] Nor can they provide for the
removal in certain events of Dominion judges.[310]
It has been held that provincial legislatures can
designate County Court judges to try cases of cor-
rupt practices under local option clauses of provincial liquor Acts, even outside their own counties
or districts;[311] but Ministers of Justice have
questioned the right of provincial legislatures to
appoint County Court judges as local judges and
referees under provincial statutes.[312] Provincial
legislatures may, it appears, regulate the procedure
in civil matters of Courts presided over by Dominion
judges, and the sittings of the judges of the Supreme
Court in the province.[313] Passing now to the powers
of the Dominion parliament in relation to provincial
Courts, it may impose new duties upon existing
provincial Courts and magistrates, and give them
new powers as to matters which do not come within
the classes of subjects assigned exclusively to the
legislatures of the provinces.[314] In the same way the
Dominion parliament can confer jurisdiction on a
British Vice-Admiralty Court sitting in Canada.[315]
So, too, the Dominion parliament, in respect to the
matters over which its exclusive jurisdiction extends, can interfere with the civil procedure of provincial Courts, as, for example, by taking away the
appeal to the King in Council in bankruptcy and
insolvency matters.[316] It comes, therefore, to this
that though the provinces alone have general juris-

diction over the administration of justice in the province by virtue of No. 14 of section 92 of the Federation Act, the Dominion parliament may deal with the matter so far as is necessary to the complete and effectual exercise of one of its own enumerated powers; but, of course, in the absence of such Dominion legislation the power to legislate remains in the province.[317] And it does not follow that because the Dominion parliament can impose jurisdiction on provincial Courts in Dominion matters, therefore it can divest the provincial Courts of such jurisdiction, although, of course, it can establish additional Courts of its own for the better administration of the laws of Canada under sec. 101 of the Federation Act (see *infra,* pp. 149-151), and then, perhaps, it can give such Dominion Courts sole jurisdiction on Dominion subjects.[318]

Provincial Judicial Officers. Subject to power given to the Governor-General to appoint the judges of the Superior, District, and County Courts in each province, under section 96 of the Federation Act (*supra,* pp. 137-8), the provinces may, by virtue of their power over the administration of justice in the province, appoint judicial officers, as, for example, the Ontario Division Court judges;[319] the judges of Parish Courts in New Brunswick;[320] Fire Marshals in Quebec;[321] Magistrates and justices of the peace;[322] Masters in Chambers, Masters in Ordinary; Local Masters, Judges and Referees;[323] a Railway Committee of the Executive Council.[324]

Other decisions as to powers of provincial legislatures under No. 14 of section 92 of the Federation Act. It has been decided that under this power the provinces may charge the expenses of criminal prosecutions on the municipalities;[325] they can authorize service of writs out of the jurisdiction[326] and regulate the effect of judgments and writs of execution and what can be done thereunder;[327] but provincial legislatures cannot legislate as to proceedings under Dominion Acts, unless, perhaps, in aid and furtherance thereof.[328] Lastly, it cannot be said that the prerogative of mercy is part of the administration of justice; nor that the Lieutenant-Governor of a province possesses the power of pardon because the administration of justice in the province is reserved to the provincial legislature.[329]

15. ' *The imposition of punishment by fine, penalty, or imprisonment for enforcing any law of the province made in relation to any matter coming within any of the classes of subjects enumerated in section 92 of the Federation Act.*'

(a) *Construction of this subsection.* Before considering the general subject of provincial penal laws there are certain decisions bearing on the above subsection requiring notice. Thus it has been decided that it applies to No. 16 which comes after it (*infra,* p. 143), as much as to the fourteen heads of provincial legislative power which come before it;[330] that notwithstanding the use of the disjunctive " or " provincial legislatures can authorize punishment by both fine and imprisonment;[331] that ' the imposition of punishment by fine, penalty, or imprisonment' includes the power to impose imprisonment with hard labour;[332] that forfeiture of goods may be imposed as punishment;[333] that a provision empowering the Court to sentence a debtor, who, having been arrested on a *capias,* has been enlarged on bail, to an imprisonment for an indeterminate period, if the *capias* be afterwards sustained, is *intra vires,* though this cannot be said, properly speaking, to be imposing a penalty or punishment, but simply replacing the defendant in the same position as he was in before he was let out on bail; [334] that the provinces may vest the pardoning power in the case of offences against provincial Acts in the Lieutenant-Governor; [335] and, lastly, that the provinces may delegate their powers under this subsection, as in other cases. [336]

(b) *Provincial penal laws.* [337] The general relation of this provincial power to the Dominion power over criminal law and procedure in criminal matters has already been discussed (*supra,* pp. 117-9). As there pointed out, it does not follow that when the Dominion parliament has drawn an Act into the domain of criminal law, the right of the provincial legislatures to pass laws in regard to such an Act necessarily ceases. They may still, in many instances, legislate against the same Act in another aspect. [338] Thus it is by virtue of No. 15 of sec. 92 in connection especially with No. 13 (property and civil rights, *supra,* pp. 134-7) and No. 16 (matters of a merely local or private nature in the province, *infra,* p. 143), that we get those provincial penal Acts which have sometimes been spoken of incorrectly as " provincial criminal law " and very often as " police regulation," as *e.g.,* regulating of the liquor traffic, and the closing of the taverns. [339] Thus, too, the Courts have upheld provincial penal laws regulating the selling of drugs; [340] and the assize of bread; [341] providing against frauds in the supplying of milk to cheese and butter manufactories, [342] prohibiting the selling of trading stamps; [343] regulating and controlling the time of opening and closing shops within the municipality; [344] prohibiting the use of fac-

tory chimneys sending forth smoke in such quantities
as to be a nuisance, for the offence aimed at, though
designated a nuisance, fell short of the criminal
misdemeanour of common nuisance, and the Act
concerned police regulation incidental to municipal
institutions;[345] regulating the killing and possession
of game at certain seasons of the year,[346] and even
prohibiting export as incidental to, and carrying
out the general scheme of game protection in the
province;[347] prohibiting contracts by unregistered
companies.[348] On the other hand it seems clear that
provincial legislatures cannot permit the operation
of lotteries forbidden by the criminal statutes of
Canada.[349] There seems, also, to be some doubt as
to whether provincial legislatures can deal with
gambling houses, keeping a common gaming house
being a criminal offence at common law;[350] as, also,
whether they can penalize, even incidentally to other
valid legislation, the malicious injury of property.[351]
As to the power of provincial legislatures in respect
to the matter of Sunday observance, the authorities
are not in a very satisfactory state.[352]

Provincial Penal Procedure. Provincial legislatures alone have power to regulate the procedure under provincial penal laws. For as
an offence under such provincial Acts is not a
" crime " within the proper meaning of No. 27 of
Section 91 of the Federation Act (*supra,* pp. 116-9),
so neither is the procedure applicable to the prosecution of such offences "criminal procedure" within
the meaning of that clause.[353]

Predominance of Dominion Parliament. We
have already referred to cases illustrating the
dominance of Dominion criminal legislation over
provincial laws when the two are really *in*

eadem materia and directly conflicting: see *supra,* pp. 117-8.[354]

16. ' *Generally all matters of a merely local or private nature in the province.*' This subsection "appears to have the same office which the general enactment with respect to legislation for the peace, order and good government of Canada, so far as supplementary to the enumerated subjects (of Dominion power) fulfils in section 91 (of the Federation Act). It assigns to the provincial legislature all matters in a provincial sense local or private which have been omitted from the preceding enumeration, and although its terms are wide enough to cover, they were obviously not meant to include provincial legislation in relation to subjects already enumerated." [355] "Local" does not mean here local in a spot in a province, but local in the sense of confined within the boundaries of the province, although, of course, whether an Act is *intra vires,* or not, must depend upon whether, notwithstanding its subject matter is " local," it does or does not fall within one of the enumerated classes of subjects in section 91.[356] As to the significance of the word "merely" in this subsection, it has been discussed in various arguments before the Judicial Committee of the Privy Council, and the outcome seems to be that it means "not touching by its immediate and direct operation those outside the province." [357]

SEC. XXVI. POWERS IN RESPECT TO MAKING LAWS IN RELATION TO EDUCATION. Section 93 of the Federation Act contains certain provisions in this matter which govern it so far as Quebec, Ontario, Nova Scotia, New Brunswick, Prince Edward Island and British Columbia are concerned. In the case of Manitoba the matter is somewhat differently ordered by section 22 of the (Dominion) *Manitoba Act, 1870;*

as it is also in the case of Alberta and Saskatchewan by sections 17 of the (Dominion) *Alberta and Saskatchewan Acts,* respectively (1905), 4-5 Edw. VII. ch. 3, and ch. 42.

A. *Quebec, Ontario, Nova Scotia, New Brunswick, Prince Edward Island and British Columbia.* Section 93 of the Federation Act provides as follows:—

'93. In and for each Province the Legislature may exclusively make laws in relation to Education, subject and according to the following provisions:—

'(1) Nothing in any such law shall prejudicially affect any Right or Privilege with respect to Denominational Schools which any class of persons have by law in the Province at the Union.

'(2) All the Powers, Privileges and Duties at the Union by Law conferred and imposed in Upper Canada on the Separate Schools and School Trustees of the (King's) Roman Catholic subjects shall be and the same are hereby extended to the Dissentient Schools of the Queen's Protestant and Roman Catholic subjects in Quebec.

'(3) Where in any Province a system of Separate or Dissentient Schools exists by law at the Union or is thereafter established by the Legislature of the province, an Appeal shall lie to the Governor-General in Council from any Act or decision of any Provincial authority affecting any Right or Privilege of the Protestant or Roman Catholic Minority of the Queen's subjects in relation to Education.

(4) In case any such provincial law as from time to time seems to the Governor-General in Council requisite for the due execution of the provisions of this section is not made, or in case any decision of the Governor-General in Council or any Appeal under this section is not duly executed by the proper

provincial Authority in that Behalf, then and in every such case, and as far only as the circumstances of such case require, the parliament of Canada may make remedial laws for the due execution of the provisions of this section and of any decision of the Governor-General in Council under this section.' [358]

As to subsection 1 of this section, by " denominational schools " is meant schools which were permanently, and by law, denominational, not schools which were merely *de facto* denominational for a time, because the whole inhabitants of a district or a great majority of them, happened to belong to that denomination.[359] As to the import of the words " prejudicially affect any right or privilege" in the above section, see *infra*, pp. 147-8. As to the meaning of the words "any class of person," the Judicial Committee of the Privy Council have recently decided that " the class of persons to whom the right or privilege is reserved must, in their lordships' opinion, be a class of persons determined according to religious belief, and not according to race or language "; and that " In relation to denominational teaching, Roman Catholics together form within the meaning of the section a class of persons, and that class cannot be subdivided into other classes by considerations of the language of the people by whom that faith is held;" and that " persons joined together by the union of language, and not by the ties of faith, do not form a class of persons within the meaning of the Act." [360] It will be noticed that the " right or privilege with respect to denominational schools " must .be such as any class of persons " have *by law* in the province at the Union." It is not sufficient that the concurrence of certain exceptional and accidental circumstances enabled certain schools to be denominational by reason of the teacher instructing the children exclusively in doctrines of a particular denomination, or using the prayers, or books, or daily teaching the catechism peculiar to such denomination. This could not confer any legal right or privilege within the meaning of the section.[361] Note also that subs. 1 of the above sec. 93 does not prohibit all legislation respecting denominational schools, but only legislation which affects such rights and privileges with regard thereto.[362] It has moreover been held that mere acquiescence will be no bar to proceedings under this section, as *e.g.*, the applicant having acquiesced for many years in a system of schools by which he, with other members of his religious denomination, was taxed for schools common to all Protestants.[363]

As to subsections 3 and 4 of the above section 93, note that the system of separate or dissentient schools must have existed *by law* at the Union.[364] As to the words " provincial authority "· the legislature of the province must be considered included.[365] And it must not be supposed that these subsections oust the jurisdiction of the ordinary tribunals to act under subsection 1.[366] Nor are they to be construed as merely giving parties aggrieved an appeal to the Governor in Council concurrently with the right to resort to the Courts in case the provisions of subs. 1 are contravened. They are not confined to rights and privileges existing at the Union, and they give an appeal only where the right or privilege affected is that· of the " Protestant or Roman Catholic minority," and not " with respect to denominational schools," but " in relation to education." They constitute a substantive enactment, and are not designed merely as a means of enforcing the provisions of subs. 1.[367]

Manitoba. Section 22 of the Dominion Act establishing the province of Manitoba, 33 Vict. (1870), c. 3, is as follows:—

' 22. In and for the province, the said (provincial) legislature may exclusively make laws in relation to education, subject and according to the following provisions:—

' (1) Nothing in any law shall prejudicially affect any right or privilege with respect to denominational schools, which any class of persons have by law *or practice* in the province at the Union.[368]

' (2) An appeal shall lie to the Governor-General in Council from any act or decision of the legislature of the province, or of any provincial authority, affecting any right or privilege of the Protestant or Roman Catholic minority in relation to education.

' (3) (Is identical with subs. 4 of section 93 of the Federation Act, as to which see *supra*, p. 146)'.[369] As to the words " or practice " which are added to the words " by law " in subs. 1 of the above section, but are not found in sec. 93 of the Federation Act (*supra*, pp. 144-5), the word "practice" must not be read as meaning "custom having the force of law." The intention was to preserve every legal right or privilege, and every benefit or advantage in the nature of a right or privilege, with respect to denominational schools, which any class of persons practically enjoyed at the time of the Union.[370] It is in view of the distinctions which exist between subs. 2 of sec. 22 of the Manitoba Act and subs. 3 of sec. 93 of the Federation Act, with which it is in other respects identical, that their lordships conclude in *Brophy* v. *Attorney-General of Manitoba*, that one is intended to be a substitute for the other, and they explain the reason for the differences.[371] It extends in terms to "any" right or privilege of the minority affected by an Act passed by the legislature, and therefore embraces all rights and privileges existing at the time when such Act was passed.[372]

Alberta, Saskatchewan. In these provinces the subject of education is dealt with by a special section, in the *Alberta Act* (1905), 4-5 Edw. VII. (D.) c. 3, and in the *Saskatchewan Act,* 4-5 Edw. VII (D) c. 42, which is in each Act identical, and in each Act sec. 17. It runs as follows:—

'17. Section 93 of the British North America Act, 1867, shall apply to the said province, with the substitution for paragraph (1) of the said section 93, of the following paragraph:—

'(1) Nothing in any such law shall prejudicially affect any right or privilege with respect to Separate Schools which any class of persons have at the date of the passing of this Act, under the terms of chapters 29 and 30 of the Ordinances of the North-West Territories passed in the year 1901 or with respect to religious instruction in any Public or Separate School as provided for in the said ordinances.

'(2) In the appropriation by the legislature or distribution by the Government of the province of any moneys for the support of schools organized and carried on in accordance with the said chapter 29, or any Act passed in amendment thereof, or in substitution therefor, there shall be no discrimination against schools of any class described in the said chapter 29.

'(3) Where the expression 'by law' is employed in paragraph 3 of the said section 93 it shall mean the law as set out in the said chapters 29 and 30, and where the expression 'at the Union' is employed in the said paragraph 3, it shall be held to mean the date at which this Act comes into force.'

Both Acts came into force on September 1st, 1905, (see sec. 25 of both Acts).[373]

SEC. XXVII. AGRICULTURE AND IMMIGRATION. There is the following special provision in the Federation Act as to these matters:—

'95. In each province the legislature may make laws in relation to agriculture in the province, and to immigration into the province; and it is hereby declared that the parliament of Canada may from time to time make laws in relation to agriculture in all or any of the provinces, and to immigration into all or any of the provinces, and any law of the legislature of a province relative to agriculture or to immigration shall have effect in and for the province as long and as far only as it is not repugnant to any Act of the parliament of Canada.'

As Mr. Joseph Chamberlain said in a despatch to the Governor-General of January 22nd, 1901:[374]

'Though the power to legislate for promotion and encouragement of immigration into the provinces may have been properly given to the provincial legislatures, the right of entry into Canada of persons voluntarily seeking such entry is obviously a purely national matter, affecting as it does the relation of the Empire with foreign states.'[375]

SEC. XXVIII. DOMINION COURTS. By section 101 of the Federation Act it is enacted:—

'101. The parliament of Canada may, notwithstanding anything in this Act, from time to time provide for the constitution, maintenance, and organization of a General Court of Appeal for Canada, and for the establishment of any additional

Courts for the better administration of the laws of
Canada.'

It was under this section that in 1875 there was
established, and still exists a Supreme Court of
Canada, consisting of a Chief Justice and five
puisne judges, who are appointed by the Governor-
General in Council. They hold office during good
behaviour, but are removable by the Governor-
General on address of the Senate and House of
Commons of Canada. This Court possesses an
appellate civil and criminal jurisdiction within and
throughout Canada. There is, indeed, no such
thing in Canada as a Court of Criminal Appeal
such as now exists in England, but any questions
of law arising in the course of a trial for a criminal
offence, may be reserved and brought before the
provincial Court of Appeal on a stated case; and
if the provincial Court of Appeal be not unanimous,
the person convicted may then appeal to the Supreme Court of Canada: R. S. C. 1906, c. 146, secs.
1013-1024, as amended Dom. Stats. 1909, c. 9. As
to civil cases, speaking generally, an appeal lies to
the Supreme Court of Canada from all final judgments of the highest Court of final resort, subject
to certain limitations, depending, e.g., on the amount
involved, or whether the title to land is called in
question, which differ in the case of different provinces, and are set out in the Supreme Court Act,
R. S. C. 1906, c. 146, or in amendments thereto.[376]

It is, however, quite competent for the Dominion
parliament to allow an appeal to the Supreme Court
from judgments of provincial Courts, even though
such judgments be not final, nor such Courts Courts
of final resort,[377] nor can provincial legislation take
away, or impair, the jurisdiction conferred upon the
Supreme Court by Dominion Act.[378] As to the con-

cluding words of the above section 101, which give the parliament of Canada power to provide ' for the establishment of any additional Courts for the better administration of the laws of Canada,' it is still an undecided point whether the expression ' laws of Canada ' means Dominion, *i.e.*, federal laws only, or whether it also embraces the laws of the various provinces.[379]

(SEC. XXIX. DOMINION AND PROVINCIAL PROPERTY UNDER THE BRITISH NORTH AMERICA ACT.

A. *Dominion Property.* Section 108 of the Federation Act enacts as follows:—

108. ' The public works and property of each province, enumerated in the third schedule to this Act, shall be the property of Canada.'[380]

The third schedule referred to is as follows:—

' Third Schedule—Provincial Public Works and Property to be the Property of Canada.

' 1. Canals with lands and water power connected therewith.[381]

' 2. Public Harbours.[382]

' 3. Lighthouses and piers and Sable Island.

' 4. Steamboats, dredges, and public vessels.

' 5. Rivers and lake improvements.[383]

' 6. Railways and railway stocks, mortgages, and other debts due by railway companies.

' 7. Military roads.

' 8. Custom houses, post offices, and all other public buildings, except such as the Government of Canada appropriate for the use of the provincial legislatures and governments.[384]

' 9. Property transferred by the Imperial Government, and known as Ordnance property.

' 10. Armouries, drill sheds, military clothing, and munitions of war, and lands set apart for general public purposes.

B. *Provincial property.*

Section 109 of the Federation Act is as follows:—

' 109. All lands, mines, minerals, and royalties belonging to the several provinces of Canada, Nova Scotia, and New Brunswick at the Union, and all sums then due or payable for such lands, mines, minerals, or royalties, shall belong to the several provinces of Ontario, Quebec, Nova Scotia, and New Brunswick, in which the same are situate or arise subject to any trusts existing in respect thereof, and to any interest other than that of the province in the same.[385]

Of course when public land with its incidents is described as "the property of" or as "belonging to" the Dominion or a province, these expressions merely import that the right to its beneficial user, or to its proceeds, has been appropriated to the Dominion, or the province, as the case may be, and is subject to the control of its legislature, the land itself being vested in the Crown.[386]

1. *Indian lands.* As to Indian lands, and as to lands in Ontario surrendered by the Indians by treaty belonging in full beneficial interest to the Crown as representing the province, or more properly as represented by the provincial Government, subject only to any privileges of the Indians reserved by the treaty, see *supra*, p. 113.[387]

On the whole the cases are against the view that the provincial authorities have any power to extinguish Indian title.[388]

2. ' *All lands, mines, minerals, and royalties.*' Whatever proprietary rights were at the time of the British North America Act possessed by the pro-

vinces remained vested in them, except such as are
by any of its express enactments transferred to the
Dominion of Canada.[389]

As to Indian lands, see *supra,* p. 113; and as to
Fisheries, see *supra,* p. 108. Whether the word
" royalties " extends to royal rights besides those
connected with lands, mines, and minerals, or not,
it certainly includes royalties in respect to lands,
such as escheats, and ought not to be restrained
to rights connected with mines and minerals only.
Lands escheated for defect of heirs belong, therefore, to the province.[390]

The word " royalties " also includes prerogative
rights to gold and silver mines.[391] It does not,
apparently, include the right to establish or create
ferries between a province and any British or
foreign country, or between two provinces.[391a]

3. *' Subject to any trusts existing in respect
thereof and to any interest other than that of the
province in the same.'* Without supposing that the
word " trust " in the first part of the above clause
of sec. 109 of the Federation Act was meant to be
strictly limited to such proper trusts as a Court
of Equity would undertake to administer, it must,
at least, have been intended to signify the existence
of a contractual or legal duty incumbent upon the
holder of the beneficial estate, or its proceeds, to
make payment, out of one or other of these, of the
debt due to the creditor to whom that duty ought
to be fulfilled. On the other hand ' an interest other
than that of the province in the same ' appears to
denote some right or interest in a third party, independent of, and capable of being vindicated in
competition with, the beneficial interest of the old
province.[392]

Sec. XXX. Controversies Between the Dominion and the Provinces—The Rule of Law in Canada. By section 32 of the Exchequer Court Act, R. S. C. 1906, c. 140, it is enacted that—

' 32. When the legislature of any province of Canada has passed an Act agreeing that the Exchequer Court shall have jurisdiction in cases of controversies:

(a) Between the Dominion of Canada and each province;

(b) Between such province, and any other province or provinces, which have passed a like Act; the Exchequer Court shall have jurisdiction to determine such controversies.

2. An appeal shall lie in such cases from the Exchequer Court to the Supreme Court.'

It is scarcely necessary to add that in such a case a further appeal may be taken to the Judicial Committee of the Privy Council by special leave there obtained.[392a]

When a dispute between the Dominion and a province of Canada, or between two provinces, comes before the Exchequer Court under the above provisions, it must be dealt with on recognized legal principles, and not merely on what the judge of the Court considers fair and just between the parties.[393]

Sec. XXXI. Some concluding remarks. The British North America Act, 1867, may be claimed as a great triumph of British constructive statesmanship. It not only successfully combined responsible parliamentary self-government in Canada with a federal system, but it did so without disturbing or endangering,—rather, indeed, as experience has shown, greatly strengthening,—its organic connection with the Empire as a whole. Furthermore, it has endowed the Dominion with a Constitution possessing such potentialities of growth and adaptation, that it seems unnecessary that it should ever be fundamentally disturbed. At the same time it leaves it to the future to settle such modifications as circumstances may dictate in the form of the relations of Canada to the Motherland and the Empire at large. There are fundamental differences between the Constitution of Canada and that of the United States, resulting from and embodying the expressed intention of its framers to adhere to the principles of the British Constitution as then developed; many have been mentioned in the text and notes, and some it may be well to recall here. Thus it retains parliamentary responsible government alike in the federal and in the provincial systems, in place of a separation of governmental powers. Again there are no such restrictions upon legislative action by provisions of the fundamental law as exist in the United States; *all* legislative powers whatever over the internal affairs of the Dominion are distributed between the federal parliament on the one hand and the provincial legislatures on the other. Moreover there is no residuary sovereignty left to the provinces, except over ' matters of a merely local or private nature in the province.' For the rest the provinces have only certain defined and enumerated powers of legislation assigned to them, in all cases exclusively, while a general residuary legislative power over matters of Dominion interest in relation to all matters not thus assigned to the provincial legislatures, is conferred upon the Dominion parliament. Both federal and provincial legislatures have, not merely power to do certain things, but a wide power to make laws in relation to the various broad subject matters of legislation committed to their jurisdiction. All express powers of legislation thus conferred are conferred exclusively on the one or the other, and there are only two subjects of legislation over which concurrent power exists, namely, agriculture and immigration; and there too, as in all other cases, if there is irreconcilable conflict, Dominion legislation prevails over provincial. Then, again, Canadian legislatures are not to be considered as mere delegates or agents of the Imperial parliament from which they derive their power, but within their respective spheres of jurisdiction they exercise authority as plenary and as ample as the Imperial parliament in the plenitude of its power, possessed or could bestow; and can delegate their authority just as freely. No reserve of power is recognized either in the people of the Dominion at large or in the people of the provinces in particular, any more than in Great Britain, though it is in the United States. And in indicating the classes of subjects in relation to which Dominion or province respectively might legislate, the framers of the British North America Act not only abstained from imposing fundamental legislative restrictions of their own, but used vague general language and overlapping descriptions, thus allowing as free scope as in the nature of the case was possible, for that process of organic growth of the national institutions, in harmony with national needs and circumstances, which is one great virtue of the Constitution of the United Kingdom; and no attempt is made to crystallize by statutory enactment the flexible system of precedents and conventions which make up the customary law of England. In a word the Fathers of Confederation did their best to secure to Canadians as a heritage for ever the precious forms of British liberty.[394]

NOTES

1. IS CANADA REALLY A FEDERATION? It has been recently pointed out by the Judicial Committee of the Privy Council, speaking through the mouth of Viscount Haldane, that Canada is not a federation in the strict sense in which the United States and the Commonwealth of Australia, are federations: that the natural and literal interpretation of the word "federation" confines its application to cases in which self-contained States, while agreeing on a measure of delegation, yet in the main continue to preserve their original Constitution: that in the preamble of the B. N. A. Act 1867, which recites that the then provinces had expressed their desire to be "federally" united into one Dominion with a Constitution similar in principle to that of the United Kingdom, the word "federally" is used in a loose sense: that in fact the principle actually adopted by that Act was not that of federation in the strict sense, but one under which the Constitution of the provinces had been surrendered to the Imperial parliament for the purpose of being refashioned, with the result of establishing wholly new Dominion and provincial governments with defined powers and duties, both derived from the statute which was their legal source, the residual powers and duties being taken away from the old provinces and given to the Dominion, a distribution between the Dominion and the provinces which extends not only to legislative but to executive authority: *Attorney-General for the Commonwealth of Australia* v. *Colonial Sugar Refining Co. Ltd.* [1914] A. C. 237, 252-4; *Bonanza Creek Gold Mining Co.* v. *Rex* [1916] A. C. 566, 579. Professor Jethro Brown ('The Nature of a Federal Commonwealth,' L. Q. R. July, 1914) contends that this reveals an entirely erroneous view of the nature of a federation, and confuses federate with confederate unions: and Judge Clement (Law of Canadian Constitution, 3rd ed., p. 337) says, 'The true federal idea is clearly manifest, to recognize national unity with the right of local self-government; the very same idea that is stamped on the written Constitution of the United States.' And in a famous passage in the judgment of the Privy Council in *Liquidators of the Maritime Bank of Canada* v. *Receiver-General of New Brunswick* [1892] A. C. 437, 441-2, Lord Watson, delivering judgment, says:—"The object of the Act was neither to weld the provinces into one nor to subordinate provincial governments to a central authority, but to create a federal government in which they should all be

represented." See, also, as to federation properly so called, Bryce's *Studies in History and Jurisprudence* (ed. 1901), pp. 392-3; 408-9.

² These Orders-in-Council are set out verbatim in the Appendix to Lefroy's "Canada's Federal System," and Clement's "Law of the Canadian Constitution." In their judgment in *Attorney-General for British Columbia* v. *Attorney-General for Canada* [1914] A. C. 153, 163, the Privy Council state the history of the Constitution of British Columbia.

³ These Orders-in-Council and statutes will be found set out *in extenso* in the Appendices to Canada's Federal System, and Clement's Law of the Canadian Constitution. The Yukon Territory was constituted a separate Territory by the Act of 1898, 61 Vict. c. 6, D., amended by the Act of 1901, 1 Edw. VII. c. 42, D. See, also, *Constitutional Status of N.-W. Territories*, 4 C. L. T. 1, 49.

⁴ Clement has a useful chapter on the constitutional history of the North-West Territories, *op. cit.*, pp. 847-862. Munro's Constitution of Canada (Cambridge, 1889) in ch. 2 contains a short and useful statement of the constitutional history of the Canadian provinces.

Other works dealing with the Constitution of Canada are: " Canada's Federal System, being a Treatise on Canadian Constitutional Law under the British North America Act," A. H. F. Lefroy, Carswell Co. Ltd., Toronto, 1913; "Leading Cases in Canadian Constitutional Law," A. H. F. Lefroy, Carswell Co. Ltd., Toronto, 1914; " The Canadian Constitution," E. R. Cameron, Butterworth & Co., 1915; "Legislative Power in Canada," A. H. F. Lefroy, The Bryant Press, Toronto, 1898 (out of print); "Parliamentary Procedure and Government in Canada," J. G. Bourinot, 2nd ed., Montreal, 1892; "Documents Illustrative of the Canadian Constitution," William Houston, Toronto, 1891; "Confederation Law of Canada," G. J. Wheeler, London, 1897; "Documents of the Canadian Constitution," W. P. M. Kennedy, Oxford University Press, 1918.

⁵ All these British North America Acts are printed *in extenso* in the appendix to "Canada's Federal System."

⁶ Maple Leaves, at p. 37, being a paper on Responsible Government in Canada, by J. G. Bourinot, 1890-1.

⁶ᵃ B. N. A. Act, 1867, sec. 51. As to the words "aggregate population of Canada" in this section, see *Attorney-General of Prince Edward Island* v. *Attorney-General for the Dominion*, [1905] A. C. 37. By 51 (a) added by Imp. B. N. A. Act, 1915, s. 2, a province is always to be entitled to a number of members in the House of Commons not less than the number of senators representing such province.

⁷ Pope's article on Federal Government in " Canada and its Provinces," p. 297. See, also, p. 60, and n. 40, *infra.* As to the Dominion Senate, see Pope, *ibid.* p. 281. See as to *Oaths Bill,* Keith's R. G. in D. p. 1131.

⁸ I owe this convenient expression " Crown (Dominion)" to signify the Crown as represented by the Dominion Government, as distinguished from the " Crown (Imperial)" and " the Crown (provincial)" to Judge Clement.

⁸ᵃ The *Supreme Court Act* provides:—"The judgment of the Court shall, in all cases, be final and conclusive, and no appeal shall be brought from any judgment or order of the Court to any Court of Appeal established by the Parliament of Great Britain and Ireland, by which appeals or petitions to His Majesty in Council may be ordered to be heard, *saving any right which His Majesty may be graciously pleased to exercise by virtue of his royal prerogative.'* As to criminal cases, sec. 1025 of the Dominion *Criminal Code,* R. S. C. 1906, c. 146, purports to forbid appeals to the Privy Council. The Judicial Committee has not, apparently, passed upon the effect of this section to bind the Royal Prerogative. See *Toronto Railway Company* v. *The King,* [1917] A. C. 630; and *cf.* Keith's *Imperial Unity,* pp. 367-9.

⁹ They will be found discussed at some length in the introductory chapter to the present writer's work on Legislative Power in Canada.

¹⁰ PARAMOUNT AUTHORITY OF THE IMPERIAL PARLIAMENT. Thus in *Smiles* v. *Belford,* 23 Grant, (U. C.) 590, 1 O. A. R. 436, it was held that Imp. 5-6 Vict. c. 45, as to copyright, which by section 29 was extended to every part of the British Dominions, applied to Canada notwithstanding No. 23 of section 91, B. N. A. Act, 1867, which assigns power over copyright to the Dominion parliament, and an injunction was granted to the holder of an English copyright under the Imperial Act to restrain a Canadian reprint. And see *Routledge* v. *Low,* L. R. 3 H. L. 100, also a case of copyright.

The Canadian power over copyright in view of Imperial Acts and treaties has been the subject of much discussion and negotiation between the Dominion and Imperial Governments. Its course may be followed in Dom. Sess. Pap. 1875, No. 28; 1890, No. 35; 1892, No. 81; 1894, No. 50; 1895, No. 81; 1896, No. 8, b.; Lefroy's Legislative Power in Canada, pp. 225-31; Keith's Responsible Government in the Dominions, Vol. III, pp. 1216-1237. The new Imperial Copyright Act, 1911, is expressed not to extend to a self-governing Dominion unless declared by the legislature of that Dominion to be in force therein. It has not yet been accepted in Canada.

So, again, in *Reg.* v. *College of Physicians, etc.,* 44 U. C. R. 564, it was held that the Imperial Medical Act of 1868 applied to Canada, and overrode the provincial Act of 1874 as to the examination of applicants for registration as medical practitioners in Ontario.

It is, however, unnecessary to cite the numerous cases wherein the supremacy of the Imperial parliament is recognized. ,The matter is beyond dispute, and the (*Imp.*) *Colonial Laws Validity Act, 1865*, is a clear statutory recognition of it. As to the origin of this Act, see Poley's Federal Systems, pp. 209-210. Reference, may, however, be made on the subject to Todd's Parl. Gov. in Brit. Col. (2nd ed.) c. 7; Lewis' Essay on Government of Dependencies, ed. 1891, at pp. 91-2, 155-6; Professor A. V. Dicey in L. Q. R., Vol. XIV, p. 198; Imp. 6 Geo. III, c. 12; 31 Geo. III. c. 31, s. 46. See also *Callender Sykes & Co.* v. *Colonial Secretary of Lagos* [1891] A. C. 460, 466-7; *New Zealand Loan and Mercantile Agency Co.* [1898] A. C. 349, at pp. 357-8. The repeal or amendment by the British parliament of an Imperial Act extending to a colony may, if proper construction so requires, be operative therein: *Reg.* v. *Mount* (1875) L. R. 6 C. P. 283.

For an appeal since Confederation by a provincial Government to the supreme jurisdiction of the Imperial parliament, see Dom. Sess. Pap. 1877, No. 86.

Thus the view expressed by a few judges that "exclusively" in sections 91 and 92 B. N. A. Act 1867, means exclusively of the Imperial Parliament, is entirely overruled by authority. See for such view *Reg.* v. *Taylor*, 36 U. C. R. 183; *Holmes* v. *Temple*, 8 Q. L. R. 351. It is expressly referred to and disapproved of in *Angers* v. *Queen Ins. Co.*, 16 Can. L. J. 204; *Smiles* v. *Belford*, 1 O. A. R. 442, 447, 448; *Tai Sing* v. *Maguire*, 1 B. C. (pt. 1) 107.

A contention was advanced on behalf of the Dominion Government by Sir J. Thompson in the course of negotiations with the Imperial Government as to copyright, that it is in the power of the Dominion parliament and provincial legislatures respectively to repeal Imperial statutes passed prior to Confederation and dealing with any of the subjects within the legislative powers granted to them by the B. N. A. Act: Dom. Sess. Pap. 1890, No. 35. But the Imperial Government has expressly dissented from it, pending a decision on the point by the Judicial Committee of the Privy Council, Dom. Sess. Pap. 1892, No. 12; and it is opposed to the decision of the Ontario Court of Appeal in *Smiles* v. *Belford*, 23 Grant 590, 1 O. A. R. 436. See, however, *Imperial Book Co.* v. *Black* (1905), 35 S. C. R. 488. See further as to it some articles on Federal Government in Canada, 9 Can. L. T. 193, 198; Todd's Parl. Gov. in Brit. Col. (2nd ed.) p. 502; and *Gordon* v. *Fuller*, 5 U. C. (O.S.) 182, 187, 192, 193. The intention of an Imperial Act to apply to self-governing colonies must be clearly expressed or implied; and in practice the paramount power of legislation by the Imperial Parliament is only exercised by Acts conferring constitutional powers, or dealing with a limited class of subjects of special Imperial or international concern, such as merchant shipping. *Cf.* despatch of Lord Carnarvon of Oct. 18th, 1875: Hodg. Dom. and Prov. Legisl. 67; and Dom. Sess. Pap. 1890, No. 35, p. 8. And see as to the whole subject of this note Lefroy's Legislative Power in Canada, pp. 208-31; and Canada's Federal System, pp. 51-58. Keith (*op. cit.* Vol. 2, pp. 1003-1031) has a chapter upon the general subject of 'Imperial control over Dominion administration and legislation.' Imperial control over Canadian (Dominion) legislation may be exercised in two ways, either by Bills being reserved for the Royal assent,—or, which is equivalent thereto, containing a suspending clause until called into force by Order in Council, or by disallowance within the two years allowed. As to Imperial control over the internal affairs of the Dominions, Mr. Keith deals with that: *op. cit.* Vol. II. pp. 1032-1053, and shows that there has been a practically complete abnegation of Imperial control since the grant of parliamentary responsible government. See reports and Imperial despatches relating to Imperial supervision over Dominion legislation collected, Hodg. Prov. Legisl. 1867-1895, pp. 6-60, and *infra*, n. 13. As to Imperial interference to protect rights of foreigners, see *infra*, n. 13, and, also, *infra*, n. 40.

11 For more detailed information as to the pre-confederation Constitutions and constitutional history of the several Canadian provinces, see the return to an address of the Dominion House of Commons for copies of the charters or Constitutions granted by the Crown or the Imperial Parliament to the several colonies: Dom. Sess. Pap. 1883, No. 70, printed also in an appendix to Vol. 3 of Cartwright's Cases; Munro's Constitution of Canada, pp. 13-39, 313-24; Clement's Canadian Constitution, 3rd ed. pp. 316-334. See, also, Professor Kennedy's Historical Introduction, *supra*.

12 *Supra*, p. 47.

13 Mr. A. B. Keith, in his Responsible Government in the Dominions, has a chapter (Vol. III, Pt. V, c. XII) on 'Imperial Legislation for the Dominions' in which these statutes are mentioned, and their purport briefly stated. He there says: 'the general rule regarding Imperial legislation is that it will not be passed save where it is necessary for the satisfactory carrying out of foreign policy and treaty obligations or other matters of Imperial interest, in which either uniformity, or extra-territorial application is required.' Several of such Acts provide for Imperial co-operation in judicial matters. One very important function of the Imperial parliament, Mr. Keith points out, is the validating of laws invalidly passed by Colonial legislatures. In 1907 a final *ex post facto* validation was given by 7 Edw. VII, c. 7 (Imp.) to every Act passed by a colonial or

state parliament if assented to by the Governor and not disallowed, or reserved and assented to by the Crown, whether or not the proper forms had in each case been adopted. See, also, R. S. O. 1897, Vol. III, Appendix Pt. IV, where is to be found a Table of 'Imperial Statutes (other than those relating to criminal law introduced by the Quebec Act, 1774) appearing to be in force in Canada *ex proprio vigore* at the end of 1901.' It is stated in a note that this table is not to be considered as exhaustive, or exclusive, but that it is intended for convenience of reference, See, further, as to this, n. 27 *infra*.

14 *Trimble* v. *Hill* (1879) 5 App. Cas. 342.

15 *Macdonald* v. *Macdonald* (1886) 11 O. R. 187; *Jacobs* v. *Beaver* (1908) 17 O. L. R. 496, 498-9,, 501; *McDonald* v. *Elliott* (1886) 12 O. R. 98; *Gentile* v. *British Columbia Electric R. W. Co.* (1913) 18 B. C. 307; *McDonald* v. *British Columbia Electric R. W. Co.* (1911) 16 B. C. 386. *Cf.*, also, *Charbonneau* v. *Pagot* (1917) 11 W. W. R. 1327, a Saskatchewan case. In *Coulson* v. *O'Connell* (1878) 29 U. C. C. P. 341, a Canadian decision being upon a point of practice, was adhered to by the full Court though placing a construction on an Ontario statute different from that put upon substantially similar language in an English Act by the English Courts.

16 *Geiger* v. *Grand Trunk R. W. Co.* (1905) 10 O. L. R. 511, 514; *Henderson* v. *Canada Atlantic R. W. Co.* (1898) 25 O. A. R. 437, 444-5.

17 *Doe d. Anderson* v. *Todd* (1845) 2 U. C. R. 82, 83 *seq.*, 90 *seq.*; *Shea* v. *Choat* (1836) 2 U. C. R. 211, 221; Blacks. 1 Comm. 107; *Cooper* v. *Stuart* (1889) 58 L. J. P. C. 93, 96, where Lord Watson says, after citing the above passage in Blackstone: "If the learned author had written at a later date he would probably have added that as the population, wealth and commerce of the colony increase, many rules and principles of English law which were unsuitable to its infancy will gradually be attracted to it; and that the power of remodelling its law belongs also to the colonial legislature."

18 *Regina* v. *Roblin* (1862) 21 U. C. R. 352, 356; *Lawless* v. *Chamberlain* (1889) 18 O. R. 309; *Fraser* v. *Kirkpatrick* (1907) 6 Terr. L. R. 403, 407; *Hodgins* v. *McNeil* (1902) 9 Gr. 305, 309.

19 *Reg.* v. *McCormick* (1859) 18 U. C. R. 131, where it was held that the *Nullum Tempus Act*, 9 Geo. III. c. 16, was in force in Ontario, but did not apply to the waste lands of the Crown.

20 *Shea* v. *Choat* (1836) 2 U. C. R. 211, 221.

21 *S.* v. *S.* (1877) 1 B. C. (pt. 1) 25; *Corporation of Whitby* v. *Liscombe* (1876) 23 Gr. 1.

[22] *Regina* v. *Row* (1864) 14 U. C. C. P. 307; *Le Syndicat Lyonnais* v. *McGrade* (1905) 36 S. C. R. 251; *Hesketh* v. *Ward* (1867) 17 U. C. C. P. 667.

[23] Judge Clement, in his Canadian Constitution (p. 1060 *seq.*), has made a useful collection of cases in the various provincial Courts holding English statutes from Magna Charta onwards in force, or not in force, in their respective provinces.

[24] *Uniacke* v. *Dickson* (1848) James 287, 291. Haliburton, C.J., there lays down that—"Every year should render the Courts more cautious in the adoption of laws that had never previously been introduced into the colony"; and that "we must hold it to be quite clear that an English statute is applicable and necessary for us before we decide that it is in force here." The principles thus laid down in this case were quoted and acted upon in *Smyth* v. *McDonald* (1863) 5 N. S. 274, 278, and *The Queen* v. *Porter* (1888), 20 N. S. 352, 357; also in *Reg.* v. *Burdell* (1861), 5 N. S. (1 Oldr.) 126. The Statute of Uses, for example, has been held in force in Nova Scotia: *Shey* v. *Chisholm* (1853) 2 N. S. 52, as it has also been in New Brunswick: (1836) *Doe d. Hanington* v. *McFadden*, 2 N. B. 260, and in Manitoba: *Sinclair* v. *Mulligan* (1886) 3 Man. 481, 5 Man. 17. It has always been accepted in Ontario as in force without question. But the Statute of Enrolments, 27 Hen. VIII, c. 16, has been held not in force in Nova Scotia: *Berry* v. *Berry* (1882) 16 N. S. 66, 76; nor in Manitoba: *Sinclair* v. *Mulligan* (1886) 3 Man. 481, 490-1, 5 Man. 17; but has been held to be in force in New Brunswick: *Doe d. Hanington* v. *McFadden*, *supra*. *Cf.* Clement's Canadian Const. 3rd ed. pp. 280-1.

[25] (1817) 2 Mer. 143.

[26] Thus this principle was applied in *Doe d. Hanington* v. *McFadden* (1836) 2 N. B. 260; and in *Kavanagh* v. *Phelon* (1842) 1 Kerr. 472. Several English statutes regulative of the practice in the Courts at Westminster have been accepted in New Brunswick as operative within the province in relation to the Superior Courts there: Clement *op. cit.* p. 282. So in Ontario: *Whitby* v. *Liscombe* (1876) 23 Gr. 1, 14.

[27] In *Doe d. Anderson* v. *Todd* (1845) 2 U. C. R. 82, 86 Robinson, C.J., said: "Looking in the first place at the words of this statute" (U. C. 32 Geo. III. c. 1), "it is my opinion that they do not place the introduction of the English law on a footing materially different as regards the extent of the introduction from what would have been, or rather from what was, the effect of the proclamation of October 7th, 1763, in those territories to which it extended, or from the footing on which the laws of England stand in those colonies in which they are merely assumed to be in force on the principles of the common law by reason of such colonies having been first inhabited and

planted by British subjects." He further says (p. 87): "These words" (*sc.* the words of the section) "it must be remarked, are not such as expressly introduce the whole civil law of England; they seem rather intended to be more prudently limited to the purpose of giving the principles of English law, modified, of course, as they may have been by statutes, as the rule of decision for settling questions as they might arise relative to property and civil rights." See also *per* McLean, J., S.C., at p. 90. In this case the Mortmain Act (Imp.), 9 Geo. II. c. 36, was held to be in force in Ontario, but only on the ground of its implied recognition by the colonial legislature. It has been held not in force in New Brunswick: *Doe d. Hazen* v. *Rector of St. James* (1879) 2 P. & B. 479. *Cf.* also as to 32 Geo. III. c. 1, *Baldwin* v. *Roddy* (1833) 3 U. C. R. (O.S.) 166, 169; *Corporation of Whitby* v. *Liscombe* (1876), 23 Gr. 1, 37. In the recent case of *Keewatin Power Co.* v. *Kenora* (1908) 16 O. L. R. 184, 189, Moss, C.J., with, apparently, the concurrence of the rest of the Court, expressed great difficulty in acceding to the above *dicta* of Robinson, C.J., and said that he could "not but think that, under a statute framed as ours, a much larger body of the law, especially of the broad and well understood doctrines and principles of the common law with regard to property and civil rights, is introduced than is to be deemed to be carried with them by the settlers or colonists of a new uninhabited country." And he adds: "To what extent such an enactment introduces local Acts of parliament, or local customs or usages·not forming part of the common law, or how far they are to be deemed modified by circumstances is another question." This judgment held that the English common law rule that a grant of land bordering upon a non-tidal stream or body of water carries with it the grantor's title to the middle thread of the stream unless there be clear words of exclusion, and that there is no public right of navigation over such non-tidal waters, applies in Ontario. See as to this case Clement's Canadian Constitution, 3rd ed. pp. 291-2. The Statute of Frauds has always been held in force in Ontario. It is not in force in Manitoba because not enacted till seven years after the date of the Hudson Bay Company's Charter: *Sinclair* v. *Milligan* (1886) 3 Man. 481, 491, see *infra*, n. 32. The Act of U. C., 32 Geo. III. c. 1, introduced the laws of marriage as existing in England at that date (except some clauses of 26 Geo. II. c. 33), and so much of the canon law as had been adopted by the law of England: *Hodgins* v. *McNeil* (1862) 9 Gr. 307; *Regina* v. *Roblin* (1862) 21 U. C. R. 355; *O'Connor* v. *Kennedy* (1888), 15 O. R. 22; *Lawless* v. *Chamberlain* (1889) 18 O. R. 309. The Statutes of Elizabeth, 13 Eliz. c. 5, and 27 Eliz. c. 4, as to fraudulent and voluntary conveyances, have always been held in force in Ontario; also in Nova Scotia: *Tarratt* v. *Sawyer* (1835), 1 Thomps. (2nd ed.)

46; *Moore* v. *Moore* (1880) 1 R. & G. 525; *Graham* v. *Bell* (1884) 5 R. & G. 90. *Cf.* Clement *op. cit.* pp. 288-292. In 1902, the Ontario legislature by 2 Edw VII., c 13, revised, classified, consolidated and published as Vol. III of R. S. O. 1897, all such Imperial statutory enactments as had by the Act of 1792, or by later provincial Acts, been incorporated into the statute law of the province, enacting that such consolidation 'shall be deemed to include and comprise all provisions contained in any Imperial statute relating to property and civil rights which have heretofore been incorporated into the statute law of this province,' and which remain in force, except those referred to in Schedule C. This last schedule names eight statutes, not repealed, revised, or consolidated but left standing as they were, amongst them being the *Habeas Corpus Act*, 31 Car. 2, c. 2, the Lord's Day Act, 21 Geo. III. c. 49, and two statutes relating to British subjects born abroad; and in addition all Acts or parts of Acts in force relating to marriage, and to ecclesiastical property. This then is a legislative declaration of what Imperial enactments are now incorporated in the statute law of Ontario (other than those in force *proprio vigore*, see *supra*, p. 50), although s. 12 provides that the consolidation of an Imperial enactment in this Vol. III of the R. S. O. 1897, is not to be construed as a declaration that it was in force immediately *before* the coming into force of the said Revised Statutes. When the Ontario statutes were again revised in 1914, the statutory provisions contained in this volume of the R. S. O., so far as not in the meanwhile repealed, were distributed as provisions in other Ontario statutes *in eadem materia*, excepting certain which are set out in an appendix, and comprise *inter alia*, the provisions of the Statute of Monopolies (21 Jac. 1, c. 3), the Statute of Quia Emptores (18 Edw. I., c. 1), and the Statute of Uses, 27 Hen. VIII, c. 10.

28 There is no provision in the Code abrogating local enactments of criminal law existing at Confederation in the different provinces not repealed or altered since Confederation, nor inconsistent with the provisions of the Code.

29 See proclamation of Governor Douglas of Nov. 19th, 1858, and B. C. Act No. 70 of 34 Vict. (1871). The English Matrimonial Causes Act of 1857 was held to have been thus introduced: *S.* v. *S.* (1877) 1 B. C. (pt. 1) 25, and governs the proceedings for the British Columbia Divorce Court: *Watts* v. *Watts*, [1908] A. C. 573. See Clement *op. cit.* pp. 296, 544-5. So, also, in Manitoba: *Walker* v. *Walker* (1918), 39 D. L. R. 731; and in Saskatchewan, *Fletcher* v. *Fletcher* (1918). The law of England as to the right of the public to fish in tidal waters is the law of the province, subject only to regulation by the Dominion parliament: *Attorney-General for British Colum-*

vìa v. *Attorney-General for Canada* [1914] A. C. 153. A great many old English statutes are printed with R. S. B. C. 1911, *e.g.*, Magna Charta, the Habeas Corpus Acts, The Thellusson Act, the Dower Act of 1833. It is a curious fact that Ontario, New Brunswick, Nova Scotia, and Prince Edward Island have never adopted the provision of the English Dower Act, 1833, as to no widow being entitled to dower out of any land which has been absolutely disposed of by her husband in his life time or by will. The Imp. Dower Act, 1833, is not in force in Manitoba, Alberta, Saskatchewan, the Yukon Territory, or the Northwest Territories; but a widow is to have the same right in her deceased husband's land as if it were personal property: 57-58 Vict. c. 28, s. 6, D. (R. S. C. 1906, c. 100, s. 12); R. S. M. 1913, c. 54, s. 19; and see Manitoba Dower Act, 1918, Alberta Dower Act, 1917. For the Order in Council admitting British Columbia into the Dominion, see Dom. Stats. 1872, pp. lxxxii-lxxxv; Canada's Federal System, p. 844.

30 Dominion statutes 1872, pp. lxiii-lxvii; Canada's Federal System, p. 838. As to laws in force in N.-W. Territories, see 4 C. L. T. at pp. 12-15.

31 This enactment has been uniformly treated as introducing into Manitoba the law of England as it stood at the date mentioned: Clement's Canadian Constitution, p. 295. As to the reception of English law into the Northwest Territories, see *Fraser* v. *Kirkpatrick* (1907) 6 Terr. L. R. 402, 5 W. L. R. 287; *Syndicat Lyonnais* v. *McGrade* (1905) 36 S. C. R. 251; *Brand* v. *Griffin* (1908), 1 Alta. 510. As to the above section of the North-West Territories Act having introduced the (Imp.) *Divorce and Matrimonial Causes Act, 1857*, into the Northwest on the same construction as applied to similar words by the Privy Council in *Watts* v. *Watts*, [1908] A. C. 573, in the case of British Columbia,—and that, therefore, the Supreme Courts of Manitoba, Saskatchewan, and Alberta are free to exercise the Divorce jurisdiction given by that Act, see Article by Mr. Bram Thompson, 37 C. L. T. 687. See, also, *ib.*, pp. 679-680; 807-9. *Contra*, see 53 C. L. J. 362. The Manitoba Courts have now so held: *Walker* v. *Walker* (1918), 39 D. L. R. 731, and likewise the Saskatchewan: *Fletcher* v. *Fletcher* (1918), not yet reported.

32 *Sinclair* v. *Mulligan* (1888) 3 Man. 481, 5 Man. 17, contains interesting judgments as to what was the law in what is now the province of Manitoba at different times. The Statute of Uses was held to be in force, but not the Statute of Enrolments (26 Hen. VIII, c. 10), because inapplicable. Other cases dealing with English law in force in Manitoba are *Re Bremner* (1889) 6 Man. 73; *Re Tait* (1890) 9 Man. 617; *Thomson* v. *Wishart* (1910) 19 Man. 340, in which last case it was held that the criminal law of maintenance and cham-

perty was not in force, as these had become obsolete as crimes in England in 1870.

33 *The Scope and Interpretation of the Civil Code of Lower Canada*, by F. P. Walton (Montreal, 1907), p. 34.

34 Walton *op. cit.* p. 130, *seq.* The Quebec *Civil Code* (ed. 1898) s. 1206 provides, in an enactment originating in the Quebec Act 25 Geo. III, c. 2, s. 10:—'When no provision is found in this code for the proof of facts concerning commercial matters recourse must be had to the rules of evidence laid down by the laws of England.'

35 Walton *op. cit.* pp. 108-9; Article by P. B. Mignault on *L'Autorité Judiciaire*, in La Revue Legale, vol. 6, p. 145: Article on *The Legal System of Quebec*, by F. P. Walton, in 13 Columbia Law Rev. p. 213.

36 See *In re Johnson, Roberts* v. *Attorney-General* [1903] 1 Ch. 821, *per* Farwell, J., at p. 389; *Attorney-General of Canada* v. *Cain* [1906] A. C. 542, at pp. 545-6, as to which, see n. 203, *infra*. For a striking illustration of this unity of the Crown, see *Williams* v. *Howarth*, [1905] A. C. 551. See also *In re Samuel* [1913[A. C. 514; Keith, R. G. in D., Vol. III. p. 1456. On the general subject of petitions of right, see Keith *op. cit.* p. 1626. As to the general relation of the Crown to the Courts, see the very important case of *The Eastern Trust Co.* v. *McKenzie, Mann & Co.* [1915] A. C. 750, and Clement (L. of C. C. 3rd ed. pp. 589-595). As to province being unable to bind Crown (Dom.), see *Gauthier* v. *The King* (1918), 56 S. C. R. 176. And see Note to S. C. in 40 D. L. R. 353.

37 *The Queen* v. *Bank of Nova Scotia* (1885), 11 S. C. R. 1, at p. 17. See, also, *Attorney-General of Canada* v. *Attorney-General of Ontario* (1894), 28 S. C. R. 458, at p. 469; and the two Australian cases. *The King* v. *Sutton* (1908), 5 C. L. R. 789, and *Attorney-General of New South Wales* v. *Collector of Customs* (1908) *ibid.* 818. For the distinction between *majora* and *minora regalia*, see Blacks. Comm. (ed. 1770 in Osgoode Hall library), I. 241; and *infra* n. 41 *ad ex.*

38 THE PREROGATIVE OF HONOUR is not one of those the exercise of which is delegated to the Governor-General: Todd's Parl. Gov. in Brit. Col. 2nd ed. p. 313. It is essentially one for the direct exercise of the Crown (Imperial). As to the practice at the present time in regard to conferring Imperial honours upon Canadians, see Canada's Federal System, p. 22, n. 2 b. In Canada the provincial governments do not recommend names for Imperial honours, though in Australia the State governments do: Keith's R. G. in D., Vol. 2, p. 808; Article in Jl. of Soc. of Comp. Legisl. N.S., 1903, p. 125. Upon the subject of "Honours" generally, including precedence, see Keith *op. cit.* Vol. III, pp. 1299-1315. As to precedence the law officers of the Crown definitely advised on April 30th, 1859,

that it is proper for a colonial governor to regulate precedence (in default of special instructions) according to local conditions; precedence by birth or title in the United Kingdom does not automatically convey similar precedence in a colony: Keith *op. cit.* Vol. III, p. 1624. Judge Clement (L. of C. C. 3rd ed., pp. 116-164) devotes a long chapter to the royal prerogatives in relation to the colonial dominions.

THE PREROGATIVE OF MERCY. This is specially delegated to tne Governor-General in his instructions, but not since 1905 as to offences against provincial laws: Keith *op. cit.* Vol. 1, pp. 1565-6. And on whole subject, see *ibid.* Vol. 3, pp. 1386-1422. It would seem that, with regard to the exercise of the power of pardon by the Governor-General of Canada, though the advice of his ministers is necessary in capital cases, the Governor-General is not bound to follow that advice: *Framework of Union* (Cape Town, 1908), citing from a despatch by the Colonial Secretary to Lord Dufferin when Governor-General of Canada, in which it is said—'Advice having thus been given to the Governor, he has to decide for himself how he will act.' The following references in connection with this prerogative may also be of use: Can. Sess. Pap. 1869, No. 16; *ibid.* 1875, No. 11; *ibid.* 1877, No. 13; Ont. Sess. Pap. 1888, No. 37; Imp. Hans. April 16th, 1875 (3rd Ser. Vol. 223, p. 1065 seq.); Imp. Parl. N. Am. 1879, No. 99. As to the Shortis case, where the Governor-General of Canada pardoned, the Council abstaining from advising one way or the other, see 32 C. L. J. 53.

PREROGATIVE OF JUSTICE. As to the general subject of the prerogative of the Crown to hear appeals from the Courts of the Dominion, see Keith *op. cit.* Vol. III, p. 1357, *seq.;* Keith's *Imperial Unity,* pp. 367-388; and *infra,* p. 169, n. 41.

39 *Liquidators of the Maritime Bank of Canada* v. *Receiver-General of New Brunswick* [1892] A. C. 437. See, also, *Queen v. Bank of Nova Scotia* (1885), 11 S. C. R. 1; *Exchange Bank* v. *The Queen* (1886), 11 App. Cas. 157; *Legislative Power in Canada,* pp. 72-86.

40 B. N. A. Act 1867, s. 56. Mr. Keith discusses Imperial control over Dominion legislation in R. G. in D., Vol 2, pp. 1007-1021, 1031, 1219-1222. He says that the exercise of the power was threatened in one case of a private Bill unless the promoters allowed adequate opportunity for the consideration of objections by the government department concerned, and adds that 'the use of the refusal of the royal assent on the advice of ministers seems clearly proper in a suitable case like that.' There is now no Imperial veto power over the Acts of Canadian provincial legislatures. As to reservation of Bills for the pleasure of the Crown (Imperial) and refusal of assent by it, see Keith's *Imperial Unity and the Dominions,* pp. 143-9.

[41] *Queen's Counsel Case*, [1898] A. C. 247, 23 O. A. R. 792. See also n. 42. A colonial Act assented to by the Crown through its authorized representative can regulate and interfere with the exercise of the prerogative of the Crown as the fountain of justice, so far as the rights of those under its jurisdiction are concerned, as by restricting the right of appeal to the King in Council: *Cuvillier* v. *Aylwin* (1882), 2 Kn. P. C. 72; *In re Wi Matua's Will*, [1908] A. C. 448; *Cushing* v. *Dupuy* (1880), 5 App. Cas. 409. But in addition to cases which are brought before the Judicial Committee of the Privy Council on appeal, it is provided by sec. 4 of Imp. 3-4 Wm. IV. c. 41, that His Majesty may refer to the Judicial Committee any such matters whatsoever other than appeals as His Majesty shall think fit, and the Committee shall thereupon hear and consider the same, and shall advise His Majesty thereon, as in the case of regular appeals. See as to this Keith *op. cit.* Vol. II^r, p. 1382, *seq.* Mr. Keith seems to think that the effect of this is that an appeal to the Privy Council cannot be absolutely barred except by an Imperial Act: *Ibid.* Vol. III, p. 1357 *seq.* See, also, Clement L. of C. C., 3rd ed., pp. 157-164, who considers the question whether a colonial legislature has power to legislate in derogation of the Crown's prerogative in connection with Colonial appeals not yet definitely decided, but inclines to the view that they have such power. As to the constitution of the Judicial Committee of the Privy Council, see Keith *op. cit.* Vol. III, pp. 1373-1383. And see *Ibid.* p. 1526 *seq.* for a concise account of the discussion at the Imperial Conference of 1911 of a new Imperial Court of Appeal. As to the distinction between *majora* and *minora regalia*, and the mistaken idea that only the *minora regalia* can be regulated by local colonial law, see Keith *op. cit.* Vol i. pp. 362-3; *Legislative Power in Canada*, pp. 79, 182, n. 2; Chitty on the Prerogative p. 25; Chalmer's Opinions, pp. 50, 373. *Cf.*, also, Keith's *Imp. Un.* Ch. XIV.

[42] *Liquidators of the Maritime Bank of Canada* v. *Receiver General of New Brunswick* [1892] A. C. 437. For the authorities generally see *Legislative Power in Canada*, pp. 90-122. It would seem that the Lieutenant-Governor of the North West Territories has only power to approve or reserve measures, but none to withhold assent: Hodgins' Prov. Legisl. 1867-1895, p. 1279. As to when he should do so, see *Ibid.* pp. 1276-7. The B. N. A. Act, 1867, secs. 12, 65, has made a distribution between the Dominion and the provinces of executive authority which in substance follows that of legislative powers, subject to certain express provisions in that Act and to the supreme authority of the Sovereign, who delegates to the Governor-General and through his instrumentality to the Lieutenant-Governors the exercise of the prerogative in terms defined in their commissions: *Bonanza Creek Gold Mining Co.* v. *Rex*

[1916] A. C. 566, 579. For acts done in their private capacity, or done *qua* governor, but beyond their powers as such, colonial governors are liable to be prosecuted criminally, or sued civilly, in the Courts of their colony, or in England; but for acts done *qua* governor and within their authority as such, they incur no liability, either *ex contractu* or in tort: *Hill* v. *Bigge* (1841), 3 Mo. P. C. 465; *Musgrave* v. *Pulido* (1880), L. R. 5 App. Cas. 102; *Macbeth* v. *Haldimand* (1786) 1 T. R. 172; *Reg.* v. *Eyre* (1868) L. R. 3 Q. B. 487. And see, generally, Clement's L. of C. C., 3rd ed. pp. 131-133; and Anson's *Law and Custom of the Constitution.* In the Australian cases of *King* v. *Governor of the State of South Australia* (1907) 4 C. L. R. 1497, and *Horwitz* v. *Connor* (1908) 6 C. L. R. 39 (and see *Electric Development Co.* v. *Attorney-General for Ontario* (1917) 38 O. L. R. 383, 389) the High Court of the Commonwealth held that no *mandamus* lay to the Governor of a State, or to the Governor in Council, even while performing an act enjoined upon him by a Commonwealth statute. But for a *mandamus* to the Provincial Secretary requiring him to perform a purely ministerial duty, see *Re The Massey Manufacturing Co.* (1886) 11 O. R. 446. See, also, 38 C. L. T. See, also, on the general subject of the representatives of the Crown in Canada, Canada's Federal System, pp. 25-29. Clement (L. of C. C. 3rd ed. pp. 589-895) discusses the general subject of the Crown in the Courts. As to a colonial governor being bound in the exercise of prerogative power by the constitutional practice of the colony, see *Commercial Cable Co.* v. *Government of Newfoundland* [1916] A. C. 610.

43 This does not inhibit a statutory increase of powers and duties germane to the office being imposed on the Lieutenant-Governor, as, *e.g.*, the power of commuting and remitting offences against the laws of the province: *Attorney-General of Canada* v. *Attorney-General of Ontario* (1890) 20 O. R. 222, 247. As to this restriction on the provincial power of amending the Constitution of the province, see *Re Initiative and Referendum Act* (1916), 27 Man. 1.

44 Since 1875, it has been the practice of the Imperial Government to appoint Colonial governors by an instrument embodied in three documents: the Letters Patent, the Commission, and the Instructions. The Letters Patent define the duties of the office; the Commission refers to the terms of the Letters Patent and contains the formal act of appointment; whilst the Instructions detail more fully the powers and functions of the office, especially with regard to the appointment of and dealing with the Executive Council, the rules for assenting to, dissenting from, or reserving for the Queen's pleasure proposed Colonial legislation, and the right to pardon and

reprieve offenders: *Framework of Union*, pp. 82-91, *q.v.* generally as to the Governor-General of Canada. See Can. Sess.
Pap. 1906, No. 18, for a Return setting out the Instructions
of Canadian Governors from 1791 to 1867. As to how, in deference to the wishes of the Canadian Minister of Justice in
1876, the Instructions to the Governor-General of Canada were
remodelled so as to omit any mention of the reservation of
special classes of Bills, 'but it was clearly intimated that
reservation was not being given up, but merely that reservation
as a fixed rule was abandoned,' and a case of its use occurred
in 1886, see Keith's R. G. in D., Vol. II, p. 1010. In 1915, the
Lieutenant-Governor of British Columbia reserved a provincial
Act for the pleasure of the Governor-General on the ground
that it affected aliens in the province: Report of Minister of
Justice of Jan 25th, 1916. *The Colonial Laws Validity Act*, 1865,
Imp. 28-29 Vict. c. 63, s. 4, expressly provides that a colonial
Act duly assented to by the Governor shall not be affected by
any instructions with reference to such law theretofore given
to such Governor, even though such instructions may be referred
to in the Letters Patent or Instrument authorizing such governor to concur in passing or to assent to laws for the peace,
order, and good government of the colony. The theory which
has been sometimes advanced that the Governor-General of
Canada and the provincial Lieutenant-Governors respectively
are entitled *virtute officii*, and without express statutory enactment or delegation from the Crown, to exercise the royal prerogatives in such a fashion as to cover the whole of the fields,
both federal and provincial, to which the self-government of
Canada extends, and which would make viceroys of them in the
full sense, does not appear to be sound. For the measure of their
powers the words of their Commissions, and of the Federation
Act itself must be looked at. It is quite consistent with this to
hold that executive power is in many situations which arise under the statutory Constitution of Canada conferred by implication
in the grant of legislative power, so that where such situations arise the two kinds of authority are correlative. See, on
this subject, *Bonanza Creek Gold Mining Co.* v. *The King*
[1916] A. C. 566, at pp. 585-7; Canada's Federal System, pp.
28-29; Keith's R. G. in D., Vol. II, pp. 564-664; *Ibid.* Vol. I. pp.
105-146; Clement's L. of C. C., 3rd ed., pp. 360-4. A colonial
Governor should not act on a mere personal discretion against
the views of a responsible Government; if necessary he should
ask the Imperial Secretary of State for instructions: Keith
op. cit., Vol. II, 1015 n., and the despatch of the Secretary of
State for the Colonies to the Governor of Newfoundland quoted
by him at pp. 1042-7. In the case of a Governor of a colony, as
in the case of the King, a dissolution of the legislature without
the advice of ministers is an impossibility: Keith *op. cit.* Vol.

172 CANADIAN CONSTITUTIONAL LAW.

III, p. 1627. On the other hand, no such practice prevails in
the Dominions, as in the United Kingdom, that ministers shall
receive a dissolution whenever they ask for it: *Ibid.* p. 1460;
also *ibid.* Vol. I, pp. 182-190. As to dismissal of Ministers by
colonial Governors in Canada and elsewhere, see Keith *op. cit.*
Vol. I, p. 223 *seq.*, and 237-245. As to Governors exercising the
prerogative power of incorporating companies, see *Bonanza
Creek Gold Mining Co.* v. *The King* [1916] A. C. 566, at p. 580.
But see *infra* n. 287. In an appendix to Vol. III of his R. G. in D.,
at pp. 1561-1613, Mr. Keith gives *in extenso* the forms of letters
patent, instructions, and commissions now issued to governors in
Canada, Australia, South Africa, New Zealand, the Australian
States and Newfoundland.

45 *Bank of Toronto* v. *Lambe* (1887) 12 App. Cas. 575, at p.
587. As to the Dominion veto power generally, see Canada's
Federal System, pp. 30-44; Legislative Power in Canada, pp.
185-203. Provincial Acts cannot be disallowed in part only;
if an Act is disallowed, it must be disallowed altogether: Hodg.
Prov. Legisl. Vol. I, at pp. 674-5. Partial disallowance is not
unknown in Crown colonies: Keith *op. cit.* Vol. II, p. 1019. Such
disallowance must be absolute; it cannot be conditional: Hodg.
Prov. Legisl., 1867-1895, p. 1146. The Dominion House of Commons cannot constitutionally interfere by resolution: *ibid.* pp.
701-2.

46 For examples, see Canada's Federal System, pp. 33-4; and
infra, p. 174, n. 54.

47 See Canada's Federal System, pp. 34-44; *The Corporation
of Three Rivers* v. *Sulte* (1882) 5 L. N. 332, at pp. 334-5;
Debates (Canadian) House of Commons, March 1st, 1909.
Vol. 89, pp. 1750-1758; Prov. Legisl., 1899-1900, pp. 5-9, 17-19,
24-36, 44-45, 1901-3, pp. 4, 46; *ibid.* 1899-1900, p. 52 *seq.; ibid.*
1904-5, pp. 91-99, 148-9; Opinion of Mr. A. V. Dicey in reference
to the Disallowance of Provincial Acts as unjust and confis-
catory (1909), 45 C. L. J. 457; *In re Companies* (1913), 48 S.
C. R. 331, per Idington, J., at p. 381, who says: "When the
legislation proposed would manifestly improperly affect people
elsewhere, or corporations created outside the province such as
Dominion corporations resting upon the residual power of Parliament, or those of other provinces, and thus affect the people
of the whole Dominion, surely the exercise of the power in that
regard ought to be, and to be held, practicable." The foreboad-
ings of Mr. A. A. Dorion, in the Debates before Confederation,
that the federal veto power would be exercised in the interest
of the party in power at Ottawa, do not seem to have been
realized: Egerton and Grant's Constitutional Documents, pp.
451-2.

48 Provincial Legislation, 1904-1906, pp. 148-149; Canada's
Federal System, pp. 40-42.

[49] Printed in the "Times" of January 23rd, 1899. See extracts from it in Canada's Federal System, pp. 45-48. Reference may be made to an Article on Treaty-making Powers of the Dominions by Sir C. Hibbert Tupper in Jl. of Society of Compar. Legisl. (N.S.), Vol. 17, p. 5.

[50] Canada's Federal System, pp. 33-4; 45-48; Keith's R. G. in D. Vol. II, pp. 1026-1031; Report of Committee of (Dominion) Privy Council, April 27th, 1909; Reports of Minister of Justice as to proposed Ontario legislation of October 18th, 1909, and March 23rd, 1911.

[51] *Cf.* Keith, R. G. in D., Vol. II, pp. 739-741, 972; House of Common Debates, 1910-11, pp. 2769, *seq.*

[52] Canada's Federal System, pp. 48-49. The whole subject of the immigration of coloured races into the Dominions is elaborately treated by Keith, R. G. in D., Vol. II, pp. 1075-1100, who remarks that ' No question at present exceeds in difficulty the question of the relations of the Imperial Government and the Dominion Governments with regard to the immigration of coloured persons into the Dominions and their treatment while there.' At p. 1081 he quotes from Mr Joseph Chamberlain's statesmanlike speech on the subject at the Colonial Conference of 1897. At p. 1087-1091, Mr. Keith deals especially with legislation in Canada which has caused ' serious trouble both as regards Indians and Japanese,' and adds—' British Columbia as usual is the cause of the disturbance of peace.'

[53] *Hodge* v. *The Queen* (1883) 9 App. Cas. 117; *Liquidators of the Maritime Bank of Canada* v. *Receiver-General of New Brunswick* [1892] A. C. 437; *Attorney-General of Canada* v. *Cain* [1906] A. C. 542, which shows that the same principle applies as to executive powers: *The Queen* v. *Burah* (1878) 3 App. Cas. 889; *Powell* v. *Apollo Candle Co.* (1885) 10 App. Cas. 282, at p. 290; *Dobie* v. *Temporalities Board* (1882) 7 App. Cas. 136, 146; *Union Colliery Co.* v. *Bryden* [1899] A. C. 580, 584-5; Canada's Federal System, pp. 64-67. Contrast the former inferior status of colonial legislatures fettered in their activities by irresponsible Executives, and by Legislative Councils the members of which were appointed by the Crown, and which had no complete control over the public revenues, or the civil list, or the regulation of trade and commerce: Bourinot's Manual of the Constitutional History of Canada, ed. 1901, pp. 1-37. In 1870, speaking of the Jamaica Assembly. the judges of the Exchequer Chamber say: "We are satisfied that a confirmed Act of the local legislature lawfully constituted, whether in a settled or a conquered colony, has as to matters within its competence, and the limits of its jurisdiction, the operation and force of sovereign legislation, though subject to be controlled by the Imperial parliament": *Phillips* v. *Eyre* (1870) L. R. 6 Q. B. 1, 20,

cited Clement's L. of C. C. 3rd ed. p. 93. In connection with
this subject, it is necessary to cite the recent decision of the
Manitoba Court of Appeal in *Re Initiative and Referendum
Act* (1916) 27 Man. 1, holding the Manitoba *Initiative and Referendum Act ultra vires* on the ground that only provincial
" legislatures " have powers given them by s. 92 of the B. N. A.
Act, and " legislature " connotes, at any rate, a representative
House; and on the ground that the power of amending the provincial Constitution given by No. 1 of section 92, does not
extend to an absolute departure from the principle of the Act in
regard to the provincial Constitutions, by giving the power to
make laws to the body of voters in a referendum, who are not
a " legislature." But this case will doubtless be carried 'to the
Privy Council, and see *Canadian Law Times* for May, 1917, Vol.
37, pp. 334-6.

54 In *In re Nakane and Okazaka* (1908) 13 B. C. 370, a provincial Act was held inoperative as against provisions of an
Imperial treaty which had been sanctioned by a Dominion Act
pursuant to its powers under s. 132. Nothing is said in this
section,' as to the nature and extent of these obligations in the
event of the Canadian parliament and Government taking no
steps to recognize and meet them. And manifestly no treaty-
making power is conferred by the section': Clement, L. of C. C.,
3rd ed., pp. 134-5. The Canadian Government has accepted the
position that they are bound in respect of any treaties which
were binding on the colonies before federation, so far as regards
such colonies as were bound: Keith, R. G. in D. Vol. II, pp.
992-3. Mr. A. B. Keith (*op. cit.* Vol. III, p. 1122) further says
that s. 132 appears to be interpreted to mean, and must apparently have meant, at least as regards treaties concluded before
1867, that the existence of a treaty, whatever the subject
matter, confers full powers upon the Dominion parliament:
that under constitutional practice the Canadian Government
does not adhere to new treaties where the matter concerned
is one which is within the exclusive legislative competence of
the provincial legislature unless the provincial Governments
consent to such adherence: that adherence must be declared
for the Dominion as a whole, and is constitutionally declared at the request of the Dominion Government alone.
The whole subject of treaty relations in connection with the
self-governing Dominions is dealt with by Keith, *op. cit.* Vol.
III, pp. 1101-1157. As he there says, there is no real doubt
that treaties made by the Crown are binding on the colonies
whether or not the colonial Governments consent to such treaties; but it is an essential part of the Constitution of the
Empire that so far as is practicable no treaty obligations
shall be imposed without their concurrence on the self-governing Dominions. At pp. 1126-1130, Keith deals specially

with the ratifications of treaties: and at pp. 1114-1122 with commercial negotiations with regard to the Dominions. See, also, Keith *op. cit.* Vol. II, pp. 796 *et seq.;* Legislative Power in Canada, pp. 256-9; Clement, L. of C. C., 3rd ed., pp. 135-6, who cites Todd's Parl. Gov. in Brit. Col., ed. 1880, p. 196.

55 *Hodge* v. *The Queen* (1883) 9 App. Cas. 117, 132. Of course they can delegate no powers which they have not themselves got: *Liquor Prohibition Appeal*, 1895 [1896] A. C. 348, 364. And see as to *Re Initiative and Referendum Act* (1916) 27 Man. 1, *supra*, p. 174, n. 53. See, also, *Rex* v. *Weldon* (1914), 18 D. L. R. (B.C.) 109, 114, where McPhillips, J.A., expresses the opinion that the Dominion parliament could not confer on a provincial legislature the power to enact legislation of the nature of criminal law. *Sed quœre.*

56 *Cf., Kerley* v. *London and Lake Erie Transportation Co.* (1912) 26 O. L. R. 588; *Ouimet* v. *Bazin* (1912), 46 S. C. R. 502, 514; Canada's Federal System, pp. 71-73; Legislative Power in Canada, pp. 694-5.

57 See, also, Canada's Federal System, pp. 74-5.

58 *City of Fredericton* v. *The Queen* (1880) 3 S. C. R. 505, 532-3; *Russell* v. *The Queen* (1882) 7 App. Cas. 829, 838-40; Canada's Federal System, pp. 210-213. But as to its being proper to construe Acts of parliament giving the Crown power to invade private rights strictly, see *Allen* v. *Foskett* (1876) 14 N. S. W. 456.

59 *Russell* v. *The Queen* (1882) 7 App. Cas. 829, 841-2.

60 *E.g.*, a pretended license Act which was in substance a Stamp Act and indirect taxation: *Attorney-General for Quebec* v. *Queen Insurance Co.* (1878) 3 App. Cas. 1090, as to which case, see *In re Companies* (1913) 48 S. C. R. 331, 418; *Colonial Building and Investment Association* v. *Attorney-General of Quebec* (1883) 9 App. Cas. 157, 165; *Union Colliery Co.* v. *Bryden* [1889] A. C. 587, in connection with *Cunningham* v. *Tomey Homma* [1903] A. C. 151, 157. See, also, Canada's Federal System, pp. 76-82. The judges will not entertain allegations that a private Act was obtained by fraud or improper practices: *Lee* v. *Bude and Torrington R. W. Co.* (1871) L. R. 6 C. P. 576, 582. At pp. 80-81 of Canada's Federal System, the question is discussed whether provincial legislation may be *ultra vires* because it is attempting to produce piecemeal an aggregate result which is *ultra vires*. *Cf.*, Hagarty, C.J.O., in *Clarkson* v. *Ontario Bank* (1888) 15 O. A. R. 166, 181.

61 *Madden* v. *Nelson and Fort Sheppard R. W. Co.* [1899] A. C. 626, 627-8; *In re Companies* (1913) 48 S. C. R. 331, 341; *Attorney-General of Canada* v. *Attorney-General of Ontario*

(1890) 20 O. R. 222, 246, 19 O. A. R. 31, 38; Legislative Power in Canada, pp. 386-392.

62 *L'Union St. Jacques* v. *Belisle* (1874) L. R. 6 P. C. 31; *Hodge* v. *The Queen* (1883) 9 App. Cas. 117, 131-2; *Liquidators of Maritime Bank* v. *Receiver-General of New Brunswick* [1892] A. C. 437, 441-2; *McGregor* v. *Esquimalt and Nanaimo R. W. Co.* [1907] A. C. 462. *Cf.,* *Florence Mining Co.* v. *Cobalt Lake Mining Co.* [1909] 18 O. L. R. 275, aff. by the Privy Council, 102 L. T. 375; *Royal Bank* v. *The King* [1913] A. C. 283; *Supreme Court Reference Case* [1912] A. C. 571. See, too, *McNair* v. *Collins* (1912) 27 O. L. R. 44, and Law of Legislative Power in Canada, pp. 279-288, and especially the *dicta* of the Privy Council in the *Fisheries case* [1898] A. C. 700. So in the United States, Bryce's American Comm., ed. 1914, Vol. 1. p. 447. Canadian legislatures, moreover, are not restricted by such limitations as restrict "the right of eminent domain" under the United States Constitution: Kent's Comm., 12th ed., Vol. 2, at p. 340. See, also, *Riel* v. *The Queen* (1885) 10 App. Cas. 675, 678; *Re Carrie Bradbury* (1916) 30 D. L. R. (N.S) 756.

63 *John Deere Plow Co.* v. *Wharton* [1915] A. C. 330, 338 *seq.* As Judge Clement observes (L. of C. C., 3rd ed., p. 345), there is a division of "powers" rather than a division of "power" in the Canadian Constitution.

64 Canada's Federal System, pp. 86-89; *The Thrasher Case* (1882) 1 B. C. (Irving) 170, 209, 211; *Reg.* v. *Wing Chong* (1886) 2 B. C. (Irving) 150, 156; *Poulin* v. *Corporation of Quebec* (1881) 7 Q. L. R. 337, 339, in app. 9 S. C. R. 185.

65 *John Deere Plow Co.* v. *Wharton* [1915] A. C. 330, 338 *seq.; Citizens Insurance Co.* v. *Parsons* (1881) 7 App. Cas. 96, 109; *Attorney-General of Ontario* v. *Attorney-General of Canada* [1912] A. C. 571, 581, 583.

65a As to whether the B. N. A. Act, 1867, should be construed in respect to the distribution of legislative powers, and of public property, as always speaking, or as having spoken once for all on July 1st, 1867, when it was brought into force, see the Annotation to *Attorney-General of Canada* v. *Ritchie Contracting Co.* (1915) 26 D. L. R. 51, 69, the conclusion reached being that it cannot be so construed as to the latter, but that, in the case of the former, the phrases used must acquire a more extended connotation as the inventions of science and developments of the national life extend their significance beyond what they comprehended when the Constitution was originally framed.

66 *Cf. City of Fredericton* v. *The Queen* (1880) 3 S. C. R. 505, 562, 566, *et seq.*

67 *Cf.* Clement, L. of C. C., 3rd ed., pp. 450-3.

68 *Liquor Prohibition Appeal* [1896] A. C. 348, 360-1; *City of Montreal* v. *Montreal Street Railway* [1912] A. C. 333, 343-4; *Attorney-General for Canada* v. *Attorney-General for Alberta* [1916] A. C. 588. And so in this last case, the Privy Council held *ultra vires* sec. 4 of the Dominion Insurance Act, 1910, which purported to prohibit private persons or provincial insurance companies from carrying on the business of insurance within Canada, unless holding a license from the Dominion Minister under the Act, to the prejudice of their civil rights, although insurance was not included in any of the enumerated Dominion powers. The mere magnitude and importance of insurance business did not bring it under the Dominion residuary power: S. C.

69 *Attorney-General for Canada* v. *Attorney-General for Alberta* [1916] A. C. 588, 595. *Russell* v. *The Queen* (1882) 7 App. Cas. 829, is an instance of such a case. There the Court considered that the particular subject-matter in question lay outside the provincial powers. Another example of *intra vires* legislation by the Dominion under its residuary power is to be found in *Re Wetherell & Jones* (1883) 4 O. R. 713, being an Act providing for taking evidence in the province for use out of the province. But see a similar provincial Act held *intra vires* in *Re Alberta and Great Waterways R. W. Co.* (1911) 20 Man. 697.

70 *Liquor Prohibition Appeal* [1896] A. C. 348, 360-1. And see argument in the *Insurance Companies Case* [1916] A. C. 588, Martin, Meredith & Co.'s Transcript, 2nd day, p. 68; and Canada's Federal System, pp. 202-209. Dominion legislation will then no longer trench upon the provincial field: but whether such a condition of things in fact exists must, it would seem, if the occasion ever arises, be for the Courts to determine, whatever the awkwardness, inconvenience, and difficulty of such an enquiry: *per* Anglin, J., in *In re Insurance Act* (1910), 48 S. C. R. 200, at pp. 310-311. In *Russell* v. *The Queen* (1882) 7 App. Cas. 829, 840, their lordships say: "There is no ground or pretence for saying . . . that parliament, under colour of general legislation, is dealing with a provincial matter only. It is, therefore, unnecessary to discuss the considerations which a state of circumstances of this kind might present." But, of course, it is not open to a Court to substitute its own opinion as to whether any particular enactment is calculated, as a matter of fact and good policy, to secure peace, order, and good government for the decision of the legislature: Keith, R. G. in D., Vol. I, p. 419.

71 *Russell* v. *The Queen* (1882) 7 App. Cas. 829, 840. This decision must be accepted as an authority to the extent to which it goes: *Liquor Prohibition Appeal* [1896] A. C. 348, 362;

The Insurance Companies Case (Attorney-General for Canada v. Attorney-General for Alberta [1916] A. C. 588, at pp. 595-6), where what must be considered the final explanation of *Russell* v. *The Queen* was given. *Russell* v. *The Queen* was much discussed and criticized· during the argument of that case: see *verbatim* notes of argument (Martin, Meredith & Co.'s transcript) 1st day, pp. 32-33; 2nd day, p. 93; 3rd day, pp. 81-2, 86, 89; 4th day, p. 18. On the argument in *Attorney-General for British Columbia.* v. *Attorney-General for Canada* [1914] A. C. 153 (*verbatim* report, p. 176), Haldane, L. Ch., referring to *Russell* v. *The Queen*, says: " It became the custom never to cite that case. We cannot overrule it, but we never cite it."

72 See last note. Mr. Upjohn's illustration, however, is suggested by the passage in their judgment in *Russell* v. *The Queen* (1882) 7 App. Cas. 829, 838-9, where the Privy Council say: " Laws which make it a criminal offence for a man wilfully to set fire to his own house on the ground that such act endangers the public safety, or to overwork his horse on the ground of cruelty to the animal, though affecting in some sense property and the right of a man to do as he pleases with his own, cannot properly be regarded as legislation in relation to property and civil rights. Nor could a law which prohibited or restricted the sale or exposure of cattle having a contagious disease be so regarded." *Cf. Rex* v. *Davis* (1917), 40 O. L. R. 352, 354.

73 [1916] A. C. 588, 3rd day, p. 31. See note 71.

74 (1885) 10 App. Cas. 675. In this case, the Privy Council say, at p. 678, that they are " of opinion that there is not the least colour of contention " that " if a Court of law should come to the conclusion that a particular enactment was not calculated as matter of fact and policy to secure peace, order, and good government, that they would be entitled to regard any statute directed to those objects, but which a Court should think likely to fail of that effect, as *ultra vires* and beyond the competency of the Dominion parliament to enact."

74a (1882) 7 App. Cas. 829.

75 Lord Davey's expression of opinion was in the course of the argument in *Fielding* v. *Thomas* [1896] A. C. 600: MS. transcript from Cock and Kight's notes, p. 23. See Legislative Power in Canada, p. 699, n. 1. And as to the power of every colonial representative legislature to make laws respecting the constitution, power, and procedure of such legislature, see Colonial Laws Validity ·Act, 1865, s. 5, and Keith, R. G. in D., Vol. 1, p. 425. On the argument before the Privy Council on the *Supreme Court References case* [1912] A. C. 571, Lord Loreburn, L.C., said: " It is not, I suppose, contended that the words ' peace, order and good government ' involve the faculty of re-writing the whole Constitution;" and Lord Atkinson

said: "Surely you cannot say that the legislature under this power can practically tear up sections of the B. N. A. Act." And in the judgment itself, their lordships say: "All depends upon whether such a power" (sc. a power to place upon the Supreme Court the duty of answering questions of law or fact when put by the Governor in Council) "is repugnant to the B. N. A. Act." So, also, as against any such power, except on certain minor points in which power of alteration is expressly given by the Act, see Keith, R. G. in D. Vol. II, p. 99; Clement, L. of C. C., 3rd ed., pp. 40 *seq.* 49; Keith, *Imp. Unity and the Dominions,* pp. 391-2.

[76] *Attorney-General for Ontario* v. *Attorney-General for Canada* (Supreme Court References case) [1912] A. C. 571, at p. 581. As Lord Chancellor Haldane is reported as having said on the argument in *Attorney-General for British Columbia* v. *Attorney-General for Canada* [1914] A. C. 153 (*verbatim* report, pp. 90-91) referring to these words: "It is not an expression which you must ride to death because in the case of the Constitution of Canada, enormous though the powers are, there are some things that are not delegated with regard to succession to the Crown and matters of that kind. They belong to the Sovereign parliament, they are not delegated. . . " And it must be admitted that the proposition is not literally true if the decision of the Manitoba Court of Appeal in *Re Initiative and Referendum Act* (1916) 27 Man. 1, holding that Act *ultra vires* is good law. See, however, the comments on this decision in 37 C. L. T. at pp. 334-7. See, also, *per* Meredith, J.A., in *The King* v. *Brinckley* (1907) 14 O. L. R. 435, 454.

[77] *The Thrasher Case* (1882) 1 B. C., (Irving) 170, at p. 195.

[78] Torrance, J., in *Angers* v. *Queen's Insurance Co.* (1877) 21 L. C. J. 77, 80. The Australian Commonwealth has modelled its Constitution largely on that of the United States. There the Commonwealth has, as a rule, only a definite sphere of legislative activity, the residual legislative power belonging to the States: Imp. 63-64 Vict. c. 12, s. 107; Keith's R. G. in D., Vol. 1, p. 867, Vol. 2, p. 973. For a detailed comparison between the Constitution of Canada and that of the United States, see the introductory chapter to Legislative Power in Canada. See also, *supra,* pp. 66-7, 70, 78-9, 105-6, 125.

[79] *Valin* v. *Langlois* (1879) 5 App. Cas. 115, 119; *Bank of Toronto* v. *Lambe* (1887) 12 App. Cas. 587, 588. But, of course, this does not mean that there must be found vested in one single authority, the power to legislate wholly with regard to a given subject, *e.g.*, through traffic passing first over a provincial railway and then over a federal railway with which the provincial railway connects. Concurrent legislation by the provincial legislatures, or even by the federal and the provincial legislatures, may be necessary: *Canadian Pacific R. W. Co.* v.

Ottawa Fire Insurance Co. (1907) 39 S. C. R. 443, 465; *City of Montreal* v. *Montreal Street Railway* [1912] A. C. 333, 346; *In re Insurance Act* (1913) 48 S. C. R. 290, 298; *In re Companies* (1913) 48 S. C. R. 331, 431; Clement's L. of C. C., 3rd ed., pp. 394-7.

80 Many of the cases are discussed in Legislative Power in Canada, pp. 322-338. See, also, Clement, L. of C. C., 3rd ed., pp. 65-115. This limitation, however, must not be insisted upon in such a manner as to render the grant of legislative power ineffectual: *Attorney-General of Canada* v. *Cain and Gilhula* [1906] A. C. 542; 'Keith, R. G. in D., Vol. I, 393 *seq.*, who discusses, in connection with this Privy Council decision, *Reg.* v. *Lesley* (1860) Bell, C. C. 220, 29 L. J. M. C. 97. See, also, Keith, *op. cit.* Vol. III, p. 1454. In *Reg.* v. *Brinkley* (1907) 14 O. L. R. 435, 454, Meredith, J.A., points out that it is altogether too narrow a proposition to say that the legislative power of a Canadian legislature is strictly limited to matters wholly within the territorial limits, and he instances the *Extradition Act*, the *Deportation Act*, the enactment against bringing stolen property into Canada, and the legislation respecting officers in England and other countries maintained by Canada for political and commercial purposes: cited Clement, *op. cit.* at p. 112. See Keith, R. G. in D., Vol. I, p. 372, *seq.*, and *Imp. Unity*, pp. 312-4, on the territorial limitation of Dominion legislation. See, also, on the subject generally, Canada's Federal System, pp. 101-106. As to the doctrine that there are certain subjects of so Imperial a character that they cannot be regarded as falling within the purview of any colonial legislature whatever, *e.g.*, that no colonial legislature could enact that the governor should exercise his prerogative of pardon only in accordance with the voice of a plebiscite, or alter the relations between the governor and the legislature, or establish a legislative council which the Crown could not dissolve—see Keith, R. G. in D., Vol. 1, pp. 361-2, who refers also to Jenkins' British Rule and Jurisdiction Beyond the Seas, pp. 69 *seq.*; Professor Harrison Moore in Jl. Soc. Comp. Legisl. Vol. II, p. 289 *seq.*; and *supra* n. 76. As to Canadian Acts at variance with Imperial Treaties, see *supra*, p. 65. As to political as distinguished from commercial treaties, see Keith's *Imp. Unity*, pp. 281-300. See, also, Poley's Federal Systems of the United States and British Empire, p. 337; Parl. Pap. 1902, Cd. 1587.

81 Thus the *Commonwealth of Australia Constitution Act, 1900*, gives the Australian Federal parliament (s. 51), the power to make laws for the peace, order, and good government of the Commonwealth with respect to 'fisheries in Australian waters beyond territorial limits,' 'external affairs,' and 'the relations of the Commonwealth with the islands of the Pacific.' See Keith, R. G. in D., Vol. 1, pp. 399-401, as to the extra-territorial

character of these Australian powers: also *ibid.* Vol. III, pp.
1124-6 as to the power over 'external affairs.' Also see *ibid.,*
Vol. III, pp. 1197-1215.

[82] *Per* Turner, L.J., in *Low* v. *Routledge* (1865) L. R. 1
Ch. 42, 46-7, where, however, the point actually decided was that
a colonial legislature cannot affect an alien's rights under an
Imperial Act expressed to extend to the colonies. In favour of
the legislatures having such a power to bind "their own subjects" everywhere, see *In re Criminal Code Sections relating
to Bigamy* (1897) 27 S. C. R. 461; *Regina* v. *Brierly* (1887) 14
O. R. 525, 533. In the opinion of the law officers of the Crown
with reference to British Guiana in 1855 (referred to in Keith,
R. G. in D., Vol. I, pp. 372-3, 394) there was a suggestion that
the laws of a colony might be applied outside its limits to persons domiciled in the colony. See, also, *In re Award of Wellington Cooks and Stewards Union*, (1906) 26 N. Z. L. R. 394; also
Keith, *op. cit.* Vol. I, p. 145 *seq.,* and Clement, L. of C. C., 3rd
ed., pp. 91-115. See, also, *Macleod* v. *Attorney-General New
South Wales* [1891] A. C. 454, as specially discussed in Legislative Power in Canada, pp. 336-8; Keith, R. G. in Vol. I, pp.
375, 397-8; Clement, L. of C. C., 3rd ed., pp. 104, 114-5; and
especially an article on *The Limitations of Colonial Legislatures,*
33 L. Q. R. 117 (1917) by John W. Salmond, who favours a certain power of extra-territorial legislation by colonial Legislatures, and cites the above New Zealand case. For the
contrary view that the legislatures have no such power, see
Keith, ad loc. cit., and Vol. I, p. 376; Despatch of Secretary of
State for the Colonies of Dec. 17th, 1869; Hodg. Prov. Legisl.
1867-1895, p. 7; *Attorney-General of the Commonwealth* v. *Ah
Sheung* (1906) 4 Comm. L. R. 949, cited Clement, *op. cit.* p. 165,
n.; Article on Extraterritorial Criminal Legislation of Canada,
19 C. L. T. pp. 1, 38. See, also, *Gavin Gibson and Co.* v.
Gibson [1913] 3 K. B. 379, 392, where Atkin, J., declined to
recognize a person born in a British colony as a subject of that
colony. But see as to a person *naturalized* in a colony: *Rex* v.
Francis (1918), 34 T. L. R. 273 (Divl. Court). As to statutes
authorizing the initiation of legal proceedings against defendants out of the jurisdiction and the cases relating thereto, see
Canada's Federal System, p. 104, n. 23. See, also, *Re Alberta
and Great Waterways R. W. Co.* (1910), 20 Man, 697; *Wetherell*
v. *Jones* (1884) 4 O. R. 713; Keith's *Imp. Unity,* pp. 311-314.

[83] See *Asbury* v. *Ellis* [1893] A. C. 339; *Rex* v. *Meikleham*
(1905) 11 O. L. R. 366; *Regina* v. *Brierly* (1887) 14 O. R. 525,
531; *In re Criminal Code Sections relating to Bigamy* (1897)
27 S. C. R. 461, 482; *Niboyet* v. *Niboyet* (1879) L. R. 4 P. D.
20; *Gavin Gibson and Co.* v. *Gibson, supra;* Clement, L. of C. C.,
3rd ed., pp. 87-91; *Rex* v. *Francis* (1918) 34 T. L. R. 273.

84 *E.g.*, an Act respecting bills of lading might be passed by a provincial legislature as a matter relating to property and civil rights while the Dominion parliament might pass a similar Act as a necessary or convenient matter to be dealt with in the regulation of trade and commerce: *Beard* v. *Steele* (1873) 34 U. C. R. 43; *Reg.* v. *Taylor* (1875) 36 U. C. R. 191, 206. See generally as to concurrent powers of legislation, Canada's Federal System, pp. 107-111.

85 *Regina* v. *Stone* (1892) 23 O. R. 46. *Cf.*, *Regina* v. *Wason* (1890) 17 O. A. R. 221. And so, although the Ontario Lord's Day Act, treated as a whole, has been held to be *ultra vires* by the Privy Council as legislation upon criminal law, an exclusively Federal subject, in *Attorney-General for Ontario* v. *Hamilton Street R. W. Co.* [1903] A. C. 524, this does not mean that provincial legislatures cannot pass Sunday Observance laws, closing places of amusement, and prohibiting trading or industrial work on Sunday, as police regulations for the locality (see *supra*, pp. 141-2); *Tremblay* v. *Cité de Quebec* (1910) R. J. Q. 38 S. C. 82, 37, S. C. 375. See, however, now *Rodrigue* v. *Parish of Ste. Prosper* (1917) 37 D. L. R. (Que.) 321; 40 D. L. R. 30; and *infra*, n. 351; *Rex* v. *Davis* (1917) 40 O. L. R. 352, 354.

86 Thus the extent of the provincial power of legislation over 'property and civil rights in the province' cannot be ascertained without also ascertaining the powers and rights conferred upon the Dominion parliament: *Attorney-General for Ontario* v. *Mercer* (1883) 8 App. Cas. 767, 776; 'solemnization of marriage' given to the provincial legislatures by section 92 must be considered as excepted out of the general subject of 'marriage and divorce,' given to the Dominion parliament by section 91, and 'direct taxation within the province in order to the raising of a revenue for provincial purposes' as excepted out of the 'raising of money by any mode or system of taxation,' the former being given to the provincial legislatures, the latter to the Federal parliament: *Citizens Insurance Co.* v. *Parsons* (1881) 7 App. Cas. 96, 108; *Bank of Toronto* v. *Lambe* (1887) 12 App. Cas. 575, 581. And so *Hodge* v. *The Queen* (1882) 7 O. A. R. 246, 274. See, generally, Canada's Federal System, pp. 112-122. It is because of the way in which the connotation of the expressions used in secs. 91 and 92 overlap, that it is a wise course for Courts not to attempt exhaustive definitions of their meaning and scope, but to decide each case which arises without entering more largely upon an interpretation of the statute than is necessary for the decision of the particular question in hand: *Citizens Insurance Co.* v. *Parsons* (1881) 9 App. Cas. 96, 109; *John Deere Plow Co.* v. *Wharton* [1915] A. C. 330, 338 *seq.*

87 *John Deere Plow Co.* v. *Wharton* [1915] A. C. 330, 339, 340. So on the argument in this case (Notes of Proceedings, p. 150), Haldane, L.C., is reported as saying: " Without expressing a final opinion about it, I should say ' civil rights ' was a residuary expression. It was intended to bring in a variety of things not comprised in the other heads, including what was not touched by section 91 in the specifically enumerated heads there." See, also, *Bonanza Creek Gold Mining Co.* v. *The King* (1915) 50 S. C. R. 534, 563, 573; *Dulmage* v. *Douglas* (1887) '4 Man. 495; *Reg.* v. *Taylor* (1875) 36 U. C. R. 183, 201.

88 *Grand Trunk R. W. Co.* v. *Attorney-General of Canada* [1907] A. C. 65, 67-9; *City of Montreal* v. *Montreal Street R. W. Co.* [1912] A. C. 333, 343; *Rex* v. *Hill* (1907) 15 O. L. R. 406; *Canadian Northern Ry. Co.* v. *Pszeniczy* (1916) 54 S. C. R. 36, 25 Man. 655. But it is only so far as the provisions come into collision that one Act is affected by the other: *Re Rex* v. *Scott* (1916) 37 O. L. R. 453, 455.

89 *Citizens Insurance Co.* v. *Parsons* (1881) 7 App. Cas. 96, 109; *Russell* v. *The Queen* (1882) 7 App. Cas. 829, 836; *Dobie* v. *Temporalities Board* (1882) 7 App. Cas. 136, 149; *Bank of Toronto* v. *Lambe* (1887) 12 App. Cas. 575, 581. The Privy Council thus corrects the rule as laid down by Gwynne, J., in *City of Fredericton* v. *The Queen* (1880) 3 S. C. R. 505, 564-5; and *Queen* v. *Robertson* (1882) 6 S. C. R. 52, 64, in so far as he predicates of every valid provincial Act that it " does not involve any interference with any of the subjects enumerated in sec. 91 ": see *supra*, pp. 95-6; also Clement, L. of C. C., 3rd ed., pp. 412-3; Legislative Power in Canada, pp. 499-500. " If what has been done is legislation within the general scope of the affirmative words which give the power, and if it violates no express condition or restriction by which that power is limited (in which category would, of course, be included any Act of the Imperial parliament at variance with it), it is not for any Court of Justice to enquire further or to enlarge constructively those conditions or restrictions ": *Queen* v. *Burah* (1878) 3 App. Cas. 889, 903-5. At pp. 483-4 of his L. of C. C., 3rd ed., Judge Clement seems to take the view that, though legislation be within the first 15 enumerated classes of sec. 92, it may fall to be dealt with by the Dominion under its residuary clauses, ' as a matter which is of, or which has attained, such dimensions, as to affect the body politic of the Dominion.' In this, it is respectfully submitted, he is wrong. These provincial powers are exclusive, and cannot in any event be exercised by the Federal parliament: *supra*, p. 96. No. 16 of sec. 92 is in a different position. It places in the exclusive power of the provincial legislatures ' generally all matters of a merely local or private nature in the province.' If a matter has assumed such a general importance to the whole Dominion that it has *ceased to be a*

matter 'of a merely local or private nature in the province,' then the Dominion may legislate on it: *supra*, p. 143.

⁹⁰*Attorney-General of Ontario* v. *Attorney-General of Canada* [1894] A. C. 189 (Dominion ancillary legislation); *Liquor Prohibition Appeal* [1896] A. C. 348 (Dominion residuary legislation); *La Compagnie Hydraulique de St. Francois* v. *Continental Heat and Light Co.* [1909] A. C. 194 (Dominion legislation under an enumerated power: see *per* Duff, J., *In re Companies* (1913) 48 S. C. R. 331, 437, 440); *Tennant* v. *Union Bank of Canada* [1894] A. C. 31 (Dominion enumerated power); *Grand Trunk R. W. Co.* v. *Attorney-General of Canada* [1907] A. C. 65, 68 (Dominion ancillary legislation); *Crown Grain Co.* v. *Day* [1908] A. C. 504, 507 (Dominion legislation as to the Supreme Court of Canada under sec. 101 of the Federation Act). With deference, it is submitted that Davies, J., is mistaken, when in *In re Companies* (1913) 48 S. C. R. 331, 345, he suggests that, while Dominion legislation under this residuary Dominion power is not paramount unless when exercised with reference to a subject matter which has attained national importance (indeed as we have seen, *supra*, p. 75, such Dominion legislation " ought to be strictly confined to such matters as are unquestionably of Canadian interest and importance "), when so legislating upon matters of unquestionably national interest and importance, the Dominion can "trench upon" the enumerated powers of the provincial legislatures, under sec. 92; although Judge Clement (L. of C. C. 3rd ed. pp. 469-470), seems to express a similar view. But their lordships' words in the *Liquor Prohibition Appeal* [1896] A. C. 348, 360 are explicit that " the exercise of legislative power by the parliament of Canada in regard to all matters not enumerated in sec. 91, ought to be strictly confined to such matters as are unquestionably of Canadian interest and importance, *and* ought not to trench upon provincial legislation with respect to *any* of the classes of subjects enumerated in sec. 92." See *supra*, pp. 74-7. Provincial legislation is only affected by Dominion, so far as the two enactments come into collision: *Re Rex* v. *Smith* (1916) 37 O. L. R. 453, 455. And see *Rex* v. *Thorburn* (1917) 41 O. L. R. 39, 39 D. L. R. 300.

⁹¹ *L'Union St. Jacques de Montreal* v. *Belisle* (1874) L. R. 6 P. C. 31, 36-7; *Liquor Prohibition Appeal* [1896] A. C. 348, 366-7, 369; Legislative Power in Canada, at pp. 529-530.

⁹² *Rex* v. *Massey-Harris Co.* (1905) 6 Terr. L. R. 126, 131,

⁹³ Legislative Power in Canada, pp. 534-537.

⁹⁴ *Attorney-General of Canada* v. *Attorney-General of the Provinces* (Fisheries case) [1898] A. C. 700, 715-716.

⁹⁵ A curious question may be raised as to what law governs Dominion subjects in Canada, when and so far as the Dominion

parliament has not legislated on them. There seems no doubt that, in the absence of Dominion legislation relating to them, such Dominion subjects will be subject to any general provincial legislation relating to property and civil rights in each province: Clement, L. of C. C., 3rd ed., pp. 466-7, citing *Canadian Southern R. W. Co.* v. *Jackson* (1890) 17 S. C. R. 316, and *Beard* v. *Steele* (1873) 34 U. C. R. 43. And so *Cook* y, *Dodds* (1903) 6 O. L. R. 608, as to the law of negotiable instruments. But, apart from statute law, the circumstance that the private law of one province, that of Quebec, is derived from a different source to that of the other provinces, seems to make it impossible to say that there is any law underlying Dominion subjects generally prevalent throughout the Dominion: *City of Quebec* v. *The Queen* (1894) 24 S. C. R. 420, 426-430. This would suggest that behind the Dominion legislative powers in Quebec, there is the French law, and in the others the common law. If, on the other hand, there is to be considered to be any one body of law upon Dominion subjects behind Dominion legislation, it seems clear it must be the English common law. See Canada's Federal System, p. 127, n. 7; *Province of Ontario* v. *Dominion of Canada* (1909) 42 S. C. R. 1, 102, [1910] A. C. 637, 645. *Cf.*, Keith, R. G. in D., Vol. 2, p. 793, as to whether there can be said to be a common law of the Commonwealth of Australia. He thinks not, save so far as the prerogatives of the Crown are concerned. Whether there is a common law of the United States—a federal common law—is a disputed question: Article on The Legal and Political Unity of the Empire, by J. H. Morgan, 30 L. Q. R. at p. 397. *Cf.*, also, *per* Duff, J., in British Columbia Electric R. W. Co. v. Victoria, Vancouver, and Eastern R. W. Co. (1913) 48 S, C. R. 98, 122, 13 D. L. R. 308, 322·

⁹⁶ *In re Prohibitory Liquor Laws* (1895)' 24 S. C. R. 170, 232-4; *Queen* v. *Mayor, etc. of Fredericton* (1879) 3 Pugs. & B. (19 N. B.) 139, 168-9; *Dupont* v. *La Cie de Moulin* (1888) 11 L. N. 224; *Bank of Toronto* v. *Lambe* (1885) M. L. R. 1 Q. B. 123, 146. It is noticeable to how great an extent the framers of the Federation Act, as compared with the Constitution of the United States, in fixing the exclusive legislative powers of the Dominion parliament, minimized the disadvantages in the economic and industrial sphere which are inseparable from federal government and divided jurisdictions: Article by Professor Leacock of McGill, published among the Proceedings of the American Political Science Association, 1909. As to whether all Dominion legislation must be of a general character, see *supra*, pp. 88-90.

⁹⁷ *Liquor Prohibition Appeal* [1896] A. C. 348, 359-360; *City of Montreal* v. *Montreal Street Railway* [1912] A. C. 333, 343-4.

98 [1899] A. C. 367, *verbatim* report of argum⸱⸱⸱, pp. 9-10. See same extracted in Canada's Federal System, pp. 136-138.

99 *Quirt* v. *The Queen* (1891) 19 S. C. R. 510, 517, 521-2; S. C. (*sub nom. Reg.* v. *County of Wellington*) 17 O. A. R. 421, 443, 17 O. R. 615, 618; *L'Union St. Jacques de Montreal* v. *Belisle* (1874) L. R. 6 P. C. 31, 36; *The Picton* (1879) 4 S. C. R. 648. It must be admitted, however, that although there is an indication in favour of this view in the passage above referred to in *L'Union St. Jacques de Montreal* v. *Belisle,* and although it seems clearly sound by reason of the exclusive character of these Dominion powers and the *non obstante* clause, there is not as yet any direct decision of the Privy Council on the point. Moreover, the words of the judgment in *Riel* v. *The Queen* (1885) 10 App. Cas. 675, 678, cited *supra,* p. 77, must not be forgotten. In Jl. of Society of Comp. Legisl. Vol. 16, p. 90, A. B. K. (doubtless Mr. Berriedale Keith) says: " the statement based on *Quirt* v. *The Queen,* that the division of legislative power between the provinces and the Dominion does not refer to area, but to subject-matter, requires some qualification in view of the express terms of s. 92 of the B. N. A. Act and *Woodruff* v. *Attorney-General for Ontario,* [1908] A. C. 508."

99a (1874) L. R. 6 P. C. 31-36.

100 (1880) 5 App. Cas. 409.

101 Clement, L. of C. C. 3rd ed. pp. 414-5; *Colonial Building and Investment Association* v. *Attorney-General of Quebec* (1883) 9 App. Cas. 157; *La Compagnie Hydraulique de St. Francois* v. *Continental Heat and Light Co.* [1909] A. C. 194; *Quirt* v. *The Queen* (1891) 19 S. C. R. 510.

102 The matter has been considerably discussed in various arguments before the Judicial Committee in a manner tending to confirm this view. See Legislative Power in Canada, pp. 574-581; Canada's Federal System, pp. 145-147. At the same time, on the argument in *Union Colliery Co.* v. *Bryden* (Martin Meredith and Henderson's Transcript, pp. 34-35), Lord Watson is reported to have said that he thought that, where the question had been discussed at the Bar in some of the cases, the consensus of opinion had been that the Dominion parliament would not have such a power: see the passage quoted, Canada's Federal System, p. 147.

103 *In re Henry Vancini* (1904) 34 S. C. R. 621. As, *e.g.,* by imposing upon the Supreme Court of Canada the duty of answering questions of law or fact when put by the Governor-General in Council: *Attorney-General for Ontario* v. *Attorney-General for Canada* [1912] A. C. 571, 584, 587; or conferring upon provincial Courts jurisdiction with respect to controverted elections to the Dominion House of Commons: *Valin* v. *Langlois* (1879) 5 App. Cas. 115; or conferring a new jurisdiction

upon a British Vice-Admiralty Court in Canada, though an Imperial Court: *Attorney-General of Canada* v. *Flint* (1884) 16 S. C. R. 707, 3 R. & G. 453; or imposing upon a municipality the duty of contributing to the cost of protecting by gates or otherwise, level crossings of railways subject to Dominion jurisdiction: *City of Toronto* v. *Canadian Pacific R. W. Co.* [1908] A. C. 54. *Cf., Re Grand Trunk R. W. Co. and City of Kingston* (1903) 8 Ex. C, R. 349. See, for other cases, Legislative Power in Canada, pp. 512, 517. There is a point of distinction here between our Constitution and that of the United States, where Congress cannot vest jurisdiction in State Courts, nor State legislatures give jurisdiction to the Federal Courts. As, however, Ritchie, C.J., pointed out in *Mercer* v. *Attorney-General of the Dominion* (1881) 5 S. C. R. 538, 638, there is not to be found one word in section 91 of the Federation Act, expressing or implying a right in the Dominion parliament to interfere with provincial executive authority, when acting, of course, under valid provincial Acts, and in connection with matters proper to exclusive provincial jurisdiction.

104 Judge Clement (L. of C. C. 3rd ed. pp. 535-7) inclines to the view that, apart from s. 101, the Dominion parliament can so divest the provincial Courts of jurisdiction over Dominion subject-matters, preferring the dictum of Taschereau, J., in *Valin* v. *Langlois* (1879) 3 S. C. R. 1, 76, to the contrary opinion expressed by Wilson, C.J., in *Crombie* v. *Jackson* (1874) 34 U. C. R. 575, 579-580, But see *supra*, pp. 138-9; *infra*, n. 318.

105 *In re County Courts of British Columbia* (1872) 21 S. C. R. 446.

106 *Citizens Insurance Co.* v. *Parsons* (1881) 7 App. Cas. 96, 109; *Russell* v. *The Queen* (1882) 7 App. Cas. 829, 836; *Bank of Toronto* v. *Lambe* (1887) 12 App. Cas. 575, 587-8.

107 But Ramsay, J., in *Dobie* v. *Temporalities Board* (1880) 3 L. N. 244, 250, says that "there is a sort of floating notion that by conjoint action of different legislatures the incapacity of a local legislature to pass an Act may be in some sort extended." See, too, *In re Prohibitory Liquor Laws* (1895) 24 S. C. R. 170, 241.

108 *Doyle* v. *Falconer* (1866) L. R. 1 P. C. 328; *Barton* v. *Taylor* (1886) 11 App. Cas. 197. See, also, *Landers* v. *Woodworth* (1878) 2 S. C. R. 158. The actual case of a Canadian legislature exercising such inherent powers does not seem yet to have come before the Board. The (Imp.) *Colonial Laws Validity Act, 1865*, s. 5, enacts that every representative colonial legislature 'shall, in respect to the colony under its jurisdiction have, and be deemed at all times to have had, full power to make laws respecting the constitution, power, and procedure of such legislature, provided that such laws shall have been

passed in such manner and form as may from time to time be required by any Act of parliament, letters patent, order in council, or colonial law for the time being in force in the colony.' Where a colonial legislative assembly, as by statute, has power to commit by a general warrant for contempt and breach of privilege of the assembly, there is incident to these powers and privileges vested in the assembly the right of judging for itself what constitutes a contempt, and of ordering the commitment to prison of persons adjudged by the House to have been guilty of contempt and breach of privilege by a general warrant, without setting forth the specific grounds of such commitment, and in that case the Courts have no power to discharge him out of custody: *Speaker of Legislative Assembly of Victoria* v. *Glass* (1871) L. R. 3 P. C. 560. As to the privileges of colonial legislatures generally, see Keith's R. G., in D., Vol. 1, pp. 446-457.

[109] *Doyle* v. *Falconer, ubi sup.,* at p. 339. As to the *lex et consuetudo parliamenti* not applying to colonial legislatures, see further *per* Pollock, C.B., in *Fenton* v. *Hampton* (1858) 11 Moo. P. C. 347, 397. So American legislative bodies, which, like colonial, are not clothed with judicial functions, as the parliament of the United Kingdom is, are held not to possess the general power to punish for contempt: Cooley's Constitutional Limitations, 6th ed, pp. 159-160.

[110] *Fielding* v. *Thomas* [1896] A. C. 600, at pp. 610-611. For the earlier history of this case, see 21 C. L. T. 503. See Legislative Power in Canada, at pp. 741-750, for Canadian and Australian decisions. In *Fielding* v. *Thomas,* the Privy Council state that they "are disposed to think that the House of Assembly (of Nova Scotia) could not constitute itself a Court of Record for the trial of criminal offences"; but that it had power to provide, as it had done by the Act in question in the case before them, that members of the House should be relieved from civil liability for acts done and words spoken in the House, whether it could or could not so relieve them from liability to a criminal prosecution. *Cf. Hill* v. *Weldon* (1845) 3 Kerr (N. B.) 1. In the case of the "Ian McLean" letter in 1914 the N. S. legislature acted as the authority of *Fielding* v. *Thomas.*

[111] As to this section, and its explanation, see *Fielding* v. *Thomas* [1896] A. C. 600, 610, *sub nom. Thomas* v. *Haliburton,* 26 N. S. 55, 59; and an Article by Professor Harrison Moore, 16 L. Q. R. at p. 43. See, also, Memorandum by the late Sir John Bourinot: Hodgins' Prov. Legisl. 1867-1895, App. B., at pp. 1316-7. As to the occasion of the passing of Imp. 38-39 Vict. c. 38, above cited, see Clement, L. of C. C. 3rd ed. p. 44, n. 1.

[112] *Liquidators of the Maritime Bank of Canada* v. *Receiver-General of New Brunswick* [1892] A. C. 437, 442. See Legislative Power in Canada, pp. 705-9. It may be mentioned in this connection that a principle appears established with regard to

the disallowance of Acts by the Governor-General, that where
Acts of doubtful validity have been left to their operation in
certain provinces, similar Acts passed in other provinces should
not afterwards be disallowed: Hodgins' Prov. Legisl. 1867-
1895, at pp. 244a-244b, 817. However, the allowance of provincial legislation by the Dominion Government is not a binding admission of the validity of such legislation, having the
effect of depriving the Federal authority of the right or power
of disallowing statutes similar to those which have been permitted to go into operation: Hodgins, op. cit. p. 537. As to the
Federal power of disallowance in Canada, see supra, pp. 62-6.

113 Dobie v. The Temporalities Board (1882) 7 App. Cas.
136, 147, 150. See this case referred to in the Liquor Prohibition Appeal [1896] A. C. 348, 366-7. As the Minister of Justice points out in his report to the Governor-General of November 22nd, 1900 (Hodg. Prov. Legisl. 1899-1900, p. 16), there
can be no doubt since the Dobie case that the legislature of
Ontario or of Quebec has no power to modify or repeal the provisions of the charter of a corporation created by the legislature of the late province of Canada for the purpose of doing
business in Upper and Lower Canada. It has been held, indeed, in Quebec, in Ex parte O'Neill (1905) R. J. Q. 28 S. C.
304, 309-310, that a provincial legislature cannot repeal any
statute of the old province of Canada applicable equally to
Upper and Lower Canada, even though it be provided that such
repeal is only to take effect in so far as that province is concerned. Sed quære, if it be not a case of interfering with a
corporation incorporated to do business in both provinces, or
controlling a fund administrable in both provinces, but one of
repealing provisions of an Act of the old province of Canada
which had no application except to local and private matters in
the province repealing it. See, also, as illustrating this sec.
129, Lafferty v. Lincoln (1907) 38 S. C. R. 620, over-ruling
Rex v. Lincoln (1907) 5 W. L. R. 301; Pearce v. Kerr (1908)
9 W. L. R. 504; Beaulieu v. La Cite de Montreal (1907) R. J. Q.
32 S. C. 97; McKinnon v. McDougall (1907) 3 E. L. R. 573;
Reg. v. Peters, Stev. N. Br. Dig. 3rd ed. p. 138; Valin v. Langlois (1879) 3 S. C. R. 1, 20-2; Leg. Power in C., pp. 368-371.
As to repeal of Dom. Stats. affecting pre-Confed. Stats. see 38
C. L. T. 163.

114 Russell v. The Queen (1882) 7 App. Cas. 829, 837; a
judgment explained and approved in Hodge v. The Queen
(1883) 9 App. Cas. 117, 129-130, and again interpreted in the
Insurance Companies case (Attorney-General for Canada v.
Attorney-General for Alberta) [1916] A. C. 588, 595-6. For
numerous Canadian cases illustrating the subject generally of
ancillary powers and powers by implication, see Legislative
Power in Canada, pp. 425-468.

115 *E.g., City of Toronto* v. *Bell Telephone Co.* [1905] A. C. 52, which decides that the Dominion parliament have exclusive jurisdiction, not only to incorporate a work or undertaking falling within the exceptions in No. 10 of sec. 92 of the Federation Act, but also to grant the powers required for the construction and establishment of the proposed work, even if, in granting such powers, there be involved an apparent invasion of matters otherwise within exclusive provincial jurisdiction: *Toronto and Niagara Power Co.* v. *Corporation of the Town of North Toronto* [1912] A. C. 834. See *supra,* pp. 119-122. See, also, *Ontario Power Co.* v. *Hewson* (1903) 6 O. L. R. 11, 15; aff. 8 O. L. R. 88, 36 S. C. R. 596; *Regina* v. *County of Wellington* (1890) 17 O. A. R. 421, 440; *Bradburn* v. *Edinburgh Life Assurance Co.* (1903) 5 O. L. R. 657; *In re Railway Act* (1905) 36 S. C. R. 136, 143; and dissenting judgment of Duff, J., in *British Columbia Electric Ry. Co.* v. *Vancouver, Victoria and Eastern Ry. Co.* (1913) 48 S. C. R. 98, 121-2, 13 D. L. R. 321-2: in app. [1914] A. C. 1067. Judge Clement (L. of C. C. 3rd ed. p. 506) suggests that 'the various cases in which so called ancillary legislation has been upheld are cases in which the enactment in controversy dealt with an aspect of the subject upon which provincial legislation would have been incompetent; in other words, the subject in the aspect dealt with fell strictly within one of the enumerated classes of s. 91' of the Federation Act. At all events the Privy Council cannot, perhaps, be said to have encouraged us to go as far as the two dissenting judges in the Australian case of *The King* v. *Barger* (1908) 6 C. L. R. 41, and to say that even the enumerated powers of the federal parliament are to be construed in as full a manner as if the federal parliament were that of a unitary State. In Australia the Courts have, it would appear, on the other hand, established a doctrine of an implied prohibition of interference by the Commonwealth parliament in matters reserved to the State parliaments: Article on the Legal Interpretation of the Commonwealth Constitution by A. B. Keith in J. C. Comp. Legisl. N.S. Vol. XII, pp. 105-127. As to Congress in the United States being entitled to use all proper and suitable means for carrying the powers conferred by the Constitution into effect, see Bryce's Amer. Comm. ed. 1914, Vol. 1, p. 381, n. 2. In conferring some benefit or creating some right, the Dominion parliament may impose as a condition upon those who avail themselves of that benefit, or that right, something which it would be *ultra vires* for it to enact otherwise: *Aitcheson* v. *Mann* (1882-3) 9 O. P. R. 253, 473; *Wilson* v. *Codyre* (1886) 26 N. B. 516; *Flick* v. *Brisbin* (1895) 26 O. R. 423. For a like principle applied to provincial legislatures, see *Kerley* v. *London and Lake Erie Transportation Co.* (1912) 26 O. L. R. 588, reversed on appeal, but not on this point: 28 O. L. R. 606.

116 *City of Toronto* v. *Canadian Pacific R. W. Co.* [1908]
A. C. 54, 58. *Cf. Re Grand Trunk R. W. Co. and City of Kingston* (1903) 8 Ex. C. R. 349.

117 *Montreal Street R. W. Co.* v. *City of Montreal* (1910)
43 S. C. R. 197, 248.

118 [1912] A. C. 333, 344-5.

119 [1896] A. C. 348, 359-360.

120 *Per* Rose, J., in *Doyle* v. *Bell* (1884) 11 O. A. R. 326,
335. See Canada's Federal System, pp. 169-179. A similar
construction seems to have been placed on that provision of the
Constitution of the United States (Art. 1, sec. 8 (18), which
gives power to Congress ' to make all laws which shall be necessary and proper for carrying into execution the foregoing powers, and all other powers vested by this Constitution in the
Government of the United States, or in any department or
officer thereof ': Story's Constitution of the United States, 5th
ed. Vol. 2, at p. 143. " It cannot be too strongly put that with
the wisdom or expediency, or policy of an Act, lawfully passed,
no Court has a word to say ": *Supreme Court References Case*
[1912] A. C. 571, 583. And in estimating the proper relation
of Dominion legislation to provincial powers, the actual conditions of Canada should be borne in mind: *City of Toronto* v.
Canadian Pacific R. W. Co. [1908] A. C. 54, 58 ; *In re Railway
Act* (1905) 36 S. C. R. 136, 145-6. See the general subject of
Dominion intrusion on the provincial area, and the functions
of the Court in that matter discussed *per* Duff, J., in *British
Columbia Electric R. W. Co.* v. *Vancouver, Victoria and Eastern R. W. Co.* (1913) 48 S. C. R. 98, 115-116, 120, 13 D. L. R.
308, 318, 321. The actual decision in that case was overruled
by the Privy Council: [1914] A. C. 1067.

121 *Bank of Toronto* v. *Lambe* (1887) 12 App. Cas. 575, 586;
The Fisheries Case [1898] A. C. 700, 715-716; *Queen* v. *City of
Fredericton* (1879) 3 P. & B. (19 N. B.) 139, 187; *Regina* v.
Wason (1890) 17 O. A. R. 221, 232; Canada's Federal System,
pp. 180-183.

122 Speaking generally, prov. stats. can operate only in provincial territory (see *supra*, 79-80), which, where bounded by
the ocean, appears to extend to but not beyond the three-mile
limit. *Cf.*, the two Newfoundland decisions, reported J. W.
Withers, Queen's Printer, St. John's, N.F., 1897, *Rhodes* v. *Fairweather* (1888) at p. 321, and *Queen* v. *Delepine* (1889) at p.
378; *The Ship "North"* v. *The King* (1906) 37 S. C. R. 385,
11 Ex. C. R. 141, 11 B. C. 473; *The Ship "Frederick Gerring
Jr."* v. *The Queen* (1897) 27 S. C. R. 271; *The Farewell* (1881)
7 Q. L. R. 380. As to the Great Lakes, see *Rex* v. *Meikleham*
(1905) 11 O. L. R. 366. As to a local option by-law covering a

public harbour, see *Mathews* v. *Jenkins* (1907) 3 E. L. R.
(P.E.I.) 577. The Privy Council, however, declined to deal with
the question of the ownership of the land subjacent to the three-
mile limit, and remarked upon the obscurity of the whole
topic, in the recent case regarding the British Columbia Fisheries, *Attorney-General of British Columbia* v. *Attorney-General
for Canada* [1914] A. C. 153, 174-5. But in *In re Quebec
Fisheries* (1917), R. J. Q. 36 K. B. 289, 35 D. L. R. 1, four
out of six judges of the Quebec Court of K. B. held that the
province owns the *solum* of the three mile limit, or, at any
rate, the fisheries therein; and that there was no public
right of fishing in tidal waters in Quebec, the same, if it
ever existed, having been taken away by legislation in that province before Confederation. See the Annotation by the present
writer at 35 D. L. R. p. 28.

123 *Bank of Toronto* v. *Lambe* (1887) 12 App. Cas. 575,
586-7, where a comparison is drawn with the United States
Constitution; followed in *Great North-Western Telegraph Co.* v.
Fortier (1903) R. J. Q. 12 Q. B. 405; *Liquidators of The Mari-
time Bank of Canada* v. *Receiver-General of New Brunswick*
[1892] A. C. 437, 441-3. Thus the provinces may tax salaries of
Dom. officials: *Abbott* v. *City of St. John* (1908) 40 S. C. R. 597;
Webb v. *Outrim* [1897] A. C. 81; *Toronto* v. *Morson* (1917) 40 O.
L. R. 227; or they may require brewers, though holding Domin-
ion licenses, to also take out provincial licenses: *Brewers and
Maltsters' Association of Ontario* v. *Attorney-General of Ontario*
[1897] A. C. 231. *Cf. Fortier* v. *Lambe* (1895) 25 S. C. R. 422.
But, *quære*, if the Dominion licenses embodied Federal statutory authority to carry on business all over Canada: *John
Deere Plow Co.* v. *Wharton* [1915] A. C. 330. See n. 243 *infra*. Or,
again, provincial legislatures may pass local liquor legislation,
although of such character that, in its practical working, it must
interfere with Dominion revenue, and, indirectly, at least, with
business operations outside the province: *Attorney-General of
Manitoba* v. *Manitoba License Holders Association* [1902] A. C.
73.

124 *Bank of Toronto* v. *Lambe, ubi sup.; Union Colliery Co.*
v. *Bryden* [1899] A. C. 580, 585; *The Fisheries Case* [1898]
A. C. 700, 713. *Cf.* despatch of Mr. Joseph Chamberlain to the
Governor of Newfoundland of Dec. 5th, 1898, quoted at length,
Keith, R. G. in D., Vol. II, pp. 1042-7. See, also, *Smith* v. *City
of London* (1909) 20 O. L. R. 133; *Beardmore* v. *City of Toronto* (1909-10), 20 O. L. R. 165, 21 O. L. R. 515; *Electric Development Co.* v. *Attorney-General for Ontario* (1917) 38 O. L.
R. 383.

125 *L'Union St. Jacques de Montreal* v. *Belisle* (1874) L. R.
6 P. C. 31, which itself affords another illustration of the same

constitutional principle. See Canada's Federal System, pp. 193-198.

126 *Union Colliery Co.* v. *Bryden* [1899] A. C. 580, 588.

126a *Hodge* v. *The Queen* (1883) 9 App. Cas. 117, 130; *Attorney-General of the Dominion* v. *Attorney-General of the Provinces* [1898] A. C. 700, 716; *Union Colliery Co.* v. *Bryden* [1899] A. C. 580, 587. Thus as the Privy Council themselves explain in *The Insurance Companies Case* [1916] A. C. 588, 595-6, although the Canada Temperance Act contemplated in certain events, the use of different licensing boards and regulations in different districts, and to this extent legislated in relation to local institutions, yet in *Russell* v. *The Queen* (1882) 7 App. Cas. 829, their lordships thought that this purpose was subordinate to a still wider and legitimate purpose of establishing a uniform system of legislation for prohibiting the liquor traffic throughout Canada excepting under restrictive conditions. The decisions, in fact, which have arisen in connection with laws prohibiting or regulating the liquor traffic—matters which are not to be found specifically mentioned either in sec. 91 or in sec. 92—illustrate in a remarkable way the principle under discussion, a principle, however, which as their lordships say in *The Insurance Companies case, supra,* "ought to be applied only with great caution." See, in addition to *Hodge* v. *The Queen,* and *Russell* v. *The Queen,* above cited, the *Liquor Prohibition Appeal 1895* [1896] A. C. 348; *Brewers and Maltsters Association* v. *Attorney-General for Ontario* [1897] A. C. 231; *The Dominion Liquor License Acts, 1883-4* (the McCarthy Act case): Cass. Dig. S. C. 509; *Attorney-General of Manitoba* v. *Manitoba License Holders' Association* [1902] A. C. 73, 78; *Rex* v. *Thorburn* (1917) 41 O. L. R. 39, 39 D. L. R. 300. See, also, Canada's Federal System, pp. 200-209.

WHOLESALE AND RETAIL. The Privy Council finds that nothing turns, so far as legislative power is concerned, upon the fact that those affected by the statutory provisions deal in wholesale, and not in retail quantities. *In the matter of the Dominion License Acts, 1883-4, supra,* the Privy Council so held; referring to which in the *Queen* v. *McDougall* (1889) 22 N. S. 462, 491, Townshend, J., says: "The distinction between wholesale and retail so far as making it a test of the respective powers of the two legislatures under the British North America Act, has been abandoned." See, further, as to this point, Legislative Power in Canada, pp. 726-730; Canada's Federal System, pp. 436-438. For further illustrations of different aspects of legislation, see Legislative Power in Canada, pp. 411-415, in connection especially with municipal police regulation as contrasted with criminal law. See, also, *City of Montreal* v. *Beau-*

194CANADIAN CONSTITUTIONAL LAW.

vais (1909) 42 S. C. R. 211; *Attorney-General of Ontario* v. *Hamilton Street R. W. Co.* [1903] A. C. 524; *Kerley* v. *London and Lake Erie Transportation Co.* (1912) 26 O. L. R. 588; Pomeroy on Constitutional Law, 1st ed. p. 218, cited by Fournier, J., in *Citizens Insurance Co.* v. *Parsons* (1880) 4 S. C. R. 215, 260; Clement's L. of C. C. 3rd ed. pp. 572-582.

127 *Russell* v. *The Queen* (1882) 7 App. Cas. 829, 838, 840. In this case the Privy Council held that, although the Dominion of Canada *Temperance Act*, the constitutionality of which they upheld, was to be brought into force in those localities only which adopted it by local option exercised in the prescribed manner, yet " the objects and scope of the legislation are still general, namely, to promote temperance by means of a uniform law throughout the Dominion." So in *Attorney-General of Quebec* v. *Queen Insurance Co.* (1878) 3 App. Cas. 1090, their lordships held that a Quebec Act which purported to impose a license on persons carrying on the business of assurance in the province, was virtually a Stamp Act, and, imposing taxation which was not " direct " (see *supra*, pp. 125-6), was, therefore, *ultra vires.* They say: " It is not in substance a License Act at all; it is nothing more nor less than a simple Stamp Act on the policies." And so Lord Watson said on the argument on the *Liquor Prohibition Appeal, 1895* [1896] A. C. 348: " We are always inclined to stand on what is the main substance of the Act in determining under which of these provisions it really falls. That must be determined *secundum subjectam materiam*, according to the purpose of the statute as that can be collected from its leading enactments ": Canada's Federal System, p. 212; *Tai Sing* v. *Maguire* (1878) 1 B. C. (Irving), 101, 104.

128 *Valin* v. *Langlois* (1879) 5 App. Cas. 115, 118.

129 *L'Union St. Jacques de Montreal* v. *Belisle* (1874) L. R. 6 P. C. 31.

130 *Hamilton Powder Co.* v. *Lambe* (1885) M. L. R. 1 Q. B. 460, 466; Legislative Power in Canada, pp. 261-269.

131 And so *Dallaire* v. *La Cité of Quebec* (1907) R. J. Q. 32 S. C. 118, 120. And cf. *City of Fredericton* v. *The Queen* (1880) 3 S. C. R. 505, 545. And so in the United States, where it is Congress whose powers are enumerated, Chief Justice Marshall laid it down that every power alleged to be vested in the national government, or any organ thereof, must be affirmatively shown to have been granted: Bryce, Amer. Comm. ed., 1914, Vol. 1, p. 379. But this doctrine is based on the position of Congress as an agent authorized by the people to exercise enumerated powers, whereas our provincial legislatures, though they have received their powers from the Imperial parliament, do not exercise them as its agents: *supra*, pp. 66-9.

[132] *Citizens Insurance Co.* v. *Parsons* (1881) 7 App. Cas. 96, 116; S. C. 4 S. C. R. 215, 279-280. *Cf. Canadian Pacific R. W. Co.* v. *James Bay R. W. Co.* (1905) 36 S. C. R. 42, 89-90; Legislative Power in Canada, pp. 237-238. But in the Insurance Companies Case (*Attorney-General for Canada* v. *Attorney-General for Alberta* [1916] A. C. 588) when counsel strove to uphold section 4 of the Dominion Insurance Act 1910, on the ground that since 1867 both the Dominion and provincial authorities have treated insurance as a matter within the legislative authority of the Dominion, the following took place:—

Lord Haldane: "Crutches are very helpful to a man who cannot walk without them, but they are not any use to those who can."

Lord Parker of Waddington: "All you mean is this: if there is a doubtful question on the true construction of secs. 91 and 92, it is permissible to refer to what has been done as showing the interpretation which throughout has been put upon the Act of Parliament."

The Lord Chancellor: "You must first look at secs. 91 and 92 and see if there is a doubt."

And on a similar line of argument in *Attorney-General of British Columbia* v. *Attorney-General of Canada* [1914] A. C. 153 (*verbatim* report p. 195) Lord Haldane, L.C., said: "It shows the view which the Dominion took, but it does not cast much light on the question."

[133] *Per* Taschereau, J., in *Mercer* v. *Attorney-General for Ontario* (1881) 5 S. C. R. 538, 673. But, of course, it is futile for the Dominion parliament, or provincial legislatures, or Imperial officials, to assume to declare authoritatively the proper interpretation of the British North America Act: *Lenoir* v. *Ritchie* (1879) 3 S. C. R. 575, 639-640; *Valin* v. *Langlois* (1879) 3 S. C. R. 1, 73-74.

[134] *Valin* v. *Langlois* (1879) 3 S. C. R. 1, 26; Provincial Legislation, 1895, p. 753.

[135] Report of the Judicial Committee in the matter of the Dominion Liquor License Acts, 1883-4: Cass. Dig. S. C. 509; 4 Cart. 342, n. 2; Dom. Sess. Pap. 1885, No. 85; *Corporation of Three Rivers* v. *Sulte* (1882) 5 L. N. 330, 332; *Dobie* v. *The Temporalities Board* (1880) 3 L. N. 244, 251; *King* v. *Commonwealth Court of Conciliation* (1910) 11 C. L. R. 1, 22; Keith, R. G. in D., Vol. 2, pp. 861, 871.

[136] Legislative Power in Canada, pp. 293-299; *In re Dominion Insurance Act*, 1910 (1913) 48 S. C. R. 260, 285. But in the Australian case of the *S.S. Kalibia and Wilson* (1910) 11 C. L. R. 689, the High Court of Australia held that when the legislature assumed jurisdiction over a whole class of ships over some of which it had and over others it had not jurisdiction in point of law, and plainly asserted its intention to place them

on the same footing, the Court would be making a new law if it gave effect to the statute as a law intended to apply to part only of the class; and, therefore, it held that the whole Act was invalid: cited Keith, *op. cit.* Vol. 2, p. 871.

137 *Colonial Building and Investment Association* v. *The Attorney-General of Quebec* (1882) 27 L. C. J. 295, 304; *Regina* v. *Mohr* (1881) 7 Q. L. R. 183, 190. In both these cases the Privy Council on appeal held the Acts *intra vires* in all respects: (1883) 9 App. Cas. 157; [1905] A. C. 52.

138 *Bourgoin* v. *La Compagnie du Chemin de Fer de Montreal* (1880) 5 App. Cas. 381, 406; *Theberge* v. *Laudry* (1876) 2 App. Cas. 102. *Cf.* Cooley's Constitutional Limitations, 6th ed. p. 222.

ESTOPPEL FROM SETTING UP UNCONSTITUTIONALITY OF A STATUTE. There is some authority for saying that one may, under certain circumstances, be estopped from setting up the unconstitutionality of a statute: *Ross* v. *Guilbault* (1881) 4 L.N. 415; *Ross* v. *Canada Agricultural Ins. Co.* (1882), 5 L. N. 23; *Forsyth* v. *Bury* (1888) 15 S. C. R. 543; *McCaffery* v. *Ball* (1889) 34 L. C. J. 91; *Belanger* v. *Caron* (1879) 5 Q. L. R. 19, 25. See, *contra*, however: *Valin* v. *Langlois* (1879) 5 Q. L. R. 1, 15; *L'Union St. Jacques de Montreal* v. *Belisle* (1872) 20 L. C. 29, 39; Clement, L. of C. C. 3rd ed. p. 377. *Cf.*, also, *City of Toronto* v. *Bell Telephone Co.*, 6 O. L. R. 335, 344, 349-50; *L'Association Pharmaceutique* v. *Livernois* (1900) 30 S. C. R. 400; *City of Fredericton* v. *The Queen* (1880) 3 S. C. R. 505, 545; *Gibson* v. *Macdonald* (1885) 7 O. R. 401, 416. See, also, *King* v. *Joe* (1891) 8 Haw. Rep. 287.

139 *Attorney-General for the Dominion* v. *Attorney-General for the Provinces* (The Fisheries case) [1898] A. C. 700, 709-711; *St. Catharines Milling and Lumber Co.* v. *The Queen* (1888) 14 App. Cas. 46. As to the general subject of Dominion and provincial property under the British North America Act, see *supra*, pp. 151-3.

140 *The Fisheries Case* (*supra*, n. 139). Their lordships must not be understood as meaning, for example, that under its power to legislate in relation to Dominion railways, the Dominion parliament cannot provide for the expropriation of lands, for this legislative power necessarily implies such a right to interfere with private property, and even with provincial Crown lands: *Attorney-General of British Columbia* v. *Canadian Pacific R. W. Co.* [1906] A. C. 204, 11 B. C. 289. Neither must they be understood as impugning the power of provincial legislatures to deal freely with vested rights and private property in the province, other than Dominion Crown property: *The Florence Mining Co.* v. *Cobalt Lake Mining Co.* (1910) 102 L. T. 374.

141 *Windsor and Annapolis R. W. Co.* v. *Western Counties
R. W. Co.* (1878) Russ. Eq. 307; in appeal (1882) 7 App. Cas.
178; *Queen* v. *Moss* (1896) 26 S. C. R. 322. But see Canada's
Federal System, pp. 228-229.

142 *Bank of Toronto* v. *Lambe* (1887) 12 App. Cas, 575, 581;
City of Montreal v. *Montreal Street Railway* [1912] A. C. 333,
344; *John Deere Plow Co.* v. *Wharton* [1915] A. C. 330, 340.
The numbers of the various Dominion powers which follow
correspond to the actual numbers of the various items or sub-
sections of sec. 91 of the Federation Act by which they are
conferred. It is to be remembered that the section states that
all these Dominion powers 'notwithstanding anything in this
Act' are 'exclusive.'

143 *Citizens Insurance Co.* v. *Parsons* (1881) 7 App. Cas.
96, 112, in which case they held that a provincial Act intended
to regulate the business of fire insurance companies in the province with a view to securing uniform conditions in their policies fell within No. 13 of sec. 92 ('property and civil rights in
the province') and not within No. 2 of sec. 91 now under consideration. *Cf. Re Dominion Marble Co. in Liquidation* (1917) 35
D. L. R. 63, 66 (Que.). On the argument in the *John Deere Plow
Co. case, supra* (Notes of Proceedings, p. 154), the following is reported as taking place as to this reference to the Union between
England and Scotland:—
Haldane, L.C.: "I should be very sorry to pursue this
reference. I think it is misleading."
Lord Moulton: "It is very misleading."
Haldane, L.C.: "Why it was introduced in Sir Montague
Smith's judgment I do not know. I can conceive nothing more
dangerous."
Sir Robert Finlay: "He only meant to give an illustration of the words 'regulation of trade' which shows it did not
apply to regulating a particular trade locally. That is the point
that Sir Montague Smith was on, and he develops it in the following paragraph."
Lord Moulton: "I think all he wanted to say was, making
certain prescriptions as to the form of contract in a particular
trade is not within the trade and commerce. I do not think
it went further."

144 *Smylie* v. *The Queen* (1900) 27 O. A. R. 172; *Stark* v.
Shuster (1904) 14 Man. 670; *De Varennes* v. *Le Procureur
Général* (1907) R. J. Q. 16 K. B. 571, 31 S. C. R. 444; *City of
Montreal* v. *Beauvais* (1909) 44 S. C. R. 211; and numerous other
Canadian decisions collected, Canada's Federal System, p. 326,
n. 18; Legislative Power in Canada, pp. 455-6, 559, n. 3. *Cf.*
as to the power of Congress to 'regulate commerce with foreign nations, and among the several States, and with the Indian
tribes': Story on the Constitution, 5th ed. Vol. 2, p. 14, which

power has been construed to include legislation regarding
every kind of transportation of goods and passengers, whether
from abroad or from one State to another, regarding navigation, maritime and internal pilotage, maritime contracts, etc.,
together with the control of all navigable waters not situate
wholly within the limits of one State, the construction of all
public works helpful to commerce between States or with foreign countries, the power to regulate or prohibit immigration, and finally power to establish a railway commission and
control of all inter-State traffic: Bryce, Amer. Comm. (ed. 1914)
Vol. 1, p. 383.

145 *Attorney-General for Canada* v. *Attorney-General for
Alberta* (the Insurance Companies case) [1916] A. C. 588;
Hodge v. *The Queen* (1883) 9 App. Cas. 117; *Dominion License
Acts case,* Cass. Dig. S. C. 509, 4 Cart. 342, n. 2; Dom. Sess.
Pap. 1885, No. 85. And see *supra,* n. 143.

146 *The Insurance Companies case* [1916] A. C. 588. And
so, *per* Idington, J., in the Court below, 48 S. C. R. 277.

147 *Cf. per* Idington, J., *In re Companies* (1913) 48 S. C. R.
331, 376. Until *The British Possessions Act,* Imp. 9-10 Vict. c. 94,
the colonies in America were prohibited from imposing duties on
British goods beyond the rates which the Colonial Office deemed
necessary for revenue purposes, and were compelled by the terms
of the *Navigation Acts* (repealed in 1849) to ship their produce in
British ships. In return until 1852, when all preferential duties
were abolished, much colonial produce enjoyed a valuable preference in British markets: so Keith, R. G. in D., Vol. III, pp. 1156-
1187, which comprise a long chapter on 'Trade Relations and
Currency' in the Dominions.

148 *Citizens Insurance Co.* v. *Parsons* (1881) 7 App. Cas.
96, 112; *Bank of Toronto* v. *Lambe* (1887) 12 App. Cas. 575,
586; *Liquor Prohibition Appeal, 1895* [1896] A. C. 348, 373. The
prohibitive enactments of the *Canada Temperance Act* cannot
be regarded as regulations of trade and commerce: *Liquor Prohibition Appeal, 1895* [1896] A. C. 348. On the argument before
the Privy Council in *Russell* v. *The Queen* in 1882 (transcript
from the shorthand notes, 2nd day, p. 18), counsel suggested
that any such matters as embargo laws, intercourse between
different provinces, or coasting regulations, would come within
the power. Imp. 7-8 Edw. VII. c. 64, permitted the Governor
in Council to reciprocate by admitting foreign vessels to the
coasting trade of Canada when British ships were admitted to
their coasts.

149 *Attorney-General for Canada* v. *Attorney-General for
Alberta* (the Insurance Companies case) [1916] A. C. 588, 597.
And so *Farmers' Mutual* v. *Whittaker* (1917) 37 D. L. R. 705
(Alta.)

150 *John Deere Plow Co.* v. *Wharton* [1915] A. C. 330, 340-341. See this judgment discussed at length by the present writer in 35 C. L. T. 148 *seq.* This case shows that under the power we are discussing, the Dominion parliament can authorise all companies incorporated by it to carry on their business throughout Canada, and can give such companies power to sue and be sued, and to contract by their corporate name, and to acquire and hold personal property for the purposes for which they were created, and to exempt individual members of the corporation from personal liability for its debts, obligations, or acts, if they do not violate the provisions of the Act incorporating them (these being things enacted in the sections of the Dominion Companies Act and the Interpretation Act successfully relied on by the John Deere Plow Co. in that case), subject, however, in the case of Dominion companies not incorporated under one of the exclusive enumerated powers, to the general law of the province to the extent above mentioned. But it is to be observed that the Privy Council, in this case, do not pass upon the contention raised that under this power to 'regulate trade and commerce,' the Dominion can incorporate companies. It would be a serious thing if this contention were sustained, because incorporations under an enumerated Dominion power can exercise the powers conferred upon them in independence of provincial legislation: *supra*, p. 120. The question presents itself on this John Deere Plow case: Can then the Dominion under this power prescribe to what extent *individuals* may exercise the power of trading throughout the Dominion, and what limitation should be placed on such powers? If so, being the exercise of an exclusive Dominion power, it will take effect in spite of any provincial legislation. The incorporation of companies under the residuary power is a different matter, for this residuary power only extends to 'matters not coming within the classes of subjects assigned exclusively to the legislatures of the province.' *Supra* pp. 120-1. See, also, *infra*, p. 231, n. 244.

151 As to such legislation by the Dominion, see an Article by F. A. Acland, Deputy-Minister of Labour, entitled 'Canadian Legislation concerning Industrial Disputes,' 36 C. L. T. 207. In *Weidman* v. *Spragge* (1912) 46 S. C. R. 1, the Supreme Court of Canada apparently regard the restraint of trade clauses in the Criminal Code as based on the Dominion jurisdiction over trade and commerce.

152 *Bank of Toronto* v. *Lambe* (1887) 12 App. Cas. 575, 586.

153 *Brewers and Maltsters Association of Ontario* v. *Attorney-General of Ontario* [1897] A. C. 231.

154 *Attorney-General of Manitoba* v. *Manitoba License Holders' Association* [1902] A. C. 73. See, however, *Gold Seal Ltd.* v.

Dominion Express Co. (1917) 37 D. L. R. 769; *Hudson Bay Co.* v. *Heffernan* (1917), 39 D. L. R. 124.

155 *Hull Electric Co.* v. *Ottawa Electric Co.* [1902] A. C. 237.

156 *Hodge* v. *The Queen* (1883) 9 App. Cas. 117. See *supra* pp. 141-2, as to such provincial power.

157 *Citizens Insurance Co.* v. *Parsons* (1881) 7 App. Cas. 96, 108. As to what is "direct" taxation, see *supra*, pp. 125-6.

157a *Attorney-General of Canada* v. *Attorney-General of the Provinces* [1898] A. C. 700, 713-4; *Angers* v. *Queen Insurance Co.* (1887) 16 C. L. J. N. S. 198, 204-5; *Severn* v. *The Queen* (1878) 2 S. C. R. 70, 101.

158 *Algoma Central R. W. Co.* v. *The King* (1901) 7 Ex. C. R. 239. Sec. 122 of the Federation Act expressly places customs and excise laws under the Dominion jurisdiction. Sec. 121 enacts that 'All articles of the growth, produce, or manufacture, of any one of the provinces shall, from and after the Union, be admitted free into each of the other provinces.' *Cf.* 18 Yale L. R. 17-20.

159 As Judge Clement says (L. of C. C. 3rd ed. p. 774), any construction of this exclusive Dominion power other than 'census, and statistics in relation thereto,' would land one in difficulties. 'So construed, it has reference to the census required to be taken every ten years by sec. 8 of the Act, and to the compilation of statistics in reference to nationality and creed, the increase or decrease of population and kindred matters.' There seems to be no reported expression of judicial opinion as to the scope of this item. Yet it is well to have a Dominion power to provide for the collection and collation of statistics from the various provinces, and for the dissemination of information even on matters of provincial jurisdiction, as *e.g.*, education.

160 *City of Montreal* v. *Gordon* (1905) Coutlee's Cases, 343, reversing the Court below, R. J. Q. 24 S. C. 465.

161 *Cunningham* v. *Tomey Homma* [1903] A. C. 151. As to taxing soldiers and sailors, see *Tully* v. *Principal Officers of Her Majesty's Ordnance* (1847) 5 U. C. R. 7, 14; as to which case, *cf.*, Keith R. G. in D., Vol. 1, p. 361, n. 2. See, also, an Article on 'the Law applicable to the Militia of Canada,' by W. E. Hodgins (1901) 21 C. L. T. 169; and another on the same subject, 37 C. L. J. 214. Keith, *op. cit.* Vol. III, pp. 1248-1298, has a long chapter on the subject of military and naval defence in connection with the Dominions; and Clement (L. of C. C. 3rd ed. pp. 201-210) has also a useful chapter entitled 'The Army and Navy.' He prints in an Appendix (p. 1053) the (Imp.) *Colonial Naval Defence Act, 1865*, 28-29 Vict, c. 14, which empowers colonial legislatures with the approval of His Majesty

in Council to provide, at the expense of the colony, for a colonial organized naval force.

¹⁶² As to the provincial power to tax the salaries of Dominion officials, see *supra*, p. 127, and *infra*, n. 263.

¹⁶³ *The Fisheries case* [1898] A. C. 700, 717, affirming 26 S. C. R. 444. *Cf.*, a similar power in Congress by virtue of its right to regulate commerce with foreign nations and among the several States: Story on the Constitution, 5th ed. Vol. 2, pp. 16-17, n. (a).

¹⁶⁴ *McMillan* v. *Southwest Boom Co.* (1878) 1 P. & B. 715. A provincial Act whereby certain persons were authorized to erect piers and booms in a river, provided there was no interference with navigation, was held *intra vires* in *McCaffrey* v. *Hall* (1891) 35 L. C. J. 38. If such a provincial Act permits interference with navigation it will be *ultra vires: Queddy River Driving Boom Co.* v. *Davidson* (1883) 10 S. C. R. 222. *Cf.*, report of Minister of Justice of February 23rd, 1910, in reference to a New Brunswick Act authorizing the City of St. John to build a bridge across the harbour of St. John: Canada's Federal System, pp. 243-4; also Legislative Power in Canada, p. 641, n. 2. So the provincial grant of a water-lot extending into navigable waters cannot authorize the grantee to erect a wharf interfering with navigation: *Wood* v. *Esson* (1884) 9 S. C. R. 239. *Cf. Reg.* v. *Fisher* (1891) 2 Ex. R. 365; *Central Vermont R. W. Co.* v. *Town of St. Johns* (1886) 14 S. C. R. 288; *Queen* v. *St. Johns Gas Light Co.* (1895) 4 Ex. C. R. 326, 346; *In re Provincial Fisheries* (1896) 26 S. C. R. 444, 575; *Normand* v. *St. Lawrence Navigation Co.* (1879) 5 Q. L. R. 215; *Lake Simcoe Ice Co.* v. *McDonald* (1900) 29 O. R. 247, 26 O. A. R. 411, 31 S. C. R. 130. There is a valuable discussion of *Caldwell* v. *McLaren* (1884) 9 App. Cas. 392, and the law generally as to the right of navigation of streams in Canada to be found in the *verbatim* report of the argument before the Privy Council in *Attorney-General for British Columbia* v. *Attorney-General for Canada* [1914] A. C. 153, (King's Printer, Victoria, B. C.) p. 140 *seq*. As to a river down which only loose logs could be floated, not being a "navigable and floatable" river within Art. 400 of the Civil Code of Lower Canada, see *Maclaren* v. *Attorney-General for Quebec* [1914] A. C. 258. As to a public right to navigate non-tidal navigable rivers in Canada, see *Fort George Lumber Co.* v. *Grand Trunk Pacific R. W. Co.* (1915) 24 D. L. R. 527, 528.

¹⁶⁵ *Re Lake Winnipeg Transportation, Lumber and Trading Co.* (1891) 7 M. R. 255, 259. As to the validity of the Dominion Act respecting navigation of Canadian waters, and the applicability of its provisions to collisions occurring therein, see *The Eliza Keith* (1877) 3 Q. L. R. 143; *The Hibernian*, L. R. 4 P. C. 511, 516-7. *Cf.* also *The Farewell* (1881) 7 Q. L. R.

380; Legislative Power in Canada, p. 641, n. 2. It is apparently not material at what port a British vessel is registered. whether, *e.g.*, she is registered in the Dominion, or in Great Britain: *Rhodes* v. *Fairweather* (1888) Nfd. Decisions, p. 337. As to the coasting trade of Canada, see (Imp.) Merchant Shipping Act, 1894, sec. 736; and (Dom.) 7-8 Edw. VII. c. 64, brought into force by Proclamation of Oct. 17th, 1908: Can. Gaz. 1908, p. 1100. As to there being a public right of navigation in Canadian non-tidal waters, see *Fort George Lumber Co.* v. *Grand Trunk Pacific Ry.* (1915) 32 W. L. R. 309; and *per* Anglin, J., in *Keewatin Power Co.* v. *Town of Kenora* (1906) 13 O. L. R. 237, 249-263; and *Leamy* v. *The King* (1915) 15 Ex. C. R. 189. In the *Fort George Lumber Co. case, supra,* Clement, J., expresses the opinion that the Dominion parliament cannot create a public right of navigation over provincial Crown lands covered by water when no public right of navigation now exists. *Sed quære,* see *Attorney-General of British Columbia* v. *Canadian Pacific R. W. Co.* [1906] A. C. 204 and *supra,* pp. 121 and 224, n. 233.

166 *Macdougall* v. *Union Navigation Co.* (1887) 21 L. C. L. 63. See, also, *Union Navigation Co.* v. *Couillard* (1875) 7 R. L. 215.

167 Report of Minister of Justice of February 23rd, 1910: Canada's Federal System, pp. 243-4. It is competent for the Dominion parliament to incorporate under Dominion charter the members of such a provincial company, and so enlarge the scope of their powers and operations: see Legislative Power in Canada, p. 633, n. 2; Canada's Federal System, pp. 480-483; and *supra,* p. 133.

168 Report of Minister of Justice of January 28th, 1889: Hodg. Prov. Legisl. 1867-1895, p. 582. *Cf. ibid.* at pp. 946-7. In *Longueuil Navigation Co.* v. *City of Montreal* (1888) 15 S. C. R. 566, a Quebec Act authorizing the levy of a tax upon ferryboats, including steamboats carrying passengers and goods between Montreal and places not distant more than nine miles, was held *intra vires.*

169 *The Picton* (1879) 4 S. C. R. 648. *Cf. Attorney-General* v, *Flint* (1884) 16 S. C. R. App. 707. The Dominion parliament may confer jurisdiction on a Vice-Admiralty Court on any matter of shipping and navigation within the territorial limits of the Dominion: *The Farewell* (1881) 7 Q. L. R. 380. For a general discussion of the Dominion power in respect to shipping, see *Algoma Central R. W. Co.* v. *The King* (1901) 7 Ex. C. R. 239. In the *King* v. *Martin* (1904) 36 N. B. 448, the Supreme Court of New Brunswick held *intra vires* a Dominion enactment forbidding, under penalty of imprisonment, enticing seamen to desert from their ship or harbouring such deserters. Judge Clement (L. of C. C. 3rd ed. pp. 211-247) has a useful chapter on merchant shipping, in which he discusses the leading provisions of the Imperial *Merchant Shipping Act, 1894,* and

the Imperial and Canadian legislation subsidiary thereto. See, also, *supra*, n. 165. The power of the Commonwealth parliament in Australia to make laws with respect to navigation and shipping, covers only navigation between States: *S.S. Kalibia and Wilson* (1910) 11 C. L. R. 689. Until the Constitution is amended it will, seemingly, be impossible for the Commonwealth parliament to pass any really effective merchant-shipping legislation: Keith, R. G. in D., Vol. II, 868 *seq.*

170 How far precisely this Dominion exclusive power over Quarantine extends has not yet been authoritatively determined. The preservation of public health in a province may, as Mr. Poley says (Federal Systems, p. 329), appear to be a matter of local concern, but one can easily understand how in the case of infectious diseases and epidemics it may assume a Dominion importance. Mr. Poley (*ad loc. cit.*) states that in 1869 a Vaccination Bill was introduced into the Dominion parliament, but not proceeded with on account of its doubtful constitutional validity.

171 Clement (L. of C. C. 3rd ed. p. 714, n. 5) calls attention to the curious error into which Lord Chancellor Selborne fell in *L'Union St. Jacques* v. *Belisle* (1874) L. R. 6 P. C. 31, 37, in not treating "sea coast" as an adjective, and speaking of the whole sea coast as put within the exclusive cognizance of the Dominion legislature. In the argument before the Privy Council in *Attorney-General of British Columbia* v. *Attorney-General of Canada* [1914] A. C. 153, "sea coast" is treated throughout as meaning "sea-coast fisheries," not "sea fisheries," "coast fisheries." Thus (*verbatim* report: William H. Cullin, King's Printer, Victoria, B.C. p. 94) Sir Robt. Finlay speaks of the jurisdiction of the Dominion parliament over "sea coast fisheries," and says: "Sea coast" is used as an adjective there." So, again, *ibid. p.* 45.

172 *Attorney-General of the Dominion* v. *Attorney-General of the Provinces* (The Fisheries case) [1898] A. C. 700, affirming S. C. 26 S. C. R. 444; *Queen* v. *Robertson* (1882) 6 S. C. R. 52. Clement (L. of C. C. 3rd ed. p. 714) expresses the view that laws as to the improvement and increase of the fisheries belonging to a province are no doubt within provincial competence, so long as they do not conflict with federal regulations. It may also be, as Gwynne, J., says (26 S. C. R. at p. 545), that provincial legislation in aid of legislation of the Dominion parliament for the protection of fisheries would be *intra vires*. A provincial Act incorporating a company with power to catch and cure fish was held *intra vires* in *Re Lake Winnipeg Transportation and Lumber Co.* (1891) 7 Man. 255. In *Young* v. *Harnish* (1904) 37 N. S. 213, the Supreme Court of Nova Scotia held that the Dominion *Fisheries Act* was *ultra*

vires in so far as it empowered the grant of exclusive fishing
rights even over a public harbour, and that fisheries do not
necessarily constitute a part of such a harbour. As to public
harbours generally, see *infra*, p. 266, n. 382. On the other hand
in *Miller* v. *Webber* (1910) 8 E. L. R. 460, Graham, E.J., held a
Dominion enactment that ' No one shall use a bag-net, trap-net,
or fish-pound, except under a special license, granted for cap-
turing deep-sea fish other than salmon,' *intra vires* even as
applied to a net set in waters (not being a public harbour)
within three miles of the shore; and says (p. 464) that a distinction may be drawn, and, perhaps, should have been drawn
in *Young* v. *Harnish, supra*, between leases and licenses. As
regards inland waters, the above Privy Council decision settled
the matter, and since 1898 the provinces of Quebec and Ontario
issue all fishery licenses in non-tidal waters, the making and
enforcing the regulations governing the times and methods of
fishing remaining with the Dominion. *Cf. Dion* v. *La Compagnie
de la Baie d' Hudson* (1917) R. J. Q. 51 S. C. 413, holding a Quebec loi de pêche *intra vires*. Nevertheless in a communi-
cation of May 14th, 1901, to the Dominion Government
(Prov. Legisl. 1899-1900, at p. 47), the premier of Ontario expresses dissatisfaction with the position in which it leaves the
provinces in respect to the protection of their property in the
provincial fisheries, and suggests securing an amendment of the
Federation Act in that direction. See Canada's Federal System, pp. 257-259.

[173] *The King* v. *The Ship " North "* (1906) 37 S. C. R. 385,
11 Ex. C. R. 141, 148-150, 11 B. C. 473. As to its being legal
to prevent foreigners from fishing within three miles of the
coast, ' such being the distance to which, according to the marine interpretation and usage of nations, a cannon shot is supposed to reach' (see Opinion of Queen's Advocate in 1854 in
reference to the Falkland Islands, cited Keith, R. G. in D., Vol.
1, p. 373). See also *Reg.* v. *Keyn* (1876) 2 Ex. D. 152, and the
(Imp.) *Territorial Waters Jurisdiction Act, 1878*, 41-42 Vict.
c. 73, as referred to Clement, L. of C. C. 3rd ed. p. 109; also see
supra, pp. 79-80, and Canada's Federal System, p. 259, n. 55 a;
and generally as to Canadian territorial waters and the three-
mile limit: Clement's L. of C. C. 3rd ed. pp. 242-6. As to fishing
in tidal waters being a public right subject only to regulation by
the Dominion parliament, and that in respect to that nothing
is included within the domain of the provincial legislatures:
see *Attorney-General of British Columbia* v. *Attorney-General for
Canada* [1914] A. C. 153, 172-3. The object and effect of sec.
91 of the Federation Act was to place the management and
protection of the cognate public rights of navigation and fishing
in the sea and tidal waters exclusively in the Dominion parliament: *ibid.* That since Magna Charta, no new exclusive fish-

ery can be created by Royal grant in tidal waters: see S. C. p. 170. As to the rights of fishing in non-tidal waters, belonging to the proprietor of the soil, see S. C. p. 171; the question whether such non-tidal waters are navigable or not has no bearing on the question: S. C. p. 173. As to the public having a right to fish in tidal waters, whether on the foreshore, or in creeks, estuaries, and tidal rivers, which since Magna Charta cannot be restricted by prerogative by royal grant or otherwise, and as to provincial legislatures having no right to alter these public rights, see S. C. 171, 173. As to the right of fishing in the sea being a right of the public in general which does not depend on any proprietary title, and that the Dominion has the exclusive right of legislating with regard to it, see S. C. p. 173 *seq.* As to foreshore fisheries, and that a grant of the foreshore does not carry with it the incorporeal hereditament of fishing, see the *verbatim* report of the argument in this Privy Council appeal, which contains a most valuable discussion of all the above points, p. 82 *seq.* It is published, as already intimated, by William H. Cullin, King's Printer, Victoria, B.C. In their judgment [1914] A. C. 153, 174-5, their lordships declined to deal with the alleged proprietary title in the province to the shore around its coast within a marine league. So below, in the Supreme Court, Duff, J. (47 S. C. R. 493, 502), held it unnecessary to deal with it. For the views of the Supreme Court judges in the case generally, see Canada's Federal System, pp. 254-7. Six out of fourteen judges in *Reg.* v. *Keyn* (1876) 2 Ex. D. 63, held the sea within three miles of the coast part of the territory of England. The others did not pass on the point. As to Quebec fisheries, however, see *In re Quebec Fisheries in Tidal Waters* (1917) 34 D. L. R. 1, in which four out of five judges of the Quebec K. B. decide that any public right of fishing in tidal waters in Quebec was abolished by local Act before Confederation, and that the provincial legislature can authorize the provincial Government to grant exclusive rights of fishing therein. The three-mile limit and the ownership of the fisheries therein is also discussed in that case. See the Annotation, *ib,* at p. 28. As to fishery rights generally in the Railway Belt in British Columbia, see the judgment [1914] A. C. at p. 171 *seq.* As to the right of fishing in navigable and floatable rivers in Quebec being exclusively in the Crown, see *Wyatt* v. *Attorney-General of Quebec* [1911] A. C. 489. Under their general taxing-power (*supra*, p. 105) the Dominion parliament can impose a tax by way of license as a condition of the right to fish: S. C. [1914] A. C. 153, 713-4.

[174] *In re International and Interprovincial Ferries* (1905) 36 S. C. R. 206; over-ruling the decision in *Perry* v. *Clergue* (1905) 5 O. L. R. 357, that the right to grant a ferry was a pre-

rogative of the Crown, and a 'royalty.' within the meaning of s. 109 of the Federation Act (*supra*, pp. 153-3), and that it, therefore, belonged to the province. 'In any case, it is clear that the prerogative is not a living one at the present day': Keith, R. G. in D., Vol. 2, p. 682, citing *Dewar* v. *Smith* [1900] S. A. L. R. 38.

175 As to the intervention of the Crown (Imperial) in currency matters in the Dominions, see Keith, R. G. in D., Vol. III, pp. 1183-1187. 'Not only has the Crown a paramount power as to coinage throughout the Empire, which has never yet been abridged by any Act, but the power is one which has been and still is regularly used in respect of the self-governing Dominions when required': *Ibid.* p. 1186.

176 *Canadian Pacific R. W. Co.* v. *Ottawa Fire Insurance Co.* (1907) 39 S. C. R. 405, 425.

177 *Tennant* v. *Union Bank of Canada* [1894] A. C. 31. *Cf. Merchants Bank* v. *Smith* (1884) 8 S. C. R. 512. 'Paper money,' the Privy Council held in the above case, necessarily means the creation of a species of personal property carrying with it rights and privileges which the law of the province did not and could not attach to it. In his report of May 23rd, 1911, the Minister of Justice says that in his opinion, the expression "banking" is intended to describe not only such powers as are inherently banking powers, but, also, those which were, under the laws of the provinces at the time of the Union, exercised by the banks in the carrying on of their business: Canada's Federal System, p. 268.

178 Prov. Legisl. 1904-1906, p. 25. So Hodgins's Prov. Legisl. 1867-1895, p. 1268. *Cf.*, also, Prov. Legisl. 1899-1900, p. 86.

179 Prov. Legisl. 1904-1906, p. 38. See, too, report of the Minister of Justice of January 7th, 1910, and January 12th, 1911, and May 23rd, 1911, upon Quebec Acts of 1909 and 1911, incorporating a company by the name of 'The General Trust,' and conferring upon it the powers of carrying on the business of money-lending, receiving deposits at interest, purchasing bills of exchange, and generally doing an exchange business with other countries: Canada's Federal System, pp. 267-269.

180 *Bank of Toronto* v. *Lambe* (1887) 12 App. Cas. 575; *Town of Windsor* v. *Commercial Bank of Windsor* (1882) 3 R. & S. 420, 427. As to the validity of a provincial Act forbidding the transfer of property till taxes paid, and its applicability to bank shares, see *Heneker* v. *Bank of Montreal* (1895) R. J. Q. 7 S. C. 257.

181 *Cie de C. F. de la Baie des Chaleurs* v. *Nantel* (1896) Q. O. R. 5 Q. B. 64, 71. *Cf.*, also *per* Maclennan, J.A., in *Regina* v. *County of Wellington* (1890) 17 O. A. R. 421, 449-451; Bouri-

not's Parliamentary Procedure and Practice, 2nd ed., at pp. 130, 674; *per* Dorion, C.J., in *Colonial Building and Investment Association* v. *Attorney-General of the Province of Quebec* (1882) 27 L. C. J. 295, 303. In *Reg.* v. *County of Wellington* (1890) 17 O. A. R 421, 428, Hagarty, C.J.O., and in S. C. in the Supreme Court (*sub nom. Quirt* v. *The Queen*) 19 S. C. R. 510, 514, Ritchie, C.J., considered that the Dominion Act there in question, which, reciting the insolvency of the Bank of Upper Canada, provided for its winding-up, was valid under this Dominion power over banking and the incorporation of banks. See, as to this case, *supra*, pp. 88-9, n. 99. Provincial legislation is not " banking legislation " merely because it may relate to money deposited in a bank: *King* v. *Royal Bank of Alberta* (1912) 4 Alta. 249, in app. [1913] A. C. 283; Canada's Federal System, pp. 270-272.

[182] In *Re Bread Sales Act* (1911) 23 O. L. R. 238, 245, Meredith, J., expresses an opinion, *obiter*, that an Ontario enactment that, except as therein excepted, ' no person shall make bread for sale or sell or offer for sale bread except in loaves weighing 24 ounces or 48 pounds avoirdupois ' might be supported under this power. *Sed quære*. *Cf.*, however, *Rex* v. *Kay* (1909) 39 N. B. 278.

[183] Hodgins' Prov. Legisl. 1867-1895, pp. 212-4. *Cf. ibid*, at p. 196; and *per* Allen, C.J., in *The Queen* v. *City of Fredericton* (1879) 3 P. & B. (19 N. B.) 139.. As to the opinion expressed by Taschereau, J., in *Valin* v. *Langlois* (1879) 3 S. C. R. 1, 74, that by virtue of this power and of s. 101 of the Federation Act empowering the Dominion parliament to establish ' any additional Courts for the better administration of the laws of Canada,' parliament could require all judicial proceedings on promissory notes and bills of exchange to be taken before a Federal Court, see *supra*, p. 139, and *infra*, p. 252. n. 318. Clement (L. of C. C. 3rd ed. p. 801)', says ' no question has been raised as to the scope of this class ' (*sc.* of Dominion power) ' or as to the validity of any of the provisions of the Federal Bills of Exchange Act ': (R. S. C. 1906, c. 119).

[184] Canada's Federal System, pp. 274-279.

[185] *Lynch* v. *Canada North-West Land Company* (1881) 19 S. C. R. 204, 212, where it was held that it does not prevent a provincial legislature imposing the addition of a percentage upon all municipal taxes unpaid by a certain date: thus over-ruling *Morden* v. *South Dufferin* (1890) 6 Man. 515; *Ross* v. *Torrance* (1879) 2 L. N. 186; *Schultz* v. *City of Winnipeg* (1884) 6 Man. 40; *Murne* v. *Morrison* (1882) 1 B. C. (pt. 2) 120. See, also, *per* Patterson, J., S. C., at p. 225; *per* Burton, J.A., in *Edgar* v. *The Central Bank* (1888) 15 O. A. R. 193, 202.

[186] *Bradburn* v. *Edinburgh Assurance Co.* (1903) 5 O. L. R. 657. A precisely similar enactment is contained in the Ontario

statute, R. S. O. 1897, c. 205, s. 25. It was argued in the above case that the Dominion power was to legislate as to rate, as to usury, leaving details and matters affecting contracts to the provinces. The learned judge, however, (Britton, J.,) says: " It is one thing to legislate when the contract has sole reference to security for money lent at interest, and quite a different thing to legislate in reference to other contracts when interest is only an incident": pp. 664-6. See, further, as to the constitutionality of such legislation: Can. Hans. 1886, p. 440; Bourinot's Parliamentary Procedure and Practice, 2nd ed. p. 671; Legislative Power in Canada, p. 389, n. 1. It is no infringement of the Dominion power for a provincial Act to authorize municipalities to issue debentures bearing interest not exceeding seven per cent. or any other rate: *Schultz* v. *City of Winnipeg* (1884) 6 Man. 35, 45. *Cf. per* Gwynne, J., in *Lynch* v. *Canada North-West Land Co.* (1891) 19 S. C. R. 204, 223; and *Royal Canadian Insurance* v. *Montreal Warehousing Co.* (1880) 3 L. N. 155, 157. On the argument before the Privy Council in the recent *Insurance Companies case* [1916] A. C. 588, the following is reported to have taken place (*verbatim* report, 3rd day, p. 27 *seq.*) :—

Lord Parker of Waddington: " . . Take enumeration No. 19 of sec. 91, which is ' interest.' Do you say it would be impossible to pass something like the Money Lenders Act in this country under that."

Sir Robert Finlay " . . I very much doubt whether the business of a money-lender would be within the scope of the enactment."

The Lord Chan.: " The question is whether the power to regulate interest under sec. 91 is confined to the regulation of interest in all transactions in which money lending is involved, or whether it can be applied to a particular trade, the trade of money lending. Is it general?

Sir Robt. Finlay: " I think the power as to interest would need to be general."

The Lord Chan.: " They must regulate the interest on the loan whoever lends the money."

187 An historical distinction exists between bankruptcy and insolvency laws. The former were passed for the protection of creditors against insolvent and fraudulent traders; the latter for the protection of ordinary private debtors,—poor and distressed, but honest: Poley's Federal Systems, p. 97. As to its being proper to assign the widest meaning to the words ' bankruptcy and insolvency' in this subsection, so as to include the right to declare certain things acts of insolvency, or evidence of insolvency, though not previously regarded as such, see *Re Colonial Investment Co.* (1913) 23 Man. 871, 15 D. L. R. 634.

188 *Attorney-General for Ontario* v. *Attorney-General for Canada* [1894] A. C. 189. *Cf. Tooke Bros. Limited* v. *Brock and*

Patterson, Limited (1907) 3 E. L. R. (N.B.) 270, 272. Their lordships had previously said in *L'Union St. Jacques* v. *Belisle* (1874) L. R. 6 P. C. 31, 36-37: "Bankruptcy and insolvency are well-known legal terms expressing systems of legislation with which the subjects of this country and probably of most other civilized communities are perfectly familiar. The words describe in their known sense provisions made by law for the administration of the estates of persons who may become bankrupt or insolvent, according to rules and definitions prescribed by law, including of course the conditions in which that law is to be brought into operation, the manner in which it is to be brought into operation and the effect of its operation." Clement (L. of C. C. 3rd ed. p. 804), italicizes the words " according to rules and definitions prescribed by law," and says—' the phrase in italics indicates that bankruptcy and insolvency— for the terms are really synonymous—is a purely legal concept which the Dominion parliament alone can create.' A provincial Act providing for the relief of debtors imprisoned on process out of the County Courts does not infringe the Dominion exclusive power: *Johnson* v. *Poyntz* (1881) 2 R. & G. 193 ; nor does one to wind up a company on the ground that it is heavily embarrassed and cannot extricate itself without having recourse to the double liability of the shareholders: *In re Wallace Huestis Grey Stone Co.* (1881) Russ. Eq. 461. *Queen* v. *Chandler* (1869) 1 Hann. 548, seems wrongly decided in holding *ultra vires* a provincial Act providing for the discharge of insolvent debtors, after examination, where their inability to pay was shewn, and they had made no fraudulent transfer or undue preference. The Dominion can legislate under this power for the distribution of the estate of the debtor either with or without a discharge of his liabilities: *Dupont* v. *La Cie de Moulin a Bardeau Charfréné* (1888) 11 L. N. 255. But ante-Confederation legislation on bankruptcy and insolvency is an unreliable guide to the scope of this Dominion power. *Cf. Crombie* v. *Jackson* (1874) 34 U. C. R. 575, 580; *per* Maclennan, J.A., in *Regina* v. *County of Wellington*, 17 O. A. R. 421, 452-3. Certainly the British North America Act "must not be read by the light of an Ontario candle alone," without reference to what the law was in other parts of the Dominion: *per* Ritchie, C.J., in *Severn* v. *The Queen* (1878) 2 S. C. R. 70, 99.

[189] See 43 Vict. c. 1, D., respecting the existing legislation. The Dominion Winding-up Acts are insolvency legislation, and are properly made applicable to companies, though incorporated under provincial legislation: *Re Eldorado Union Store Co.* (1886) 6 R. & G. 514 ; *Schoolbred* v. *Clarke* (1890) 17 S. C.

R. 265; *Re Clark* v. *Union Fire Ins. Co.* (1887) 14 O. R. 618,
16 O. A. R. 161; *Re Farmers Bank, Lindsay's case* (1916) 35
O. L. R. 470, *q. v.* as to the Dominion parliament having power
to determine the machinery by which such corporations shall be
wound up, as by referring and delegating to any officer of the
Court any of the powers conferred upon the Court by the
Act; and in *Allen* v. *Hanson* (1890) 13 L. N. 129, 16 Q. L. R.
78, a provision in the Dominion Winding-up Act making that statute applicable to incorporated trading companies
' doing business in Canada, no matter where incorporated,' was
held *intra vires*, all the Act seeking to do in the case of foreign
corporations being to protect and regulate the property in Canada, and to protect the rights of creditors of such corporations upon their property in Canada. But this must not be
understood as meaning that the Dominion Act can authorize the making of an original winding-up order of a
company incorporated under the Imperial Joint Stock Companies Act and never incorporated in Canada: S. C. at p.
674; *Merchants Bank of Halifax* v. *Gillespie* (1885) 10 S.
C. R. 312. *Cf. per* Henry, J., S.C., p. 334; Lindley's Law of Companies, 6th ed. pp. 840, 1225. See, also *per* Strong, J., in *Allen*
v. *Hanson* (1890) 18 S. C. R. 667. But in *Re Briton Medical
Life Association* (1886) 12 O. R. 441, 447-8, Dominion enactments requiring foreign insurance companies doing business in
Canada to make a certain deposit with the Minister of Finance
were held *intra vires*, and an order made, on petition, for the
distribution of the deposit made by an English company among
the Canadian policy holders, notwithstanding that proceedings
to wind up the company were pending before the English Courts.
By virtue of its exclusive power over bankruptcy and insolvency, the Dominion parliament can provide for the winding-
up in insolvency, of a single institution: *Quirt* v. *The Queen*
(1891) 19 S. C. R. 510, affirming the decisions of the Courts
below reported *sub nom. Regina* v. *County of Wellington*, 17
O. R. 615, 17 O. A. R. 421. Maclennan, J.A., however, dissented:
17 O. A. R. at pp. 452-3. *Cf.* Legislative Power in Canada, pp.
568-571.

190 *Cushing* v. *Dupuy* (1880) 5 App. Cas. 409. *Cf. Attorney-
General of Ontario* v. *Attorney-General of Canada* [1894] A. C. 189;
Thrasher Case (1882) 1 B. C. (Irving) 170, 208. For Canadian
decisions and *dicta* illustrating the same point, see Legislative
Power in Canada, at pp. 439-442.

191 *Hodge* v. *The Queen* (1882) 7 O. A. R. 246, 274.

192 *Attorney-General of Canada* v. *Sam Chak* (1909) 44 N.
S. 19; *In re Henry Vancini* (1904) 34 S. C. R. 621; *Geller* v.
Loughrin (1911) 24 O. L. R. 18, 25, 33; Canada's Federal Sys-
tem, pp. 148-151; Legislative Power in Canada, pp. 511-517.

¹⁹³ *Supra,* pp. 97-8. And so *per* Osler, J.A·, in *Clarkson* v. *Ontario Bank* (1888) 15 O. A. R. 166, 191.

¹⁹⁴ *In re De Veber* (1882) 21 N. B. 397, 398-9, 425.

¹⁹⁵ *Parent* v. *Trudel* (1887) 13 Q. L. R. 136, 139.

¹⁹⁶ *Attorney-General of Ontario* v. *Attorney-General of Canada* [1894] A. C. 189; *In re Killam* (1878) 14 L. J. N. S. at pp. 242-3. In *Baie des Chaleurs R. W. Co.* v. *Nantel* (1896) R. J. Q. 9 S. C. 47, 5 Q. B. 65, the Quebec Court of Queen's Bench held that a provincial statute which provided for the sequestration of the property of a railway company subsidized by the province, when such company was insolvent, and that the sequestrator should take possession, complete and work the railway, and that, if he had not the means at his disposal for that, the Court might order the sheriff to seize and sell the road and its rolling stock, applied to, and was *intra vires* as applying to, a Dominion railway company. *Sed quære*, See *Re Iron Clay Brick Manufacturing Co.* (1889) 19 O. R. 113, 119-120; Reports of Minister of Justice of Nov. 11th, 1899, and January 8th, 1904: Prov. Legisl. 1899-1900, at p. 49, and 1901-3, at p. 27; Legislative Power in Canada, p. 457, n, 2, where *In re Dominion Provident Benevolent and Endowment Association* (1894) 25 O. R. 619, is discussed. There would seem, however, no objection to provincial legislation providing for the liquidation of the affairs of companies, under special circumstances, and irrespective of whether they be insolvent or not: *McClanaghan* v. *St. Ann's Mutual Building Society* (1880) 24 L. C. J. 162. *Cf. L'Union St. Jacques de Montreal* v. *Belisle* (1874) L. R. 6 P. C. 31. On the other hand, as to the Dominion Winding-up Act only applying where there is insolvency, since otherwise it would be *ultra vires*, see *Re Cramp Steel Co. Limited* (1908) 16 O. L. R. 230, But see *Re Colonial Investment Co.* (1913) 23 Man. 871. The correctness of the view taken in this last case is doubted: Clement, L. of C. C. 3rd ed. p. 810. As to Dominion bankruptcy legislation, though free to deal with civil rights in the province as regards creditors or contributories or assets of the company, it is not free to deal with the rights of third parties not creditors or contributories of the company, *e.g.*, parties asserting merely a legal or equitable right to property which they claim, and which the company holds in trust for them: *per* Davies, J., in *Stewart* v. *Le Page* (1916) 53 S. C. R. 337, 342-3. The judgments of the other judges, however, cannot be said to support this view.

¹⁹⁷ In *In re Bell Telephone Co.* (1884) 7 O. R. 605, 612, Osler, J.A., held *intra vires* sec. 28 of the Dominion Patent Act, 1872, which, after specifying certain cases in which patents are to be null and void, provided that in case dispute should arise

under that section, it should be settled by the Minister of Agriculture, whose decision should be final. *Cf. per* Henry, J., in *Smith* v. *Goldie* (1882) 9 S. C. R. 46, 68, 69; *per* Ritchie, C.J., in *Valin* v. *Langlois* (1879) 3 S. C. R. 1, 23-24; and *supra*, pp. 138-9. The decision also may be justified upon the principle illustrated and acted upon in *Aitcheson* v. *Mann* (1882-3) 9 P. R. 253, 472; *Wilson* v. *Codyre* (1886) 26 N. B. 516; and *Flick* v. *Brisbin* (1895) 26 O. R. 423, namely, that, in conferring some benefit or creating some right, the Dominion parliament may impose as a condition upon those who avail themselves of that benefit or right, something which it would be *ultra vires* for it to enact otherwise. For the application of a like principle to provincial legislatures, see *Kerley* v. *London and Lake Erie Transportation Co.* (1912) 26 O. L. R. 588; reversed on app., but not on this point, 28 O. L. R. 606. As to whether the Attorney-General for the province or for Canada, is the proper person to institute proceedings in the nature of a *scire facias* to set aside a patent of invention, see *Reg.* v. *Pattee* (1871) 5 O. P. R. 292; *Mousseau* v. *Bate* (1883) 27 L. C. J. 153. Clement (L. of C. C. 3rd ed. pp. 589-595), discusses generally the subject of the Crown in the Courts. By the Ontario Execution Act (9 Edw. VII, c. 47, s. 16), all rights under letters patent of invention and any equitable or other right, property, interest, or equity of redemption therein may be seized and sold under execution by the sheriff: notice of the seizure is to be given to the patent office, and the interest of the debtor 'shall be bound from the time when the notice is received there.' In *Felt Gas Compressing Co.* v. *Felt* (1914) 5 O. W. N. 821, Falconbridge, C.J., held the section *intra vires*, treating it as legislation in regard to 'property and civil rights in the province.'

[198] *Smiles* v. *Belford* (1873) 23 Gr. 590, 1 O. A. R. 436. See *per* Burton, J.A., 1 O. A. R. at p. 443; *per* Moss, J.A., *ibid.* at pp. 447-8. See, also, *Anglo-Canadian Music Publishers Association* v. *Suckling* (1889) 17 O. R. 239; *Black* v. *Imperial Book Co.* (1903) 5 O. L. R. 184.

[199] *Hubert* v. *Mary* (1906) R. J. Q. 15 K. B. 381; *Smiles* v. *Belford, supra;* Imperial Copyright Act 1911, and the speech of Mr. Sydney Buxton in introducing the Bill into the House of Commons, on July 26th, 1910; Legislative Power in Canada, pp. 222-231; Canada's Federal System, pp. 51-53, 56, 295; Dom. Sess. Pap. 1894, No. 50, p. 7; Articles on Canadian Copyright, in 49 Amer. L. R. 675, and 24 C. L. J. 307, 347 (1904).

[200] The Dominion Constitution leaves the Indians in the same position as any other persons with regard to the franchise, but there are certain restrictions in some of the pro-

vinces with regard to the Indians being enrolled as electors, though these restrictions are only partial: see, generally, Keith, R. G. in D., Vol. II, pp. 1055-7, who deals in the same chapter with the general subject of the treatment and position of the native races in all the Dominions.

201 *St. Catherines Milling and Lumber Co.* v. *The Queen* (1888) 14 App. Cas. 46, 59. And see *per* Patterson, J.A., S. C. 13 O. A. R. 148, 170. See, also, *Ontario Mining Co.* v. *Seybold* [1903] A. C. 73; reported below 32 S. C. R. 1, 32 O. R. 801, 31 O. R. 386. See, too, *Caldwell* v. *Fraser* (1898) unreported, apparently, except in McPherson and Clark's Law of Mines, pp. 15-24, but referred to at some length in Canada's Federal System, pp. 299-301; approved of by Boyd, C., in *Ontario Mining Co.* v. *Seybold* (1899) 31 O. R. at p. 400. On the argument before the Privy Council in *The Bonanza Creek Gold Mining Co. case* [1916] A. C. 566 (7th day, p. 72, Martin Meredith and Co.'s transcript), Mr. Newcombe referring to the *St. Catherines Milling and Lumber Co. case*, says:—"It will be the other way about, I submit, when the surrender is in one of the new provinces. They are exempted under sec. 91, under 'Public debt and property.' The local authority has no legislative jurisdiction over the public property of Canada."

Viscount Haldane: "No, they have legislative jurisdiction over the whole territory, and they have some power to make laws there, but they cannot legislate with regard to the title."

As to when lands are 'lands reserved for Indians' within this item, see *Attorney-General for Canada* v. *Giroux* (1916) 53 S. C. R. 172, 30 D. L. R. 123. Idington, J., held in this case (30 D. L. R. at p. 132) that for this Dominion legislative power to apply, the alleged reserve must have been duly constituted on or before July 1st, 1867.

202 *Church* v. *Fenton* (1880) 28 C. P. 384, 4 O. A. R. 159, 5 S. C. R. 239. But Indians may possess an interest in lands 'other than that of the Province in the same' within the meaning of sec. 109 of the Federation Act (*supra*, pp. 152-3) as *e.g.* the constituted rents of a seigniory in the province of Quebec, in which case it will be for the Dominion Government (it having the administration of the affairs and property of Indians in Canada, as an implication from its legislative power) to sue for and collect the arrears of such rents: *Mowat* v. *Casgrain* (1896) R. J. Q. 6 Q. B. 12. Whether the legislative power of the provinces over lands when divested of the Indian title is controlled and limited by the provisions of any treaties made with the Indians at the time of their surrender does not appear to have come up for decision: but, in any case, the Dominion Government would, no doubt, always protect the rights

of the Indians under such treaties by its power of disallowance. *Cf.* Hodgins' Prov. Legisl. 1867-1895, pp. 1024-8, *q.v.* on
the general subject of the Indian title. As to any right of
indemnity of the Dominion against the province for expenditure involved in obtaining surrender of Indian lands, see *Dominion of Canada* v. *Province of Ontario* [1910] A. C. 637. For
a case where Indians surrendered their beneficial interest in
trust under a special instrument without destroying it, see *per*
Duff, J., in *Attorney-General for Canada* v *Giroux* (1916) 30
D. L. R. 123, 140, 53 S. C. R. 172.

203 *Cunningham* v. *Tomey Homma* [1903] A. C. 151. As
to Indians being subject to the general laws of the province, see
Rex v. *Hill* (1907) 15 O. L. R. 406; *Rex* v. *Martin* (1917), 39 D.
L. R. 635. As to the power of the Dominion parliament to remove Indians from the scope of provincial laws, see *per* Osler,
J.A., S. C. at p. 410. But, *cf.*, *per* Meredith, J.A., S. C., at
p. 414.

204 *Cunningham* v. *Tomey Homma* [1903] A. C. 151. Accordingly their lordships refused to hold that a British Columbia Act which enacted that no Japanese, whether naturalized or not, should have his name placed on the register of
voters, or be entitled to vote at the elections for the provincial
legislature was *ultra vires*. In the previous case of *Union Colliery
Co.* v. *Bryden* [1899] A. C. 580, they had observed that the subject of naturalization seems *primâ facie* to include the power
of enacting what shall be the consequences of naturalization,
but they expressly guarded themselves against being supposed
to be defining the precise meaning of "naturalization" in the
clause under consideration. They observed that it could hardly
have been intended to give the Dominion parliament the exclusive right to legislate for the children of naturalized aliens,
who are not aliens requiring to be naturalized, but are natural
.born Canadians, but that sub-s. 25 of sec. 91 might properly
be construed as conferring that power in the case of naturalized aliens after naturalization. They say, at p. 586: "Every
alien when naturalized in Canada becomes, *ipso facto*, a Canadian subject of the Queen." See now The (Imp.) *British Nationality and Status of Aliens Act 1914*, 4-5 Geo. V. c. 17, under
which 'the Government of any British possession shall have the
same power to grant a certificate of naturalization as the Secretary of State has under this Act,' subject in the case of Canada,
however, to the adoption by the Dominion parliament of this
enactment. It was adopted in Canada by the Naturalization
Act, 1914, 4-5 Geo. V, c. 44, amended 5 Geo. V, c. 7. See Article
on the Effect of a Certificate of Naturalization, by F. B. Ed-
wards, 30 L. Q. R. 433. 'Prior to the Imperial *British Nationality and Status of Aliens Act, 1914*, no colonial Act could, it is
conceived, alter the status of an alien or—which is the same

thing—confer full Imperial nationality': Clement, L. of C. C.
3rd. ed. p. 670. 'Naturalization, in these days, has very seldom,
if ever, any other object than to confer political privileges;
that is to say, to give to a person really identified by residence
with the nation's affairs, a voice in its government. All else is
a negligible quantity': Clement's L. of C. C. 3rd ed. pp. 677-8.
See, further, on the general subject, Article *sub voce* "British
Subject" in Encyclopedia of Laws of England, 2nd ed. Vol. 2,
p. 413 *seq.;* Article by John W. Salmond on Citizenship and
Allegiance (1901) 17 L. Q. R. 270, 18 L. Q. R. 49; and one on
Naturalization of Aliens (1905) 25 C. L. T. 181, by N. W.
Hoyles; Keith's Responsible Government in the Dominions,
Vol. III, pp. 1322-4. As to the right of the Dominion to legislate
for the deportation of aliens and others see *Attorney-General* v.
Cain [1906] A. C. 542, as commented on in Jl. of Comp. Legisl.
Vol. 16, pp. 89-91; and Keith's *Imp. Unity and the Dom.* (1916)
pp. 130-1; *R. G. in D.*, Vol. 1, p. 394. See, also, Jl. of Comp.
Legisl. Vol. XI., pp. 235-7.

205 *Cunningham* v. *Tomey Homma* [1903] A. C. 151, referred
to in the last note; *Union Colliery Co.* v. *Bryden* [1899] A. C.
580, where the Board held *ultra vires* the provisions of section
4 of the British Columbia *Coal Mines Regulation Act*, as
amended in 1890, which prohibited Chinamen, naturalized or
not, of full age from employment in underground coal workings; decided the other way below, *sub nom. Coal Mines Regulation Amendment Act, 1890*, (1896) 5 B. C. 306. See for a discussion of these cases, and generally as to this Dominion
power: Canada's Federal System, pp. 303-314. They are discussed also in *In re Coal Mines Regulation Act* (1904) 10 B. C.
408, and in *Quong Wing* v. *The King, infra.* See also *Rex* v.
Priest (1904) 10 B. C. 436. Clement seems to agree with the
summarization of the results of the cases in the text: L. of C. C.
3rd ed. p. 678. Note that in *Quong Wing* v. *The King* (1914)
49 S. C. R. 440, the Supreme Court (Idington, J., dissenting)
held *intra vires* a Saskatchewan enactment that 'No person
shall employ in any capacity any white woman or girl, or permit any white woman or girl to reside or lodge in or to work
in or, save as a *bona fide* customer in a public apartment
thereof only, to frequent any restaurant, laundry, or other place
of business or amusement owned, kept or managed by any . . .
Chinaman . .'; and on May 19th, 1914, leave to appeal to the
Privy Council was refused. The Supreme Court held the legislation primarily directed to the protection of white children
and girls in the province; and that it was not an Act dealing
with aliens or naturalized subjects as such. The reason given
by the Judicial Committee for refusing leave to appeal was
that—"In their lordships' opinion this is too wide a question
to raise in a case of this kind in which an individual subject is

complaining "; but they stated they would reconsider the question of giving leave if the Attorney-General of the Dominion came and said he desired to have the constitutional question raised in this case. In 1899 a British Columbia Act providing that no person other than a British subject might thereafter be recognized as having any right or interest in any of the mining properties to which the British Columbia *Placer Mining Act* applied was disallowed, after the Secretary of State of the Colonies had objected to it as *ultra vires*: Prov. Legisl. 1899-1900 p. 120. In *Reg.* v. *Wing Chong* (1886) 1 B. C. (pt. 2) 150, noted Wheeler's Confederation Law at p. 122, a British Columbia Act was held *ultra vires* as imposing unequal taxation on Chinese (see *supra*, pp. 63-5), and contrary to Imperial treaty. The Privy Council gave leave to appeal, but the appeal was not proceeded with. See Canada's Federal System p. 310, n. 162, a. For other cases of disallowance of provincial legislation as *ultra vires* on the principle of *Union Colliery Co.* v. *Bryden* [1899] A. C. 580, see Prov. Legisl. 1904-1906, pp. 130-131, 138; *ibid.* 1899-1900, pp. 134-8; also pp. 104, 123. *Cf.*, also, Prov. Legisl. 1901-1903, pp. 64, 74-75. It would seem that the status of individual aliens resident in the colonies must be determined by the law of England, but the rights and liabilities incidental to such status must be determined by the law of the colony: *In re Adams* (1837) 1 Mo. P. C. 460; *Donegani* v. *Donegani* (1835) 3 Kn. 63, 85. *Cf. Regina* v. *Brierly* (1887) 14 O. R. 525, 533. As to the power of the Dominion parliament to legislate for the expulsion of aliens, see *Attorney-General of Canada* v. *Cain* [1906] A. C. 542, commented on Keith (R. G. in D., Vol. I, p. 393 *seq.*,); Articles in (1899) 33 Amer. L. R. 90; (1905) 25 C. L. T. 487; and Jl. of Comp. Legisl. N.S. Vol. II, pp. 235-8. An alien has no power to sue on account of non-admittance into a British colony: *Musgrove* v. *Chun Teong Toy* [1891] A. C. 272. See, also, Keith, R. G. in D., Vol. III, p. 1621, and Judge Clement, L. of C. C. 3rd ed. pp. 190-200; *Robtelmes* v. *Brenan* (1906) 4 C. L. R. 395; *McKelvey* v. *Meagher* (1906) *ibid.* p. 265; *The Canadian Prisoners' case* (1839) 5 M. & W. 32, reported as *Leonard Watson's case*, 9 A. & E. 731, is discussed at length in Legislative Power in Canada, pp. 323-5. In no view does that case carry the matter involved in it beyond the power of the legislature of Upper Canada to legislate for transportation in criminal cases, such power being rested upon special recognition by the Imperial parliament. As to the power of a provincial legislature to provide for the deportation of alien insane paupers, see Hodg. Prov. Legisl. 1867-1895, p. 1325. 'The validity of provincial Acts debarring aliens from acquiring Crown land by pre-emption or direct purchase, has not been questioned in any reported case': Clement, L. of C. C. 3rd ed.

p. 676, n. 8. Strong, C.J., however, in *In re Criminal Code sections relating to Bigamy* (1897), 27 S. C. R. 461, 475, says: " The effect of alienage upon the local tenure of land may be dealt with by a colonial legislature." The Privy Council point out in *Union Colliery Co.* v. *Bryden, supra*, that the abstinence of the Dominion parliament from legislating to the full limit of its powers could not have the effect of transferring to any provincial legislature any legislative power assigned to the Dominion exclusively by section 91 of the B. N. A. Act, 1867.

206 *Attorney-General for Canada* v. *Attorney-General for Alberta* (The Insurance Companies case) [1916] A. C. 597.

207 See, however, Prov. Legisl. 1904-1906, p. 3. See. further. as to such legislation, Legislative Power in Canada, pp. 459-460. See, also, *per* Strong, C.J., *In re Criminal Code sections relating to Bigamy* (1897) 27 S. C. R. 461, 474-5.

208 Mr. Keith (R. G. in D. Vol. III, pp. 1238-1247) has a chapter on ' Divorce and Status.' He begins with the remarks that: 'Questions of marriage degrees and of divorce have arisen chiefly in the case of the Australian colonies, probably because there only has there been no body of opinion sufficiently strong to prevent the matter becoming the subject of advanced legislation. Such legislation was rendered impossible once and for all in Canada since 1867, and the date of admission of the provinces of British Columbia and Prince Edward Island, by the transfer to the Dominion of the sole power of legislating upon this topic, and the existence of the Roman Catholic population of Quebec and elsewhere in the Dominion. Newfoundland, with a large Catholic population, is in like case.'

209 *In re Marriage Legislation in Canada* [1912] A. C. 880, reported below 46 S. C. R. 132. *Cf. Citizens Insurance Co.* v. *Parsons* (1881) 7 App. Cas. 96, 108. See, also, Legislative Power in Canada, p. 488, n. 3.

210 But note the provincial power extends only to ' solemnization in the province.' This is not saying that a provincial legislature can validly enact that the inhabitants of the province of which it is the legislature, shall not be validly married if they cross the border and are married according to the solemnities and under the conditions prescribed by the legislature of another province for marriages within the borders of that province. *Cf. Swifte* v. *Attorney-General of Ireland* [1912] A. C. 276. For the opinion of the law officers of the Crown in England in 1870 as to the scope of these Dominion and provincial powers, see Dom. Sess. Pap. 1877, No. 89, p. 340; Canada's Federal System, p. 318. As to marriages of Catholics by Protestants in Quebec, see Keith's R. G. in D., Vol. III, p. 1625.

211 See *May* v. *May* (1910) 22 O. L. R. 559, 565; *Malot* v. *Malot* (1913) 4 W. N. 1405; *Peppiatt* v. *Peppiatt* (1916) 34 O. L. R. 121, 36 O. L. R. 427—discussed in 35 C. L. T. 505, 36 C. L. T. 795-797. *Cf. T.* v. *B.* (1907) 15 O. L. R. 224, where Boyd, C., held that the Court has no jurisdiction to entertain an action to have a marriage declared void by reason of alleged incapacity and impotence of one of the parties. *Cf.* Clement, L. of C. C., 3rd ed., pp. 557-562, who seems on the whole to favour the view that the provincial Act is valid. As to the jurisdiction, dating from before Confederation, of the Divorce Courts in British Columbia and Nova Scotia, see *Watts* v. *Watts* [1908] A. C. 573, 13 B. C. 281; *Sheppard* v. *Sheppard* (1908) 13 B. C. 486. *Cf.* 14 B. C. 142. As to the British Columbia legislature having no jurisdiction to confer on the full Court of the province any appellate jurisdiction in divorce matters, see *Scott* v. *Scott* (1891) 14 B. C. 316. As to the provincial legislatures in New Brunswick not being able to legislate as to the rules of evidence by which a right of divorce is to be established, see Hodg. Prov. Legisl. 1896-8, p. 52. In Prince Edward Island, under local statute 5 Wm. IV, c. 10 (1836), the Lieutenant-Governor and Council have jurisdiction in all matters touching marriage and divorce; this power, however, has been disused in the Island for a century: Keith, *Imperial Unity*, p. 456. See Article on Divorce, by N. W. Hoyles, 37 C. L. J. 481 *seq.;* and one upon *Peppiatt* v. *Peppiatt and the Marriage Act of Ontario*, by Alfred B. Morine, K.C., in 52 C. L. J. 369. See, also, Article on *The Law of Divorce in Saskatchewan and Other Western Provinces*, by Bram Thompson, M.A., (T.C.D.) 37 C. L. T. 687, contending that the Supreme Court in such provinces has jurisdiction to grant divorce under the *Imp. Matrimonial Causes Act*, 1857, (20-21 Vict,, c. 85). See, also, 37 C. L. T. 679-680. Apart from what is stated above, divorce can only be obtained through the medium of a Dominion Act of Parliament following upon a favourable report of the Senate Divorce Committee, a fact tending to make divorce a privilege of the well-to-do, by reason of the cost. There have been recent cases of the House of Commons debating and rejecting Divorce Bills even after favourable reports of the Senate Committee, *e.g.*, in the cases of the Power Divorce Bill in 1913, and of the Kennedy and Gordon Divorce Bills in 1917. See now as to Man., *Walker* v. *W.*, 39 D. L. R. 731; as to Sask., *Fletcher* v. *F.* (1918), not reported.

212 *Attorney-General for Ontario* v. *Hamilton Street R. W. Co.* [1903] A. C. 524, reported below (1902) 1 O. W. R. 312. The Privy Council in this case held the Ontario *Lord's Day Act* " treated as a whole " *ultra vires* as legislation upon criminal law. It was followed in *In re Legislation respecting Abstention from Labour on Sunday* (1905) 35 S. C. R. 581; *Rex* v. *Yaldon* (1908) 17 O. A. R. 179; see, also, as to it, *Ouimet* v.

Bazin (1912) 46 S. C. R. 502, 528. See, also, as to it, *Rodrique* v.
Parish of Ste. Prosper (1917) 40 D. L. R. 30, 37 D. L. R. 321,
where Sup. Ct. of Can. held that a municipal corporation cannot by by-law close restaurants on Sunday, such being legislation
on a criminal matter on the principle of *Ouimet* v, *Bazin*. As to
the words " treated as a whole," see *Couture* v. *Panos* (1908) R.
J. Q. 17 K. B. 560, 564. Notwithstanding, Boyd, C., held in
Kerley v. *London and Lake Erie Transportation Co.* (1912) 26
O. L. R. 588, that provincial legislatures can require provincial
companies, as a condition of their incorporation, not to work
on Sunday.

213 *Rex* v. *Lee* (1911) 23 O. L. R. 490, where Meredith, J.A.,
suggests (pp. 495-6), that the proper rule may be: " Parliament
has power to prohibit and punish any act as a crime provided
it does not violate any exclusive powers of legislation conferred upon the legislatures of the provinces; and the Courts
cannot consider the question further than to see whether there
has been a violation of such exclusive powers." The distinction
between *malum in se* and *malum prohibitum* was drawn by
Allen, C.J., in *Queen* v. *City of Fredericton* (1879) 3 P. & B.
139, 188-9; and by Street, J., in *Regina* v. *Wason* (1889) 17
O. R. 58, 64. Archambault, J. reiterates it in spite of the above
Privy Council judgment: *Ouimet* v. *Bazin* (1910) R. J. Q. 20
K. B. 416, 433.

214 *Cf.* the words of Lord Davey upon the argument in
Attorney-General for Ontario v. *Hamilton Street R. W.* [1903]
A. C. 524, as reported in Marten Meredith, Henderson and White's
Shorthand Notes, 2nd day, pp. 25-26, quoted Canada's Federal
System, pp. 324-6. But note *per* Anglin, J., in *Ouimet* v. *Bazin*
(1912) 46 S. C. R. 502, 528, where he says that he cannot " ac-
cede to an argument which involves the view that legislation
held to be criminal in one province of Canada may be regarded
as something different in another province." In *Weidman* v.
Spragge (1912) 46 S. C. R. 1, the Supreme Court apparently
regards the restraint of trade clauses in the Criminal Code as
based on the Dominion jurisdiction over criminal law.

215 Report of Sir J. Thompson as Minister of Justice, of
February 12th, 1894, on some Quebec Acts: Hodg. Prov. Legisl.
1867-1895, p. 461; *L'Association St. Jean Baptiste* v. *Brault*
(1900) 30 S. C. R. 598; *Thomson* v. *Wishart* (1910) 19 Man.
340. On the other hand, if a thing is within the exclusive
competency of the provincial legislature, it would not seem
that the Dominion parliament could indirectly take that away
from the province by making it a crime to do that which the
provincial legislatures had authority to say might be done:
Canada's Federal System, pp. 325-6. But with regard to the
exclusive provincial power under No. 16 of sec. 92, it must

always be remembered that it is only over matters of a 'merely local or private nature in the province': see Legislative Power in Canada, pp. 383-5, and supra, p. 143.

[216] The Queen v. Halifax Electric Tramway Co. (1888) 30 N. S. 469; McDonald v. McGuish (1883) 5 R. & G. 1, followed in The Queen v. Wolfe (1886) 7 R. & G. 24; per Osler, J.A., in Reg. v. Eli (1886) 13 O. A. R. 526, 533, cited per Moss, C.J.O., in In re Boucher (1879) 4 O. A. R. 191; Reg. v. Lake (1878) 43 U. C. R. 515; Reg. v. Toland (1892) 22 O. R. 505.

[217] Per Osler, J.A., in Reg. v. Wason (1890) 17 O. A. R. 221, 241. See the subject discussed in 10 C. L. T. at p. 223 seq. On the other hand parliament can declare that what previously constituted a criminal offence shall no longer do so, although a procedure in form criminal be kept alive, as was done in the case of certain common nuisances by sec. 223 of the Criminal Code, R. S. C. c. 146: Toronto Railway Company v. The King [1917] A. C. 630.

[218] Dallaire v. La Cite de Quebec (1907) R. J. Q. 32 S. C. 118; and supra, p. 98, supra, pp. 141-2. In re Rex v. Scott (1916) 37 O. L. R. 453, 456, a provincial enactment declaring that a person found drunk in a public place in a municipality in which a local option by-law is in force, or in which no tavern or shop license is issued, is guilty of an offence, was held intra vires. But, see contra, Beaulieu v. La Cité de Montreal (1907) R. J. Q. 32 S. C. 97.

[219] Ward v. Reed (1882) 22 N. B. 279, specially referred to in Pigeon v. Mainville (1893) 17 L. N. 68, 72. Cf. Clemens v. Bemer (1871) 7 C. L. J. 126; Curran v. Grand Trunk R. W. Co. (1898) 25 O. A. R. 407; Ex parte Perkins (1884) 24 N. B. 66, 70; Ex parte Porter (1889) 28 N. B. 587. Quære, as to the view expressed in this last case, that if the provincial legislature has established a Court for the trial of certain criminal offences, the Dominion must either make use of that Court or establish a Dominion Court under sec. 101 of the B. N. A. Act, but cannot select some other provincial Court in lieu of the one so established by the provincial legislature: see supra, p. 90. As to appeals in criminal cases, see infra, n. 376.

[220] Reg. v. Bittle (1892) 21 O. R. 605. And see Legislative Power in Canada, at pp. 464, n. 1, 463-8; Reg. v. Fox (1899) 18 O. P. R. 343; McMurrer v. Jenkins (1907) 3 E. L. R. 149; Ex parte Duncan (1872) 16 L. C. J. 188, 191. As to the provision of the Criminal Code (R. S. C. 1906, c. 146, s. 13) that 'no civil remedy for any act or omission shall be suspended or affected, by reason that such act or omission amounts to a criminal offence' being ultra vires as assuming to bind provincial civil tribunals, see Paquet v. Lavoie (1898) R. J. Q. 7 Q. B. 277;

cf. Richer v. *Gervais* (1894) R. J. Q. 6 S. C. 254, as to a Dominion Act declaring a non-juridical day: *contra*, Clement, L. of C. C., 3rd ed. p. 588 *seq*. As to the power of the Dominion parliament to include within the criminal law of Canada acts of Canadian subjects committed abroad, see *In re Criminal Code Sections relating to Bigamy* (1897) 27 S. C. R. 461, and *supra*, pp. 79-80. See, also, *Chandler* v. *Main* (1863) 16 Wisc. 422. As to the Dominion power over criminal law, not debarring a provincial legislature preventing and punishing obstruction to the business of legislation, although the interference or obstruction be of a character involving the commission of a criminal offence or bringing the offender within reach of the criminal law, see *Fielding* v. *Thomas* [1896] A. C. 600; Legislative Power in Canada, p. 784, n. 1, and *supra*, pp. 91-2. As to the right of disposal of fines, forfeitures, and penalties under provincial penal laws belonging to the provincial legislatures, and under Dominion criminal law, to the Dominion parliament, see Report of Mr. David Mills, as Minister of Justice, of August 12th, 1898; Hodg. Prov. Legisl. 1896-8, pp. 118-9. As to the latter point, however, and the right to legislate respecting the forfeiture of goods of a felon, see *Dumphy* v. *Kehoe* (1891) 21 R. L. 119.

221 (1906) 12 O. L. R. 1. See, also, *Reg.* v. *O'Rourke* (1882) 32 C. P. 388, 1 O. R. 464, and *Reg.* v. *Prevost* (1885) M. L. R. 1 Q. B. 477; *Sproule* v. *Reginam* (1886) 2 B. C. (Irving) Pt. II. 219; *Hubbard* v. *City of Edmonton* (1917) Alta., 3 W. W. R. 732, in which the Appellate Division, (Stuart, J., diss.) held that the right to a jury is not a substantive right as distinguished from a matter of procedure. Stuart, J., holds that the question whether a jury shall be present to determine the issues of fact is a matter of the constitution of the Court, not of procedure in the Court, citing *inter alia*, *Reg.* v. *O'Rourke, supra*.

222 So, too, *Queen* v. *Cox* (1898) 31 N. S. 311, where Ritchie, J., says (p. 314): "In many cases the procedure of the Court is so combined with its constitution and organization that it seems very difficult, if not impossible, to define clearly the line separating them." In *Copeland-Chatterson Ltd.* v. *Business Systems Ltd.* (1908) 16 O. L. R. 481, the Court of Appeal held that the issue of a writ of sequestration against the property of defendants for contempt of Court in disobeying an injunction in a civil matter was not within No. 27 of sec. 91 of the B. N. A. Act 1867.

223 *Reg.* v. *Bradshaw* (1876) 38 U. C. R. 564. Followed *Queen* v. *Malloy* (1900) 4 Can. Cr. Cas. 116. As to there being no appeal to the Privy Council from the judgment of the Supreme Court of Canada in a criminal case, see *infra*, n. 376. Fixing dates when Courts shall sit is "organization of the Courts," not

"procedure": *King* v. *Cook* (1914) 19 D. L. R. 318, *per* Ritchie, J.

224 *In re Chantler* (1905) 9 O. L. R. 529. *Cf.* Report of Minister of Justice of May 10th, 1892, upon provincial Acts dealing with the right of jurors to affirm, the rights of challenge of jurors, the right of jurors to separate in certain cases, in connection with criminal trials, being *ultra vires*: Hodg. Prov. Legisl. 1867-1895, p. 1125. *Cf.*, however, *Regina* v. *Levinger* (1892) 22 O. R. 690, overruling *Reg.* v. *Toland* (1892) 22 O. W. N. 505, and holding a provincial Act authorizing the General Sessions of the Peace to try persons charged with forgery to be *intra vires*. As to a provincial legislature authorizing Industrial Schools as places of confinement for persons convicted of criminal offences under the Dominion criminal law, see report of Minister of Justice of December 13th, 1910: Canada's Federal System, p. 578.

225 *Ex parte Vancini* (1904) 36 N. B. 456; followed *Geller* v. *Loughrin* (1911) 24 O. L. R. 18, see at pp. 23, 33. 35. *Ex parte Vancini* went to the Supreme Court, 34 S. C. R. 621, where, however, it was found unnecessary to pass upon the constitutionality of the provincial Act. See Canada's Federal System pp. 336-7.

226 The legislative jurisdiction of the parliament of Canada under this head cannot be in any way limited, restricted, or affected by any provincial legislation in the province, whether before or after Confederation: *In re New Brunswick Penitentiary* (1880), Coutlee's Sup. Ct. Cas. 24. A Dominion Act establishing a Boys' Industrial Home as a prison, was held *intra vires* in *In re Goodspeed* (1903) 36 N. B. 91.

227 Judge Clement (L. of C. C. 3rd ed. p. 50) thinks, all the same, that legislation by the parliament of Canada as regards the office of Lieutenant-Governor would be 'repugnant to the spirit of the British North America Act,' referring to *Liquidators of the Maritime Bank of Canada* v. *Receiver-General of New Brunswick* [1892] A. C. 437, 443. As to Lieutenant-Governors, see *supra*, pp. 61-2.

228 See an annotation dealing with every aspect of subs. (c) in *Can. Ry. Cas.*, Vol. 20, pp. 128-134, being an annotation to *Hamilton, Grimsby and Beamsville R. W. Co.* v. *Attorney-General for Ontario* [1916] 2 A. C. 583, 29 D. L. R. 521, *infra*, n. 238-9. On the argument in *John Deere Plow Co.* v. *Wharton* [1915] A. C. 330, the contention was raised, although their lordships did not find it necessary to pass expressly upon it, that the enterprise of such a company as the John Deere Plow Co.—a trading company dealing throughout the Dominion in agricultural implements and machinery, and doing a general agency, commission and mercantile business, was a "work or under-

taking extending beyond the limits of the province" within
the above clause of the Act; and that, therefore, the incorporation of such a company fell under the above enumerated Dominion power, No. 29 of sec. 91: (Notes of Proceedings,
p. 82). Their lordships evidently rejected the contention, because, if they had approved of it, they could not have held the
John Deere Plow Co., as they did, subject to the general laws
of the provinces. *Cf. In re Companies* (1913) 48 S. C. R. 331,
at p. 440. In *City of Montreal* v. *Montreal Street Railway*
[1912] A. C. 333, 342, their lordships observed that the works
and undertakings referred to in No. 10 of sec. 92, were "physical things, not services." On the argument in the *John Deere
Plow Co. case, supra* (Notes of Proceedings, p. 84), Halsbury,
L.C., is reported as saying: "Some of the physical enterprises
'connect,' others 'extend.' For instance, a canal, you might
say, 'extended beyond the limits of the province,' naturally,
whereas a line of steamships might 'connect' the provinces
when they were separated by water. I do not think the use of
the word 'extend' as an alternative to 'connect' by any
means shuts out the notion that there is a physical genus you
are dealing with." On the same argument, Sir Robt. Finlay
argued that one reason for the introduction of the word "extending" as well as "connecting," was that "connecting" was
obviously applicable only to means of transit or of communi-
cation, whereas by waterworks or by sewage works you have
works "extending" over parts of two provinces, and it was
necessary to include such works, although they could not be
said to "connect" the one province with the other. In *Dow*
v. *Black* (*sub nom.* Queen v. *Dow*) (1873) 1 Pugs. 300. Fisher,
J., held that the words "extending beyond the limits of the
province," refer to extension into another province, not extension into a foreign country: *sed quære.* See *per* Garrow, J.A.,
City of Toronto v. *Bell Telephone Co.* (1903) 6 O. L. R. 335,
343; *per* Davies, J., *Hewson* v. *Ontario Power Co.* (1905) 36
S. C. R. 596, 606. On general subject of legislative power as to
companies, see 54 C. L. J. 81.

229 *Montreal Street Ry. case* [1912] A. C. 333, 43 S. C. R. 197.
The power thus given to the Dominion parliament is to make
laws in relation to "railways" connecting the province with any
other or others of the provinces, or extending beyond the limits of the province, and not merely in relation to railway companies. *Canadian Pacific R. W. Co.* v. *Corporation of Bonsecours*
[1899] A. C. 367 (*supra*, p. 121, n. 235) illustrates this. Until
1903, a Committee of the Cabinet, styled the Railway Committee of the Privy Council, administered the Dominion Railway
Act, thus exercising a certain supervision and control over all
Canadian railways. The Dominion parliament then abolished
this committee, and appointed in its stead a Board composed

of three Railway Commissioners (the number was afterwards
increased to six). This Board regulates Dominion railways
under large powers. For Dominion jurisdiction generally in respect to railways, see Canada's Federal System, pp. 337-371.

230 *Toronto and Niagara Power Co.* v. *Corporation of the
Town of North Toronto* [1912] A. C. 831; *City of Toronto* v. *Bell
Telephone Co.* [1905] A. C. 52, reported below 6 O. L. R. 335,
3 O. L. R. 465, overruling *Regina* v. *Mohr* (1881) 7 Q. L. R. 183.
This *Bell Telephone case*, in the Court below, brings up the
curious question of the possibility and effect of a Dominion
corporation consenting that its powers should in certain respects
be limited and defined by a provincial Act: per Garrow, J.A.,
6 O. L. R. at p. 344, against any such power; per Maclennan, J.A.,
6 O. L. R. at pp. 349-50, 352, in favour of such power, and the
binding effect of such consent. The Privy Council state simply
that they do not find any trace of such agreement.

231 Per Garrow, J.A., in *City of Toronto* v. *Bell Telephone
Co.* (1903) 6 O. L. R. 335, 342; per Maclennan, J.A., S. C. 6 O.
L. R. 335, 347; *La Cie Hydraulique St. Francois* v. *Continental
Heat and Light Co.* [1909] A. C. 194, *supra*, pp. 84-5. *Cf. Tennant*
v. *Union Bank of Canada* [1894] A. C. 31. See, also, *Canada
Atlantic R. W. Co.* v. *Montreal & Ottawa R. W. Co.* (1901) 2
O. L. R. 336; *Montreal & Ottawa R. W. Co.* v. *City of Ottawa*
(1902) 4 O. L. R. 56, as to railway companies which have taken
proper proceedings under the Dominion Railways Act, and been
duly authorized thereunder to cross highways in a city, not
being bound to make compensation to the municipality therefor. As to the provincial power to tax Dominion corporations,
see *supra*, p. 127.

232 *Citizens Insurance Co.* v. *Parsons* (1881) 7 App. Cas.
96; *Colonial Building and Investment Association* v. *Attorney-
General of Quebec* (1883) 9 App. Cas. 157; per Idington, J., in
Canadian Pacific R. W. Co. v. *Ottawa Fire Insurance Co.* (1907),
39 S. C. R. 405, 442, and *In re Companies* (1913) 48 S. C. R.
331, 374; Legislative Power in Canada, pp. 618-623, 626-7. And
as to provisions of the Quebec Civil Code relating to pledge and
hypothec not being interfered with by such Dominion incorporation, see *Re Dominion Marble Co. in Liquidation* (1917)
35 D. L. R. 63, 66. It does not follow that the Dominion Government might not, on occasion, veto a provincial Act affecting such
Dominion companies, as was done in 1907 with some Nova
Scotia legislation: Canada's Federal System, p. 343, n. 235.

233 *Attorney-General of British Columbia* v. *Canadian Pa-
cific R. W. Co.* [1906] A. C. 204: reported below 11 B. C. 289.
But as to this case, see per Duff, J., in *Attorney-General for
Canada* v. *Ritchie Contracting and Supply Co.* (1915) 26 D. L.
R. 51, 66. *Cf. Booth* v. *McIntyre* (1880) 31 C. P. 183, 193. But

when a provincial Act sought to expropriate Dominion public
lands for the purposes of a provincial railway, the Act was disallowed by the Dominion Government: Hodgins' Prov. Legisl.
1867-1895, at pp. 855-6. "When you have an existing Dominion
railway, all matters relating to the physical interference with
the works of that railway or the management of the railway
should be regarded as wholly withdrawn from provincial authority": per Duff, J., in In re Alberta Railway Act (1913) 48
S. C. R. 9, 38.

234 See supra, pp. 94-5; City of Montreal v. Montreal Street
R. W. Co. [1912] A. C. 333, reported below 43 S. C. R. 197,
where the Privy Council held a provision of the Dominion Railway Act, 1906, as to through traffic, not thus necessarily incidental and, therefore, ultra vires. Cf. in the Court below, per
Duff, J., at pp. 227-8. On the other hand, in Grand Trunk R.
W. Co. v. Attorney-General of Canada [1907] A. C. 65, referred
to Couture v. Panos (1908) R. J. Q. 17 K. B. 561, the Privy
Council held intra vires, as so necessarily incidental, Dominion
enactments prohibiting "contracting out" on the part of Dominion railway companies from liability to pay damages for personal injury to their servants. The Dominion parliament may
possibly even have power to bind Dominion railways as to the
terms upon which they shall carry goods delivered to them in a
foreign country: Macdonald v. Grand Trunk R. W. Co. (1900)
31 O. R. 663, 665. The Dominion can regulate generally the
liability of federal railways to their employees for negligence:
In re Railway Act (1905) 36 S. C. R. 136, see, especially, at pp.
141, 143, 144-5. So Curran v. Grand Trunk R. W. Co. (1898)
25 O. A. R. 407, as to Dominion provisions in respect to damages recoverable. Cf., also, as to provisions of provincial
Workmen's Compensation Acts, relating to railway frogs applying only to provincial railways: per Osler, J.A., Washington v.
Grand Trunk R. W. Co. (1897) 24 O. A. R. 183, 185-186; Monk-
house v. Grand Trunk R. W. Co. (1883) 8 O. A. R. 637; Legislative Power in Canada, p. 596, n. 1. But cf. Canada Southern
R. W. Co. v. Jackson (1890) 17 S. C. R. 316, where the provisions of a provincial Act giving railway employees a right of
action under certain circumstances for the negligence of fellow
servants was held applicable to a railway which had been declared a work for the benefit of Canada under sub-s. 10 (b) of
section 92 of the Federation Act; see supra, p. 122. Legislation providing for the safety of the public at or upon a line of
railway is a matter relating to such work or undertaking: Re
Canadian Pacific R. W. Co. and County and Township of York
(1918) 25 O. A. R. 65, 79. Thus, again, the Dominion parliament may forbid directors of a federal railway company being
interested in contracts with the company: Macdonald v. Rior-

dan (1899) 30 S. C. R. 619: reported below, R. J. Q. 8 Q. B. 555. *Cf.* as to this case, *per* Anglin, J., in *Montreal Street R. W. Co.* v. *City of Montreal* (1910) 43 S. C. R. 197. And the Privy Council have held *intra vires* provisions of the Dominion *Railway Act* authorizing the Railway Committee of the Privy Council to require federal railways to protect crossings over streets or highways by watchmen, or gates, or otherwise, and to apportion the costs of such protection between the railway company and any persons interested therein, as *e.g.*, the municipality: *City of Toronto* v. *Canadian Pacific R. W. Co.* [1908] A. C. 54; *Grand Trunk R. W. Co.* v. *Attorney-General of Canada* [1907] A. C. 65. *Cf. Re Canadian Pacific R. W. Co. and County and Township of York* (1896-8) 27 O. R. 559, 25 O. A. R. 65. But this does not mean that everyone benefited may be so assessed for improvements: *British Columbia Electric R. W. Co.* v. *Vancouver, Victoria & Eastern R. W. Co.* [1914] A. C. 1067, overruling the Court below: 48 S. C. R. 98, where see *per* Duff, J., at pp. 114-5, 118, 121-2. See the above Privy Council decisions cited and applied to the matter of immigration: *In re Narain Singh* (1908) 13 B. C. 477. *Cf. Toronto Railway Co.* v. *Corporation of the City of Toronto* (1916) 53 S. C. R. 222; *British Columbia Electric R. W. Co.* v. *Vancouver, Victoria, and Eastern R. W. Co.* [1914] A. C. 1067. For other cases illustrating the Dominion incidental powers when legislating with respect to federal railways, see *Grand Trunk R. W. Co.* v. *Hamilton Radial Electric Co.* (1897) 29 O. R. 143, respecting legislation regarding railway crossings, as to which see Canada's Federal System, p. 352, n. 253; *In re Portage Extension of the Red River Valley Railway,* Cas. Sup. Ct. Dig. 487; *City of Toronto* v. *Grand Trunk R. W. Co.* (1906) 37 S. C. R. 232, as to which see *per* Idington, J., in *Montreal Street R. W. Co.* v. *City of Montreal* (1910) 43 S. C. R. 197, 219, where Anglin, J., at pp. 238-248, discusses very thoroughly what Dominion legislation will in different cases be held necessarily incidental to the complete and effective control of federal railways; *Grand Trunk R. W. Co.* v. *City of Toronto* (1900) 32 O. R. 120, 127, *seq.; In re Alberta Railway Act* (1913) 48 S. C. R. 9; *McArthur* v. *Northern Pacific Junction R. W. Co.* (1888-1890), 15 O. R. 723, 17 O. A. R. 86, where a six-month limitation imposed by Dominion enactment for damage actions against Dominion railway companies was upheld by three judges, two *contra*. See it referred to in *Montreal Street R. W. Co.* v. *City of Montreal* (1910) 43 S. C. R. 197, 243. This legislation was also upheld in *Levesque* v. *New Brunswick R. W. Co.* (1889) 29 N. B. 588, and *Canadian Northern Ry. Co.* v. *Pszenienzy* (1916) 54 S. C. R. 36, 25 Man. 655, where *held* that the Dominion parliament has power to provide a limitation of one year for the recovery of damages for injury sustained by reason of the construction or operation of a Dominion railway; and that the fact that a Manitoba *Employers Liability Act* allowed two years for bringing an action under it did not affect the matter. *Cf.*, lastly, *Keefer* v. *Todd* (1885) 2 B. C. (Irving) 249, 255, where Dominion Acts for the preservation of peace in the vicinity of public works were upheld,

²³⁵ *Canadian Pacific R. W. Co.* v. *Corporation of Bonsecours* [1899] A. C. 367, 373, reported below R. J. Q. 7 Q. B. 121. See following this decision: *Grand Trunk R. W. Co.* v. *Therrien* (1900) 30 S. C. R. 485, 492. But the Privy Council have held *ultra vires* provincial legislation enacting that a Dominion railway company should be responsible for cattle injured or killed on their tracks unless they erected proper fences on their railway: *Madden* v. *Nelson and Fort Sheppard R. W. Co.* [1899] A. C. 626. And see as to these two cases, *per* Davies, J., in *In re Railway Act* (1905) 36 S. C. R. 136, 146-7. A provincial legislature would have no power to ratify the transfer of a federal railway, with its property, liabilities, and rights to the provincial government and so to a new company, to be governed by provincial legislation: *Bourgoin* v. *La Compagnie du Chemin de Fer de Montreal* (1880) 5 App. Cas. 381.

²³⁶ *Attorney-General for Alberta* v. *Attorney-General for Canada* [1915] A. C. 363. Provincial legislation cannot override, interfere with, or control or affect the crossing or right of crossing of a Dominion railway by a provincial railway: *In re Alberta Railway Act* (1913) 48 S. C. R. 9, 38. See, further, *Rex* v. *Canadian Pacific R. W. Co* (1905) 1 W. L. R. 89, holding *intra vires*, even as applied to Dominion railways, the *Prairie Fire Ordinance* forbidding people, under penalty, kindling a fire or letting it run at large on any land not their own: *Grant* v. *Canadian Pacific R. W. Co.* (1904) 36 N. B. 528, holding *intra vires*, similarly, certain provincial enactments against starting fires near any forests or woodlands during certain seasons; *Canadian Pacific R. W. Co.* v. *The King* (1907) 39 S. C. R. 476, holding certain North West Ordinances *ultra vires* as seeking to impose a duty upon Dominion railways to use smoke stacks on the engines, and construct fire-guards of ploughed lands in prairie country, Idington, J., dissenting, pp. 488, 490-5. As to a lien under a provincial *Mechanics and Wage Earners Lien Act* not being enforcible against a Dominion company, see *Crawford* v. *Tilden* (1907) 14 O. L. R. 572, 13 O. L. R. 169; and *cf.*, *Larsen* v. *Nelson and Fort Sheppard R. W. Co.* (1895) 4 B. C. 151. As to a provincial Act which merely provided a procedure in order to obtain a judicial sale in the case of a Dominion insolvent railway, there being no Dominion law, being held *intra vires*, see *Baie des Chaleurs R. W. Co.* v. *Nantel* (1896) R. J. Q. 9 S. C. 47, 5 Q. B. 65. As to the sale of a Dominion railway under a

writ of *fi. fa.:* see *Redfield* v. *Corporation of Wickham* (1888)
13 App. Cas. 467. And *cf. Wile* v. *Bruce Mines R. W. Co.*
(1906) 11 O. L. R. 200. As to provincial Sunday legislation
not applying to Dominion railways, see *In re Lords Day Act of
Ontario* (1902) 1 O. W. R. 312. The Privy Council on appeal
sub nom. Attorney-General for Ontario v. *Hamilton Street R. W.
Co.* [1903] A. C. 524, treated the legislation in question as criminal legislation, and therefore exclusively for the Dominion: *supra*
n. 212. As to this Privy Council decision and as to a provincial legislature imposing Sunday observance conditions when
incorporating a provincial railway, see *Kerley* v. *London and
Lake Erie Transportation Co.* (1912-3) 26 O. L. R. 588, 28 O. L.
R. 606. Certainly a provincial legislature is not competent to
interfere with the operations of a company whose undertaking
is subject to the exclusive legislative authority of the Dominion
parliament: *City of Toronto* v. *Bell Telephone Co.* [1905] A. C.
52, 57; *Kerley* v. *London and Lake Erie Ry. and Transportation
Co.*, *supra*, 13 D. L. R. 365, 372. See, also, *Johnson* v. *Can.
Northern* (1918) 14 O. W. N. 159.

237 As to the need of the regulation of railroads, as respects
both their methods of operation and their rates, by one law
and one administrative authority, *cf.* Bryce, Amer. Comm. Vol.
1, pp. 358-9. " Railways, telegraph lines and like works from
the practical point of view must for some purposes be regarded
as entireties, and the law recognizes that by treating them so in
many instances. The B. N. A. Act seems to treat them so in
those provisions as subjects of legislative jurisdiction. . . .
But the Dominion when it assumes jurisdiction, must assume
jurisdiction of the work or undertaking as a whole": *per* Duff,
J., in *British Columbia Electric R. W. Co.* v. *Vancouver, Victoria, and Eastern Ry. Co.* (1913) 48 S. C. R. 98, 116, 13 D. L.
R. 308, 319.

238 *City of Montreal* v. *Montreal Street Railway* [1912] A.
C. 333, 339. Their lordships in this case indicate that it is
proper for such declaration to be made when the circumstances
of a provincial railway are such " as to affect the body politic
of the Dominion." In *City of Toronto* v. *Bell Telephone Co.*
[1905] A. C. 52, 58, the Privy Council has definitely over-ruled
the contention, supported by some *dicta* in the Canadian Courts
(Canada's Federal System, p. 364, n. 276), that such declaration
is not permissible unless the work referred to has been completed. Note the words ' *before or after* their execution' in
No. 10 (c) of section 92 of the Federation Act. The assumption by
the Dominion of jurisdiction over works obviously of only local
interest by declaring them to be for the ' general advantage of
Canada,' became a few years ago a grave scandal: *per* Duff, J.
in *In re Companies* (1913) 48 S. C. R. 331, 426; Canada's Federal System, p. 371, n. 289; *per* Meredith, J.A., in *Kerley* v.

London and Lake Erie Ry. & Transportation Co. (1913) 13 D.
L. R. 365, 374. In *Hamilton, Grimsby and Beamsville R. W.
Cô.* v. *Attorney-General for Ontario* [1916] A. C. 583, Sir Robt.
Finlay contended that such declarations must refer to specific
works either existing or in course of construction, or about to
be constructed, and would not justify a general Dominion enactment that every railway which in the future might cross a
Dominion railway would be a railway for the public advantage
of Canada, but in the view their lordships took of that case it
became unnecessary for them to deal with this contention.
Street, J., held the contrary in *Grand Trunk R. W. Co.* v. *Hamilton Electric Co.* (1897) 29 O. R. 143. Notwithstanding such
a declaration a provincial railway will, apparently, continue to
work under the provincial Acts applying to it until they are
altered or amended by Dominion legislation: *per* Street, J., in
City of Toronto v. *Bell Telephone Co.* (1902) 3 O. L. R. 465,
473-4: in app. 6 O. L. R. 335, [1905] A. C. 52, 58. So also, *per*
Ramsay, J., in *Corporation of St. Joseph* v. *Quebec Central R. W.
Co.* (1885) 11 Q. L. R. 193. However, such declaration may
affect the right of the provincial Attorney-General to bring
action for the cancellation of its charter: *Attorney-General of
British Columbia* v. *Vancouver, etc., Railway and Navigation
Co.* (1902) 9 B. C. 338. And, after such a declaration, any
power of the company to acquire land for branch lines must
be exercised in accordance with the Dominion Railway Act:
In re Columbia and Western R. W. Co. and The Railway Acts
(1901) 8 B. C. 415. *Cf.* a general treatment of declarations by
the Dominion parliament under sec. 92, subs. 10 (c) in an
annotation by the present writer to the above *Hamilton, Grimsby and Beamsville Co.* case, as reported in *Canadian Railway
Cases*, Vol. 20, pp. 123, 128.

239 *Hamilton, Grimsby and Beamsville R. W. Co.* v. *Attorney-General for Ontario* [1916] A. C. 583.

240 *Hewson* v. *Ontario Power Co.* (1905) 36 S. C. R. 596;
Windsor and Annapolis R. W. Co. v. *Western Counties R. W.
Co.* (1878) 3 R. & C. 377, 415. *Contra, per* Davies, J., in *Hewson*
v. *Ontario Power Co. supra*, at p. 605; *Re Grand Junction R. W.
Co.* v. *County of Peterborough* (1880) 45 U. C. R. 302, 316-7,
6 O. A. R. 339, 341, 349. And see Legislative Power in Canada,
at pp. 601-606. For an attempt by a provincial legislature to
provide that on such declaration being made a provincial company shall forfeit powers and privileges under its charter,
see Prov. Legisl. 1899-1900, p. 106; Canada's Federal System, pp.
367-8, 370. As to a provincial legislature imposing a charge
on the lands of a railway company after such declaration, Prov.
Legisl. 1901-1903, p. 57; Canada's Federal System, pp. 368-9;
or attempting nevertheless to retain the right to fix the maxi-

mum rates: Prov. Legisl. 1901-1903, p. 63; Canada's Federal System, p. 369.

241 The Department of the Secretary of State at Ottawa has consistently refused to incorporate educational institutions of any kind, hospitals, and eleemosynary institutions, and certain other bodies whose purposes are clearly within provincial jurisdiction.

242 Citizens Insurance Co. v. Parsons (1881) 7 App. Cas. 96, 116-7; Colonial Building and Investment Association v. Attorney-General of Quebec (1883) 9 App. Cas. 157, 165-6, commented on at length per Duff, J., in Canadian Pacific R. W. Co. v. Ottawa Fire Insurance Co. (1907) 39 S. C. R. 405, 463-8; John Deere Plow Co. v. Wharton [1915] A. C. 330, 343-4. Re Dominion Marble Co. in Liquidation (1917) 35 D. L. R. 63 (Que.) where held that parliament could not empower a Dominion trading company to hypothecate, mortgage, and pledge its property in a province contrary to the law of the province in such matters. See, also, per Idington, J., S. C. at p. 442. Cf. Story on the Constitution of the United States, 5th ed. Vol. 2, p. 153, quoted Legislative Power in Canada, p. 627, n. 2. Cf. Cooper v. McIndoe (1887) 32 L. C. J. 210; Waterous Engine Works Co. v. Okanagan Lumber Co. (1908) 14 B. C. 238; Rex v. Massey-Harris Co. (1905) 6 Terr. L. R. 126, 133-4; per Idington, J., in In re Companies, 48 S. C. R. 260, 286.

243 John Deere Plow Co. v. Wharton [1913] A. C. 330. The company in that case was a company trading in agricultural implements and machinery and doing a general agency commission and mercantile business. Sir Robt. Finlay vainly raised the contention on the argument, (Notes of Proceedings, p. 101), that the power of the Dominion parliament does not extend to creating one company, or nine companies, with power to carry on purely local business in the different provinces, that being reserved to the legislature of each province. The Privy Council did not find it necessary to pass upon, nor did they pass upon the contention that the Dominion can claim any power of incorporation under 'regulation of trade and commerce' in No. 2 of section 92; and they evidently rejected the contention raised, (Notes of Proceedings, pp. 55, 57), that the incorporation of companies with other than provincial objects must be held to be expressly excepted out of the provincial powers, and, therefore, to fall under No. 29 of section 91 of the Federation Act; for this being an enumerated power, if they had so held, they could not have held such companies subject to any general provincial laws directly affecting their operations: cf. supra p. 120. See this case referred to in Attorney-General for Canada v. Attorney-General for Alberta [1916] A. C. 588, 597. In

1908 the Privy Council held as a proposition too plain for serious discussion that a colonial Act incorporating a company may validly empower it to carry on its business "in or out of" the colony: *Campbell* v. *Australian Mutual Provident Society* (1908) 77 L. J. P. C. 117, 118-119, cited Clement, L. of C. C. 3rd ed. p. 107. Dominion laws are, of course, binding on foreign and provincial corporations carrying on business in Canada, as much as on Dominion corporations. *Cf. per* Duff, J., in *In re Companies* (1913) 48 S. C. R. 331, 410. On the argument in the *John Deere Plow Co. case* [1915] A. C. 330 (Notes of Proceedings p. 46) the following is reported:—

Haldane, L.C.: "Just let me ask you this: Could the Dominion incorporate a company for some purpose not within the specified heads to trade exclusively in Manitoba or British Columbia, or not? Would that be a provincial company?"

Mr. Newcombe: "I would suppose that would be a provincial company."

Haldane, L.C.: "I think it would be a provincial company."

Cf. per Duff, J., in *In re Companies* (1913) 48 S. C. R. 331, 446-7. In reliance on the judgment of the Privy Council in this John Deere Plow Co. case, Anglin, J., held in *Linde Canadian Refrigerator Co.* v. *Saskatchewan Creamery Co.* (1915) 24 D. L. R. 703, 708-710, that it is *ultra vires* of a provincial legislature to penalise a Dominion company for not registering under the provincial statute by denying it the right to maintain actions in the Courts of the province upon its contracts; while the Prince Edward Island Supreme Court in *Willett-Martin Co.* v. *Full* (1915) 24 D. L. R. 672, held *intra vires* a local Act requiring every company not incorporated in the Island to transmit full information, upon oath, to the provincial secretary as to its capital, stock subscribed, amount paid up, etc., before beginning business in the province.

244 *John Deere Plow Co.* v. *Wharton* [1915] A. C. 330. See this case discussed at length by the present writer in 35 C. L. T. 148 *seq.* In *Harman* v. *A. Macdonald Co. Ltd.* (1916) 30 D. L. R. 640 (N.S.) Elwood, J., held that the license fees imposed on corporations by the Companies Act of Saskatchewan for carrying on business in the province are "direct taxation," and applicable to Dominion companies, and *intra vires*, inasmuch as the penalties prescribed by the Act for carrying on business without being registered or licensed, do not interfere with the status of a corporation, or prevent it from exercising the powers conferred upon it by its Dominion letters patent. And see now on the same point, *Davidson* v. *Great West Saddlery Co.* (1917) 27 M. R. 576. But some judges hold a provincial enactment that so long as a company is unlicensed it shall not be capable of suing in any Court in the province in respect of a contract made

therein in its business *ultra vires:* S. C. and n. 243. But see
Currie v. *Harris Lith. Co.* (1917) 6 O. W. N. 327, 40 O. L. R. 290.

245 *La Cie Hydraulique St. Francois* v. *Continental Heat &
Light Co.* [1909] A._C. 194. It may have been that their lordships in this case held the Dominion incorporation to be under
enumerated power No. 29 of section 91; and in *In re Companies*
(1913) 48 S. C. R. 331, 437, Duff, J., says that he thinks it was
on this hypothesis that the judgment of the Privy Council proceeded. And so, again, S. C. at p. 440. But since the John
Deere Plow Co. case, *supra*, it may be deemed that the decision
would have been the same even if the incorporation were under
the Dominion residuary power only,—and even if the Dominion
incorporation had been subsequent to the provincial Act and
not previous. As to various other provincial attempts to interfere with the business of Dominion corporations, and the action
of Ministers of Justice taken thereon, see Canada's Federal
System, pp. 377-381.

246 *Citizens Insurance Co.* v. *Parsons* (1881) 7 App. Cas.
96, 117; *Colonial Building and Investment Association* v. *Attorney-General of Quebec* (1883) 9 App. Cas. 157, 164-5. It is of
course, competent for the Dominion parliament to incorporate
under Dominion charter the members of a provincial company,
and so enlarge the scope of their operations and powers: Todd's
Parl. Gov. in Brit. Col., 2nd ed. p. 437; but the Dominion parliament cannot otherwise enlarge the charter powers of a provincial company: *Canadian Pacific R. W. Co.* v. *Ottawa Fire
Insurance Co.* (1907) 39 S. C. R. 405, 415, 433-4. And there
may be objects for which only a provincial legislature could
incorporate a company because of their necessarily provincial
character: *Forsyth* v. *Bury* (1888) 15 S. C. R. 543, 549, 551;
Citizens Insurance Co. v. *Parsons* (1880) 4 S. C. R. 215, 310;
Legislative Power in Canada, p. 375, n. 2. It is questionable
whether provincial legislatures can enlarge or affect the powers
of a Dominion company: Canada's Federal System, p. 382, n.

247 *Colonial Building and Investment Association* v. *Attorney-General of Quebec* (1883) 9 App. Cas. 157, 174; *City of
Toronto* v. *Bell Telephone Co.* [1905] A. C. 52, 58.

248 The numbering in the text follows the numbering of
section 92 of the Federation Act. As to the vast importance
which the future promises to give to the functions and powers
of provincial legislatures, see, *per* Idington, J. in *In re Companies* (1913) 48 S. C. R. 331, 385.

249 The (Imp.) *Colonial Laws Validity Act, 1865*, expressly
provides (sect. 5) that ' . . every representative legislature shall, in respect to the colony under its jurisdiction, have
and be deemed at all times to have had, full power to make

laws respecting the constitution, powers, and procedure of such
legislature; provided that such laws shall have been passed
in such manner and form as may from time to time be required
by any Act of parliament, letters patent, order in council, or
colonial law from the time being in force in the said colony.'
As to which provision see Keith's R. G. in D., Vol. 1, p. 425,
who says that it was always necessary that a colonial Constitution should be altered expressly, referring to *Cooper* v. *Commissioners of Income Tax* (1907) 4 C. L. R. 1304, and expresses
the opinion that a change of the Constitution of a Canadian
province under this provision of the Federation Act must still
be enacted *as such.* As to the application of the above section
of the *Colonial Laws Validity Act* to a provincial legislature,
see *Fielding* v. *Thomas* [1896] A. C. 600, 610. See, also, as to
it, *Doyle* v. *Falconer* (1866) L. R. 1 P. C. 328, 341.

250 (1875) 19 L. C. J. 210, 224-5; Legislative Power in Canada, p. 699, n. 1, 755, n. 1.

251 Per Boyd, C. in *Attorney-General of Canada* v. *Attorney-
General of Ontario* (1890) 20 O. R. 222, 247: affirmed 19 O. A.
R. 31, 23 S. C. R. 458. But see Hodgins' Prov. Legisl. 1867-1895,
p. 338; Canada's Federal System, pp. 385-387. And see further
as to Lieutenant-Governors of provinces, *supra*, pp. 61-2.

252 *Fielding* v. *Thomas* [1896] 600, 610-1. See Legislative
Power in Canada, pp. 746-749.

253 *Cunningham* v. *Tomey Homma* [1903] A. C. 151, reported below 7 B. C. 368, 8 B. C. 76. In *Re Initiative and Referendum Act* (1916) 27 Man. 1, however, the Manitoba Court
of Appeal has held that provincial legislatures cannot, under
this power, enact that (the preliminary conditions prescribed
by the Act being fulfilled) laws may be made or repealed
by direct vote of the people, for this is to give the law-making
powers of the legislature to others, and to substitute a new
Constitution founded on new principles, and to interfere with
the office of the Lieutenant-Governor, because the passing of
the Bill by the legislature is a condition precedent to its receiving his assent. *Sed quære.* See 37 C. L. T. pp. 334-337.
As to the tendency in the Australian Commonwealth and States
to adopt the Referendum: see Keith's R. G. in D., Vol. 1, pp.
370-1.

254 *Citizens Insurance Co.* v. *Parsons* (1881) 7 App. Cas.
96, 108; *Bank of Toronto* v. *Lambe* (1887) 12 App. Cas. 575,
581. In the same way the Dominion power in relation to the
regulation of trade and commerce must be so construed as to
leave proper scope to this provincial power: *Bank of Toronto*
v. *Lambe, supra*, p. 587. See Canada's Federal System, pp. 390-
1. *Cf.*, also, *Weiler* v. *Richards* (1890) 26 C. L. J. N. S. 338.

See, also, as to the concurrent power of taxation between the
Dominion parliament and the provincial legislatures: *Attorney-
General of the Dominion* v. *Attorney-General of the Provinces*
(The Fisheries case) [1898] A. C. 700, 713-714; *per* Strong, J.,
in *Severn* v. *The Queen* (1878) 2 S. C. R. 70, 111; *per* Dorion,
C.J., in *Dobie* v. *Temporalities Board* (1880) 3 L. N. 244, 254;
the argument before the Supreme Court upon the Dominion
Liquor License Acts, 1883-4: Dom. Sess. Pap. 1885, No. 85, at
p. 98; Todd's Parl. Gov. in Brit. Col. 2nd ed. p. 564.

255 Kent's Comm. 10th ed. Vol. 2, p. 331; Legislative Power
in Canada, pp. 254-5, 270, n. 1. At the same time the Dominion
Government has objected to provincial Acts discriminating in
the matter of taxation against extra-provincial companies or
individuals doing business in the province, although not re-
sorting to disallowance: Prov. Legisl. 1901-1903, pp. 96-98; 1904-
1906, p. 25. As to discrimination against aliens, see *Regina* v.
Wing Chong (1885) 2 B. C. (pt. 2) 150; Wheeler's Confederation
Law, p. 122. This provincial power "must be taken to enable
the provincial legislature wherever it shall see fit, to impose
direct taxation for a local purpose upon a particular locality
within the province": *Dow* v. *Black* (1875) L. R. 6 P. C. 272,
282. Besides No. 2 above, provincial legislatures have certain
powers of raising revenue by Nos. 9 (*supra*, p. 128) and 15
(*supra*, p. 140): *Reed* v. *Mousseau* (1883) 8 S. C. R. 408, 431;
and, possibly, under No. 16 (*supra*, p. 143). By sec. 124 of the
Federation Act, New Brunswick is specially authorized to continue to levy existing lumber dues on New Brunswick lumber,
an exception to the general rule that provincial legislatures
have no power of indirect taxation: *Attorney-General of Quebec*
v. *Reed* (1882) 26 L. C. J. 331, 355. An imposition under a provincial Act under the name of "interest" may be really a tax:
Lynch v. *Canada North-West Land Co.* (1891) 19 S. C. R. 204.

256 *Bank of Toronto* v. *Lambe* (1887) 12 App. Cas. 575, 581-
3, holding valid as direct taxation a Quebec Act imposing as a
tax on every bank carrying on business within the province, a
sum varying with the paid-up capital, with an additional sum
for each office or place of business. See, also, *Brewers and
Maltsters Association of Ontario* v. *Attorney-General for Ontario* [1897] A. C. 231, holding valid as direct taxation a provincial Act imposing a license fee on brewers and maltsters
and other persons (although duly licensed by the Dominion)
for licenses to sell within the province the liquors manufactured by them: followed in *Rex* v. *Neiderstadt* (1905) 11 B.C.
347; *Attorney-General for Quebec* v. *Queen Insurance Co.* (1878)
3 App. Cas. 1090, holding as not direct taxation a stamp duty
on policies, renewals, and receipts, which does not necessarily
mean that stamp duties are necessarily always indirect taxa-

tion; *Attorney-General of Quebec* v. *Reed*, 3 Cart. 190, 220-1;
Choquette v. *Lavergne* (1893) R. J. Q. 5 S. C. 108, 122-3; *per*
Lacoste, C.J., S. C. in App. R. J. Q. 3 Q. B. 303, 308-9; *Attorney-
General of Quebec* v. *Reed* (1883) 10 App. Cas. 141, holding not
a direct tax a stamp duty of ten cents imposed on every exhibit
produced in Court in an action, where their lordships say:
" the best general rule is to look to the time of payment and
if, at the time, the ultimate incidence is uncertain, then it cannot, in this view, be called direct taxation within the meaning
of No. 2 of sec. 92 of the Federation Act"; *Cotton* v. *Rex* [1914]
A. C. 176, 190, holding the taxation imposed by the Quebec *Succession Duties Act, 1906*, not to be " direct taxation." American decisions as to what are " direct " taxes within the United
States Constitution are inapplicable in Canada, because of the
provision of that Constitution (Art. 1, sec. 8) that ' no capita-
tion or other direct tax shall be laid unless in proportion to
the census or enumeration hereinbefore directed to be taken;
hence a " direct " tax in the United States must be capable
of such apportionment: Story on the Constitution, 5th ed. Vol.
1, pp. 703-4; Legislative Power in Canada, p. 720, n. 1. It may
be added that in *In re Yorkshire Guarantee and Securities Corporation* (1895) 4 B. C. 258, 274, the Court held that a tax imposed by the Provincial Assessment Act upon mortgages was
a direct tax, though the company required their mortgagors to
recoup the amount; and in *Le College de Médecins* v. *Brigham*
(1888) 16 R. L. 283, it was held that a provincial Act requiring
all members of the College of Physicians and Surgeons of the
province to pay $2 for the use of the College was *intra vires*.
See, further, Hodg. Prov. Legisl. 1867-1895, p. 1229; Canada's
Federal System, p. 399, n. 34. It seems possible that the provinces may have some restricted powers of imposing indirect
taxation if of ' a merely local or private nature in the province '
within the meaning of No, 16 of section 92 (*supra*, p. 143), or
if incidental to the exercise of the other express powers conferred by section 92, as, *e.g.*, ' the maintenance of public and
reformatory prisons in and for the province ' (No. 6), ' the
maintenance ' of provincial Courts (No. 14): *Bank of Toronto*
v. *Lambe* (1885) M. L. R. 1 Q. B. 122, 145, 192, 197-91; *Attorney-
General of Quebec* v. *Reed* (1884) 10 App. Cas. 141, 144-5, 8
S. C. R. 408, *sub nom. Reed* v. *Mousseau; Dow* v. *Black* (1875)
L. R. 6 P. C. 272, 282; Legislative Power in Canada, pp. 730-741;
Canada's Federal System, pp. 411-414. See, however, *Dal-
mage* v. *Douglas* (1887) 4 Man. 495. *Cf. Crawford* v. *Duffield*
(1888) 5 Man. 121. But any such provincial power, if any such
exists, is greatly restricted by sec. 121 of the Federation Act,
which provides for free trade between the provinces in articles
of their own growth, produce, or manufacture; and by sec. 122,

which places customs and excise laws under Dominion control. As to the explanation and interpretation of this provincial power, and that the terms " direct taxation " ought to be liberally and not narrowly construed, see *per* Middleton, J. in *Treasurer of Ontario* v. *Canada Life Ass. Co.* (1915) 22 D. L. R. (Ont.) 428, 434. And so, in that case, he held an Ontario Act *intra vires* in imposing a tax upon the gross premiums received by any insurance company in respect of business transacted in Ontario, including every premium which by the terms of the contract is payable in Ontario, or which is in fact paid in Ontario, or is payable in respect to a risk undertaken in Ontario, or in respect of a person or property resident or situate in Ontario at the . time of payment. He also held that all taxation is for the purpose of the B. N. A. Act to be regarded as either direct or indirect. It depends on the dominant intention of the legislature; not on any special agreements or covenants of the parties.

[257] *Dow* v. *Black* (1875) L. R. 6 P. C. 272. Some judges had construed the clause in the narrower fashion: Legislative Power in Canada, p. 722, n. 1. ' This decision is a warrant for the whole system of municipal taxation in operation to-day throughout the Canadian provinces ': Clement's L. of C. C. 3rd ed. p. 366. . Whether a province has any power of taxation except for provincial, municipal, or local purposes, as *e.g.*, for erecting wharves, piers, and docks in harbours, or for supplementing the sum paid during the annual drill of the militia, though ' militia and defence,' ' navigation and shipping ' are exclusively Dominion subjects, may be questionable: Prov. Legisl. 1901-2, pp. 20-21.

[258] *Woodruff* v. *Attorney-General for Ontario* [1908] A. C. 508, 513, reported below, 15 O. L. R. 416. As to the *situs* of stock in a company, see *Nickle* v. *Douglas* (1875) 35 U. C. R. 126, 37 U. C. R. 51, where held that the *situs* of stock in a bank was where the head office of the bank was. See, too, on this subject Keith's R. G. in D. Vol. 1, p. 395, n. And *cf. Lambe* v. *Manuel* [1903] A. C. 68. A province cannot by legislative declaration make anything property within the province which would not otherwise be such according to the recognized principles of English law: *Lovitt* v. *The King* (1910) 43 S. C. R. 106, 160-1. See, also, *Treasurer of Province of Ontario* v. *Patten* (1910) 22 O. L. R. 184.

[259] *Bank of Toronto* v. *Lambe* (1887) 12 App. Cas. 575, 584-5. But see *Cotton* v. *Rex* [1914] A. C. 176, 193, as to taxation by way of succession duty. The phrase " succession duty " is not one with a well-known and definite legal significance. Its real meaning must be gathered from the statute in which it is used: the real character of the tax, whatever it may be styled, depends upon its intended incidence as disclosed by the

statute itself: *Re Doe* (1914) 16 D. L. R. 740 (B.C.). As to
the Imperial *Finance Act 1894*, which provides for a reduction
of duty in the case of assets situated in a colony if duty has
been paid there on death, provided the colony reciprocates, see
Keith *op. cit.* Vol. II, pp. 1029-1030. As to *Cotton* v. *Rex*, see
Keith's *Imperial United*, pp. 375-8.

260 *Rex* v. *Lovitt* [1912] A. C. 212, reported below, 43 S. C. R.
106, 37 N. B. 558. The property must be locally situate inside the
province, though the deceased be domiciled outside: *Cotton* v.
Rex [1914] A. C. 176, 193; *Woodruff* v. *Attorney-General for
Ontario* [1908] A. C. 508; *Smith* v. *Rural Municipality of Ver-
million Hills* (1914) 49 S. C. R. 563, 565, 568, 575. For the Manitoba *Succession Duty Act* held *intra vires* as constituting direct
taxation, see *Standard Trusts Co.* v. *Treasurer of Manitoba*
(1915) 23 D. L. R. 811, 817, 820-1, 823, 830.

261 (1912) 45 S. C. R. 469; reported below R. J. Q. 20 K.
B. 162. Davies and Anglin, JJ. dissented. See *per* Anglin, J.
at pp. 540-541. The case went to the Privy Council [1914]
A. C. 176, but they disposed of the appeal by holding that the
taxation imposed by the Succession Duty Act in question was
not "direct" taxation, and therefore *ultra vires*. *Cf. Re Ren-
frew* (1898) 29 O. R. 565, 569. In *Standard Trust Co.* v. *Treasurer of Manitoba* (1915) 23 D. L. R. 811, 824, 51 S. C. R. 428,
Duff, J., expresses the view that the result of Lord Moulton's
reasoning in *Cotton* v. *Rex* [1914] A. C. 176, at p. 195, 15 D. L.
R. 283, at p. 293, is that any attempt on the part of a province to
exact succession duties in respect to property not situate within
the province, and without respect to the domicil of the bene-
ficiary, must fail as necessarily indirect taxation. But payment
of a succession duty as a condition for local probate on property
situate within the province may be required under provincial
legislation: *per* Brodeur, J., in *Standard Trusts Co.* v. *Treasurer
of Manitoba* (1915) 23 D. L. R. 811, 832, 51 S. C. R. 428, and *Re
Doe* (1914) 16 D. L. R. (B.C.) 740, 742, where Clement, J., observes that a tax upon land is in law a direct tax, though according to a certain school of economists it is considered as the most
scientific form of indirect taxation; and referring to the Privy
Council decisions, he says: "That a tax can be laid on property
and that such a tax may be direct taxation is, in my opinion,
not negatived by any of those cases." *Aliter*, if the Act makes
the executor or administrator liable for the succession duty,
and not the property devolving: *Re Cust* (1914) 18 D. L. R. 647
(Alta.). As to debts constituting property in the province subject to succession duty, though arising from a contract to erect
buildings in another province, or out of agreements to sell lands
situated in another province, see *Standard Trust Co. case,
supra*. For an ingenious attempt to indirectly impose succession duties on property outside the province, see the report of

Doherty, M.J., on Manitoba Act, 1911, c. 60; and see too, Act of
Nova Scotia 1912, c. 13, and report of Doherty, M.J., thereon
of March 12th, 1913. *Cf. Standard Trusts Co.* v. *Treasurer of
Manitoba, supra.*

262 This exemption is for the protection of the interest of
the Crown only, and does not debar the province from taxing
any interest in Crown lands, Dominion or provincial, legal or
equitable, which the Crown has conferred on a subject: *Rud-
dell* v. *Georgeson* (1893) 9 Man. 407; *Calgary and Edmonton
Land Co.* v. *Attorney-General of Alberta* (1911) 45 S. C. R.
170, 2 Alta. 446; *Canadian Pacific R. W. Co.* v. *Rural Municipality of Cornwallis* (1891) 7 Man. 1, 24, in app. 19 S. C. R.
702, 710; *Smith* v. *Rural Municipality of Vermilion* (1914) 49
S. C. R. 563, 572, 576, aff. [1916] A. C. 569. *Cf. Southern Alberta Land Co.* v. *Rural Municipality of McLean* (1916) 53 S.
C. R. 151; *Whelan* v. *Ryan* (1891) 20 S. C. R. 65, 73; *Rural
Municipality of Norfolk* v. *Warren* (1892) 8 Man. 481; *Alloway*
v. *Rural Municipaltiy of Morris* (1908) 18 Man. 361.

263 *Abbott* v. *City of St. John* (1908) 40 S. C. R., 597, 606,
616, 619; followed *Toronto* v. *Morson* (1917) 40 O. L. R. 227.
This overruled a number of previous Canadian decisions: Canada's Federal System, p. 417, n. 72. And so under the Australian
Constitution: *Webb* v. *Outrim* [1907] A. C. 81; Keith R. G. in D.
Vol. III, pp. 1368-1372, where a contrast is drawn between the
position of the States of the Australian Commonwealth and those
of the American Union which applies equally to the provinces of
Canada, notwithstanding the latter have only certain specific enu-
merated powers. *Cf. Bank of Toronto* v. *Lambe* (1887) 12 App.
Cas. 575, 587; *Baxter* v. *Commissioners of Taxation* (1907) 4
C. L. R. 1087; Article on Constitution of United States and
Canada (1912) 32 C. L. J. 849. *Coté* v. *Watson* (1877) 3 Q. L.
R. 157, would no longer be sustainable in holding *ultra vires*
a provincial Act imposing a tax on the sum realized from the
sale of an insolvent's effects when made under the Dominion
Insolvent Act. See, also, Legislative Power in Canada, pp.
671-8. *Cf. Fillmore* v. *Colburn* (1896) 28 N. S. 292. It may
still be good law, however, that a provincial legislature has no
power to declare liable to seizure the salaries of employees of
the Federal Government: *Evans* v. *Hudon* (1877) 22 L. C. J.
268; Prov. Legisl. 1904-1906, p. 12. As to taxing soldiers and
sailors, *cf. per* Robinson, C.J. in *Tully* v. *Principal Officers of
Her Majesty's Ordnance* (1847) 4 U. C. R. 7, 14. As to the right
of a province to compensate Dominion officials, when the Dominion has not done so: *Re Toronto Harbour Commissioners*
(1881) 28 Gr. 195.

264 *Bank of Toronto* v. *Lambe* (1887) 12 App. Cas. 575,
586-7; *Great North Western Telegraph Co.* v. *Fortier* (1903) R. J.

Q. 12 K. B. 405; *Town of Windsor* v. *Commercial Bank of Windsor* (1882) 3 R. & G. 420, 427; *Canadian Pacific R. W. Co.* v. *Corporation of Bonsecours* [1889] A. C. 367, 372-3. *Cf. Angers* v. *Queen Insurance Co.* (1877) 21 L. C. J. 77, 81; *Heneker* v. *Bank of Montreal* (1895) R. J. Q. 7 S. C. 257, 262.

265 *Brewers and Maltsters Association of Ontario* v. *Attorney-General of Ontario* [1897] A. C. 231, followed *Rex* v. *Neiderstadt* [1905] 11 B. C. 347; *Fortier* v. *Lambe* [1895] 25 S. C. R. 422. The distinction between wholesale trading and retail trading seems to mark no line of cleavage in Canadian constitutional law: Canada's Federal System, pp. 204, n. 14, 436-8. *Cf. Attorney-General of Manitoba* v. *Manitoba License Holders Association* [1902] A. C. 73.

266 The appointment of Queen's Counsel is an appointment to an office within this sub-section: *Attorney-General for the Dominion* v. *Attorney-General for Ontario* (Queen's Counsel case) [1898] A. C. 247; *Lenoir* v. *Ritchie* (1879) 3 S. C. R. 575; Legislative Power in Canada, pp. 88-9, 133-5. Under section 134 of the Federation Act, providing for the appointment of executive officers for Ontario and Quebec, until the provincial legislatures otherwise provide, the Lieutenant-Governors of those provinces can create Queen's Counsel for the purposes of the provincial Courts: Canada's Federal System, p. 424, where the opinion of the law officers of the Crown in 1887 to this effect is referred to.

267 Thus, though the regulation of fisheries is an exclusively Dominion subject, the terms and condition upon which provincial fisheries may be granted, leased, or otherwise disposed of appear proper subjects of provincial legislation under this clause: *Attorney-General of the Dominion* v. *Attorney-General of the Provinces* [1898] A. C. 700, 715-6; and so does a restriction that all pine timber cut under provincial licenses shall be manufactured into sawn lumber in Canada: *Smylie* v. *The Queen* (1900) 31 O. R. 202, 27 O. A. R. 172. As to Indian lands, see *supra*, p. 152, and notes.

268 *Attorney-General of Ontario* v. *Attorney-General of the Dominion* (Liquor Prohibition Appeal, 1895) [1896] A. C. 348, 363-4. Premonitions of this view had been given in the course of the arguments before the Privy Council in *Hodge* v. *The Queen* (Dom. Sess. Pap. 1884, Vol. 17, No. 30 at p. 67), and *In re Dominion License Acts* 1883 and 1884: see extracts given Canada's Federal System, pp. 427-429. The matter does not depend, as was at one time supposed by some judges, upon the municipal institutions which existed, or the powers which were exercised by municipal corporations in this, that, or the other province, before Confederation. See for cases illustrating this superseded view: Legislative Power in Canada, pp. 45-46, 59-61, 706 n 1.

²⁶⁹ *Hodge* v. *The Queen* (1883) 9 App. Cas. 117, 132.

²⁷⁰ *Schultz* v. *City of Winnipeg* (1889) 6 Man. 40, 57; *Reg. ex rel. McGuire* v. *Birkett* (1891) 21 O. R. 162, where it was held they had power to invest the Master in Chambers at Toronto with authority to try controverted municipal election cases. *Cf. Crowe* v. *McCurdy* (1885) 18 N. S. 301; *Clarke* v. *Jacques* (1900) R. J. Q. 9 Q. B. 238. Provincial legislation enacting that no Chinaman, Japanese, or Indian shall be entitled to vote at municipal elections would seem to be *intra vires*; Prov. Legisl. 1899-1900, p. 139 (see, however, *ibid.* p. 144); *Cunningham* v. *Tomey Homma* [1903] A. C. 151. It would seem that the Dominion parliament can confer upon municipal corporations, powers and functions in respect to matters not of provincial competence: *Hart* v. *Corporation of County of Missisquoi*, (1876) 3 Q. L. R. 170; *Cooey* v. *Municipality of the County of Brome* (1872) 21 L. C. J. 182, 186; *Township of Compton* v. *Simoneau* (1891) 14 L. N. 347; *In re Prohibitory Liquor Laws* (1885) 24 S. C. R. 170, 247. Clement (L. of C. C. 3rd ed. p. 796) refers to the Canada Temperance Act as a notable example of powers conferred and duties imposed upon municipalities by federal legislation. But it would not seem that the Dominion parliament can give new corporate powers to municipal corporations, or confer on them capacities not conferred by the provincial legislation such as to acquire and make new streets across Dominion railways: *Grand Trunk R. W. Co.* v. *City of Toronto* (1900) 32 O. R. 120, 125. As to the Dominion power to compel municipalities to contribute to the cost of protecting railway crossings over federal railways, see *City of Toronto* v. *Canadian Pacific R. W. Co.* [1908] A. C. 54; *In re Canadian Pacific R. W. Co. and County and Township of York* (1896) 27 O. R. 559, 569. See *supra*, n. 233.

²⁷¹ These cases are collected in Legislative Power in Canada, pp. 27, n. 1, 726, n. 2. See, also, *City of Halifax* v. *Western Assurance Co.* (1885) 18 N. S. 387. *Lee* v. *De Montigny* (1889) R. J. Q. 15 S. C. 607, a provincial Act authorizing the City of Montreal to require laundries to take out a license, was held to be *intra vires*, on the strength, however, of No. 8, 'municipal institutions,' which seems clearly an error (*supra*, p. 127). In *Re Foster and Township of Raleigh* (1910) 22 O. L. R. 26, 342, a provincial Act exacting an annual license fee for keeping billiard tables for hire, was held valid.

²⁷² Thus in *Russell* v. *The Queen* (1882) 9 App. Cas. 829, their lordships speak of "licenses granted under the authority of subs. 9 by the provincial legislature for the sale or carrying of arms"; in the *Fisheries case* [1898] A. C. 700, they speak of provincial legislatures being able to impose licenses as a condition of the right to fish; in the *Brewers and Maltsters'*

Association, case [1898] A. C. 700, they hold that at any rate the *genus* will include brewers' and distillers' licenses, thus destroying the authority of *Severn* v. *The Queen* (1878), 2 S.C.R. 70. In *John Deere Plow Co.* v. *Wharton*, [1915] A. C. 330. 348, they say that: " a Dominion company . . cannot . . escape the payment of taxes, even though they may assume the form of requiring, as the method of raising a revenue, a license to trade which affects a Dominion company in common with other companies." *Cf.* also *International Text Book* v. *Brown* (1907), 13 O. L. R. 644.

273 *Brewers and Maltsters Association of Ontario* v. *Attorney-General for Ontario* [1897] A. C. 231. Some Canadian judges, however, had held that taxation by means of licenses under this subsection was indirect taxation: see Legislative Power in Canada, p. 361, n. 2. The fact that there might be doubt as to this may be the explanation of the subsection: so *per* Spragge, C.J., in *Regina* v. *Frawley* (1882) 7 O. A. R. 246. Provincial legislatures must not under colour of licenses tax indirectly: *Attorney-General of Quebec* v. *Queen Insurance Co.* (1878) 3 App. Cas. 1090; *Brewers and Maltsters Association case, supra,* p. 357. But if taxation under this subsection can be indirect, it will nevertheless be valid: *In re Companies* (1913) 48 S. C. R. 331, 418.

274 *Brewers and Maltsters Association of Ontario* v. *Attorney-General for Ontario* [1897] A. C. 231; *Queen* v. *McDougall* (1889) 22 N. S. 462, 491; *In re Dominion License Acts, 1883-4,* Cas. Dig. S. C. 509; *Regina* v. *Halliday* (1893) 21 O. A. R. 42, 44; *Liquor Prohibition Appeal, 1895* [1896] A. C. 348, 367-8; Canada's Federal System, pp. 436-8. It had been thought otherwise in Canadian Courts, and that wholesale trade had a quasi-national, rather than municipal character, and comprised the trade and commerce of the country in some fuller sense than the retail trade: *Severn* v. *The Queen* (1878) 2 S. C. R. 70; Legislative Power in Canada, p. 727, n. 3. See, further, as to *In re Dominion License Acts, 1883-4,* Legislative Power in Canada, pp. 403-6, 727-9. It was discussed on the argument before the Privy Council on the recent Insurance Companies case (*Attorney-General for Canada* v. *Attorney-General for Alberta* [1916] A. C. 588); see *e.g.* Martin, Meredith, & Co.'s Transcript, 3rd day, p. 86.

275 *Severn* v. *The Queen* (1878) 2 S. C. R. 70, 108-9; *Russell The Queen* (1882) 7 App. Cas. 829, 837. But quite apart from this subsection 9, there seems nothing to prevent provincial legislatures imposing the necessity of obtaining licenses as a method of police regulation (as to which see *supra*, pp. 141-2): *O'Danaher* v. *Peters* (1889) 17 S. C. R. 44; *Hamilton Powder Co.*

C.C.L.—16

v. *Lambe* (1885) M. L. R. 1 Q. B. 460. See, also, *City of Montreal* v. *Walker* (1885), M. L. R. 1 Q. B. 469. See also as to the power of police regulation extending to wholesale trade, *Keefe* v. *Mc-Lennan* (1876) 2 R. & C. 5, 12: *contra Severn* v. *The Queen* (1878) 2 S. C. R. 70, 100-2, 105-6, 115. *Cf. per* Strong, J. in *In re Prohibitory Liquor Laws* (1895) 24 S. C. R. 170, 204. It must not, apparently, be supposed, though some Canadian judges have been of that opinion (see cases collected Legislative Power in Canada, at pp. 44-49; Canada's Federal System, p. 441, n. 152) that in taxing by means of licenses under No. 9 of section 92 provincial legislatures are confined to licenses of the same kind as those in existence in the provinces before Confederation: per Strong, J. in *Severn* v. *the Queen* (1878) 2 S. C. R. 70, 109, who says: "I think everything indicates that co-equal and co-ordinate legislative powers in every particular were conferred by-the (Federation) Act on the provinces" (see *supra,* p. 93). See, however, *per* Strong, J., in *Huson* v. *Township of South Norwich* (1895) 24 S. C. R. 145, 150-1. As to whether provincial legislatures may discriminate against aliens in the granting of licenses, see Prov. Legisl. 1899-1900, at pp. 134-138.

276 *Attorney-General for the Dominion* v. *Attorney-General for the Provinces* [1898] A. C. 700, 713-4; *Severn* v. *The Queen* (1878) 2 S. C.-R. 70, 101; *Angers* v. *Queen Insurance Co.* (1877) 16 C. L. J. N. S. 198, 204-5; *In re Local Option Act* (1891) 18 O. A. R. 572, 580; Canada's Federal System, pp. 443-4.

277 Sub-divisions (a) (b) and (c) have been dealt with in connection with Dominion powers, *supra,* pp. 119-122. As to the Dominion power to withdraw local works and undertakings from provincial jurisdiction, see *supra,* pp. 119-124. As to the Dominion power to control crossings by provincial railways of Dominion railways, see nn. 236, 279. In *Quong Wing* v. *The King* (1914) 49 S. C. R. 440, 461, there is the, perhaps, somewhat surprising *dictum* of Duff, J. that a provincial enactment forbidding the employment of white women in Chinese restaurants, laundries, etc., might "plausibly be contended" to be legislation in relation to 'local works and undertakings' under the above sub-section of section 92.

278 *Pro: European and North American R. W. Co.* v. *Thomas* (1871) 1 Pugs. 42; *contra*: *Hewson* v. *Ontario Power Co.* (1905) 36 S. C. R. 596, 608, *per* Davies, J. who, however, speaks as though this sub-section contained the expression "undertakings of a local and private nature" which it does not: see Canada's Federal System, pp. 447-449; *Dow* v. *Black* (1873) 14 N. B. 300, *sub nom. The Queen* v. *Dow; City of Toronto* v. *Bell Telephone Co.,* 6 O. L. R. 335, 343; Prov. Legisl. 1899-1900, p. 138; 1901-1903, p. 58. See, also, Canada's Federal System, p. 452, n. 176.

279 As to provincial legislatures, quite apart from any question of the Dominion veto power, not being able to authorize a provincial railway company to expropriate and cross Dominion Crown lands, see Hodg. Prov. Legisl. 1867-1895, at pp. 855-6; Canada's Federal System, p. 453.

280 *Kerley* v. *London and Lake Erie Transportation Co.* (1912) 26 O. L. R. 588, refusing to follow *In re Legislation Respecting Abstention from Labour on Sunday* (1905) 35 S. C. R. 581. " If the company accept a charter with such a limitation wherein is the Constitutional Act offended against?": *per* Boyd, C. 26 O. L. R. at p. 598. See *supra*, n. 212. On appeal in the Kerley case (28 O. L. R. 606) the constitutional point was not dealt with.

281 *Attorney-General for Ontario* v. *Hamilton Street R. W. Co.* [1903] A. C. 524.

282 Prov. Legisl. 1901-1903, pp. 58, 64. *Cf.* Prov. Legisl. 1899-1900, pp. 104, 112, 122-3; Canada's Federal System, pp. 457-460.

283 *Schoolbred* v. *Clarke* (1890) 17 S. C. R. 265, 274. And see *St. Francois Hydraulic Co.* v. *Continental Heat and Light Co.* [1909] A. C. 194. As Duff, J. says in *British Columbia Electric R. W. Co.* v. *Vancouver, Victoria, and Eastern R. W. Co.* (1913) 48 S. C. R. 98, 116, 13 D. L. R. 308, 318, a provincial railway is subject to provincial legislative jurisdiction in respect to matters properly comprehended within railway legislation, but not in respect to matters which fall under some other head of sec. 91 of the B. N. A. Act. *Cf.* as to a corporation created by Act of the old province of Canada being bound by provincial legislation passed after Confederation: *Hamilton Powder Co.* v. *Lambe* (1885) M. L. R. 1 Q. B. 460. As to a provincial legislature when carrying out by statute a scheme for the financial re-organization of a local work or undertaking having power to legislate respecting debenture bonds held out of the jurisdiction, see *Jones* v. *Canada Central R. W. Co.* (1881) 46 U. C. R. 250, 260. *Cf. per* Savary, Co.J. in *In re Killam* (1878) 14 C. L. J. N. S. 242. See, also, now *Royal Bank of Canada* v. *The King* [1913] A. C. 283 (*infra*, n. 303); and Canada's Federal System, pp. 454-5.

284 Probably it was intended by this sub-section " to preclude the contention that if the power of incorporation should be regarded as a substantive and distinct head of legislative jurisdiction, it was wholly vested in the Dominion parliament as part of the residuum under the ' peace, order, and good government' provision of section 91 because not expressly mentioned in the enumeration of provincial powers.": per Anglin, J. in *In re Companies* (1913) 48 S. C. R. 331, 450.

285 *Per* Duff, J., in *In re Companies* (1913) 48 S. C. R. 331, at p. 411, 446.

286 [1916] A. C. 566,

287 The words are from the judgment of the Privy Council in *Bonanza Creek Gold Mining Co.* v. *The King* [1916] A. C. 566, 577. For confirmation see *per* Davies, J. in *Canadian Pacific R. W. Co.* v. *Ottawa Fire Insurance Co.* (1907) 39 S. C. R. 405, 412-3; *per* Fitzpatrick, C. J. in *Bonanza Creek Gold Mining Co.* v. *The King* (1915) 50 S. C. R. 534, 539; *per* Davies, J. S. C. at p. 542; *per* Duff, J. S. C. p. 574. The point actually decided by the majority of the Supreme Court in *Canadian Pacific R. W. Co.* v. *Ottawa Fire Insurance Co.*, *supra*, was that a company incorporated under the authority of a provincial legislature to carry on the business of fire insurance is not inherently incapable of entering outside the boundaries of its province of origin into a valid contract of insurance of property also outside its limits. As to this case and for previous provincial decisions to the same effect, see Canada's Federal System, pp. 466-475. In the *Bonanza Creek Gold Mining Co. case*, *supra*, the Supreme Court held that a mining company incorporated under the law of the province of Ontario has no power or capacity to carry on its business in the Yukon territory, and that an assignment to it of mining leases and agreements for leases there is void. Ministers of Justice had always taken strong ground that companies with power to transact business beyond the limits of the province are not companies 'with provincial objects' within the clause of the Federation Act under consideration: Canada's Federal System, pp. 476-479. The contention that by "provincial objects" was meant "public provincial objects" was long ago discouraged by the Privy Council in *Citizens Insurance Co.* v. *Parsons* (1881) 7 App. Cas. 96, 116, and does not seem to have been ever again revived. And so *per* Idington, J. in *Bonanza Creek Gold iMning Co.* v. *The King*, (1915) 50 S. C. R. 534, 552. See, also, Keith, R. G. in D., Vol. 1, p. 119.

288 Their lordships discuss in this judgment *Ashbury Railway Carriage and Iron Co.* v. *Riche*, L. R. 7 H. L. 653, and hold (p. 582) that its doctrine "does not apply where a company purports to derive its existence from the act of the Sovereign, and not merely from the words of the regulating statute." See as to the *Bonanza Creek Gold Mining Company case*, *Attorney-General for Canada* v. *Attorney-General for Alberta* (the Insurance Companies' Case) [1916] A. C. 588, 597. See, also, *Re Companies Incorporation* (*Attorneys-General of Ontario and other provinces* v. *Attorney-General for the Dominion*) [1916] A. C. 598. In 1908 it was held by the Privy Council as a proposition too plain for serious discussion that a Colonial Act incorporating a company may validly empower it to carry on its business "in or out of" the Colony: *Campbell* v. *Australian Mutual Provident Society* (1908) 77 L. J. P. C. 117, cited Clement L. of C. C., 3rd ed.,

p. 107. See these cases discussed by Victor E. Mitchell, K.C., in a pamphlet entitled *Canadian Companies Incorporation* (Financial Times Press, Montreal, 1917), where he contends that the capacity to accept powers and rights *ab extra* does not mean that the company can be authorized *ab extra* to carry on a business with purposes and objects different from those it is authorized to carry on by its charter. See, also, his *Treatise on the Law Relating to Canadian Commercial Corporations* (Montreal: Southam Press, Ltd., 1916.) Mr. Keith (R. G. in D. Vol. 1, p. 119) takes the view that Governors have never had authority delegated to them to incorporate companies, but adds that they have done so in the past, as *e.g.* in New Brunswick, referring to 1 Hann. *Hist. N. Br.* 151. So in the 1st ed. of R. G. in D. in one Vol., he says (p. 254) 'the prerogative of granting charters of incorporation is never delegated.' See, also, *Kittles* v. *Colonial Assurance Co.* (1917) 28 Man. 47. Several provinces, as *e.g.* Man., 7 Geo. V., c. 12, Ont. 6 Geo. V., c. 35, have now specially enacted that every corporation or company heretofore or hereafter created shall, unless otherwise expressly declared in the Act creating it, 'have,' as the Manitoba Act puts it, 'and be deemed to have had from its creation, the capacity of a natural person to exercise its powers beyond the boundaries of the province'; and, as the Ontario Act puts it,—'have and be deemed from its creation to have had, the general capacity which the common law ordinarily attaches to corporations created by charter.'

289 *Per* Dorion, C.J., *Dobie* v. *Temporalities Board* (1880), cited Doutre on Constitution of Canada, p. 260. Some Ministers of Justice, however, have taken up a different position: Prov. Legisl. 1904-1906, pp. 175-7; Canada's Federal System, pp. 481-482.

290 (1905) 36 S. C. R. 596, 608-9.

291 *Per* Fitzpatrick, C.J., in *Canadian Pacific Railway Co.* v. *Ottawa Fire Insurance Co.* (1907) 39 S. C. R. 405, 415. *Per* Davies, J., S. C. at pp. 433-4. *Cf.* Hodg. Prov. Legisl. 1904-6, p. 60. As to there being objects of so necessarily a provincial character that only a provincial legislature could incorporate a company for them, see Canada's Federal System, p. 382, n. As to a statute enlarging powers and extending the business of a company being binding on all the shareholders whether assenting or not to the application for it, see *Canada Car and Manufacturing Co.* v. *Harris* (1875) 24 C. P. 380.

292 *Colonial Building and Investment Association* v. *Attorney-General of Quebec* (1883) 9 App. Cas. 157, 165; *per* Dorion, C. J. in *Dobie* v. *Temporalities Board* (1880) cited Doutre on The Constitution of Canada at p. 260. See *supra*, pp. 69-70, as to colourable legislation. As to provincial legislatures when incorporating having power to say what are the rights of the parties under the incorporation see *In re Dominion Provident and*

Endowment Association (1894) 25 O. R. 619, 620, as commented on Canada's Federal System, pp. 486-7. See, also, Legislative Power in Canada, p. 458, n.

293 *Citizens Insurance Co.* v. *Parsons* (1881) 7 App. Cas. 96, 108. See Legislative Power in Canada, p. 488, n. 3.

294 *In re Marriage Legislation in Canada* [1912] A. C. 880: reported below, 46 S. C. R. 132. Under this sub-section, also, the provincial legislatures have the power of legislating upon the subject of the publication of banns, and the issue of marriage licenses: Opinion of the Law Officers of the Crown in England (1869-1870), Dom. Sess. Pap. 1877, No. 89, p. 340, who observe that the phrase 'the laws respecting the solemnization of marriage in England' occurs in the preamble of the Marriage Act (Imp. 4 Geo. IV, c. 76).

295 Canada's Federal System, pp. 316-318. *Cf.* Article by Hon. E. M. Cullen, ex-Chief Justice of the Court of Appeals, New York State, in *Case and Comment* (Vol. 22, p. 819), where speaking of legislation in the States of the Union forbidding marriage without the certificate of a physician to the physical well-being of the parties, he says that such legislation is easily avoided 'by going to another State to perform the marriage ceremony.' *Cf.* also *Swifte* v. *Attorney-General of Ireland* [1912] A. C. 276. As to divorce in N.-W. provinces, see *Jl. Comp. Leg.*, Vol. 18, p. 169.

296 As to the power of provincial legislatures to interfere with vested rights or pass *ex post facto laws*, or laws impairing the obligation of contracts, see *supra*, p. 70. As to how far Dominion corporations are subject to provincial laws in relation to property and civil rights, see *supra*, pp. 123-4.

297 *Attorney-General of Ontario* v. *Mercer* (1883) 8 App. Cas. 767, 776. Sec. 102 creates a consolidated revenue fund for Canada out of the duties and revenues over which provincial legislatures before and at the Union had power of appropriation.

298 *Cf. Hodge* v. *The Queen* (1882) 7 O. A. R. 246, 274; *Cushing* v. *Dupuy* (1880) 5 App. Cas. 409, 415-6; *Attorney-General of Ontario* v. *Attorney-General of Canada* [1894] A. C. 189, 200-1; *Tennant* v. *Union Bank of Canada* [1894] A. C. 31, 45; *City of Toronto* v. *Canadian Pacific R. W. Co.* [1908] A. C. 54-59.

299 *John Deere Plow Co.* v. *Wharton* [1915] A. C. 330, 339-340. In the course of the argument in this case (Notes of Proceedings, p. 150) Haldane, L.C., is reported as saying: "Without expressing a final opinion about it, I should say 'civil rights' was a residuary expression. It was intended to bring in a variety of things not comprised in the other heads, including what was not touched by section 91 in the specifically enumerated heads there."

300 *Supra*, pp. 93-4; *Russell* v. *The Queen* (1882) 7 App. Cas. 829, 839.

301 *Supra*, pp. 94-5; *Valin* v. *Langlois* (1879) 3 S. C. R. 1, 15. *Cf. Citizens' Insurance Co.* v. *Parsons* (1880), 4 S. C. R. 215, 242, 308; *Steadman* v. *Robertson* (1879) 2 P. & B. 580, 595-6; Canada's Federal System, pp. 495-6. The words 'property and civil rights' in the sub-section under consideration are to be understood in their largest sense: *Citizens Insurance Co.* v. *Parsons* (1881) 7 App. Cas. 96, 111. But they must not be understood as applying to such property as is necessary to the existence of a Dominion object: *Dobie* v. *Temporalities Board* (1880) 3 L. N. 244, 248. This does not mean, however, that a provincial Act can under no circumstances deal with the property and civil rights of a Dominion corporation: S. C. (1882) 7 App. Cas. 136, 152; Canada's Federal System, pp. 495-497.

302 *Queen* v. *Robertson* (1882) 6 S. C. R. 52, 65-6; *Attorney-General of British Columbia* v. *Attorney-General of Canada* (1889) 14 App. Cas. 295, 302; and see *infra*, n. 391. In *Sawyer-Massey Co.* v. *Dennis* (1907) 1 Alta. 125, Beck, J. held that the provincial legislation was competent to say that a mortgage or an agreement to give a mortgage upon land prior to recommendation for patent is void. As to the Dominion parliament having control over the disposition of fines, forfeitures, and penalties imposed under Dominion laws, see Hodg. Prov. Legisl. 1896-8, pp. 118-9. See, however, *Dumphy* v. *Kehoe* (1891) 21 R. L. 119. *Cf. In re Bateman's Trusts* (1873) L. R. 15 Eq. 355.

303 *Dobie* v. *Temporalities Board* (1882) 7 App. Cas. 136, 150-1; *Attorney-General of Ontario* v. *Attorney-General for Canada* (Liquor Prohibition Appeal, 1895) [1896] A. C. 348, 364; *Royal Bank of Canada* v. *The King* [1913] A. C. 283, in which last case referring to parties in England who had advanced monies which the provincial Act in question had assumed to confiscate, their lordships say: " Their right was a civil right outside the province, and the legislature of the province could not legislate validly in derogation of that right . . a civil right, which had arisen and remained enforceable outside of the province." Provincial legislatures evidently cannot direct their own Courts to refuse to recognize such a right in an action brought in them, notwithstanding their exclusive power over the 'administration of justice in the province,' which follows the one under discussion: pp. 137-140. See, as to this case, Canada's Federal System, pp. 504-509; Jl. of Society of Comp. Legisl. Vol. 16, pp. 90-91. Review of Historical Publications Relating to Canada, vol. 18, p. 224; Article by J. S. Ewart, K.C. in 33 C. L. T. 269 *seq.*, and letter from him in 50 C. L. J. 56. He defends the Alberta Act in question as *intra vires* under No. 10 of section 92 as relating to a " Local Work

and Undertaking."   *Cf.*, also, 9 D. L. R. at pp. 346-363. Such maxims as '*Mobilia personam sequuntur*,' or '*mobilia ossibus inhaerent*' can in no way restrict the provincial legislative power: Canada's Federal System, pp. 509-511; Legislative Power in Canada, pp. 757-759. As to the *situs* of the obligation of a bank under a deposit receipt issued by one of its branches, and of other debts and choses in action, see *Lovitt* v. *The King* [1912] A. C. 22; *per* Duff, J.S.C., 43 S. C. R. 106, 131, 133-142; *Henty* v. *The Queen* [1896] A. C. 567; *Nickle* v. *Douglas* (1875) 37 U. C. R. 51, 61-62, 71; S. C. 35 U. C. R. 126, 145. As to cases where the owner is in one province, and the property in another, and the power of the provincial legislature in the latter, see Canada's Federal System, pp. 511-513. As to the property and civil rights of a railway which, though authorized to extend beyond the province, has not done so, see *In re Windsor and Annapolis R. W. Co.* (1883) 4 R. & G. 312, 322-3. As to provincial legislation under this power affecting the rights of extra-provincial creditors, see *Clarkson* v. *Ontario Bank* (1888) 15 O. A. R. 166, 190; *Jones* v. *Canada Central R. W. Co.* (1881) 46 U. C. R. 250; Canada's Federal System, pp. 513-515. For provincial Acts which have been held or suggested by the Courts as possibly valid under the power under discussion, see *Attorney-General for Ontario* v. *Attorney-General for the Dominion* [1896] A. C. 348; *Citizens Insurance Co.* v. *Parsons* (1881) 7 App. Cas. 96; *Gower* v. *Joyner* (1896) 2 Terr. L. R. 387; *Stairs* v. *Allen* (1896) 28 N. S. 410, 418-9; *McCarthy* v. *Brener* (1896) 2 Terr. L. R. 230; *Ex parte Ellis* (1878) 1 P. and B. 593; *Re Stinson* v. *College of Physicians* (1911) 22 O. L. R. 627, 634; *Regina* v. *Wason* (1889) 17 O. R. 58, 17 O. A. R. 221, 240-1, 251. *Cf. Florence Mining Co.* v. *Cobalt Lake Mining Co.* (1909) 18 O. L. R. 275, where the Ontario Court of Appeal say that: "the right to bring an action is a civil right." But the right of voting is not a "civil right" within the meaning of the clause in question: *In re North Perth, Hessin* v. *Lloyd* (1891) 21 O. R. 538. Provincial legislatures, in legislating under this power over 'property and civil rights in the province' may in some incidental way regulate trade and commerce: *Regina* v. *Taylor* (1875) 36 U. C. R. 183, 206; just as it may in some incidental way touch the subject of bankruptcy and insolvency: *In re Killam* (1878) 14 C. L. J. N. S. 242-3; *Parent* v. *Trudel* (1887) 13 O. L. R. 136, 139. See, however, Prov. Legisl. 1899-1900, p. 49.

304 Nothing effective has yet been done in the matter of this provision. See Canada's Federal System, pp. 521-525. The Canadian Bar Association has for one of its principal objects uniformity of law in the different provinces. See, also, Articles on Uniformity of Provincial Laws by R. B. Henderson in 19

C. L. T. 209; on Uniform Legislation by W. Seton Gordon in 20 C. L. T. 187; on Uniformitty in Registration of Title Law, 37 C. L. T. 374; and a Plea for a Uniform Contract of Fire Insurance in Canada (1899) 19 C. L. T. 112. Also see 46 C. L. J. 41; 35 C. L. T. 396; 36 C. L. T. 298; 37 C. L. T. 818.

305 As to the distinction between "the constitution of provincial Courts of criminal jurisdiction," and "procedure in criminal matters," see *supra*, pp. 118-9. As to the power to appoint King's Counsel, see *supra*, p. 61, n. 41. As to the power of the Dominion parliament to create new Courts to exercise jurisdiction in federal matters, and to deprive the provincial Courts of such jurisdiction, see *supra*, p. 90, and sec. 101 of the Federation Act, *supra*, pp. 149-150. As to the predominance of Dominion criminal legislation over provincial penal laws, see pp. 117-118. As to Dominion power over provincial Courts, see *supra*, p. 90 and pp. 138-9. Judge Clement (L. of C. C. 3rd ed., pp. 508-597) has a long chapter upon the administration of justice in Canada and its provinces, and the subjects which arise for discussion under this provincial power. As to appeals to the Supreme Court of Canada, and the Judicial Committee of the Privy Council, see *supra*, p. 149, and n. 376.

306 For this report of Sir John Thompson, see Hodg. Prov. Legisl. 1867-1895, p. 358. It is, also, set out at length in Legislative Power in Canada, pp. 140-174.

307 The power to appoint County and District Court judges in section 96, appears to carry with it the power to remove, although section 99 of the Federation Act applies only to Superior Court judges: *Re Squier* (1882) 46 U. C. R. 474. See *Re Small Debts Recovery Act*, (1917) 37 D. L. R. 170, 3 W. W. R. 698, and the annotation by the present writer, at p. 183 *seq.* endeavouring to place an exact interpretation on the power of appointment of " District " and " County Court " judges in sec. 96 of the B. N. A. Act, 1867, and finding the standard of jurisdiction in that of County Court and District Court judges in Upper Canada at Confederation under C. S. U. C. (1859) c. 15, and, possibly, in that exercised by County Court judges in New Brunswick under 30 Vict. c. 10 (N.Br.). See also *Niagara Election case* (1878) 29 C.P. 261, 280. See also an Article on the Constitution of Canada, 11 C. L. T. 145 *seq.;* Todd's Parl. Gov. in Brit. Col. 2nd ed. pp. 46-7, 827 *seq.* who treats, *inter alia*, of powers of removal still existing under Imp. 22 Geo. III, c. 75; and an Article on the Right to remove County Court Judges, 17 C. L. T. 445. R. S. C. 1906, c. 138, provides for the removal of County Court Judges by order of the Governor-General in Council in certain cases. The independence of the Superior Court judges appointed under sec. 96 is secured by sec. 99, which, following cl. 3, art. 7, of the *Act of Settlement* (Imp.) 12-13 Wm. III, c. 2, provides

that they shall hold office during good 'behaviour, but be removable by the Governor-General on address of the Senate and House of Commons.

308 See *In re Small Debts Act* (1896) 5 B. C. 246, and *Bank v. Tunstall* (1890) 2 B. C. (Hunter) 12, where the Court says that the provincial legislature cannot by merely constituting a Court by special name avoid section 96. See, also, *Ganong v. Bayley* (1877) 1 P. & B. 324. Upon the general subject of provincial attempts to evade the section, see the report of Sir John Thompson upon the *Quebec District Magistrates Act* referred to in the text; also Prov. Legisl. 1901-3, p. 33; and *King v. King* (1904) 37 N. S. 294. And *cf. Re Public Utilities Act, City of Winnipeg* v. *Winnipeg Electric R. W. Co.* (1916) 26 Man. 584, where two judges of the Manitoba Court of Appeal hold a provincial Act *ultra vires* in so far as it purported to confer powers transcending those of a Superior Court judge upon an officer called a commissioner, appointed by the Lieutenant-Governor in Council and paid by the province, contrary to secs. 96 and 100 of the Federation Act, and *Colonial Investment and Loan Co.* v. *Grady* (1915) 24 D. L. R. 176, 8 A. L. R. 496, holding *intra vires*, on similar grounds, a provincial Act purporting to confer upon a Master in Chambers extraordinary powers in mortgage actions, and actions on contracts for the sale of lands. And so *Rex* v. *Laity* (1913) 18 B. C. 443. See, also, *Polson Iron Works* v. *Munns* (1915) 24 D. L. R. 18, and the annotation thereto, *ibid.* at pp. 22-5.

309 Hodg. Prov. Legisl. 1867-1895, at p. 358; Prov. Legisl. 1896-8, pp. 12-14; 1904-6, pp. 128, 135, 155, 157.

310 *E.g.* that the Lieutenant-Governor may remove County Court judges for inability, incapacity, or misbehaviour: Hodg. Prov. 1867-1895, p. 361. *Ibid.* pp. 84, 853-4. Ministers of Justice have at times taken exception to provincial Acts supplementing the salaries of Dominion judges: Hodg. Prov. Legisl. 1867-1895, pp. 93-4, 853-4, But the Ontario *Extra-Judicial Services Act, 1910,* was allowed to go into force: *ibid.* pp. 1202-3. As to provincial attempts otherwise to regulate Dominion judges as by enacting that judges of one County or District shall have jurisdiction to try cases in another County or District, see *In re County Courts of British Columbia* (1892) 21 S. C. R. 446, 453, upholding the provincial Act and overruling *Peil-ke-ark-an* v. *Reginam* (1891) 2 B. C. (Hunter) 52, and *Gibson* v. *McDonald* (1885) 7 O. R. 401; *In re Wilson* v. *McGuire* (1883) 2 O. R. 118. See other Canadian cases referred to Canada's Federal System, p. 536, n. *Cf.* also, Prov. Legisl. 1867-1895, at pp. 1032-1034, 1037-1038.

311 *Rex* v. *Carlisle* (1903) 6 O. L. R. 718. See also, *Rex* v. *Walsh* (1903), 5 O. L. R. 527.

312 Hodg. Prov. Legisl. 1867-1895, pp. 186, 244 b., 528-9. *Ibid.* 1896-8, pp. 35-6. As to a Dominion Act empowering judges in a province to take evidence required in cases being litigated before foreign Courts under commissions or orders issued by such foreign Courts being *intra vires*, see *Wetherell* v. *Jones* (1883) 4 O. R. 713. As to a provincial Act of the same kind being also *intra vires*, see *Re Alberta and Great Waterways R. W. Co.* (1911) 20 Man. 697. As to the propriety, constitutionality and otherwise, of provincial Governments appointing Superior Court judges to act as Commissioners on Royal Commissions of Enquiry, see an able Article by Mr. J. B. Coyne, K.C., in 37 C. L. T. 416, who concludes that 'there can be no question as to the power of the province to have a judge as a Royal Commissioner even though the Dominion attempted in express terms to prohibit it.' He discusses the construction and constitutionality in that connection of s. 33 of the Dominion *Judges Act*, R. S. C., 1906, c. 138.

313 *The Thrasher case* (1882) 1 B. C. (Irving) 170, 174; Cass. Dig. Sup. Ct. 480; *Re Ginsberg* (1917) 40 O. L. R. 136, where held that in a civil proceeding within provincial legislative jurisdiction, the question whether a witness should be entitled to the privilege of refusing to answer on the ground that such answer would tend to incriminate him, is a question of civil right, and within the control of the provincial legislature. See this case referred to in Todd's Parl. Gov. in Brit. Col. 2nd ed. p. 566 *seq.;* also a number of letters and Articles upon it in 18 C. L. J. esp. at pp. 181, 265; and a series of Articles on provincial jurisdiction over civil procedure: 2 C. L. T. at pp. 313, 360, 409, 456, 513, 561.

314 *Valin* v. *Langlois* (1879) 5 App. Cas. 115; S. C. below 3 S. C. R. 1, 20-22, 69; *Attorney-General for Ontario* v. *Attorney-General for the Dominion* [1912] A. C. 571; *Ex parte Vancini* (1904) 36 N. B. 456, 462-3, in app. 34 S. C. R. 621; *Geller* v. *Loughrin* (1911) 24 O. L. R. 18, 25, 33; *Attorney-General of Canada* v. *Sun Chak* (1909) 44 N. S. 19; *King* v. *Wipper* (1901) 34 N. S. 202; *Attorney-General of Canada* v. *Flint* (1884) 16 S. C. R. App. 707; *Ex parte Porter* (1889) 28 N. B. 587; *Ex parte Perkins* (1884) 24 N. B. 70; *Ryan* v. *Devlin* (1875) 20 L. C. J. 77, 83-4; *Bruneau* v. *Massue* (1878) 23 L. C. J. 60. *Ex parte Flanagan* (1899) 34 N. B. 577, must be considered over-ruled. As to what are provincial Courts, see letter of Mr. Alpheus Todd, 18 C. L. J. at p. 181. See some remarks in 11 L. N. at pp. 349-350 on the question of the expediency of vesting Dominion or Federal judicial powers in provincial Courts.

315 *Attorney-General of Canada* v. *Flint* (1884) 16 S. C. R. App. 707, reported below (1882) 3 R. & G. 453, from which it appears that the judge of the Vice-Admiralty Court at Halifax

said, in his judgment:—"If a Dominion Act were to attempt
to give this Court a jurisdiction analogous to that of Admiralty
Courts in the United States, and exceeding that of the High
Court of Admiralty in England, I would have no difficulty to
holding that such an Act was *ultra vires.*" But see *contra per*
Weatherbe, J. 3 R. & G. at p. 461. Followed in *The King* v.
Kennedy (1902), 35 N. S. 266. *Cf. The Farewell* (1881) 7 Q. L. R.
380. As to admiralty jurisdiction in the Dominions, see Keith,
R. G. in D., Vol. III, pp. 1348-1356; also Clement's L. of C. C.,
3rd ed. pp. 232-241.

316 *Cushing* v. *Dupuy* (1880) 5 App. Cas. 409. *Cf. Peek* v.
Shields (1883) 8 S. C. R. 579, where Ritchie, C.J., reiterates his
language in *Valin* v. *Langlois* (1879) 3 S. C. R. 1, 15, *q. v., Cf.*
S. C. at p. 64. *Cf.,* also, *Ward* v. *Reed* (1882) 22 N. B. 279.
On the general subject of colonial attempts to limit the
prerogative of the Crown as to judicial appeals, see Keith,
R. G. in D., Vol. III, pp. 1365-1373, who holds the view that in
face of the (Imp.) *Judicial Committee Act, 1844,* this cannot
be done except by Imperial legislation. See *Toronto Railway
Co.* v. *The King* [1917] A. C. 630, where a certain doubt as to
the power of the Dominion parliament to take away the right
of appeal to the Privy Council seems hinted at. And see on the
general subject of the Dominion power to interfere with civil
procedure in Dominion subjects: Legislative Power in Canada,
p. 427, and *Re Steinberger* (1906) 5 W. L. R. 93.

317 See *per* Crease, J., in the *Thrasher case* (1882) 1 B. C.
(Irving) 126. Provincial Courts cannot interfere with the decisions of a Dominion tribunal, such as that of the Minister of
Agriculture in the case of patents: *In re The Bell Telephone Co.*
(1885) 9 O. R. 339, at p. 346. As to the Courts not enforcing an
ultra vires order of such a tribunal, see *Re Canadian Pacific
Railway Co. and County and Township of York* (1896) 27 O. R.
559, 570. A Dominion Act declaring a non-juridical day must
be interpreted as relating only to Dominion matters: *Richer*
v. *Gervais* (1894) R. J. Q. 6 S. C. 254. Of course the Dominion
parliament cannot prescribe procedure in provincial matters:
McKilligan v. *Machar* (1886) 3 M. R. 418; *Weiser* v. *Heintzman*
(No. 2) (1893) 15 O. P. R. 407; *Re Ginsberg* (1917) 40 O. L.
R. 136. *Cf. Regina* v. *Bittle* (1892) 21 O. R. 605; *Regina* v. *Fox*
(1899) 18 O. P. R. 343. See also, *supra*, p. 94.

318 For the negative view that the Dominion cannot divest
the provincial Courts of jurisdiction, see *Ex parte Porter* (1889)
28 N. B. 587; *Crombie* v. *Jackson* (1874) 34 U. C. R. 575, 579-
580; *Ex parte Wright* (1896) 34 N. B. 127. *Cf.* also *per* Thompson, J. in *Pineo* v. *Gavaza* (1885) 6 R. & G. 487, 489, commented
on 22 C. L. J. N.S. at pp. 70-72; and Clement *op. cit.* pp. 535-7.
But see *Re North Perth, Hessin* v. *Lloyd* (1891) 21 O. R. 538;
McLeod v. *Noble* (1897) 28 O. R. 528, 24 O. A. R. 459.

319 *In re Wilson* v. *McGuire* (1883) 2 O. R. 118; *Regina* v. *Bush* (1888) 15 O. R. 398. *Cf.* Articles in 2 C. L. T. 416, 521, 561; and *In re Small Debts Act* (1896) 5 B. C. 246; Canada's Federal System, pp. 556-7.

320 *Ganong* v. *Bayley* (1877) 1 P. & B. 324, where the Court agreed in interpreting section 96 by a reference to Courts existing before Confederation. See this case referred to Prov. Legisl. 1867-1895, p. 365, 1901-1903, p. 32; Legislative Power in Canada, at pp. 169-170.

321 *Regina* v. *Coote* (1873) L. R. 4 P. C. 599.

322 *Regina* v. *Horner* (1876) 2 Steph, Dig. 450; *Regina* v. *Bennett* (1882) 1 O. R. 445; *Queen* v. *Reno* (1868) 4 O. L. R. 281; *Regina* v. *Bush* (1888) 15 O. R. 398; *Richardson* v. *Ransom* (1886) 10 O. R. 387; *The King* v. *Sweeney* (1912) 1 D. L. R. 476; *The King* v. *Basker* (1912) 1 Dom. L. R. 295; *Ex parte Vancini* (1904) 36 N. B. 456; *Geller* v. *Loughrin* (1911) 24 O. L. R. 18, 23, 33; Canada's Federal System, pp. 559-564.

323 *Regina ex rel. McGuire* v. *Birkett* (1891) 21 O. R. 162. *Cf. In re Dominion Provident Benevolent and Endowment Association* (1894) 25 O. R. 619; *Ross* v. *Canada Agricultural Ins. Co.* (1882) 5 L. N. 22; *Polson Iron Works* v. *Munns* (1915) 24 D. L. R. 18, and annotation thereto, pp. 22-5; Canada's Federal System, pp. 564-6.

324 *Cf.* Report of Minister of Justice on a Quebec Act appointing a Railway Committee of the Executive Council: Hodgins' Prov. Legisl. 1867-1895, p. 439.

325 *McLeod* v. *Municipality of King* (1900) 35 N. B. 163.

326 *McCarthy* v. *Brener* (1896) 2 Terr, L. R. 230. See, also, *Stairs* v. *Allan* (1896) 28 N.S. 410, 418-9. *Cf.* however, *Deacon* v. *Chadwick* (1901) 1 O. L. R. 346.

327 *Attorney-General of Ontario* v. *Attorney-General of Canada* [1894] A. C. 189, 198; *Ex parte Ellis* (1878) 1 P. & B. 593, as to which *cf. Re Stinson and College of Physicians* (1911) 22 O. L. R. 627. See, too, *Baie des Chaleurs R. W. Co.* v. *Nantel* (1896) R. J. Q. 9 S. C. 47, 5 Q. B. 65.

328 *Queen* v. *De Coste* (1888) 21 N. S. 216; *Regina* v. *Eli* (1886) 13 O. A. R. 526, 533. *Cf. Regina* v. *Lake* (1878) 43 U. C. R. 515; *McLeod* v. *Noble* (1897) 28 O R. 528; *The Queen* v. *O'Bryan* (1900) 7 Ex. C. R. 19. As to provincial legislation in aid and furtherance of Dominion Acts being unobjectionable, see *Ex parte Whalen* (1891) 30 N. B. 586; *Matthew* v. *Wentworth* (1895) R. J. Q. 4 Q. B. 343; Hodgins' Prov. Legisl. 1867-1895, pp. 582, 947.

329 Despatch of Lord Granville: Dom. Sess. Pap. 1869, No. 16. As to provincial legislatures, however, being able to vest the Lieutenant-Governor with power of remitting sentences for

offences against provincial penal statutes, see *Attorney-General of Canada* v. *Attorney-General of Ontario* (1892) 19 O. A. R. 31.

330 *Hodge* v. *The Queen* (1883) 9 App. Cas. 117; Canada's Federal System, pp. 574-5. As to the same power existing for other laws within provincial jurisdiction under other parts of the Constitution, *cf. Regina* v. *Harper* (1892) R. J. Q. 1 S. C. 327, 333. See, also, *per* Osler, J.A., in *Regina* v. *Wason* (1890) 17 O. A. R. 221, 243.

331 *Paige* v. *Griffith* (1873) 18 L. C. J. 119, 122; *Aubry* v. *Genest* (1895) R. J. Q. 4 Q. B. 523. *Cf.* as to the provincial·right of disposal of fines, forfeitures, and penalties imposed under this subsection, *Dumphy* v. *Kehoe* (1891) 21 R. L. 119; and Prov. Legisl. 1896-8, pp. 118-9.

332 *Hodge* v. *The Queen* (1883) 9 App. Cas. 117, 133; *Regina* v. *Frawley* (1882) 7 O. A. R. 246. See, also, *Blouin* v. *Corporation of Quebec* (1880) 7 Q. L. R. 18.

333 *King* v. *Gardner* (1892) 25 N. S. 48, 52-4; *Matthews* v. *Jenkins* (1907) 3 E. L. R. 577 (P. E. I.). As to Dominion power to impose forfeiture as punishment, see *O'Neil* v. *Tupper* (1896) R. J. Q. 4 Q. B. 315, 26 S. C. R. 122, 132.

334 *Quebec Bank* v. *Tozer* (1899) R. J. Q. 17 S. C. 303. As to provincial statutes authorizing offenders against Dominion criminal law being sent to industrial schools being *ultra vires*, see report of Minister of Justice of Dec. 13th, 1910, referred to Canada's Federal System, p. 578.

335 *Attorney-General of Canada* v. *Attorney-General of Ontario* (1890-4) 20 O. R. 322, 19 O. A. R. 31, 23 S. C. R. 458. See this case referred to 10 C. L. T. at p. 233; 26 C. L. J. at p. 459.

336 *Hodge* v. *The Queen* (1883) 9 App. Cas. 117; *Turcotte* v. *Whalen*, M. L. R. 7 Q. B. 263; Canada's Federal System, p. 580. See *supra*, pp. 68-9.

337 As to there being a vast number of acts punishable on summary conviction which nevertheless are in no sense crimes, see *Attorney-General* v. *Radloff* (1854) 10 Ex. 84, 96, cited *Ex parte Green* (1900) 35 N. B. 137, 148. As to "penal actions" for acts injurious to the community which nevertheless are not crimes, see Kenny's Criminal Law, at pp. 7-8. As to the difficulty of drawing the line between what is within No. 15 of sec. 92 of the Federation Act, and what within No. 27 of sec. 91, see Hodgins' Provincial Legisl. 1867-1895, at p. 762. *Cf.* Canada's Federal System, pp. 580-2, n. 23.

338 *Cf.* Clement, L. of C. C., 3rd ed., pp. 586-7; *Regina* v. *Boardman* (1871) 30 U. C. R. 553, 556; *Quong Wing* v. *The King* (1914) 49 S. C. R. 440, 462.

339 *Huson* v. *Township of South Norwich* (1895) 24 S. C. R. 145, 160; *Hodge* v. *The Queen* (1883) 9 App. Cas. 117; *Attorney-*

General for Ontario v. Attorney-General for the Dominion [1896]
A. C. 348, 371; Attorney-General of Manitoba v. Manitoba License
Holders Association [1902] A. C. 73; Rex v. Riddell (1912)
4 D. L. R. 662. As to police power in Canada and that the
provinces do not possess it exclusively in "the wide meaning
which the jurisprudence of the United States has given it," see
per Sedgewick, J., in In re Prohibitory Liquor Laws (1895)
24 S. C. R. 170, 248. For criticisms by members of the Judicial
Committee of the term "police regulation" see Canada's Federal
System, pp. 583-4, n. 29. Cf. Rex v. Meikleham (1905) 11 O. L. R.
366, as to the power of the Ontario Legislature to prohibit the
sale of liquor on vessels on the Great Lakes. Cf. also City of
Montreal v. Beauvais (1909) 42 S. C. R. 211, upholding early
shop-closing legislation by the Province; and Re Rex v. Scott
(1916) 37 O. L. R. 453, in which last case a provincial Act declaring that a person found drunk in a public place in a municipality in which a local option by-law is in force, or in which
no tavern or shop license has been issued, is guilty of an offence,
was held intra vires.

340 Bennett v. Pharmaceutical Association of the Province
of Quebec (1881) 1 Dor. Q. A. 336; In re Girard (1898) R. J. Q.
14 S. C. 237; In re Slavin and Village of Orillia (1875) 36 U. C.
R. 159, per Richards, C.J., at p. 173.

341 The King v. Kay (1909) 39 N. B. 278. Cf. also Re Bread
Sales Act (1911) 23 O. L. R. 238.

342 Regina v. Wason (1890) 17 O. A. R. 221, 239-240, 248,
with which contrast Regina v. Stone (1892) 23 O. R. 46, where
a Dominion Act, superficially similar, but really a public criminal law, was, also, held to be intra vires. Cf., also, Regina v.
Keefe (1890) 1 Terr. L. R. 280; Kitchen v. Saville (1897) 17
C. L. T. 91; Regina v. Fleming (1895) 15 C. L. T. (N.W.T.) 247.

343 Montreal Trading Stamp Co. v. City of Halifax (1900)
20 C. L. T. (Occ. N.) 355. The Ontario Court of Appeal held
the same of like Ontario legislation in answer to questions
submitted, infra. Aliter, however, Wilder v. La Cité de Montreal
(1905) R. J. Q. 14 K. B. 139, holding that a provincial legislature has no power to prohibit any kind of commerce not in
itself contrary either to good morals or to public order—Sed
quære, see supra, pp. 66-7. The answers of the Ontario Court
of Appeal in the above trading stamp case are set out in the
report of this last case in the Court below (R. J. Q. 25 S. C.
at p. 137), but do not appear to be elsewhere reported.

344 State v. Schuster (1904) 14 Man. 672; City of Montreal
v. Beauvais (1909) 42 S. C. R. 211, R. J. Q. 7 K. B. 420, 30 S. C.
427, in which case the Privy Council refused leave to appeal: 42
S. C. R. p. VII. See, also, Re McCoubrey (1913) 9 D. L. R. 84.

345 *Pillow* v. *City of Montreal* (1885) M. L. R. 1 Q. B. 401.
Cf. per Torrance, J. in *Ex parte Pillow* (1883) 6 L. N. 209;
Toronto Railway Co. v. *The King* [1917] A. C. 630.

346 *Queen* v. *Robertson* (1886) 3 Man. 613.

347 *Regina* v. *Boscowitz* (1895) 4 B. C. 132. But see Prov.
Legisl. 1867-1895, at pp. 929-930, 1121; *ibid.* 1899-1900, p. 85.

348 *Rex* v. *Pierce* (1904) 9 O. L. R. 374.

349 *L'Association St. Jean Baptiste* v. *Brault* (1900) 30 S.
C. R. 598. *Cf. Regina* v. *Harper* (1892) R. J. Q. 1 S. C. 333;
Pigeon v. *Mainville* (1893) 17 L. N. 68, 72.

350 *Regina* v. *Shaw* (1891) 7 Man. 518.

351 Prov. Legisl. 1867-1895, pp. 643, 994. But see *McCaffrey* v. *Hall* (1891) 35 L. C. J. 38; Canada's Federal System, p. 615.

352 Provincial statutes prohibiting sales of various kinds
of goods, or the doing of certain kinds of labour on Sunday
were held good in: *Regina* v. *Petersky* (1895) 4 B. C. 385;
Ex parte Green (1900) 35 N. B. 137; *Couture* v. *Panos* (1908)
R. J. Q. 17 K. B. (Crown side) 560, 564; *Fallis* v. *Dalthaser*
(1912) 4 D. L. R. 705. *Cf.* also *Poulin* v. *Corporation of Quebec* (1883) 9 S. C. R. 185, 7 Q. L. R. 337; and *Queen* v. *Halifax
Electric Tramway Co.* (1898) 30 N. S. 469. So, also, a municipal by-law passed under the provisions of a provincial Municipal Act closing billiard rooms on Sunday was held valid in
Re Fisher v. *Village of Carmen* (1905) 16 Man. 560. And *cf.
Tremblay* v. *Cité de Quebec* (1910) R. J. Q. 37 S. C. 375, 38
S. C. 82. On the other hand, a provincial Act covering such
prohibitions was held *ultra vires*, because " treated as a whole "
it was legislation upon criminal law: *Attorney-General for Ontario* v. *Hamilton Street Railway Company* [1902] A. C. 524,
basing themselves upon which decision the majority of the
judges in *Ouimet* v. *Bazin* (1912) 46 S. C. R. 502, held *ultra
vires* as criminal law Quebec legislation prohibiting under
penalties the giving of theatrical performances on Sunday. They
seem to hold that the question whether Sunday legislation is
exclusively for the Dominion parliament or not depends on the
point of view of the legislator in legislating. If he is legislating from a Christian point of view in order to prevent religious desecration of the Lord's Day, the legislation is for the
Dominion and not for the province. *Cf.*, also, *Audette* v. *Daniel*
(1913) 13 D. L. R. 240; *McLaughlin* v. *Recorder's Court*
(1902) 4 Q. P. R. 304; *Rodrigue* v. *Parish Ste. Prosper* (1917) 37
D. L. R. 321, 40 D. L. R. 30, and for a general discussion of the
subject, Canada's Federal System, pp. 594-612.

353 *Regina* v. *Bittle* (1892) 21 O. R. 605; *Ex parte Duncan*
(1872) 16 L. C. J. 188, 191; *Regina* v. *Wason* (1890) 17 O. A. R.

221, 232; and other cases collected, Canada's Federal System, pp. 618-623. *Regina* v. *Roddy* (1877) 41 U. C. R. 291, 296, 302, must, it would seem, be considered overruled. And so in *Weiser* v. *Heintzman* (No. 2) (1893) 15 O. P. R. 407. But *cf. Regina* v. *Hart* (1891) 20 O. R. 611, 612-14. See, also, *Regina* v. *Becker* (1891) 20 O. R. 676; *Regina* v. *Rowe* (1892) 12 C. L. T. 95.· And see, also, *O'Neil* v. *Tupper* (1896) R. J. Q. 4 Q. B. 315, 26 S. C. R. 122, 132; and *In re McNutt* (1912) 47 S. C. R. 259, where three judges held that a trial and conviction for keeping intoxicating liquor for sale contrary to the provisions of a provincial Act are proceedings on a criminal charge within the meaning of section 39 (c) of the Supreme Court Act, R. S. C. 1906, c. 139, whereby an appeal is given from the judgment in any case of *habeas corpus* 'not arising on a criminal charge.' As to this last case, see *Quong Wing* v. *The King* (1914) 49 S. C. R. 440, 459, where, as a matter of fact, the Supreme Court entertained the appeal, although it was an appeal from a conviction under a provincial penal enactment. See, also, Clement, L. of C. C. (3rd ed. p. 546 *seq.*) who dissents from the view of the three judges in the McNutt case. And in *Rex* v. *Miller* (1909) 19 O. L. R. 288, the Court held that the procedure applicable to a motion for a writ of *habeas corpus* when there has been a committal for the infraction of a provincial Act is such as may be prescribed by the provincial legislature. See, also, *Rex* v. *Graves* (1910) 21 O. L. R. 329; *Rex* v. *Gage* (1916) 36 O. L. R. 183. In *Regina ex rel. Brown* v. *Simpson Co.* (1896) 28 O. R. 231, it was held that a magistrate has no power to state a case under sec. 900 of the Dominion Criminal Code for an alleged offence against an Ontario Statute. But see *Rex* v. *Durocher* (1913) 9 D. L. R. 627. In *Copeland & Chatterson Co.* v. *Business Systems Ltd.* (1908) 16 O. L. R. 481, the Ontario Court of Appeal held an order of sequestration for disobedience of an injunction, not to be under the circumstances, an order in a 'criminal matter,' within the Ontario Judicature Act.

    354 To the cases there cited, we may add a reference to *Regina* v. *Lawrence* (1878) 43 U. C. R. 164, as to provincial legislation as to offences which are criminal offences at common law, such as tampering with witnesses and subornation of perjury: *Rex* v. *Garvin* (1908) 13 B. C. 331; *Regina* v. *Holland* (1894) 30 C. L. J. 428, 14 C. L. T. 294; *Rex* v. *Ferris* (1910) 15 W. L. R. 331; *Regina* v. *Shaw* (1891) 7 Man. 518; *Rex* v. *Laughton* (1912) 22 Man. 520; *Re Stinson and College of Physicians* (1911) 22 O. L. R. 627; Prov. Legisl. 1867-1895, at pp. 484, 581; Clement's L. of C. C. 3rd ed. pp. 583-4. At p. 569, Judge Clement remarks that there is no reported case in

which a federal penal law has been held invalid as an unauthorized encroachment upon the provincial field.

³⁵⁵ *Attorney-General for Ontario* v. *Attorney-General for the Dominion* [1896] A. C. 348, 365.

³⁵⁶ *Attorney-General of Manitoba* v. *Manitoba License Holders Association* [1902] A. C. 73, where the Privy Council held a Manitoba Act *intra vires* under this sub-section, although it purported to prohibit all use in Manitoba of spirituous fermented malt and all intoxicating liquors as beverages or otherwise, subject to certain exceptions; and although such legislation might or must have an effect outside the limits of the province, and might or must interfere with the sources of Dominion revenue, and the industrial pursuits of persons licensed under Dominion statutes to carry on particular trades.

³⁵⁷ See as to these arguments: Legislative Power in Canada, pp. 655-661. Lord Herschell incidentally observed in the course of one of these arguments, that there is scarcely anything which may be desirable and beneficial for a province to deal with locally, which may not become, some time or other, a matter of Dominion concern, and, therefore, one on which it might be necessary for the Dominion parliament to legislate for the whole Dominion, which would oust the power of the provincial legislature. Several examples of provincial Acts held valid under this sub-section have been noticed *supra*, pp. 141-2 and notes, when considering sub-section 15. The important Privy Council decision in *L'Union St. Jacques* v. *Belisle* (1874) L. R. 6 P. C. 31, and *The King* v. *Kay* (1909) 39 N. B. 378, may be added. As to provincial legislatures not being able to legislate on the enumerated subjects of section 91 of the Federation Act under the pretence or contention that the legislation is of a provincial or local character, see *supra*, p. 86; as to a provincial legislature not being incapacitated from enacting a law otherwise within its proper competency merely because the Dominion parliament might, under section 91, if it saw fit so to do, pass a general law which would embrace within its scope the subject matter of the provincial Act, see *supra*, pp. 97-8; as to whether the provinces have any power or indirect taxation under sub-section 16, see supra, n. 255; and as to matters once local and provincial ceasing to be so, and becoming of national concern so as to fall under Dominion jurisdiction, see *supra*, p. 75. See, also, Clement's L. of C. C., pp. 829-836.

³⁵⁸ The decisions under this section, and under section 22 of the Manitoba Act above referred to, have largely turned upon questions of fact, namely, whether the New Brunswick Common Schools Act, 1871, prejudicially affected rights or privileges of the Roman Catholics in the province with respect to denominational schools which they had by law at the Union:

Maher v. *Town of Portland,* before the Privy Council, July 17th, 1874, reported fully only, apparently, in Wheeler's Confederation Law, pp. 362-7, briefly noted 2 Cart. Cas. at p. 486, n; whether the Manitoba Public Schools Act of 1890 prejudicially affected any right or privilege which the Roman Catholics, by law or practice, had in that province at the Union: *City of Winnipeg* v. *Barrett* [1892] A. C. 445, 19 S. C. R. 374, 7 Man. 273; whether any rights or privileges of the Roman Catholic minority in Manitoba which accrued to them after the Union under statutes of that province, had been interfered with by the above Act of 1890, and another provincial statute of that year: *Brophy* v. *Attorney-General of Manitoba* [1895] A. C. 202, 223, 22 S. C. R. 577. *Cf.* Keith's Responsible Government in the Dominions, Vol. 2, pp. 689-696. On the general subject of the Church in the Dominions, see Keith *op. cit.* p. 1423 *seq.* As to why sec. 93 was enacted, see *Brophy* v. *Attorney-General* [1895] A. C. 202, at pp. 213-4; *Maher* v. *Town of Portland, sub nom. Ex parte Renaud,* 14 N. B. (1 Pugs.) 273, 293. For a thoughtful little Article on *Federal* v. *Provincial Control of Education* see *Mail and Empire* for May 19th, 1917. Of course it does not exclude the paramount power of the Imperial parliament to legislate: *Regina* v. *College of Physicians and Surgeons* (1879) 44 U. C. R. 564, 576, as to which see *supra*, pp. 47, 50. There is nothing in it to debar a province from establishing a national system of unsectarian education: *City of Winnipeg* v. *Barrett* [1892] A. C. 445, 454.

359 *Maher* v. *Town of Portland, supra.* And see extracts from the argument before the Privy Council, and from the judgment of Fisher, J. in the Court below (14 N. B. 273) in Canada's Federal System, pp. 636-639. And as to the reference in the sub-section being to rights and privileges in respect to denominational schools only, and not to any rights and privileges with respect to religious teaching in schools generally, see *Ex parte Renaud* (1873) 14 N. B. 273, 298. As to collegiate institutions, not being within the contemplation of section 93, see *per* Ritchie, C.J., S. C. at p. 277. For an application under it in reference to an alleged discrimination in a Quebec Act against the Protestant universities and schools of Quebec, in regard to the admission of students to the study of law, see Hodg. Prov. Legisl. 1867-1895, pp. 337-38. As to there having been at the time of the Union no schools clearly denominational, whether Roman Catholic or Protestant, in any of the four provinces which were supported by rates on all the Queen's subjects without reference to their religion, see *per* Duff, K.C., *arguendo* in *Maher* v. *Town of Portland,* Wheeler's Confed. Law, at p. 366; and as to there being nothing in the above

sub-s. 1 to prevent the legislature of Upper Canada repealing
the peculiar laws by which the Roman Catholic schools in
Upper Canada were established, see *per* Mellish, L.J. *ibid.*
Needless to say, the constitutionality of a provincial Act relating to education cannot be affected by any regulation made
under it, there being nothing unconstitutional in the Act itself;
if regulations have been made which ought not to have been
made, or not made, which ought to have been made, that may
be a case for an appeal under sub-s. 3: *Ex parte Renaud* (1873)
14 N. B. (1 Pugs.) 273, 289.

360 *Ottawa Separate Schools* v. *Machell* [1917] A. C. 62.
For a careful statement as to the points decided in this judgment in reference to the Roman Catholic Separate Schools in
Ontario, in special connection with the bilingual controversy, see
36 C. L. T. pp. 968-970; as also in the other appeal decided by
their lordships at the same time, of *Ottawa Separate School
Trustees* v. *Ottawa Corporation* [1917] A. C. 76. The intention
of the sub-section is that every class of persons having any
right or privilege with respect to denominational schools,
whether such class should be one of the numerous denomina-
tions of Protestants, or Roman Catholics, should be protected
in such rights: *Ex parte Renaud* (1873) 14 N. B. (1 Pugs.)
273, 287. See, also, *Re Ottawa Separate Schools*, 13 O. W. N.
261, 369.

361 *Ex parte Renaud* (1873) 14 N. B. (1 Pugs.) 273, 277,
292, 294.

362 *City of Winnipeg* v. *Barrett* (1891) 19 S. C. R. 374, 425;
Separate School Trustees of Belleville v. *Grainger* (1878) 25
Gr. 570, 579. *Cf. In re Roman Catholic Separate Schools*
(1889) 18 O. R. 606; *Roman Catholic Separate Schools* v. *Township of Arthur* (1891) 21 O. R. 60. Nor does the section in any
way affect or lessen the power of the provincial legislatures to
pass laws respecting the general educational system of the province: Hodg. Prov. Legisl. 1867-1895, p. 662. *Cf. per* Taylor,
C.J., in *City of Winnipeg* v. *Barrett* (1891) 7 Man. 273, 298-9,
329, 375. See, also, G. M. Weir's *Separate School Law in the
Prairie Provinces:* (Queen's Univ., Ont., 1918.)

363 *Logan* v. *City of Winnipeg* (1891) 8 Man. 3, 15, heard in
appeal with *City of Winnipeg* v. *Barrett* [1892] A. C. 445, where
the appeal being decided on other grounds, the point is not
dealt with. As to whether one may under certain circumstances be estopped from setting up the unconstitutionality
of a statute, as *e.g.* by the Act being a private one, passed on
one's own application; or because one has not pleaded the unconstitutionality, see *pro: City of Toronto* v. *Bell Telephone
Co.* (1903) 6 O. L. R. 335, 349-350, 352; *Ross* v. *Guilbault* (1881)
4 L. N. 415; *Ross* v. *Canada Agricultural Insurance Co.* (1882)

5 L. N. 23; *Forsyth* v. *Bury* (1888) 15 S. C. R. 543; *McCaffery* v. *Ball* (1889) 34 L. C. J. 91; *Belanger* v. *Caron* (1879) 5 O. L. R. 19, 25; *contra: City of Toronto* v. *Bell Telephone Co., supra,* at p. 344; *Valin* v. *Langlois* (1879) 5 Q. L. R. 1, 16; *L'Union St. Jacques de Montreal* v. *Belisle* (1872) 20 L. C. J. 29, 39: Prov. Legisl. 1867-1895, at p. 216; Clement, L. of C. C. 3rd ed. p. 377. As to the duty generally to uphold the Constitution, see *City of Fredericton* v. *The Queen* (1880) 3 S. C. R. 505, 545; *Gibson* v. *Macdonald* (1885) 7 O. R. 401, 416. See, also, *King* v. *Joe* (1891) 8 Haw. Rep. 287; Cooley on Const. Limit. 5th ed. pp. 196-7.

364 Prov. Legisl. 1867-1895, at pp. 1189-1197; Wheeler *op. cit.* at p. 338.

365 *Brophy* v. *Attorney-General of Manitoba* [1895] A. C. 202, 221. *Cf. Separate School Trustees of Belleville* v. *Grainger* (1878) 25 Gr. 570, 581.

366 *City of Winnipeg* v. *Barrett* [1892] A. C. 445, 452. What is there stated is spoken of sub-ss. 2 and 3 of sec. 22 of the Manitoba Act (*supra*, pp. 147-8), but these, so far as the present point is concerned, may be said to be identical with the sub-section we are now considering. *Cf. Brophy* v. *Attorney-General of Manitoba* [1895] A. C. 202, 213-6.

367 *Brophy* v. *Attorney-General of Manitoba* [1895] A. C. 202, 217. The parliament of Canada has no jurisdiction in relation to education, except under the conditions in sub-s. 4: *Ottawa Separate Schools* v. *Mackell* [1917] A. C. 62. See further as to this case, *Re Ottawa Separate Schools* (1917) 13 O. W. N. 261, 369.

368 As to "denominational schools," and "any class of persons," see the construction placed upon the similar words in sec. 93 of the Federation Act, *supra*, pp. 145-6.

369 As to this section 22 generally, and its origin, see *Brophy* v. *Attorney-General of Manitoba* [1895] A. C. 202, 213, 215, 219, 228. As to sub-ss. 2 and 3 not ousting the jurisdiction of the ordinary tribunals, and as to the fact that they are not to be construed as merely giving a concurrent remedy where sub-s. 1 is infringed, see *supra*, p. 146. As to sub-s. 4, in *Brophy's case, supra*, at p. 228 their lordships say: "Their lordships have decided that the Governor-General in Council has jurisdiction, and that the appeal is well founded, but the particular course to be pursued must be determined by the authorities to whom it has been committed by the statute. It is not for this tribunal to intimate the precise steps to be taken." See, also, Canada's Federal System, pp. 665-6.

370 *City of Winnipeg* v. *Barrett* [1892] A. C. 445, 452-3, 454, 357-8. In this case, their lordships decided that the Roman Catholics of Manitoba, as a matter of fact, had no right or privi-

lege with respect to denominational schools by law or practice
at the Union; and that the establishment of a national system
of education upon an unsectarian basis is not so inconsistent
with the right to set up and maintain denominational schools
that the two things cannot exist together, or that the existence
of the one necessarily implies or involves immunity from taxation for the purpose of the other.   See their judgment in this
case referred to in the subsequent one of *Brophy* v. *Attorney-
General of Manitoba* [1895] A. C. 202.

371 See S. C. [1895] A. C. 202, 221.

372 *Brophy* v. *Attorney-General of Manitoba* [1895] A. C. 202,
219, 221.   Their lordships here decided that rights or privileges
of the Roman Catholic minority in relation to education, which
accrued to them after the Union under statutes of the province,
had been affected by the Manitoba Public Schools Act, 1890.

373 Clement, L. of C. C. 3rd ed. pp. 954-959, gives extracts
from the Ordinances of the North-West Territories above referred to touching Separate Schools.   See, also, *ibid.* pp. 784-788.
Reference may also be made to the speech of Sir W. Laurier as
to Separate Schools in these provinces of February 21st, 1905:
House of Commons Debates, Vol. 69, p. 1442.   See, also, *Regina
Public School District* v. *Gratton Separate School District*
(1915) 50 S. C. R. 589 (reversing 7 W. W. R. 7, 6 W. W. R.
1088), wherein two judges of the Supreme Court hold *intra
vires* and one *ultra vires* a Saskatchewan statute authorizing
Separate School Boards to give notice to companies requiring
their taxes to be apportioned in a way prescribed between the
Separate School and the Public School Boards.

374 Prov. Legisl. 1899-1910, p. 139.   *Cf.* Keith's *Imp. Unity,*
p. 443.

375 The predominance of Dominion legislation is illustrated
by *In re Narain Singh* (1908) 13 B. C. 477.   A provincial Act
to prevent the fraudulent entry of horses at exhibitions under
false or assumed names or pedigrees or in a wrong class was
held *intra vires* under "agriculture" in this section in *Rex*
v. *Horning* (1904) 8 O. L. R. 215; so was the Dominion *Animal
Contagious Diseases Act, 1903,* in *Brooks* v. *Moore,* (1907) 13
B. C. 91.   For provincial Acts relating to immigration disallowed on the ground that the Dominion parliament had legislated, see Prov. Legisl. 1867-1895, pp. 634-5; *ibid.* 1899-1900, pp.
134-9; *ibid.* 1901-1903, pp. 64, 74-75; Canada's Federal System, 669-
671.   As to the meaning of the term "immigration," see the
Australian cases: *Attorney-General for the Commonwealth* v.
Ah Sheung (1906) 4 C. L. R. 949; *Chia Gee* v. *Martin* (1905)
3 C. L. R. 649; *Ah Yin* v. *Christie* (1907) 4 C. L. R. 1428; *Potter*
v. *Minahan* (1908) 7 C. L. R. 277; and an Article on the Legal
Interpretation of the Constitution of the Commonwealth, by

A. B. Keith, Jl. of Compar. Legisl., N.S., Vol. 11, pp. 239-242. See, also, *In re Behari Lal* (1908) 13 B. C. 415.

[876] No appeal lies of right from the Supreme Court of Canada to His Majesty in Council, but an appeal lies by special leave in every case save as regards criminal appeals, in which a Dominion enactment purports to limit the prerogative: R. S. C. 1906, c. 146, s. 1025, 'though it is a good deal more than possible that that Act might be held to be inconsistent with Imp. 7-8 Vict. c. 69, s. 1, and, therefore, *ultra vires* of the Dominion parliament': Keith's R. G. in D., Vol. II, pp. 981, 1023. As to the power to refer special matters to the Judicial Committee under 3-4 Wm. IV, c. 41, s. 4 (Lord Brougham's Act) see Keith *op. cit.* Vol. III, p. 1382 *seq.* See, also, Clement, L. of C. C. 3rd ed. pp. 157-164. Provincial statutes, however, permit litigants, in certain cases, to appeal direct to the Privy Council from the provincial Court of Appeal, without first going to the Supreme Court of Canada. Thus, *e.g.*, in Ontario, such appeal is permitted 'where the matter in controversy in any case exceeds the sum or value of $4,000, as well as in any case where the matter in question relates to the taking of any annual or other rent, customary or other duty, or fee, or any like demand of a general and public nature affecting future rights, of what value or amount soever the same may be ': R. S. O. 1914, c. 54, s. 2. See as to the other provisions, Bentinck's Privy Council Practice (London, 1912), pp. 50-64. There is nothing repugnant to sec. 101 of the Federation Act in the provisions of the Dominion Supreme Court Act authorizing the Governor-General in Council to obtain by direct request answers from the Supreme Court of Canada on any questions of law or fact; such provisions are *intra vires: Attorney-General of Ontario* v. *Attorney-General of Canada* [1912] A. C. 571. As to the different position of the Supreme Court of the United States to that of the Supreme Court of Canada, see *Attorney-General for British Columbia* v. *Attorney-General for Canada* [1914] A. C. 153, 162; and Canada's Federal System, p. 677, n. 10. As to similar legislation in Australia regarding the reference of questions by the Governor-General to the High Court, see Keith *op. cit.* Vol. II, p. 886. The opinions of judges in response to such references are not, however, binding on the Governor-General in Council or on the judges of the Supreme Court themselves in any concrete case which may arise, nor on the judge of any of the provincial Courts: *In re Supreme Court References* (1910) 43 S. C. R. 536, 550, 561, 588, 592. *Cf. Kerley* v. *London and Lake Erie Transportation Co.* (1912) 26 O. L. R. 588; *The King* v. *Brinkley* (1907) 14 O. L. R. 434, 448-452; Prov. Legisl. 1867-1895, pp. 423-4. As to counsel not being permitted to vary the questions submitted by hypothetical

limitations not to be found in legislative provisions or in the
questions which relate to them, see *Attorney-General of Alberta*
v. *Attorney-General for Canada* [1915] A. C. 363. As to any
power in the Supreme Court to avoid answering such questions,
see *Attorney-General for Ontario* v. *Attorney-General for the
Dominion* [1912] A. C. 571, 589. As to such Canadian legislation for the answering of questions not binding the Judicial
Committee, and as to the objectionable points in such procedure for "obtaining speculative opinions on hypothetical questions," and instances where the Judicial Committee have refused to answer such questions, see *Attorney-General of British
Columbia* v. *Attorney-General for Canada, supra,* at p. 162;
John Deere Plow Co. v. *Wharton* [1915] A. C. 330; *Attorney-
General for Ontario* v. *Attorney-General for Canada* [1916] A. C.
588, 601; *Attorney-General for Ontario* v. *Hamilton Street R. W.
Co.* [1913] A. C. 524, 529; *Attorney-General for the Dominion of
Canada* v. *Attorneys-General for the Provinces* [1898] A. C.
700, 717. See, also, *Attorney-General for the Dominion of Can-
ada* v. *Attorneys-General of the Provinces* [1897] A. C. 199, 208.
As to similar legislation in the United States, see Bryce, Amer.
Comm., ed. 1914, Vol. I, pp. 448-9; and as to the whole matter
generally, see Canada's Federal System, pp. 672-683.

377 *L'Association St. Jean Baptiste* v. *Brault* (1901) 31 S.
C. R. 172. And *cf.* Supreme Court Act, R. S. C. 1906, c. 139,
secs. 38, 40.

378 *Crown Grain Co.* v. *Day* [1908] A. C. 504, 507, 39 S. C.
R. 258; *Danjou* v. *Marquis* (1879) 3 S. C. R. 251, 264, 268-9.
City of Halifax v. *McLaughlin Carriage Co.* (1907) 39 S. C. R.
175. Nor have provincial legislatures any power to grant an
appeal to the Supreme Court: *Union Colliery Co.* v. *Attorney-
General of British Columbia* (1897) 17 C. L. T. 391; Prov.
Legisl. 1896-8, p. 4.

379 On the argument in *Attorney-General for Ontario* v.
Attorney-General for Canada [1912] A. C. 571, Sir Robert Finlay contended that the words included only the laws of the
Dominion as distinguished from the laws of the provinces; but
Lord Macnaghten is reported as observing: "Is that so very
clear? I am not quite sure about that. I should have thought
the 'laws of Canada' might embrace the laws of the several
provinces too": *Verbatim* argument (Wm. Briggs, Toronto,
1912), p. 11; Canada's Federal System, pp. 674-6, 685-6. The
view of the Court below in that case seems to have harmonized
with that of Lord Macnaghten: 43 S. C. R. 536. See, however,
per Davies, J. and Idington, J., pp. 552, 569, 571, 575. *Cf.* also
sec. 4 of the Federation Act, and *Prince Edward Island* v. *Attorney-General for the Dominion of Canada* [1905] A. C. 37. See,

also, in favour of the broader construction, Article in 11 C. L. T. 147, upon the Constitution of Canada; and per Strong, J. in *City of Quebec* v. *The Queen* (1894) 24 S. C. R. 420, 430. And *cf.* per Duff, J. in *Bonanza Creek Gold Mining Co.* v. *The King* (1915) 50 S. C. R. 534, 571-2, and in app. S. C. [1916] A. C. 566, 576, as to a provincial charter being included in the term "a Canadian charter," in certain Government regulations. Judge Clement, however, takes the view that Dominion or Federal laws only are meant, but that it includes the law on all subjects within federal jurisdiction, whether there has been post-Confederation legislation by the Dominion parliament or not: L. of C. C. 3rd ed. pp. 511, 528-9. See, generally, Canada's Federal System, pp. 685-687. Such Courts for the better administration of the laws of Canada, are the Exchequer Court of Canada (with original jurisdiction, *inter alia*, in matters of suit against the Crown (Dominion), and between subject and subject in patent, copyright, and trade-mark cases, and also as a Court of Admiralty: see R. S. C. 1906, chaps. 140, 141); and the Railway Committee of the (Dominion) Privy Council. See Clement *op. cit.* p. 552. There is an appeal as of right to the Judicial Committee of the Privy Council under the Imperial *Colonial Court of Admiralty Act 1890*, in respect to its exercise of Admiralty jurisdiction: Clement *op. cit.* pp. 241, 986. It was by virtue of secs. 101 and 132 of the Federation Act that the Dominion had the constitutional power to establish a Court presided over by a Commissioner named for that purpose to apply the laws relating to extradition: *Gaynor* v. *Lafontaine* (1904) R. J. Q. 14 K. B. 99. The jurisdiction of a Dominion Court may be limited to a single province: *The Picton* (1879) 4 S. C. R. 648. As to whether provincial Courts created by local legislation can, as such, interfere with the decisions of a Dominion tribunal such as the Minister of Agriculture in the case of patents, see *In re Bell Telephone Co.* (1885) 9 O. R. 339, 346, where Cameron, C.J. leans the other way, without finding it necessary to decide the point. As to the Courts not enforcing an *ultra vires* order of such a tribunal, see *Re Canadian Pacific R. W. Co. and Township of York* (1896) 27 O. R. 559, 570.

[380] As to whether in respect to the property clauses of the British North America Act, it can be construed as always speaking,—so as, for example, to signify that harbours which were not public harbours at the time of the Union, but afterwards became such, must be held as thereupon passing to the Dominion, see the annotation to *Attorney-General for Canada* v. *Ritchie Contracting Co.* (1915) 26 D. L. R. (B.C.) 51, the conclusion reached being that it cannot be so construed.

The subjects comprised in the Third Schedule "are for the most part works or constructions which have resulted from

the expenditure of public money, though there are exceptions ":
The Fisheries case [1898] A. C. 700, 710-1. They consist " of
public undertakings which might be fairly considered to exist
for the benefit of all the provinces federally united, of lands
and buildings necessary for carrying on the customs or postal
service of the Dominion, or required for the purpose of national
defence, and 'lands set apart for general public purposes'":
St. Catherines Milling and Lumber Co. v. *The Queen* (1888)
14 App. Cas. 46, 56. It seems correct to say that while, as to
legislative powers, it is the residuum which is left to the Dominion, as to proprietary rights, the residuum goes to the provinces. See, however, *per* Strong, J. in *St. Catherines Milling
& Lumber Co.* v. *The Queen* (1887) 13 S. C. R. 577, 605. By sec.
125 of the Federation Act, 'No lands or property belonging to
Canada or any province shall be liable to taxation.' As to
Dominion Crown lands becoming subject to provincial taxation
even before patent issued, see *supra*, p. 238, n. 262. In all cases
it must be taken that the Dominion became the owner of the soil
on which the works mentioned are situate: *The Fisheries case*
(1896) 26 S. C. R. 444, 564. Sec. 108 only transfers to the
Dominion the interest which the provinces had at Confederation: *Windsor and Annapolis R. W. Co.* v. *Western Counties
R. W. Co.* (1882) 7 App. Cas. 178. *Cf. Province of Ontario* v.
Dominion of Canada and Province of Quebec (1895) 25 S. C. R.
434, 532. And see *Queen* v. *Moss* (1896) 26 S. C. R. 322. As
to whether the Dominion parliament could override an interest
outstanding at Confederation in respect to the things enumerated in the Third Schedule, it is submitted that it could where
to do so was incidental to the exercise of its exclusive
power under section 91 of the Federation Act: *Canada's Federal
System*, pp. 166-9, 343, 706-7. But see the above *Windsor and
Annapolis R. W. Co.* case in the court below: Russ. Eq. 287,
307.

[381] This did not give the Dominion any proprietary rights
in the River St. Lawrence from which the water is taken for
the Cornwall Canal, beyond the right to take the water, nor
make the river itself a public work of Canada: *Macdonald* v.
The King (1906) 10 Ex. C. R. 394.

[382] Whatever is properly comprised in the term " public
harbour" became vested in the Dominion, not merely those
parts on which public works had been executed: *The Fisheries
case* [1898] A. C. 700; *Holman* v. *Green* (1881) 6 S. C. R. 707.
Nor does " public harbours" mean those harbours only which
have been declared to be such by some public executive act,
some act of the *jus regium* as to harbours. See Chitty on the
Crown, pp. 174-5; *Brown* v. *Reed* (1874) 2 Pugs. 206; *Nash* v.
Newton (1891) 30 N. B. 610, 618-620. 'So early as the reign of

King John we find ships seized by the King's officers for putting in at a place that was not a legal port': Black's Comm. (ed. 1770, Osgoode Hall Library, I. 264). The coal and other minerals under the waters and beds of Nanaimo harbour thus became the property of the Dominion: *Attorney-General of British Columbia* v. *Esquimalt and Nanaimo R. W. Co.* (1900) 20 C. L. T. 268. As to the harbour of St. John, New Brunswick, not passing to the Dominion, being vested in the city under charter of 1785, ratified by local Act 1786, see *St. John Gas Light Co.* v. *The Queen* (1895) 4 Ex. C. R. 326. In the *Fisheries case* (1896) 26 S. C. R. 444, 538-9, Taschereau, J. asks the question whether there are any private harbours? It must depend to some extent, at all events, upon the circumstances of each particular harbour what forms a part of that harbour. It does not follow that because a foreshore on the margin of a harbour is Crown property, it necessarily forms part of the harbour; if it has actually been used for harbour purposes it would no doubt do so: *The Fisheries case* [1898] A. C. 700, 711-712; *Attorney-General of British Columbia* v. *Canadian Pacific R. W. Co.* [1906] A. C. 204, 209, see *per* Hunter, C.J., S. C. 11 B. C. 289, 296, who says, "the (Dominion) jurisdiction in my opinion is latent, and attaches to any inlet or harbour as soon as it becomes a public harbour, and is not confined to such public harbours as existed at the time of the Union"; *cf.*, the *dictum* of Allen, C.J. in *Nash* v. *Newton* (1891) 30 N. B. 610, 618: but see *contra per* Davies, Duff, and Anglin, JJ. in *Attorney-General for Canada* v. *Ritchie Contracting and Supply Co.* (1915) 26 D. L. R. 51, 17 D. L. R. 778; and the annotation at 26 D. L. R. 69 *seq.*: these seem to be the only judicial *dicta* reported on this last important point. See further as to the foreshore of harbours: *Kennelly* v. *Dominion Coal Co.* (1904) 36 N. S. 495, 500; and the argument of counsel in *Attorney-General for British Columbia* v. *Canadian Pacific R. W. Co.* [1906] A. C. 204, as reported by Martin, Meredith, Henderson & White, pp. 97-100, and given in Canada's Federal System, pp. 695-6. As to the law of the foreshore with special reference to Canadian cases, see Article by Mr. Silas Alward, K.C., in 34 C. L. T. at p. 501 *seq.* It was held in *Fader* v. *Smith* (1885) 18 N. S. 433, that the provincial Government could confer no title to one of the small inlets on the shores of St Margaret's Bay, N. S., which had been used on several occasions by small vessels for loading timber, although it had neither the name nor character of a public harbour. *Sed quære.* It is questionable whether a provincial Act can incorporate a company to construct a subway beneath a public harbour: Prov. Legisl. 1867-1895, at p. 748. But see *The Queen* v. *St. John Gas Light Co.* (1895) 4 Ex. C. R. 326, 338. Opening and improving a channel through a sea wall separating a small body of water from a public harbour, may cause the former to become a public harbour: *Nash* v. *Newton* (1831) 30 N. B. 610. But a small body of water where there was a wharf but no mooring ground, and little shelter, was held not to be a "public harbour": *McDonald* v. *Lake Simcoe Ice and Cold Storage Co.* (1899) 26 O. A. R. 411. And so *cf.* *Perry* v. *Clergue* (1903) 5 O. L. R. 357, where the fact that there were wharves in an open river front, was held not to constitute it a public harbour. See further as to what is a "public harbour:" *Attorney-General for Canada* v. *Ritchie Contracting Co.* (1915), 26 D. L. R. 51, 17 D. L. R. 778; *Pickels* v. *The King* (1912) 14 Ex. C. R. 379, 7 D. L. R. 698. Fisheries therein do not necessarily constitute part of a harbour so as to enable the Dominion parliament to authorize the grant to anyone of an exclusive right of fishing therein: *Young* v. *Harnish* (1904) 37 N. S. 213, 220-221. It is no objection to a local option by-law that it includes a public harbour: *Re Sturmer and Town of Beaverton* (1911) 24 O. L. R. 65, 72. See *contra*, however, *per* Girouard, J. in *In re Provincial Fisheries* (1896) 26 S. C. R. 444, 564. As to the power of the Dominion parliament under its legislative power over 'navigation and shipping' (*supra*, pp. 106-7), to expropriate a provincial harbour, see *Attorney-General for Canada* v. *Ritchie Contracting and Supply Co.* (1915) 26 D. L. R. 51, *per* Davies, J. at p. 56, *per* Duff, J. at p. 66.

383 This means "river improvements" and "lake improvements." It does not mean that rivers or beds of rivers, not granted before Confederation, were to become the property of the Dominion: *Attorney-General for the Dominion* v. *Attorney-Generals for the Provinces* [1898] A. C. 700, 710-711. "Rivers" is probably a clerical error: *In re Provincial Fisheries* (1896) 26 S. C. R. 444, 542-4. The other view was at one time advanced by the Dominion Government: Prov. Legisl. 1867-1895, at pp. 764, 1122, 1147. The ownership of river improvements does not give the Dominion Government any right to grant a ferry across the river which did not exist apart from it: *Perry* v. *Clergue* (1903) 5 O. L. R. 357, 364-5. But as to boundary rivers, it appears that the Dominion parliament alone has jurisdiction over the establishment or creation of ferries between a province and British or foreign country, or between two provinces: *In re International and Interprovincial Ferries* (1905) 36 S. C. R. 206. However see Memorandum of Attorney-General of Ontario read in Dominion House of Commons on May 7th, 1909, to the effect that a stream being an international stream does not deprive a province of its share of jurisdiction over it: Toronto *Globe* for May 8th, 1909; Canada's Federal System, p. 703, n. 30. See, further, as to beds of navigable rivers in Quebec, even above tidewater, being in the Crown, and not in the riparian proprietors:

Dixson v. *Snetsinger* (1873) 23 C. P. 235. *Aliter* in Manitoba *Keewatin Power Co.* v. *Town of Kenora* (1908) 16 O. L. R. 184, 13 O. L. R. 237. But see *Bartlett* v. *Scotten* (1895) 24 S. C. R. 367. As to the ownership of beds of rivers in Ontario, see R. S. O. 1914, c. 130. As to provincial Attorneys-General being competent to take proceedings to restrain pollution of navigable rivers, as well as the Dominion Attorney-General, see *Attorney-General of Canada* v. *Ewen* (1895) 2 B. C. 468. As to provincial legislatures having the right to make a municipality extend to the middle of a navigable river, see *Central Vermont R. W. Co.* v. *Town of St. Johns* (1886) 14 S. C. R. 288. As to the right to cut ice in rivers in Quebec, see *Dupuis* v. *Saint Jean* (1910) R. J. Q. 38 S. C. 204. As to a river down which only loose logs could be floated not being a "navigable and floatable river" within Art. 400 of the Civil Code of Lower Canada, see *Maclaren* v. *Attorney-General for Quebec* [1914] A. C. 258. As to a public right to navigate non-tidal navigable rivers in Canada, see *Fort George Lumber Co.* v. *Grand Trunk Pacific R. W. Co.* (1915) 24 D. L. R. 527, 528.

[384] As to what amounts to an appropriation under the above clause, see Prov. Legisl. 1865-1895, pp. 757-8.

[385] This section applies *mut. mut.* to the other provinces admitted into the Union since Confederation other than Manitoba, Alberta and Saskatchewan, where the public lands are still retained by the Dominion, save that by 48-49 Vict. c. 53, s. 1, (now R. S. C. 1906, c. 99, s. 3; see, also R. S. C. 1906, c. 55, s. 5), it is provided that all Crown lands which may be shewn to the satisfaction of the Dominion Government to be swamp lands, shall be transferred to the province of Manitoba, and enure wholly to its benefits and uses. See *Attorney-General for Manitoba* v. *Attorney-General for Canada* [1904] A. C. 799, 34 S. C. R. 287, as to the effect of this statement. As to the surrender by the Imperial Government of the Crown lands in the province of Canada, the maritime provinces, and Prince Edward Island, to those colonies, see Keith, R. G. in D., Vol. II, pp. 1047-1053. *Cf.* also *ibid.* Vol. III, p. 1621. As to the practice of the United States in this respect when new States are organized out of the Territories, see Bryce's Amer. Comm. (ed. 1914) Vol. I, p. 354, n. 1. As to royalties, see *King* v. *Rithet* (1918) 54 C. L. J. 116.

[386] *St. Catherines Milling and Lumber Co.* v. *The Queen* (1888) 14 App. Cas. 46, 56; *Attorney-General for the Dominion of Canada* v. *Attorney-Generals for the Provinces* [1898] A. C. 700, 709-711. As to grants to the Dominion Government such as that of the Railway Belt in British Columbia, and their effect, see *The Queen* v. *Farwell* (1887) 14 S. C. R. 392, 425; *Attorney-General of British Columbia* v. *Attorney-General of Canada* (1889) 14 App. Cas. 295, 301-2. As to Deadman's Island near

the entrance to Burrard's Inlet in the harbour of Vancouver see *Attorney-General of British Columbia* v. *Attorney-General of Canada* [1906] A. C. 552.

³⁸⁷ For a case in which, before the title of the provinces to Indian lands had been thus decided, the Dominion Government, acting in the interests of the Dominion as a whole, had obtained the surrender of Indian lands on certain terms, and then vainly endeavoured to establish a principle of law or equity upon which they could recover indemnity from the province to whose benefit the surrender had ultimately accrued, see *Dominion of Canada* v. *Province of Ontario* [1910] A. C. 637, 42 S. C. R. 1, 10 Ex. C. R. 445. For a case where Indians surrendered their beneficial owership in trust under a special instrument, without destroying it, see *per* Duff, J., *Attorney-General for Canada* v. *Giroux* (1916) 30 D. L. R. 123, 140. As to Indian lands in British Columbia: see Canada's Federal System, pp. 711-714; Prov. Legisl. 1867-1895, pp. 1025-8. As to Indian lands in New Brunswick, see *Doe d. Burk* v. *Cornier* (1890) 30 N. B. 142, 147-150.

³⁸⁸ In favour of the provinces having such power, see *per* Burton, J.A. in *St. Catherines Milling and Lumber Co.* v. *The Queen* (1886) 13 O. A. R. 148, 167; *contra*, *per* Rose, J. in *Caldwell* v. *Fraser*, unreported except in McPherson and Clark's Law of Mines, pp. 15-24; *Dominion of Canada* v. *Province of Ontario* (1909) 42 S. C. R. 1, 93. Also an Article in 12 C. L. T. 163. The enumeration in sched. 3 of the Federation Act of provincial public works and property does not include Crown lands which are reserved for Indian use: *St. Catherines Milling & Lumber Co.* v. *The Queen* (1888) 14 App. Cas. 46, 56. Such Indian lands are before surrender vested in the Crown subject to an interest other than that of the province in the same, within the meaning of sec. 109 of the Federation Act: S. C. The Dominion cannot dispose, by permits or otherwise, of the beneficial interest in the timber, which passes to the province: S. C. at p. 60. As to native title in New Zealand, see *In re London and Whitaker Claims Act* (1872) 2 C. A. 41, 49, 50; *Wi Parata* v. *Bishop of Wellington*, 3 J. R. N.S. S. C. 72; Keith's R. G. in D., Vol. II, p. 1059 *seq.;* and as to Indian title generally, see Canada's Federal System, pp. 710-721.

³⁸⁹ *Attorney-General of Canada* v. *Attorney-General of the Provinces* (Fisheries case) [1898] A. C. 700, 709. For the distinction between *majora* and *minora regalia*, see Black.'s Comm. (ed. 1770, Osgoode Hall library) I. 241. In the last case the Supreme Court decided that under the word "lands" in the above section 109 of the Federation Act is comprised the beds of all lakes, rivers, and other waters (except public harbours, as to which see *supra*, n. 382) within the territorial

limits of the several provinces which had not been granted by the Crown before Confederation *of every description*: S. C. (1896) 26 S. C. R. 444. And see *Queen* v. *Moss* (1896) 26 S. C. R. 322. This, of course, will not prevent the Dominion parliament exercising such jurisdiction over them as is properly incidental to its exercise of its exclusive enumerated powers under section 91 of the Federation Act: *per* Gwynne, J., S. C. 26 S. C. R. 444, 541. See, however, his words at pp. 544-5. See, also, *supra*, p. 121. As to the rule of riparian ownership *ad medium filum* not applying to the great lakes of Canada, or to rivers *de facto* navigable: see *per* Strong, C.J., S. C. 26 S. C. R. at p. 530 *seq.*; and *per* Girouard, J. at p. 548 *seq.* As to the ownership of the land covered by sea within the three-mile limit, see *Attorney-General of British Columbia* v. *Attorney-General for Canada* [1914] A. C. 153, 174-5. Their lordships, however, for reasons stated declined to pronounce upon it, and point out that the question is not one which belongs to the domain of municipal law alone. As to narrow arms of the sea, bays, inlets, etc., see Clement's L. of C. C. 3rd ed. p. 246. See, further, as to the three-mile limit, the argument in the last mentioned case (printed *verbatim* by W. H. Cullin, Victoria, B.C.) pp. 62-4, 81 *seq.* 173; also *supra*, n. 173. As to a bridge constructed by an individual over the Richelieu River before Confederation reverting to the Crown in right of the province after Confederation, see *Montreal Light, Heat and Power Co.* v. *Archambault* (1907-8) R. J. Q. 16 K. B. 410, aff. 41 S. C. R. 116. See, also, *Queen* v. *Yule* (1899) 6 Ex. C. R. 103, 30 S. C. R. 24. As to a Crown grant derogating from a public right of navigation, see *Queen* v. *Fisher* (1891) 2 Ex. C. R. 365; *Queen* v. *St. John Gas Light Co.* (1895) 4 Ex C. R. 326, 346; *In re Provincial Fisheries*, 26 S. C. R. 444, 575. But see *Normand* v. *St. Lawrence Navigation Co.* (1879) 5 Q. L. R. 215.

390 *Attorney-General of Ontario* v. *Mercer* (1883) 8 App. Cas. 767, which thus affirmed *Attorney-General of Quebec* v. *Attorney-General of Dominion of Canada (Church* v. *Fenton)* (1876) 1 Q. L. R. 77, 2 Q. L. R. 236. As to this case not deciding anything in respect of personal estate which escheats for want of next of kin; and as to its not applying to escheats of land in Manitoba, and, on the same principle, in Saskatchewan and Alberta, see Prov. Legisl. 1867-1895, at pp. 838-9, 853, 856; an Article on Escheat and *Bona Vacantia* in Alberta and elsewhere, by W. S. Scott, 37 C. L. T. 764; and *Trust and Guarantee Co.* v. *The King* (1916) 54 S. C. R. 107, 15 Ex. C. R. 403, where the Supreme Court (Idington and Brodeur, JJ., dissenting) held that escheats of land in Alberta were a royalty reserved to the Dominion of Canada by sec. 21 of the *Alberta Act*, 4-5 Edw. VII, c. 3, D., and the right of the Dominion there-

to could not be affected by provincial legislation. See *supra*,
n. 385, as to Manitoba lands.

391 *Attorney-General of British Columbia* v. *Attorney-General of Canada* (the Precious Metals case) (1889) 14 App. Cas.
295; *Attorney-General* v. *Mercer* (1883) 8 App. Cas. 767. In
these cases their lordships expressly refrain from considering
whether ' royalties' in section 109, includes *jura regalia* other
than those connected with lands, mines, and minerals. In the
first they held that notwithstanding the statutory grant of the
Railway Belt by British Columbia to the Dominion, pursuant
to their Articles of Union, the expression " land" though it
carried with it the baser metals, they being *partes soli*, incidents of land, did not carry the precious metals, which remained
vested in the Crown, subject to the control and disposal of the
provincial government. Their lordships refer to this case in their
subsequent judgment in *Attorney-General for British Columbia*
v. *Attorney-General for Canada* [1914] A. C. 153, 165; *cf. Woolley*
v. *Attorney-General of Victoria* (1877) 2 App. Cas. 163; *Esquimalt and Nanaimo R. W. Co.* v. *Bainbridge* [1896] A. C. 561.
A conveyance of land from one private individual to another
when once the precious metals have passed out of the Crown,
will pass them although not specially . mentioned: *Re St. Eugene Mining Co. and the Land Registry Act* (1900) 7 B. C.
288. Lands in the railway belt can only pass from the Crown
by Dominion grant: *Queen* v. *Farwell* (1893-4) 22 S. C. R.
553, 561, 3 Ex. C. R. 171, 289; *Burrard Power Co.* v. *The King*
[1911] A. C. 87, 43 S. C. R. 27. Water rights incidental to the
lands granted passed to the Dominion: S. C.   The province
retained no power of legislation as to them: S. C. Once granted
to settlers by the Dominion, these lands revert to the same
position as if settled by the provincial Government in the ordinary course of its administration: *Precious Metals Case
supra.   Cf. McGregor* v. *Esquimalt and Nanaimo R. W. Co.*
[1907] A. C. 462.

391a *In re International and Interprovincial Ferries* (1905)
36 S. C. R. 206, overruling *Perry* v. *Clergue* (1903) 5 O. L. R.
357. See, also, No. 13 of sec. 91, *supra* p. 109.

392 *Attorney-General for the Dominion* v. *Attorney-General
of Ontario* [1897] A. C. 199, 25 S. C. R. 434. See, also, in connection with the same proceedings out of which this appeal
arose: *Province of Quebec* v. *Dominion of Canada* (1898) 30
S. C. R. 151; *Attorney-General for Ontario* v. *Attorney-General
for Quebec* [1903] A. C. 38, 31 S. C. R. 516; *Attorney-General
for Quebec* v. *Attorney-General for Ontario* [1910] A. C. 627,
42 S. C. R. 161.   These proceedings arose upon those sections
of the Federation Act, namely, sections 109, 111, 112, and 142,
which relate to the incidence after the Union of the debts and

liabilities of the old province of Canada. See further as to
them, and, also, as to Crown lands being bound by a trust,
Canada's Federal System, p. 736, n., and cases there referred
to. Such a " trust " or " interest " as referred to in sec. 109,
was the right possessed by the Canada Central Railway Company under its charter to pass over any portion of the country
between limits mentioned therein, and to carry the railway
through the Crown lands lying between the same: *Booth* v.
McIntyre (1880) 31 C. P. 183, 193-4. So was the interest in
the, public lands created by an ante-Confederation statute directing them to be set apart to be sold and the proceeds applied
to the creation of a common school fund: *Provinces of Ontario
and Quebec* v. *Dominion of Canada* (1898) 28 S. C. R. 609. The
contention that Magna Charta creates a " trust " or " interest ".
in favour of the public in land covered by tidal waters cannot
be sustained: *In re Provincial Fisheries* (1896) 26 S. C. R.
444, 509. But as to the right of Indians to enjoy the constituted
rents of a certain seigniory in Quebec being such " an interest
other than that of the province in the same," see *Mowat* v.
Casgrain (1896) R. J. Q. 6 Q. B. 12.

392a In this connection it may be pardonable to quote the
words of Mr. Bernard Holland in his " *Imperium et Libertas,*"
at pp. 10-11:—' Not long ago the Judicial Committee of the
Privy Council decided questions arising in Canada and involving large interests as between different States within the
Dominion as to rights in the Great Lakes and other waters.
Had Canada been divided like the same area in Europe into
several quite independent states, this is precisely the kind of
question which might have led to war—the worst and
most barbarous of remedies, with all its cost in life, and
wealth, and happiness, with all its legacy of bitter memories,
and ending, perhaps, in a decision in favour of the strongest,
but contrary to true justice, since might is not always identical
with right. But because the Canadian provinces all formed
part of one Empire, the questions at issue could be settled
by four or five wise elderly gentlemen seated round a table
at Whitehall, after hearing the tranquil arguments of Mr. Blake,
Q.C., and Mr. Haldane, Q.C. This is civilization on a higher
level — arbitration in lieu of war.' And see the whole question of Imperial unity and Imperial co-operation discussed in
his usual thorough way by Mr. Berriedale Keith in R. G. in
D., in Vol. III, pp. 1453-1558, where at pp. 1463 *seq.* he concisely summarises the proceedings and discussions in the suc-
cessive Colonial Conferences from 1887 to 1911.

393 *Dominion of Canada* v. *Province of Ontario* [1910] A. C. 637, 42 S. C. R. 1, 10 Ex. C. R. 445. The Judicial Committee there say (p. 645): "It may be that, in questions between a Dominion comprising various provinces of which the laws are not in all respects identical, on the one hand, and a particular province with laws of its own, on the other hand, difficulty will arise as to the legal principle which is to be applied. Such conflicts may always arise in the case of States and provinces within a union. But the conflict is between one set of legal principles and another. In the present case, it does not appear to their lordships that the claim of the Dominion can be sustained on any principle of law that can be invoked as applicable." See, also, *Attorney-General of Ontario* v. *Attorney-General of Canada* (1907) 39 S. C. R. 14, 10 Ex. C. R. 293. Ontario has passed an Act submitting to the jurisdiction of the Supreme Court of Canada and the Exchequer Court in cases of controversies between the Dominion of Canada and itself, and also 'controversies between any other province of the Dominion which may have passed an Act similar to this Act and Ontario:' R. S. O. 1914, c. 55, s. 2. For similar Acts, see R. S. M. 1913, c. 38, s. 7; C. S. N. B. 1903, c. 110, s. 1.

394 See this whole matter of comparison between the United States Constitution and that of Canada gone into in more detail in the introductory chapter to the Law of Legislative Power in Canada, and the concluding chapter of Canada's Federal System. There, too, special attention is called to the ways in which the express legislative powers conferred upon the Dominion parliament and the provincial legislatures respectively in Canada differ from those of Congress and the States in the United States. Special reference may also be made in this connection to an Article on *Judicial Review of Legislation in Canada* by Charles G. Haines, 28 Harv. L. R. 565.

APPENDIX

THE BRITISH NORTH AMERICA ACT, 1867, BEING (IMP.)
30 VICTORIÆ, CHAPTER 3.[1]

An Act for the Union of Canada, Nova Scotia, and New Brunswick, and the Government thereof: and for Purposes connected therewith.[1]

[*March 29th, 1867.*]

WHEREAS the Provinces of Canada, Nova Scotia, and New Brunswick, have expressed their desire to be federally united into one Dominion under the Crown of the United Kingdom of Great Britain and Ireland, with a Constitution similar in principle to that of the United Kingdom:

And whereas such a Union would conduce to the welfare of the Provinces and promote the interests of the British Empire:

And whereas on the establishment of the Union by authority of Parliament it is expedient, not only that the Constitution of the Legislative Authority in the Dominion be provided for, but also that the nature of the Executive Government therein be declared:

And whereas it is expedient that provision be made for the eventual admission into the Union of other parts of British North America:

Be it therefore enacted and declared by the Queen's most Excellent Majesty, by and with the advice and consent of the Lords Spiritual and Temporal, and Commons, in this present Parliament assembled, and by the authority of the same, as follows:

I.—PRELIMINARY.

1. This Act may be cited as *The British North America Act, 1867.*   Short title.

2. The provisions of this Act referring to Her Majesty the Queen extend also to the heirs and successors of Her Majesty,   Application of provisions referring to the Queen.

---

[1] Brought into force, pursuant to sec. 3, by Royal Proclamation, on July 1st, 1867. See *sub.* Imp. 30 Vict. c. 3, in "Table of Statutes Referred to," *supra.*

Kings and Queens of the United Kingdom of Great Britain and Ireland.

II.—UNION.

Declaration by proclamation of Union of Canada, Nova Scotia and New Brunswick, into one Dominion under name of Canada.

3. It shall be lawful for the Queen, by and with the advice of Her Majesty's Most Honourable Privy Council, to declare by Proclamation that on and after a day herein appointed, not being more than six months after the passing of this Act, the Provinces of Canada, Nova Scotia, and New Brunswick shall form and be one Dominion under the name of Canada; and on and after that day those three Provinces shall form and be one Dominion under that name accordingly.

Commencement of subsequent provisions of Act.

Meaning of Canada in such provisions.

4. The subsequent provisions of this Act shall, unless it is otherwise expressed or implied, commence and have effect on and after the Union, that is to say, on and after the day appointed for the Union taking effect in the Queen's Proclamation; and in the same provisions, unless it is otherwise expressed or implied, the name Canada shall be taken to mean Canada as constituted under this Act.

Four Provinces.

5. Canada shall be divided into four Provinces, named Ontario, Quebec, Nova Scotia, and New Brunswick.

[*Canada now also includes the Provinces of Manitoba, British Columbia, Prince Edward Island, Alberta and Saskatchewan, and the Yukon Territory and the North-West Territories.*]

Provinces of Ontario and Quebec.

6. The parts of the Province of Canada (as it exists at the passing of this Act) which formerly constituted respectively the Provinces of Upper Canada and Lower Canada shall be deemed to be severed, and shall form two separate Provinces. The part which formerly constituted the Province of Upper Canada shall constitute the Province of Ontario and the part which formerly constituted the Province of Lower Canada shall constitute the Province of Quebec.

Provinces of Nova Scotia and New Brunswick.

7. The Provinces of Nova Scotia and New Brunswick shall have the same limits as at the passing of this Act.

Population of Provinces to be distinguished in decennial census.

8. In the general census of the population of Canada which is hereby required to be taken in the year one thousand eight hundred and seventy-one, and in every tenth year thereafter, the respective populations of the four Provinces shall be distinguished.

III.—EXECUTIVE POWER.

Executive Power to continue vested in the Queen.

9. The Executive Government and authority of and over Canada is hereby declared to continue and be vested in the Queen.

10. The provisions of this Act referring to the Governor- Application of provisions referring to Governor General. General extend and apply to the Governor-General for the time being of Canada, or other the Chief Executive Officer or Administrator, for the time being carrying on the Government of Canada on behalf and in the name of the Queen, by whatever title he is designated.

11. There shall be a Council to aid and advise in the Gov- Constitution of Privy Council for Canada. ernment of Canada, to be styled the Queen's Privy Council for Canada; and the persons who are to be members of that Council shall be from time to time chosen and summoned by the Governor-General and sworn in as Privy Councillors, and members thereof may be from time to time removed by the Governor-General.

12. All powers, authorities, and functions, which under any All powers under Acts to be exercised by Governor General with advice of Privy Council, or alone. Act of the Parliament of Great Britain, or of the Parliament of the United Kingdom of Great Britain and Ireland, or of the Legislature of Upper Canada, Lower Canada, Canada, Nova Scotia, or New Brunswick, are at the Union vested in or exercisable by the respective Governors or Lieutenant-Governors of those Provinces, with the advice, or with the advice and consent, of the respective Executive Councils thereof, or in conjunction with those Councils, or with any number of members thereof, or by those Governors or Lieutenant-Governors individually, shall, as far as the same continue in existence and capable of being exercised after the Union in relation to the Government of Canada, be vested in and exercisable by the Governor-General, with the advice or with the advice and consent of or in connection with the Queen's Privy Council for Canada, or any members thereof, or by the Governor-General individually, as the case requires, subject nevertheless (except with respect to such as exist under Acts of the Parliament of Great Britain or of the Parliament of the United Kingdom of Great Britain and Ireland) to be abolished or altered by the Parliament of Canada.

13. The provisions of this Act referring to the Governor- Application of provisions referring to Governor General in Council. General in Council shall be construed as referring to the Governor-General acting by and with the advice of the Queen's Privy Council for Canada.

14. It shall be lawful for the Queen, if Her Majesty thinks Power to Her Majesty to authorize Governor General to appoint Deputies. fit, to authorize the Governor-General from time to time to appoint any person or any persons jointly or severally to be his Deputy or Deputies within any part or parts of Canada, and in that capacity to exercise during the pleasure of the Governor-General such of the powers, authorities, and functions of the Governor-General as the Governor-General deems it necessary

or expedient to assign to him or them, subject to any limitations or directions expressed or given by the Queen; but the appointment of such a Deputy or Deputies shall not affect the exercise by the Governor-General himself of any power, authority or function.

Command of armed forces to continue to be vested in the Queen.

15. The Command-in-Chief of the Land and Naval Militia, and of all Naval and Military Forces, of and in Canada, is hereby declared to continue and be vested in the Queen.

Seat of Government of Canada.

16. Until the Queen otherwise directs the seat of Government of Canada shall be Ottawa.

IV.—LEGISLATIVE POWER.

Constitution of Parliament of Canada.

17. There shall be one Parliament for Canada, consisting of the Queen, an Upper House, styled the Senate, and the House of Commons.

[Section 18 was repealed by Imperial Act 38 and 39 Vict. c. 38, and the following section substituted therefor.

Privileges, etc., of Houses.

18. The privileges, immunities, and powers to be held, enjoyed and exercised by the Senate and by the House of Commons and by the members thereof respectively shall be such as are from time to time defined by Act of the Parliament of Canada, but so that any Act of the Parliament of Canada defining such privileges, immunities and powers shall not confer any privileges, immunities or powers exceeding those at the passing of such Act held, enjoyed, and exercised by the Commons House of Parliament of the United Kingdom of Great Britain and Ireland and by the members thereof.]

First Session of the Parliament of Canada.

19. The Parliament of Canada shall be called together not later than six months after the Union.

Yearly Session of the Parliament of Canada.

20. There shall be a Session of the Parliament of Canada once at least in every year, so that twelve months shall not intervene between the last sitting of the Parliament in one Session and its first sitting in the next Session.

The Senate.

Number of Senators.

21. The Senate shall, subject to the provisions of this Act, consist of seventy-two members, who shall be styled Senators.

[The Senate now includes representatives of the Provinces of Manitoba, British Columbia, Prince Edward Island, Alberta and Saskatchewan and comprises ninety-six members.][2]

[2] See *supra*, p. 41.

22. In relation to the constitution of the Senate, Canada shall be deemed to consist of three divisions—

1. Ontario;

2. Quebec;

3. The Maritime Provinces, Nova Scotia and New Brunswick; which three divisions shall (subject to the provisions of this Act) be equally represented in the Senate as follows: Ontario by twenty-four Senators; Quebec by twenty-four Senators; and the Maritime Provinces by twenty-four Senators, twelve thereof representing Nova Scotia, and twelve thereof representing New Brunswick.

In the case of Quebec each of the twenty-four Senators representing that Province shall be appointed for one of the twenty-four Electoral Divisions of Lower Canada specified in Schedule A. to chapter one of the Consolidated Statutes of Canada.[2a]

23. The qualifications of a Senator shall be as follows:—

1. He shall be of the full age of thirty years:

2. He shall be either a natural-born subject of the Queen, or a subject of the Queen naturalized by an Act of the Parliament of Great Britain, or of the Parliament of the United Kingdom of Great Britain and Ireland, or of the Legislature of one of the Provinces of Upper Canada, Lower Canada, Canada, Nova Scotia, or New Brunswick, before the Union, or of the Parliament of Canada after the Union.

3. He shall be legally or equitably seised as of freehold for his own use and benefit of lands or tenements held in free and common socage, or seised or possessed for his own use and benefit of lands or tenements held in franc-aleu or in roture, within the Province for which he is appointed, of the value of $4,000, over and above all rents, dues, debts, charges, mortgages and incumbrances due or payable out of or charged on or affecting the same;

4. His real and personal property shall be together worth $4,000 over and above his debts and liabilities;

5. He shall be resident in the Province for which he is appointed;

6. In the case of Quebec he shall have his real property qualification in the Electoral Division for which he is appointed, or shall be resident in that Division.

[2a] See *supra*, p. 41.

Summoning of
Senators.

24. The Governor-General shall from time to time, in the Queen's name, by instrument under the Great Seal of Canada, summon qualified persons to the Senate; and, subject to the provisions of this Act, every person so summoned shall become and be a member of the Senate and a Senator.

Summons of
first body of
Senators.

25. Such persons shall be first summoned to the Senate as the Queen by warrant under Her Majesty's Royal Sign Manual thinks fit to approve, and their names shall be inserted in the Queen's Proclamation of Union.

Additions of
Senators in
certain cases.

26. If at any time on the recommendation of the Governor-General the Queen thinks fit to direct that three or six members be added to the Senate, the Governor-General may by summons to three or six qualified persons (as the case may be), representing equally the three divisions of Canada, add to the Senate accordingly.

Reduction of
Senate to
normal number.

27. In case of such addition being at any time made the Governor-General shall not summon any person to the Senate, except on a further like direction by the Queen on the like recommendation, until each of the three divisions of Canada is represented by twenty-four Senators and no more.

Maximum
number of
Senators.

28. The number of Senators shall not at any time exceed seventy-eight.

[*See note appended to s. 21.*]

Tenure of place
in Senate.

29. A Senator shall, subject to the provisions of this Act, hold his place in the Senate for life.

Resignation
of place in
Senate.

30. A Senator may by writing under his hand addressed to the Governor-General resign his place in the Senate, and thereupon the same shall be vacant.

Disqualification
of Senators.

31. The place of a Senator shall become vacant in any of the following cases:

1. If for two consecutive Sessions of the Parliament he fails to give his attendance in the Senate;

2. If he takes an oath or makes a declaration or acknowledgment of allegiance, obedience, or adherence to a foreign power, or does an act whereby he becomes a subject or citizen, or entitled to the rights or privileges of a subject or citizen, of a foreign power;

3. If he is adjudged bankrupt or insolvent, or applies for the benefit of any law relating to insolvent debtors, or becomes a public defaulter;

4. If he is attainted of treason or convicted of felony or of any infamous crime;

5. If he ceases to be qualified in respect of property or of residence; provided, that a Senator shall not be deemed to have ceased to be qualified in respect of residence by reason only of his residing at the seat of the Government of Canada while holding an office under that Government requiring his presence there.

32. When a vacancy happens in the Senate by resignation, death, or otherwise, the Governor-General shall by summons to a fit and qualified person fill the vacancy. Summons on vacancy in Senate.

33. If any question arises respecting the qualification of a Senator or a vacancy in the Senate, the same shall be heard and determined by the Senate. Questions as to qualifications and vacancies in Senate.

34. The Governor-General may from time to time, by instrument under the Great Seal of Canada, appoint a Senator to be Speaker of the Senate, and may remove him and appoint another in his stead. Appointment of Speaker of Senate.

35. Until the Parliament of Canada otherwise provides, the presence of at least fifteen Senators, including the Speaker, shall be necessary to constitute a meeting of the Senate for the exercise of its powers. Quorum of Senate.

36. Questions arising in the Senate shall be decided by a majority of voices, and the Speaker shall in all cases have a vote, and when the voices are equal the decision shall be deemed to be in the negative. Voting in Senate.

The House of Commons.

37. The House of Commons shall, subject to the provisions of this Act, consist of one hundred and eighty-one members, of whom eighty-two shall be elected for Ontario, sixty-five for Quebec, nineteen for Nova Scotia, and fifteen for New Brunswick.[3] Constitution of House of Commons in Canada.

38. The Governor-General shall from time to time, in the Queen's name, by instrument under the Great Seal of Canada, summon and call together the House of Commons. Summoning of House of Commons.

39. A Senator shall not be capable of being elected or of sitting or voting as a member of the House of Commons. Senators not to sit in House of Commons.

[3] See R. S. C. 1906, c. 5, and amendments, for the present composition of the House of Commons, and *supra*, p. 42.

40. Until the Parliament of Canada otherwise provides, Ontario, Quebec, Nova Scotia, and New Brunswick shall, for the purposes of the election of members to serve in the House of Commons, be divided into Electoral Districts as follows:—

1.—ONTARIO.

Ontario shall be divided into the Counties, Ridings of Counties, Cities, parts of Cities, and Towns enumerated in the first Schedule to this Act, each whereof shall be an Electoral District, each such District as numbered in that Schedule being entitled to return one member.

2.—QUEBEC.

Quebec shall be divided into sixty-five Electoral Districts, composed of the sixty-five Electoral Divisions into which Lower Canada is at the passing of this Act divided under chapter two of the Consolidated Statutes of Canada, chapter seventy-five of the Consolidated Statutes of Lower Canada, and the Act of the Province of Canada of the twenty-third year of the Queen, chapter one, or any other Act amending the same in force at the Union, so that each such Electoral Division shall be for the purposes of this Act an Electoral District entitled to return one member.

3.—NOVA SCOTIA.

Each of the eighteen Counties of Nova Scotia shall be an Electoral District. The County of Halifax shall be entitled to return two members, and each of the other Counties one member.

4.—NEW BRUNSWICK.

Each of the fourteen Counties into which New Brunswick is divided, including the City and County of St. John, shall be an Electoral District; the City of St. John shall also be a separate Electoral District. Each of those fifteen Electoral Districts shall be entitled to return one member.[4]

41. Until the Parliament of Canada otherwise provides, all laws in force in the several Provinces at the Union relative to the following matters or any of them, namely,—the qualifications and disqualifications of persons to be elected or to sit or vote as members of the House of Assembly or Legislative Assembly in the several Provinces, the voters at elections of such members, the oaths to be taken by voters, the Return-

---

[4] See R. S. C. 1906, c. 5, and amendments for the present provisions for the representations of the foregoing provinces and of those admitted subsequently to the B. N. A. Act, 1867.

ing Officers, their powers and duties, the proceedings at elections, the periods during which elections may be continued, the trial of controverted elections, and proceedings incident thereto, the vacating of seats of members, and the execution of new writs in case of seats vacated otherwise than by dissolution,—shall respectively apply to elections of members to serve in the House of Commons for the same several Provinces.

Provided that, until the Parliament of Canada otherwise provides, at any election for a Member of the House of Commons for the District of Algoma, in addition to persons qualified by the law of the Province of Canada to vote, every male British subject aged twenty-one years or upwards, being a householder, shall have a vote.[5]

42. For the first election of members to serve in the House of Commons the Governor-General shall cause writs to be issued by such person, in such form, and addressed to such Returning Officers as he thinks fit. *Writs for first election.*

The person issuing writs under this section shall have the like powers as are possessed at the Union by the officers charged with the issuing of writs for the election of members to serve in the respective House of Assembly or Legislative Assembly of the Province of Canada, Nova Scotia, or New Brunswick; and the Returning Officers to whom writs are directed under this section shall have the like powers as are possessed at the Union by the officers charged with the returning of writs for the election of members to serve in the same respective House of Assembly or Legislative Assembly.

43. In case a vacancy in the representation in the House of Commons of any Electoral District happens before the meeting of the Parliament, or after the meeting of the Parliament before provision is made by the Parliament in this behalf, the provisions of the last foregoing section of this Act shall extend and apply to the issuing and returning of a writ in respect of such vacant District. *As to vacancies before meeting of Parliament or before provision is made by Parliament in this behalf.*

44. The House of Commons on its first assembling after a general election shall proceed with all practicable speed to elect one of its members to be Speaker. *As to election of Speaker of House of Commons.*

45. In case of a vacancy happening in the office of Speaker by death, resignation or otherwise, the House of Commons shall with all practicable speed proceed to elect another of its members to be Speaker. *As to filling up vacancy in office of Speaker.*

[5] See R.S.C. 1906, caps. 6, 7, 8, and 9, and amendments thereto.

Speaker to preside.

46. The Speaker shall preside at all meetings of the House of Commons.

Provision in case of absence of Speaker.

47. Until the Parliament of Canada otherwise provides, in case of the absence for any reason of the Speaker from the chair of the House of Commons for a period of forty-eight consecutive hours, the House may elect another of its members to act as Speaker, and the member so elected shall during the continuance of such absence of the Speaker have and execute all the powers, privileges, and duties of Speaker.

Quorum of House of Commons.

48. The presence of at least twenty members of the House of Commons shall be necessary to constitute a meeting of the House for the exercise of its powers, and for that purpose the Speaker shall be reckoned as a member.

Voting in House of Commons.

49. Questions arising in the House of Commons shall be decided by a majority of voices other than that of the Speaker and when the voices are equal, but not otherwise, the Speaker shall have a vote.

Duration of House of Commons.

50. Every House of Commons shall continue for five years from the day of the return of the writs for choosing the House (subject to be sooner dissolved by the Governor-General), and no longer.

Decennial Readjustment of Representation.

51. On the completion of the census in the year one thousand eight hundred and seventy-one, and of each subsequent decennial census, the representation of the four Provinces shall be re-adjusted by such authority, in such manner and from such time as the Parliament of Canada from time to time provides, subject and according to the following rules:—

1. Quebec shall have the fixed number of sixty-five members.

2. There shall be assigned to each of the other Provinces such a number of members as will bear the same proportion to the number of its population (ascertained at such census) as the number sixty-five bears to the number of the population of Quebec (so ascertained).

3. In the computation of the number of members for a Province a fractional part not exceeding one-half of the whole number requisite for entitling the Province to a member shall be disregarded; but a fractional part exceeding one-half of that number shall be equivalent to the whole number.

4. On any such re-adjustment the number of members for a Province shall not be reduced unless the proportion which the number of the population of the Province bore to the number of the aggregate population of Canada at the then last preceding re-adjustment of the number of members for the Province is ascertained at the then latest census to be diminished by one-twentieth part or upwards.

5. Such re-adjustment shall not take effect until the termination of the then existing Parliament.[6]

52. The number of members of the House of Commons may be from time to time increased by the Parliament of Canada, provided the proportionate representation of the Provinces prescribed by this Act is not thereby disturbed. *Increase of number of House of Commons.*

Money Votes; Royal Assent.

53. Bills for appropriating any part of the public revenue, or for imposing any tax or impost, shall originate in the House of Commons. *Appropriation and tax bills.*

54. It shall not be lawful for the House of Commons to adopt or pass any vote, resolution, address, or bill for the appropriation of any part of the public revenue, or of any tax or impost, to any purpose that has not been first recommended to that House by message of the Governor-General in the Session in which such vote, resolution, address, or bill is proposed. *Recommendation of money votes.*

55. Where a bill passed by the Houses of the Parliament is presented to the Governor-General for the Queen's assent, he shall declare according to his discretion, but subject to the provisions of this Act and to Her Majesty's instructions, either that he assents thereto in the Queen's name, or that he withholds the Queen's assent, or that he reserves the bill for the signification of the Queen's pleasure. *Royal assent to bills, etc.*

56. Where the Governor-General assents to a bill in the Queen's name, he shall by the first convenient opportunity send an authentic copy of the Act to one of her Majesty's Principal Secretaries of State; and if the Queen in Council within two years after the receipt thereof by the Secretary of State thinks fit to disallow the Act, such disallowance (with a certificate of the Secretary of State of the day on which the Act was received by him) being signified by the Governor-General by speech or message to each of the Houses of the Parliament, *Disallowance by order in Council of Act, assented to by Governor General.*

---

[6] See R. S. C. 1906, c. 5.

of by proclamation, shall annul the Act from and after the day of such signification.

Signification of Queen's pleasure on bill reserved.

57. A bill reserved for the signification of the Queen's pleasure shall not have any force unless and until within two years from the day on which it was presented to the Governor-General for the Queen's assent, the Governor-General signifies, by speech or message to each of the Houses of the Parliament or by proclamation, that it has received the assent of the Queen in Council.

An entry of every such speech, message, or proclamation shall be made in the Journal of each House, and a duplicate thereof duly attested shall be delivered to the proper officer to be kept among the Records of Canada.

V.—PROVINCIAL CONSTITUTIONS.

Executive Power.

Appointment of Lieutenant Governors of Provinces.

58. For each Province there shall be an officer, styled the Lieutenant-Governor, appointed by the Governor-General in Council by instrument under the Great Seal of Canada.

Tenure of office of Lieutenant Governor

59. A Lieutenant-Governor shall hold office during the pleasure of the Governor-General; but any Lieutenant-Governor appointed after the commencement of the first Session of the Parliament of Canada shall not be removable within five years from his appointment, except for cause assigned, which shall be communicated to him in writing within one month after the order for his removal is made, and shall be communicated by message to the Senate and to the House of Commons within one week thereafter if the Parliament is then sitting, and if not then within one week after the commencement of the next Session of the Parliament.

Salaries of Lieutenant Governors.

60. The salaries of the Lieutenant-Governors shall be fixed and provided by the Parliament of Canada.

Oaths, etc., of Lieutenant Governor.

61. Every Lieutenant-Governor shall, before assuming the duties of his office, make and subscribe before the Governor-General or some person authorized by him, oaths of allegiance and office similar to those taken by the Governor-General.

Application of provisions referring to Lieutenant Governor.

62. The provisions of this Act referring to the Lieutenant-Governor extend and apply to the Lieutenant-Governor for the time being of each Province or other the chief executive officer or administrator for the time being carrying on the government of the Province, by whatever title he is designated.

63. The Executive Council of Ontario and of Quebec shall be composed of such persons as the Lieutenant-Governor from time to time thinks fit, and in the first instance of the following officers, namely:—The Attorney-General, the Secretary and Registrar of the Province, the Treasurer of the Province, the Commissioner of Crown Lands, and the Commissioner of Agriculture and Public Works, with in Quebec, the Speaker of the Legislative Council and the Solicitor-General.[7]

Appointment of executive officers for Ontario and Quebec.

64. The Constitution of the Executive Authority in each of the Provinces of Nova Scotia and New Brunswick shall, subject to the provisions of this Act, continue as it exists at the Union until altered under the authority of this Act.

Executive Government of Nova Scotia and New Brunswick.

65. All powers, authorities, and functions which under any Act of the Parliament of Great Britain, or of the Parliament of the United Kingdom of Great Britain and Ireland, or of the Legislature of Upper Canada, Lower Canada, or Canada, were or are before or at the Union vested in or exercisable by the respective Governors or Lieutenant-Governors of those Provinces, with the advice, or with the advice and consent, of the respective Executive Councils thereof, or in conjunction with those Councils, or with any number of members thereof, or by those Governors or Lieutenant-Governors individually, shall, as far as the same are capable of being exercised after the Union in relation to the Government of Ontario and Quebec respectively, be vested in and shall or may be exercised by the Lieutenant-Governor of Ontario and Quebec respectively, with the advice or with the advice and consent of or in conjunction with the respective Executive Councils, or any members thereof, or by the Lieutenant-Governor individually, as the case requires, subject nevertheless (except with respect to such as exist under Acts of the Parliament of Great Britain, or of the Parliament of the United Kingdom of Great Britain and Ireland), to be abolished or altered by the respective Legislatures of Ontario and Quebec.

All powers under Acts to be exercised by Lieutenant-Governor of Ontario or Quebec with advice of Executive Council or alone.

66. The provisions of this Act referring to the Lieutenant-Governor in Council shall be construed as referring to the Lieutenant-Governor of the Province acting by and with the advice of the Executive Council thereof.

Application of provisions referring to Lieutenant Governor in Council.

67. The Governor-General in Council may from time to time appoint an administrator to execute the office and functions of Lieutenant-Govenor during his absence, illness, or other inability.

Administration in absence, etc. of Lieutenant Governor.

[7] See now as to Ontario, R. S. O. 1914, c. 13; am. 8 Geo. V. c. 20, s. 6.

Seats of
Provincial
Governments.
68. Unless and until the Executive Government of any Province otherwise directs with respect to that Province, the seats of Government of the Provinces shall be as follows, namely,—of Ontario, the City of Toronto; of Quebec, the City of Quebec; of Nova Scotia, the City of Halifax; and of New Brunswick, the City of Fredericton.

Legislative Power.

1.—ONTARIO.

Legislature
for Ontario.
69. There shall be a Legislature for Ontario consisting of the Lieutenant-Governor and of one House, styled the Legislative Assembly of Ontario.

Electoral
districts.
70. The Legislative Assembly of Ontario shall be composed of eighty-two members to be elected to represent the eighty-two Electoral Districts set forth in the first Schedule to this Act.[8]

2.—QUEBEC.

Legislature
for Quebec.
71. There shall be a Legislature for Quebec consisting of the Lieutenant-Governor and of two Houses, styled the Legislative Council of Quebec and the Legislative Assembly of Quebec.

Constitution of
Legislative
Council.
72. The Legislative Council of Quebec shall be composed of twenty-four members, to be appointed by the Lieutenant-Governor in the Queen's name, by instrument under the Great Seal of Quebec, one being appointed to represent each of the twenty-four electoral divisions of Lower Canada in this Act referred to, and each holding office for the term of his life, unless the Legislature of Quebec otherwise provides under the provisions of this Act.

Qualification
of Legislative
Councillors.
73. The qualifications of the Legislative Councillors of Quebec shall be the same as those of the Senators for Quebec.

Resignation,
Disqualification, etc.
74. The place of a Legislative Councillor of Quebec shall become vacant in the cases *mutatis mutandis*, in which the place of Senator becomes vacant.

Vacancies.
75. When a vacancy happens in the Legislative Council of Quebec, by resignation, death, or otherwise, the Lieutenant-Governor, in the Queen's name by instrument under the Great Seal of Quebec, shall appoint a fit and qualified person to fill the vacancy.

Questions as to
Vacancies, etc.
76. If any question arises respecting the qualification of a Legislative Councilor of Quebec, or a vacancy in the Legisla-

[8] The number of members is now 106. See R. S. O. 1914, c. 5, s. 3; am. 5 Geo. V, c. 2.

tive Council of Quebec, the same shall be heard and determined by the Legislative Council.

77. The Lieutenant-Governor may from time to time, by instrument under the Great Seal of Quebec, appoint a member of the Legislative Council of Quebec to be Speaker thereof, and may remove him and appoint another in his stead. *Speaker of Legislative Council.*

78. Until the Legislature of Quebec otherwise provides, the presence of at least ten members of the Legislative Council, including the Speaker, shall be necessary to constitute a meeting for the exercise of its powers. *Quorum of Legislative Council.*

79. Questions arising in the Legislative Council of Quebec shall be decided by a majority of voices, and the Speaker shall in all cases have a vote, and when the voices are equal the decision shall be deemed to be in the negative. *Voting in Legislative Council.*

80. The Legislative Assembly of Quebec shall be composed of sixty-five members, to be elected to represent the sixty-five electoral divisions or districts of Lower Canada in this Act referred to, subject to alteration thereof by the Legislature of Quebec: Provided that it shall not be lawful to present to the Lieutenant-Governor of Quebec for assent any bill for altering the limits of any of the Electoral Divisions or Districts mentioned in the second Schedule to this Act, unless the second and third readings of such bill have been passed in the Legislative Assembly with the concurrence of the majority of the members representing all those Electoral Divisions or Districts, and the assent shall not be given to such bills unless an address has been presented by the Legislative Assembly to the Lieutenant-Governor stating that it has been so passed. *Constitution of Legislative Assembly of Quebec.*

3.—ONTARIO AND QUEBEC.

81. The Legislatures of Ontario and Quebec respectively shall be called together not later than six months after the Union. *First Session of Legislatures.*

82. The Lieutenant-Governor of Ontario and of Quebec shall from time to time, in the Queen's name, by instrument under the Great Seal of the Province summon and call together the Legislative Assembly of the Province. *Summoning of Legislative Assemblies.*

83. Until the Legislature of Ontario or of Quebec otherwise provides, a person accepting or holding in Ontario or in Quebec any office, commission, or employment permanent or temporary, at the nomination of the Lieutenant-Governor, to which *Restriction on election of holders of office.*

C.C.L.—19

an annual salary, or any fee, allowance, emolument, or profit of any kind or amount whatever from the Province is attached, shall not be eligible as a member of the Legislative Assembly of the respective Province, nor shall he sit or vote as such; but nothing in this section shall make ineligible any person being a member of the Executive Council of the respective Province, or holding any of the following offices, that is to say, the offices of Attorney-General, Secretary and Registrar of the Province, Treasurer of the Province, Commissioner of Crown Lands, and Commissioner of Agriculture and Public Works, and, in Quebec, Solicitor-General, or shall disqualify him to sit or vote in the House for which he is elected, provided he is elected while holding such office.[9]

Continuance of existing election laws. **84.** Until the Legislatures of Ontario and Quebec respectively otherwise provide, all laws which at the Union are in force in those Provinces respectively, relative to the following matters, or any of them, namely,—the qualifications and disqualifications of persons to be elected or to sit or vote as members of the Assembly of Canada, the qualifications or disqualifications of voters, the oaths to be taken by voters, the Returning Officers, their powers and duties, the proceedings at elections, the periods during which such elections may be continued, and the trial of controverted elections and the proceedings incident thereto, the vacating of the seats of members and the issuing and execution of new writs in case of seats vacated otherwise than by dissolution, shall respectively apply to elections of members to serve in the respective Legislative Assemblies of Ontario and Quebec.[10]

Provided that until the Legislature of Ontario otherwise provides, at any election for a member of the Legislative Assembly of Ontario for the District of Algoma, in addition to persons qualified by the law of the Province of Canada to vote, every male British Subject, aged twenty-one years or upwards, being a householder, shall have a vote.[11]

Duration of Legislative Assemblies. **85.** Every Legislative Assembly of Ontario and every Legislative Assembly of Quebec shall continue for four years from the day of the return of the writs for choosing the same (subject nevertheless to either the Legislative Assembly of Ontario or the Legislative Assembly of Quebec being sooner dissolved by the Lieutenant-Governor of the Province), and no longer.[12]

[9] Acts have since been passed with the view of further securing the independence of the Legislative Assembly of Ontario. See R. S. O. 1914, c. 11, secs. 7-16.
[10] See now as to Ontario, R. S. O. 1914, caps 8 and 10, and amendments.
[11] See now R. S. O. 1914, c. 8, s. 19.
[12] See now R. S. O. 1914, c. 11, s. 4.

86. There shall be a session of the Legislature of Ontario Yearly Sessions and of that of Quebec once at least in every year, so that of Legislature. twelve months shall not intervene between the last sitting of the Legislature in each Province in one session and its first sitting in the next session.[13]

87. The following provisions of this Act respecting the Speaker, House of Commons of Canada, shall extend and apply to the Quorum, etc. Legislative Assemblies of Ontario and Quebec, that is to say,— the provisions relating to the election of a Speaker originally and on vacancies, the duties of the Speaker, the absence of the Speaker, the quorum, and the mode of voting, as if those provisions were here re-enacted and made applicable in terms to each such Legislative Assembly.[14]

4.—NOVA SCOTIA AND NEW BRUNSWICK

88. The constitution of the Legislature of each of the Pro- Constitutions of vinces of Nova Scotia and New Brunswick shall, subject to Legislatures of Nova Scotia and the provisions of this Act, continue as it exists at the Union New Brunswick. until altered under the authority of this Act; and the House of Assembly of New Brunswick existing at the passing of this Act shall, unless sooner dissolved, continue for the period for which it was elected.

5.—ONTARIO, QUEBEC, AND NOVA SCOTIA

89. Each of the Lieutenant-Governors of Ontario, Quebec, First elections. and Nova Scotia shall cause writs to be issued for the first election of members of the Legislative Assembly thereof in such form and by such person as he thinks fit, and at such time and addressed to such Returning Officer as the Governor-General directs, and so that the first election of members of Assembly for any Electoral District or any subdivision thereof shall be held at the same time and at the same places as the election for a member to serve in the House of Commons of Canada for that Electoral District.

6.—THE FOUR PROVINCES

90. The following provisions of this Act respecting the Application to Parliament of Canada, namely, — the provisions relating to Legislatures of provisions appropriation and tax bills, the recommendation of money respecting votes, the assent to bills, the disallowance of Acts, and the money votes, signification of pleasure on bills reserved. — shall extend and etc. apply to the Legislatures of the several Provinces as if those

---

[13] See R. S. O. 1914, c. 11, s. 5.
[14] See secs. 44, 45, 46, 47, 48, and 49 of this Act, and R. S. O. 1914, c. 11, secs. 35, 36, 38, 62 and 63.

provisions were here re-enacted and made applicable in terms
to the respective Provinces and the Legislatures thereof, with
the substitution of the Lieutenant-Governor of the Province
for the Governor-General, of the Governor-General for the Queen
and for a Secretary of State, of one year for two years, and of
the Province for Canada.

VI.—DISTRIBUTION OF LEGISLATIVE POWERS.

Powers of the Parliament.

Legislative
authority of
Parliament of
Canada.

91. It shall be lawful for the Queen, by and with the advice
and consent of the Senate and House of Commons, to make
laws for the peace, order, and good government of Canada, in
relation to all matters not coming within the classes of subjects by this Act assigned exclusively to the Legislatures of the
Provinces; and for greater certainty, but not so as to restrict
the generality of the foregoing terms of this section, it is hereby
declared that (notwithstanding anything in this Act) the exclusive legislative authority of the Parliament of Canada extends to all matters coming within the classes of subjects next
hereinafter enumerated; that is to say:—

1. The Public Debt and Property.

2. The regulation of Trade and Commerce.

3. The raising of money by any mode or system of Taxation.

4. The borrowing of money on the public credit.

5. Postal service.

6. The Census and Statistics.

7. Militia, Military and Naval Service and Defence.

8. The fixing of and providing for the salaries and allowances of civil and other officers of the Government of
   Canada.

9. Beacons, Buoys, Lighthouses, and Sable Island.

10. Navigation and Shipping.

11. Quarantine and the establishment and maintenance of
    Marine Hospitals.

12. Sea Coast and inland Fisheries.

13. Ferries between a Province and any British or Foreign country or between two Provinces.

14. Currency and Coinage.

15. Banking, incorporation of banks, and the issue of paper money.

16. Savings Banks.

17. Weights and Measures.

18. Bills of Exchange and Promissory Notes.

19. Interest.

20. Legal tender.

21. Bankruptcy and Insolvency.

22. Patents of invention and discovery.

23. Copyrights.

24. Indians, and lands reserved for the Indians.

25. Naturalization and Aliens.

26. Marriage and Divorce.

27. The Criminal Law, except the Constitution of Courts of Criminal Jurisdiction, but including the Procedure in Criminal Matters.

28. The Establishment, Maintenance, and Management of Penitentiaries.

29. Such classes of subjects as are expressly excepted in the enumeration of the classes of subjects by this Act assigned exclusively to the Legislatures of the Provinces.

And any matter coming within any of the classes of subjects enumerated in this section shall not be deemed to come within the class of matters of a local or private nature comprised in the enumeration of the classes of subjects by this Act assigned exclusively to the Legislatures of the Provinces.

Exclusive Powers of Provincial Legislatures.

92. In each Province the Legislature may exclusively make laws in relation to matters coming within the classes of subjects next hereinafter enumerated, that is to say,— *Subjects of exclusive Provincial Legislation.*

1. The Amendment from time to time, notwithstanding anything in this Act, of the Constitution of the Province, except as regards the office of Lieutenant-Governor.

2. Direct Taxation within the Province in order to the raising of a Revenue for Provincial purposes.

3. The borrowing of money on the sole credit of the Province.

4. The establishment and tenure of Provincial offices and the appointment and payment of Provincial officers.

5. The management and sale of the Public Lands belonging to the Province and of the timber and wood thereon.

6. The establishment, maintenance, and management of public and reformatory prisons in and for the Province.

7. The establishment, maintenance, and management of hospitals, asylums, charities, and eleemosynary institutions in and for the Province, other than marine hospitals.

8. Municipal institutions in the Province.

9. Shop, saloon, tavern, auctioneer, and other licenses in order to the raising of a revenue for Provincial, local, or municipal purposes.

10. Local works and undertakings other than such as are of the following classes,—

> a. Lines of steam or other ships, railways, canals, telegraphs, and other works and undertakings connecting the Province with any other or others of the Provinces, or extending beyond the limits of the Province;

> b. Lines of steam ships between the Province and any British or Foreign country;

> c. Such works as, although wholly situate within the Province, are before or after their execution declared by the Parliament of Canada to be for the general advantage of Canada or for the advantage of two or more of the Provinces.

11. The incorporation of companies with Provincial objects.

12. The solemnization of marriage in the Province.

13. Property and civil rights in the Province.

14. The administration of justice in the Province, including the constitution, maintenance, and organization of Pro-vincial Courts, both of civil and of criminal jurisdiction, and including procedure in civil matters in those Courts.

15. The imposition of punishment by fine, penalty, or imprisonment for enforcing any law of the Province made in relation to any matter coming within any of the classes of subjects enumerated in this section.

16. Generally all matters of a merely local or private nature in the Province.

Education.

93. In and for each Province the Legislature may exclu- Legislation sively make laws in relation to education, subject and according respecting education. to the following provisions:—

1. Nothing in any such law shall prejudicially affect any right or privilege with respect to denominational schools which any class of persons have by law in the Province at the union.

2. All the powers, privileges, and duties at the uuion by law conferred and imposed in Upper Canada on the separate schools and school trustees of the Queen's Roman Catholic subjects shall be and the same are hereby extended to the dissentient schools of the Queen's Protestant and Roman Catholic subjects in Quebec.

3. Where in any Province a system of separate or dissen- tient schools exists by law at the Union or is thereafter established by the Legislature of the Province, an ap- peal shall lie to the Governor-General in Council from any Act or decision of any Provincial authority affect- ing any right or privilege of the Protestant or Roman Catholic minority of the Queen's subjects in relation to education.

4. In case any such Provincial law as from time to time seems to the Governor-General in Council requisite for the due execution of the provisions of this section is not made, or in case any decision of the Governor- General in Council on any appeal under this section is not duly executed by the proper Provincial authority

in that behalf, then and in every such case, and as far only as the circumstances of each case require, the Parliament of Canada may make remedial laws for the due execution of the provisions of this section and of any decision of the Governor-General in Council under this section.

Uniformity of Laws in Ontario, Nova Scotia and New Brunswick.

Legislation for uniformity of laws in the three Provinces as to property and civil rights and uniformity of procedure in Courts.

94. Notwithstanding anything in this Act, the Parliament of Canada may make provision for the uniformity of all or any of the laws relative to property and civil rights in Ontario, Nova Scotia and New Brunswick, and of the procedure of all or any of the Courts in those three Provinces; and from and after the passing of any Act in that behalf the power of the Parliament of Canada to make laws in relation to any matter comprised in any such Act shall, notwithstanding anything in this Act, be unrestricted; but any Act of the Parliament of Canada making provision for such uniformity shall not have effect in any Province unless and until it is adopted and enacted as law by the Legislature thereof.

Agriculture and Immigration.

Concurrent powers of Legislation respecting agriculture and immigration.

95. In each Province the Legislature may make laws in relation to Agriculture in the Province, and to Immigration into the Province; and it is hereby declared that the Parliament of Canada may from time to time make laws in relation to Agriculture in all or any of the Provinces, and to Immigration into all or any of the Provinces; and any law of the Legislature of a Province relative to Agriculture or to Immigration shall have effect in and for the Province as long and as far only as it is not repugnant to any Act of the Parliament of Canada.

VII.—JUDICATURE.

Appointment of Judges.

96. The Governor-General shall appoint the Judges of the Superior, District, and County Courts in each Province, except those of the Courts of Probate in Nova Scotia and New Brunswick.

Selection of Judges in Ontario, etc.

97. Until the laws relative to property and civil rights in Ontario, Nova Scotia, and New Brunswick, and the procedure of the Courts of those Provinces, are made uniform, the Judges of the Courts of those Provinces appointed by the Governor-General shall be selected from the respective Bars of those Provinces.

98. The Judges of the Courts of Quebec shall be selected Selection of
from the Bar of that Province. Judges in Quebec.

99. The Judges of the Superior Courts shall hold office Tenure of office
during good behaviour, but shall be removable by the Gover- of Judges of
nor-General on address of the Senate and House of Commons. Superior Courts.

100. The salaries, allowances and pensions of the Judges Salaries, etc.,
of the Superior, District, and County Courts (except the Courts of Judges.
of Probate in Nova Scotia and New Brunswick), and of the
Admiralty Courts in cases where the Judges thereof are for
the time being paid by salary, shall be fixed and provided by
the Parliament of Canada.

101. The Parliament of Canada may, notwithstanding any- General Court
thing in this Act, from time to time, provide for the constitu- of Appeal, etc.
tion, maintenance, and organization of a general Court of
Appeal for Canada, and for the establishment of any additional
Courts for the better administration of the Laws of Canada.

VIII.—REVENUES; DEBTS; ASSETS; TAXATION.

102. All duties and revenues over which the respective Creation of
Legislatures of Canada, Nova Scotia, and New Brunswick Consolidated
before and at the Union had and have power of appropriation, Revenue Fund.
except such portions thereof as are by this Act reserved to the
respective Legislatures of the Provinces, or are raised by them
in accordance with the special powers conferred on them by
this Act, shall form one Consolidated Revenue Fund, to be
appropriated for the public service of Canada in the manner
and subject to the charges in this Act provided.

103. The Consolidated Revenue Fund of Canada shall be Expenses of
permanently charged with the costs, charges, and expenses inci- collection, etc.
dent to the collection, management, and receipt thereof, and
the same shall form the first charge thereon, subject to be
reviewed and audited in such manner as shall be ordered by
the Governor-General in Council until the Parliament otherwise
provides.

104. The annual interest of the public debts of the several Interest of
Provinces of Canada, Nova Scotia and New Brunswick at the Provincial
Union shall form the second charge on the Consolidated Rev- public debts.
enue Fund of Canada.

105. Unless altered by the Parliament of Canada, the salary Salary of
of the Governor-General shall be ten thousand pounds sterling Governor
money of the United Kingdom of Great Britain and Ireland, General,
payable out of the Consolidated Revenue Fund of Canada, and
the same shall form the third charge thereon.

Appropriation of fund subject to charges.

106. Subject to the several payments by this Act charged on the Consolidated Revenue Fund of Canada, the same shall be appropriated by the Parliament of Canada for the public service.

Transfer to Canada of stocks, etc., belonging to two Provinces.

107. All stocks, cash, banker's balances, and securities for money belonging to each Province at the time of the Union, except as in this Act mentioned, shall be the property of Canada, and shall be taken in reduction of the amount of the respective debts of the Province at the Union.

Transfer of property in schedule.

108. The public works and property of each Province, enumerated in the third schedule to this Act, shall be the property of Canada.

Lands, mines, etc., belonging to Provinces to belong to them.

109. All lands, mines, minerals, and royalties belonging to the several Provinces of Canada, Nova Scotia and New Brunswick at the Union, and all sums then due or payable for such lands, mines, minerals or royalties, shall belong to the several Provinces of Ontario, Quebec, Nova Scotia and New Brunswick in which the same are situate or arise, subject to any trusts existing in respect thereof, and to any interest other than of the Province in the same.

Assets connected with Provincial debts.

110. All assets connected with such portions of the public debt of each Province as are assumed by that Province shall belong to that Province.

Canada to be liable for Provincial debts.

111. Canada shall be liable for the debts and liabilities of each Province existing at the Union.

Liability of Ontario and Quebec to Canada.

112. Ontario and Quebec conjointly shall be liable to Canada for the amount (if any) by which the debt of the Province of Canada exceeds at the Union $62,500,000, and shall be charged with interest at the rate of five per centum per annum thereon.

Assets of Ontario and Quebec.

113. The assets enumerated in the fourth Schedule to this Act belonging at the Union to the Province of Canada shall be the property of Ontario and Quebec conjointly.

Liability of Nova Scotia to Canada.

114. Nova Scotia shall be liable to Canada for the amount (if any) by which its public debt exceeds at the Union $8,000,000, and shall be charged with interest at the rate of five per centum per annum thereon.

Liability of New Brunswick to Canada.

115. New Brunswick shall be liable to Canada for the amount (if any) by which its public debt exceeds at the Union $7,000,000, and shall be charged with interest at the rate of five per centum per annum thereon.

116. In case the public debts of Nova Scotia and New Payment of Brunswick do not at the Union amount to $8,000,000 and $7,000,- interest to Nova Scotia and 000 respectively, they shall repetively receive by half-yearly New Brunswick payments in advance from the Government of Canada Interest if their public debts are less at five per centum per annum on the difference between the than the stipu- actual amounts of their respective debts and such stipulated lated amounts. amounts.

117. The several Provinces shall retain all their respective Provincial public property not otherwise disposed of in this Act, subject public property. to the right of Canada to assume any lands or public property required for fortifications or for the defence of the country.

118. The following sums shall be paid yearly by Canada Grants to to the several Provinces for the support of their Governments Provinces. and Legislatures:—.

Dollars

Ontario . . . . Eighty thousand.

Quebec . . . . Seventy thousand.

Nova Scotia. Sixty thousand.

New Brunswick . . . . Fifty thousand.

Two hundred and sixty thousand.

And an annual grant in aid of each Province shall be made, equal to eighty cents per head of the population as ascertained by the Census of 1861, and in case of Nova Scotia and New Brunswick, by each subsequent decennial census until the population of each of those two Provinces amounts to four hundred thousand souls, at which rate such grant shall thereafter remain. Such grants shall be in full settlement of all future demands on Canada, and shall be paid half-yearly in advance to each Province; but the Government of Canada shall deduct from such grants, as against any Province, all sums chargeable as interest on the Public Debt of that Province in excess of the several amounts stipulated in this Act.

119. New Brunswick shall receive by half-yearly payments Further grant to in advance from Canada, for the period of ten years from the New Brunswick for ten years. Union an additional allowance of $63,000 per annum; but as long as the Public Debt of that Province remains under $7,000,- 000, a deduction equal to the interest at five per centum per annum on such deficiency shall be made from that allowance of $63,000.

120. All payments to be made under this Act, or in dis- Form of charge of liabilities created under any Act of the Provinces of payments. Canada, Nova Scotia and New Brunswick respectively, and assumed by Canada, shall, until the Parliament of Canada otherwise directs, be made in such form and manner as may from time to time be ordered by the Governor-General in Council.

Manufactures, etc., of one Province to be admitted free into the others.   **121.** All articles of the growth, produce, or manufacture of any one of the Provinces shall, from and after the Union, be admitted free into each of the other Provinces.

Continuance of Customs and Excise Laws.   **122.** The Customs and Excise Laws of each Province shall, subject to the provisions of this Act, continue in force until altered by the Parliament of Canada.

Exportation and importation as between two Provinces.   **123.** Where Customs duties are, at the Union, leviable on any goods, wares, or merchandises in any two Provinces, those goods, wares and merchandises may, from and after the Union, be imported from one of those Provinces into the other of them on proof of payment of the Customs duty leviable thereon in the Province of exportation, and on payment of such further amount (if any) of Customs duty as is leviable thereon in the Province of importation.

Lumber dues in New Brunswick.   **124.** Nothing in this Act shall affect the right of New Brunswick to levy the lumber dues provided in chapter fifteen, of title three, of the Revised Statutes of New Brunswick, or in any Act amending that Act before or after the Union, and not increasing the amount of such dues; but the lumber of any of the Provinces other than New Brunswick shall not be subjected to such dues.

Exemption of public lands, etc., from taxation.   **125.** No lands or property belonging to Canada or any Province shall be liable to taxation.

Provincial Consolidated Revenue Funds.   **126.** Such portions of the duties and revenues over which the respective Legislatures of Canada, Nova Scotia and New Brunswick had before the Union power of appropriation as are by this Act reserved to the respective Governments or Legislatures of the Provinces, and all duties and revenues raised by them in accordance with the special powers conferred upon them by this Act, shall in each Province form one Consolidated Revenue Fund to be appropriated for the public service of the Province.

IX.—MISCELLANEOUS PROVISIONS.

General.

As to Legislative Councillors of Provinces becoming Senators.   **127.** If any person being at the passing of this Act a Member of the Legislative Council of Canada, Nova Scotia, or New Brunswick, to whom a place in the Senate is offered, does not within thirty days thereafter, by writing under his hand, addressed to the Governor-General of the Province of Canada, or to the Lieutenant-Governor of Nova Scotia or New Brunswick (as the case may be), accept the same, he shall be deemed to have declined the same; and any person who, being at the passing of this Act a member of the Legislative Council of Nova Scotia or New Brunswick, accepts a place in the Senate, shall thereby vacate his seat in such Legislative Council.

128. Every member of the Senate or House of Commons of Canada shall before taking his seat therein, take and subscribe before the Governor-General or some person authorized by him, and every member of a Legislative Council or Legislative Assembly of any Province shall before taking his seat therein, take and subscribe before the Lieutenant-Governor of the Province or some person authorized by him, the oath of allegiance contained in the fifth Schedule to this Act; and every member of the Senate of Canada and every member of the Legislative Council of Quebec shall also, before taking his seat therein, take and subscribe before the Governor-General or some person authorized by him, the declaration of qualification -contained in the same Schedule. *Oath of allegiance, etc.*

129. Except as otherwise provided by this Act, all laws in force in Canada, Nova Scotia or New Brunswick at the Union, and all Courts of civil and military jurisdiction, and all legal commissions, powers and authorities, and all officers, judicial, administrative and ministerial, existing therein at the Union, shall continue in Ontario, Quebec, Nova Scotia and New Brunswick respectively, as if the Union had not been made; subject nevertheless (except with respect to such as are enacted by or exist under Acts of the Parliament of Great Britain or of the Parliament of the United Kingdom of Great Britain and Ireland,) to be repealed, abolished or altered by the Parliament of Canada, or by the Legislature of the respective Province, according to the authority of the Parliament or of that Legislature under this Act. *Continuance of existing laws, courts, officers, etc.*

130. Until the Parliament of Canada otherwise provides, all officers of the several Provinces having duties to discharge in relation to matters other than those coming within the classes of subjects by this Act assigned exclusively to the Legislatures of the Provinces shall be officers of Canada, and shall continue to discharge the duties of their respective offices under the same liabilities, responsibilities and penalties as if the Union had not been made. *Transfer of officers to Canada.*

131. Until the Parliament of Canada otherwise provides, the Governor-General in Council may from time to time appoint *Appointment of new officers.*

such officers as the Governor-General in Council deems necessary or proper for the effectual execution of this Act.

Power for performance of treaty obligations by Canada as part of British Empire.

132. The Parliament and Government of Canada shall
have all powers necessary or proper for performing the obligations of Canada or of any Province thereof, as part of the
British Empire, towards foreign countries, arising under treaties between the Empire and such foreign countries.

Use of English and French languages.

133. Either the English or the French language may be
used by any person in the debates of the Houses of the Parliament of Canada and of the Houses of the Legislature of
Quebec; and both those languages shall be used in the respective records and journals of those Houses; and either of those
languages may be used by any person or in any pleading or
process in or issuing from any Court of Canada established
under this Act, and in or from all or any of the Courts of
Quebec.

The Acts of the Parliament of Canada and of the Legislature of Quebec shall be printed and published in both those
languages.

Ontario and Quebec.

Appointment of executive officers for Ontario and Quebec.

134. Until the Legislature of Ontario or of Quebec otherwise provides, the Lieutenant-Governors of Ontario and
Quebec may each appoint under the Great Seal of the Province the following officers, to hold office during pleasure, that
is to say:—the Attorney-General, the Secretary and Registrar
of the Province, the Treasurer of the Province, the Commissioner of Crown Lands, and the Commissioner of Agriculture
and Public Works, and in the case of Quebec the Solicitor-
General; and may, by order of the Lieutenant-Governor in
Council, from time to time prescribe the duties of those
officers and of the several departments over which they shall
preside or to which they shall belong, and of the officers and
clerks thereof; and may also appoint other and additional
officers to hold office during pleasure, and may from time to
time prescribe the duties of those officers, and of the several
departments over which they shall preside or to which they
shall belong, and of the officers and clerks thereof.

Powers, duties, etc., of executive officers.

135. Until the Legislature of Ontario or Quebec otherwise
provides, all rights, powers, duties, functions, responsibilities
or authorities at the passing of this Act vested in or imposed
on the Attorney-General, Solicitor-General, Secretary and
Registrar of the Province of Canada, Minister of Finance, Com-

missioner of Crown Lands, Commissioner of Public Works, and Minister of Agriculture and Receiver-General, by any law, statute or ordinance of Upper Canada, Lower Canada, or Canada, and not repugnant to this Act, shall be vested in or imposed on any officer to be appointed by the Lieutenant-Governor for the discharge of the same or any of them; and the Commissioner of Agriculture and Public Works shall perform the duties and functions of the office of Minister of Agriculture at the passing of this Act imposed by the law of the Province of Canada, as well as those of the Commissioner of Public Works.

136. Until altered by the Lieutenant-Governor in Council, Great Seal. the Great Seals of Ontario and of Quebec respectively shall be the same, or of the same design, as those used in the Provinces of Upper Canada and Lower Canada respectively before their Union as the Province of Canada.

137. The words " and from thence to the end of the then Construction of next ensuing Session of the Legislature," or words to the temporary Acts. same effect, used in any temporary Act of the Province of Canada not expired before the Union, shall be construed to extend and apply to the next Session of the Parliament of Canada, if the subject matter of the Act is within the powers of the same, as defined by this Act, or to the next Sessions of the Legislatures of Ontario and Quebec respectively, if the subject matter of the Act is within the powers of the same as defined by this Act.

138. From and after the Union, the use of the words As to errors in " Upper Canada" instead of "Ontario," or "Lower Canada" names. instead of "Quebec," in any deed, writ, process, pleading, document, matter or thing, shall not invalidate the same.

139. Any Proclamation under the Great Seal of the Pro- As to issue of vince of Canada issued before the Union to take effect at a Proclamations before Union, time which is subsequent to the Union, whether relating to to commence that Province, or to Upper Canada, or to Lower Canada, and after Union. the several matters and things therein proclaimed, shall be and continue of like force and effect as if the Union had not been made.

140. Any Proclamation which is authorized by any Act of As to issue of the Legislature of the Province of Canada to be issued under Proclamations after Union the Great Seal of the Province of Canada, whether relating to under authority that Province, or to Upper Canada, or to Lower Canada, and of Acts before which is not issued before the Union, may be issued by the Union. Lieutenant-Governor of Ontario or of Quebec, as its subject matter requires, under the Great Seal thereof; and from and after the issue of such Proclamation the same and the several matters and things therein proclaimed shall be and continue of the like force and effect in Ontario or Quebec as if the Union had not been made.

Penitentiary.

141. The Penitentiary of the Province of Canada shall, until the Parliament of Canada otherwise provides, be and continue the Penitentiary of Ontario and of Quebec.

Arbitration respecting debts, etc.

142. The division and adjustment of the debts, credits, liabilities, properties and assets of Upper Canada and Lower Canada shall be referred to the arbitrament of three arbitrators, one chosen by the Government of Ontario, one by the Government of Quebec and one by the Government of Canada; and the selection of the arbitrators shall not be made until the Parliament of Canada and the Legislatures of Ontario and Quebec have met; and the arbitrator chosen by the Government of Canada shall not be a resident either in Ontario or in Quebec.

Division of records.

143. The Governor-General in Council may from time to time order that such and so many of the records, books, and documents of the Province of Canada as he thinks fit shall be appropriated and delivered either to Ontario or to Quebec. and the same shall henceforth be the property of that Province; and any copy thereof or extract therefrom duly certified by the officer having charge of the original thereof shall be admitted as evidence.

Constitution of townships in Quebec.

144. The Lieutenant-Governor of Quebec may from time to time, by Proclamation under the Great Seal of the Province, to take effect from a day to be appointed therein, constitute townships in those parts of the Province of Quebec in which townships are not then already constituted, and fix the metes and bounds thereof.

X.—INTERCOLONIAL RAILWAY.

Duty of Government and Parliament of Canada to make railway herein described.

145. Inasmuch as the Provinces of Canada, Nova Scotia, and New Brunswick have joined in a declaration that the construction of the Intercolonial Railway is essential to the consolidation of the Union of British North America, and to the assent thereto of Nova Scotia and New Brunswick, and have consequently agreed that provision should be made for its immediate construction by the Government of Canada: Therefore, in order to give effect to that agreement, it shall be the duty of the Government and Parliament of Canada to provide for the commencement within six months after the Union, of a railway connecting the River St. Lawrence with the City of Halifax in Nova Scotia, and for the construction thereof without intermission, and the completion thereof with all practicable speed.

XI.—Admission of other Colonies.

146. It shall be lawful for the Queen, by and with the advice of Her Majesty's Most Honourable Privy Council, on Addresses from the Houses of the Parliament of Canada, and from the Houses of the respective Legislatures of the Colonies or Provinces of Newfoundland, Prince Edward Island, and British Columbia, to admit those Colonies or Provinces, or any of them, into the Union, and on Address from the Houses of the Parliament of Canada to admit Rupert's Land and the Northwestern Territory, or either of them, into the Union, on such terms and conditions in each case as are in the Addresses expressed and as the Queen thinks fit to approve, subject to the provisions of this Act, and the provisions of any Order in Council in that behalf, shall have effect as if they had been enacted by the Parliament of the United Kingdom of Great Britain and Ireland. *Power to admit Newfoundland, Prince Edward Island, British Columbia, Rupert's Land and Northwestern Territory into the Union by Order in Council.*

147. In case of the admission of Newfoundland and Prince Edward Island, or either of them, each shall be entitled to a representation in the Senate of Canada of four members, and (notwithstanding anything in this Act) in case of the admission of Newfoundland the normal number of Senators shall be seventy-six and their maximum number shall be eighty-two; but Prince Edward Island when admitted shall be deemed to be comprised in the third of the three divisions into which Canada, is, in relation to the constitution of the Senate divided by this Act, and accordingly, after the admission of Prince Edward Island, whether Newfoundland is admitted or not, the representation of Nova Scotia and New Brunswick in the Senate shall, as vacancies occur, be reduced from twelve to ten members respectively, and the representation of each of those Provinces shall not be increased at any time beyond ten, except under the provisions of this Act for the appointment of three or six additional Senators under the direction of the Queen. *As to representation of Newfoundland and Prince Edward Island in Senate.*

GENERAL INDEX

A.

Act of Settlement, 24, 40.
'Administration of Justice in the Province,' etc., 137-140.
Admiralty and Vice-Admiralty Courts, 138.
Agriculture and Immigration Act, 80, 91, 149.
Alberta Act, 144, 148-9.
Alberta, Province of, 38.
    Constitution of, 49.
    Created out of North-West Territories, 38.
    Criminal law in, 55.
    English law in, 50-1, 55.
Aliens—
    Deportation of alien paupers, 216.
    Provincial interference with, 129.
    Rights in Canada, 216.
Aliens and naturalization, 114-5.
American Colonies—
    Breaking out of war with, 11.
Ancillary legislation, 87-8, 93-5, 121.
Aspects of legislation, 69, 80-1, 98, 118, 141-2.
Assignments for benefit of creditors, 111-3.
Assize of bread, 141.
Australia—
    Commonwealth Constitution Act, 179, n. 78, 180, n. 81.
    Constitution compared, 190, n. 115, 203, n. 169.
Autonomy of provinces, 96-8.

B.

Bagot, Sir Charles, 27.
Baldwin, Robert, 27.
Banking, incorporation of banks, and the issue of paper money, 109-110, 206, n. 177.
Bankruptcy and insolvency, 111-3.
Beacons, Buoys, Lighthouses, and Sable Island, 106.
Bill of Rights, 40.
Bills of Exchange and Promissory Notes, 110.
Blake, Hon. Edward, 2.
Borrowing of money on the public credit, 106.
Boundaries—
    Provincial railway, electric, etc., lines extending to boundary, 128-9.
British Columbia, 44, 48.
    Admitted into Confederation, 37.
    Criminal law in, 54-5.
    English law in, 55.
    Pre-Confederation Constitution of, 48.
    Present Constitution of, 44-5.

P.

www.ingramcontent.com/pod-product-compliance
Lightning Source LLC
Chambersburg PA
CBHW031544260326

41914CB00002B/268